Contents

D0334164

Introduction

Welcome to Edexcel's BTEC National family of qualifications!

For over 20 years, the BTEC National family of Computing and IT qualifications have represented **the** practical, vocational-oriented alternative to GCE A-Level study.

During 2006 Edexcel revised their 2003 BTEC National qualification for IT Practitioners, taking into consideration invaluable feedback from various professional bodies, schools, colleges and employers.

Both its academic and vocational themes have been thoroughly revised to more appropriately reflect the changing needs of employers in the IT sector and the expectations of learners both in schools and colleges. Accordingly, part of its revised structure includes a mixture of vendor units from Microsoft, Cisco and CompTIA.

The new BTEC National qualification (encompassing an Award, Certificate and a Diploma) links firmly to its sector's National Occupational Standards (NOS) and is supported by its Sector Skills Council (SSC).

All qualifications have been accredited to the National Qualifications Framework (NQF) at level 3.

Academic pathways

The new BTEC National scheme has 4 pathways which define occupational routes in the modern IT Industry. These are:

◆ IT and Business
◆ Software Development
◆ Systems Support
◆ Networking

Although each pathway has a number of common units (e.g. Unit 1 – Communication and Employability Skills for IT), they each contain a combination of specialist units which can make the learning experience truly unique.

BTEC National Award for IT Practitioners

In order to achieve the BTEC National Award (BNA) for IT Practitioners you should pass units which total 360 Guided Learning Hours (GLH). This is the equivalent of 6 units of study. The award has no pathway options.

This is roughly equivalent to studying one GCE A-Level.

BTEC National Certificate for IT Practitioners

In order to achieve the BTEC National Certificate (BNC) for IT Practitioners you should pass units which total 720 GLH. Usually this is equivalent to 12 units of study. The Certificate is available in all 4 vocational pathways listed above.

This is roughly equivalent to studying two GCE A-Levels.

BTEC National Diploma for IT Practitioners

In order to achieve the BTEC National Diploma (BND) for IT Practitioners you should pass units which total 1080 Guided Learning Hours (GLH). Usually this is equivalent to 18 units of study. As with the Certificate, the Diploma is available in all 4 vocational pathways.

This is roughly equivalent to studying three GCE A-Levels.

What's in this book

This book includes sufficient material which is designed to help you study (and complete) the core of the BTEC National Award, Certificate or Diploma for IT Practitioners, no matter which vocational pathway you eventually follow.

Icons used in this book

 A light overview of the units contents and purpose.

 Complex topics made easy for you.

 Your target – the learning aims associated with the unit.

 Key term which you should understand in order to succeed in the unit.

 An activity – something to get you working on aspects of the unit, may be practical or theoretical.

 An opportunity to test your memory and understanding of the the unit content.

 A case study concerning a select number of realistic businesses that want to use IT but who may not know how. Your task will be to solve their problems.

 Where related material can be found.

 How to achieve the prize (completing the unit).

 A list of extra resources that can be found on the CD.

 Other books, some recommended by Edexcel which contains useful reading for the unit.

Units covered by this book

This book covers the following 14 units marked as either core (with a tick) or an "O" for optional on all versions of the qualification:

Core Units	GLH	BTEC National Award	Business & IT		Software Development		Systems Support		Networking	
			Certificate	Diploma	Certificate	Diploma	Certificate	Diploma	Certificate	Diploma
Unit 1 Communication and Employability Skills for IT	60	✓	✓	✓	✓	✓	✓	✓	✓	✓
Unit 2 Computer Systems	60	✓	✓	✓	✓	✓	✓	✓	✓	✓
Unit 3 Information Systems	60	O	✓	✓	✓	✓	✓	✓	O	O
Unit 7 IT Systems Analysis and Design	60	O	O	O	O	✓	O	O	O	O
Unit 8 Communication Technologies	60	O	O	O	O	O	O	O	✓	✓
Unit 15 Organisational Systems Security	60	O	O	✓	O	O	O	✓	O	✓
Unit 18 Principles of Software Design and Development	60	O	O	O	✓	✓	O	O	O	O
Unit 20 Event Driven Programming	60		O	O	O	✓	O	O	O	O
Unit 22 Network Management	60						O	O	O	✓
Unit 27 Principles of Computer Networks	60	O	O	O	O	O	O	O	✓	✓
Unit 28 IT Technical Support	60	O	O	O	O	O	✓	✓	O	O
Unit 29 IT Systems Troubleshooting and Repair	60	O	O	O	O	O	O	✓	O	O
Unit 34 e-Commerce	60	O	O	✓	O	O	O	O	O	O
Unit 35 Impact of the Use of IT on Business Systems	60	O	✓	✓	O	O	O	O	O	O

Assessment and Grading

Assessment for this qualification is undertaken through a series of coursework based assignments. Your tutors may use assignments developed by Edexcel, or will write assignments for you to do that meet grading criteria. These assignments, and the work you provide, are marked and checked by your own centre and are then checked through External Verification activity with a representative from Edexcel.

This qualification will now be awarded on a points system, although your certificate will show achievement at Pass, Merit or Distinction. To monitor your own progress as you undertake the course, each unit has a monitoring sheet for you to use. A full set of master grids that you can print off and use is included on the companion CD.

Each time you complete an assignment, your tutor will identify **which** grading criteria you have been awarded. You can tick off your achievement on the relevant unit sheet. Using this mechanism you will be able to identify which grading criteria you still have outstanding at each level (Pass, Merit and Distinction). **You must always remember** that to achieve a particular grade you must have been awarded **all the grading criteria available within a grade**. For a **Pass**, all **Pass** criteria must have been achieved. For a Merit grade, all Pass and all Merit criteria must have been achieved. For a **Distinction** grade, all **Pass**, all **Merit** and all **Distinction** criteria must have been achieved.

Once a unit has been completed you will then be awarded a number of points. This will be dependent on the size of the unit and the grade you achieved. Please see the following points table:

Size of Unit (GLH)	Pass Grade	Merit Grade	Distinction Grade
30	3	6	9
60	6	12	18
90	9	18	27
120	12	24	36

Table reproduced from the Edexcel Qualification Specification

The points score for each individual unit is reported to Edexcel at the end of your course. The points are then added together to give a total score. This will be the overall grade that you achieve for the qualification. It is known as your qualification grade.

Qualification grade

The qualification grade boundaries and UCAS points (as at 1st January 2007) are shown below and represent information about how your grade will be calculated, based on the number of points you have achieved in the selection of units you studied (N.B. **All** tables shown here have been reproduced from the Edexcel Qualification Specification):

Grade boundaries BTEC National Award	Overall grade BTEC National Award		UCAS points
36–59	Pass	P	40
60–83	Merit	M	80
84–108	Distinction	D	120

Grade boundaries BTEC National Certificate	Overall grade BTEC National Certificate	UCAS points
72–95	PP	80
96–119	MP	120
120–143	MM	160
144–167	DM	200
168–216	DD	240

Grade boundaries BTEC National Diploma	Overall grade BTEC National Diploma	UCAS points
108–131	PPP	120
132–155	MPP	160
156–179	MMP	200
180–203	MMM	240
204–227	DMM	280
228–251	DDM	320
252–324	DDD	360

Further information can be found on the Edexcel website at www.edexcel.org.uk. For example, you can look at the unit specification and guidance given to your tutors. Your centres have been advised by Edexcel to keep up-to-date with the latest guidance provided on the website.

Communication and Employability Skills for IT

Capsule view

Communication and Employability Skills for IT is a 60-hour unit which is designed to introduce you to the world of work. Regardless of whether you ultimately work for yourself or you are employed by someone else, you will need to develop both **technical** and **non-technical skills** to support your endeavours. The technical skills will in part be achieved through this National Diploma. The non-technical skills, such as **interpersonal skills**, **communications skills** and **self-development skills** will be explored through this unit.

It is clear that in a fast-moving world, you will need to be prepared to undergo **continual self-development** in order to remain effective and competitive. The final outcome for this unit will help you to focus on your personal progression needs.

Learning aims

1 Understand the attributes of employees that are valued by employers.
2 Understand the principles of effective communication.
3 Be able to exploit IT to communicate effectively.
4 Be able to identify personal development needs and the ways of addressing them.

1 Understanding the attributes of employees that are valued by employers

While it would be fair to say that most employers will have their own ideas about the skills and attributes they require from their employees, there are a number of skills, attitudes and abilities that most employers will agree are fundamental in an effective employee.

Key Terms

Attributes and abilities – these are the personal characteristics that employers expect you to have. Examples would be that you can **problem-solve**, can be **creative**, have **leadership qualities**, can work as **part of a team** and can work with a **minimum of supervision**.

Skills – these are relatively easy to measure. For example, do you have IT skills at a particular level? These will be evidenced through your qualifications or, in some cases, employers will give you a job-related test to measure particular skills that they expect you to have (although in many cases employers will be prepared to offer additional training, if appropriate).

Attitudes – this refers to your own personal behaviours in a work context. Examples would include that you **show an interest** in your work, that you **show a willingness** to **put in effort**, that you have a **pride** in your **personal appearance**, are **polite** and **respectful**.

Recruiting new members of staff is a time-intensive exercise and, in most cases, it will be the remit of both the human resource (HR) function and line managers to decide when and how to recruit and advertise.

A post is generally advertised because one of the following situations has arisen:

◆ The current post holder is retiring.
◆ Current post holder is leaving (has a new job, is leaving the area or their current contract is being terminated).
◆ Creation of a new post (for a fixed-term project, long-term illness, maternity etc.).
◆ Creation of a new post (ongoing to cover increased or diversifying workload).

It also has long-term ramifications if ill-defined roles are advertised and possibly **legal consequences** if any **equal opportunities** (ethnicity, religion, gender) are **breached** during the process itself.

In order to recruit suitable employees, managers need to identify the **nature of the post**, the **attitudes, attributes** and **abilities** it expects employees to have and the **exact skills** that the applicant should be able to demonstrate in order to be selected for the post.

Identification of a post

Generally, procedures vary from organisation to organisation; however it is common for a manager to produce a **written proposal** outlining the **need** for recruitment.

Typically this would state **job function, circumstances of its creation, line management** and the **salary** being offered. It may be generated as a result of business planning strategies, especially if the post is **new** or **different** to one which has just been vacated.

1.1 Specific job-related attributes

Technical knowledge

In most situations, employers will be looking for particular skills when engaging a new employee. The exact requirements will be listed in a **job description**, where a description of the tasks the employee will be expected to undertake will be listed and explained.

Describing the post

A **job description** typically consists of:

◆ **core information** about the post (title, start date, salary range/grade etc.)
◆ **job purpose** (a broad overview of the post)
◆ job **responsibilities and duties** (what the person is expected to do in the role)
◆ **information** about the **department** and **organisation**
◆ a **person specification**.

Fundamental to this process is the development of a **person specification (PS)**. The PS is used to define the **essential** (must haves) and **desirable** (would be nice) facets required from a person applying for the post. Careful use of sensible descriptors will enable an experienced manager and personnel team (or HR) to quickly whittle a large number of hopeful applications down to a manageable **shortlist** of four to six candidates for **formal interview**.

Here is a sample template for a PS as a guide.

Attributes	Essential	Desirable
Experience		
Qualifications & Training		
Abilities		
Job Circumstances (e.g. mobility/late/early working)		

Experience

Usually this is a short profile detailing the type of **previous experience** that is required to take on this type of role. It may be a **precursory role** (with a number of years' service attached) or an **identical role** (with a number of years' service attached). Emphasis should also be placed on the **vocational/industrial background** that is being sought. Experience may even be very specific ('…has developed database systems in Microsoft Visual Basic® .NET for the retail sector for at least two years').

Qualifications and training

These outline the **educational requirements** and **professional vocational qualifications** that are necessary in order to perform this job. Most industries have a **vocational guide body** to help with this sort of decision.

Abilities

These define the **personal characteristics** of the person envisaged for the role. Typical entries that may fit here include 'must be able to work in a team' or 'must be able to use own initiative to complete tasks'.

These are often seen as the **softer skills** but, as many industrial comments have shown, these are often **vitally important** to the smooth running of an organisation.

Job circumstances

Generally this section would reflect **conditions** that would make the job **less/more difficult** for some people. Common examples would include: mobile working, working in the evenings, working abroad, flexible hours, multi-site working etc.

Here is a completed PS for a systems programmer.

Attributes	Essential	Desirable
Experience	Three years' experience in a commercial environment using C++ and Microsoft Visual Basic® .NET	Java™ and C#® experience would also be useful
Qualifications & Training	Educated to National Diploma standard	Evidence of professional updating in the last two years
Abilities	Good team player, able to work unsupervised	Has experience of leading a small project team
Job Circumstances (e.g. mobility/late/early working)	Fully mobile as some travelling to visit clients may be required	Able to work to tight deadlines and stay late to get the job done

When working with a person specification you should understand that an employer will expect you to show that you have the **essential** attributes, as defined on the specification, and as **many** of the **desirable attributes as possible**. The more desirable attributes you can evidence that you have, the more likely you are to get an interview.

Working procedures and systems including health and safety

When you first go into your first job you will realise that there is a lot more to employment than physically doing your job. You will need to familiarise yourself with organisational working procedures that affect the way that you work.

An example of a working procedure might be where an employer operates a **flexible working** system or process. This is where you are able to choose your own start and finish times in your job. In addition, quite often you will be able to accrue time worked, for additional hours you need to work when the organisation is busy, that you will be allowed to **take back** when things are quieter. Most organisations that operate flexible working require employees to observe certain boundaries. For example:

◆ **You must begin work between 7.00 am and 9.30 am** – from this it should be clear that you will need to arrive at work somewhere between the times shown. You will not be allowed to start prior to 7.00 am or after 9.30 am.

◆ **You may not leave before 3.30 pm** – this is an instruction that you are not permitted to leave work before the time specified.

◆ **Your working day must be no less than 5 hours and your average working week is 35 hours over 5 days** – if you look at the timings shown (you must start by 9.30 am and may not leave before 3.30 pm), and bearing in mind that you should take a statutory 60 minutes for lunch, this would calculate out to a minimum 5-hour day. Technically, however, you should be working approximately 7 but the flexible pattern would allow you to work a minimum of 5 hours, but it could be as many as it needs to be to make an average of 35 hours across the working week! For example, you work 5 hours on a Monday, but then 8 hours on a Tuesday and Wednesday to make a combined 21 hours over 3 days (and 3 times 7 is 21).

◆ **Lunch must be for a minimum of 30 minutes and a maximum of 90 minutes and must be taken between 11.00 am and 2.00 pm** – employers often stipulate this to ensure that employees do not take very early breaks and come in later, or very late lunches to leave earlier than times required by the organisation.

It is usual that if you work a flexible working pattern, you keep a **record** (often referred to as a **time sheet**), which you will need to produce when required.

Here is a sample of a completed time sheet.

Most employers will allow you to work slightly less than your expected hours in a week, providing you **give the time back** at times when they are busy. In many cases, time sheets are checked once a month by the payroll department to ensure that no one is taking advantage of the system.

Lee Office Supplies

Name of employee: Alex Stephenson

Day/Date	Time in	Time out	Lunch	Hours worked	Running total
Monday 13/11/06	7.30 am	3.30 pm	45 mins	7 hrs 15 mins	7 hrs 15 mins
Tuesday 14/11/06	8.15 am	5.00 pm	75 mins	7 hrs 30 mins	14 hrs 45 mins
Wednesday 15/11/06	9.30 am	3.30 pm	60 mins	5 hrs	19 hrs 45 mins
Thursday 16/11/06	7.45 am	4.30 pm	60 mins	7 hrs 45 mins	27 hrs 30 mins
Friday 17/11/06	8.00 am	4.45 pm	45 mins	8 hrs	35 hrs 30 mins

Total Hours worked: 35 hours 30 minutes

Total Hours expected: 35 hours

Flexi-hours owing: 30 minutes

Figure 1.1 Sample time sheet

There will be other procedures and systems that you will need to learn to ensure that you maximise your efficiency and work within the boundaries and expectations required by the organisation. It is likely that you will receive training early in your working life with the company where many of these will be introduced and explained. However, as with most training, there will no doubt be information that will, for some reason, have been omitted. For that reason you should:

◆ ask for clarification if you are not sure about something
◆ be observant about those working around you and ask if you think it's something you should know.

Health and safety

During your school or college life you will have been introduced to the concepts of health and safety. Certainly, when you were younger, **others** would **take the responsibility** for ensuring that you were in a **safe environment**. As you get older, however, you will increasingly be expected to **take responsibility** for **your own safety and health**. By the time you go into employment, you will be expected to have an understanding of the **Health and Safety at Work Act 1974** and **The Management of Health and Safety at Work Regulations 1999**.

These Acts set out the responsibilities of both employees and employers who manage the health and safety process within the workplace, and in terms of your responsibilities as a new employee, you will be expected to know the basic health and safety issues around the job for which you are engaged (for example, wearing wrist straps when working with the insides of computers) even before you start. In addition there are more generic aspects of your responsibilities.

The most obvious and basic requirements for employees are:

◆ **Be observant** in your own working environment and identify any obvious hazards or dangers.
◆ **Report** any hazards or dangers you have identified to the relevant individuals or groups of individuals to ensure the safety of yourself and others.
◆ **Anticipate** any possible hazards and be proactive in helping the organisation overcome these.

Employers also have basic responsibilities including providing you with any health and safety equipment required by your job, and providing you with the necessary tools or circumstances to ensure you have a safe working environment.

1.2 General attributes

In addition to the job-specific attributes that will be identified, there are a number of general attributes that most employers look for in potential employees, and your ability to demonstrate that you have these skills will be influential on whether or not you ultimately get the job.

In terms of identifying and evidencing your general attributes, the most common way to do this is through the acquisition of key skills (sometimes also called core skills or essential skills). These are really transferable skills that you take with you from employer to employer and which can be applied regardless of your job and in terms of your daily life. Some examples follow.

Planning and organisational skills

The skills required under this heading can be evidenced in several ways. Firstly they form part of the wider key skills syllabus for **Improving own Learning and Performance** and **Problem Solving**, and in addition are the sorts of skills that are discussed if your school or an employer is asked to provide a reference for you.

Future employers want to be reassured that you are able to plan your time effectively and organise your work, carefully prioritising (deciding how important each task is and placing it in your plan according to how important or urgent it is) work as required to meet organisational and departmental objectives.

Being well organised is fundamental not only from an employment perspective but also from a personal one.

Time management

Time management skills, like planning and organisational skills, are developed through **Improving own Learning and Performance** and **Problem Solving** activities. Using flow charts, Gantt charting and other associated time management techniques, you will need to show that you can **identify** and **allocate relevant times** as appropriate to meet deadlines where there can often be conflicting demands on your time.

One of the key issues with good time management is to **be realistic** about what you can achieve. **Do not set** yourself **unrealistic deadlines** that you really do not have any hope of meeting. Sometimes it is easier if you can create a visual representation of a series of tasks and how you might plan their completion. The example below is a Gantt chart that suggests how a series of tasks will be handled over a given time frame. This chart represents the order of tasks for a fictitious assignment for this unit. The suggestion here is that the assignment contains five tasks.

Unit 1 Assignment	Monday	Tuesday	Wednesday	Thursday	Friday	Saturday	Sunday
Task 1	███						
Task 3				███	███		
Task 3						███	███
Task 4							
Task 5							

Figure 1.2 Gantt chart example one

The implication here is that tasks one, two and three must be completed in sequence and each must be finished before the next task begins. The same is true of tasks four and five – that task four must finish before task five can begin. However, in this example, it is clear that task four does not require tasks one, two and three to have been completed, and it implies that task four can run in parallel to task one (while it is being completed) and parallel to the beginning of task two.

An alternative might be the following.

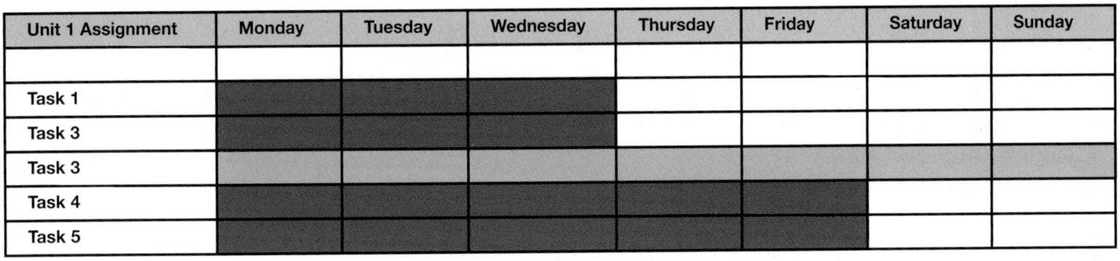

Unit 1 Assignment	Monday	Tuesday	Wednesday	Thursday	Friday	Saturday	Sunday
Task 1							
Task 3							
Task 3							
Task 4							
Task 5							

Figure 1.3 Gantt chart example two

Here the Gantt chart suggests that all tasks can be started at the same time, which implies that no task needs to be completed before another can begin. In addition, it suggests that task three will take the longest and can be carried out throughout.

This time management technique is particularly useful when planning engineering projects (where some processes must run in sequence and others may run in parallel).

Team working

These skills are part of the wider key skill **Working with others** that you may have been asked to do at your school or college. Being able to work effectively as part of a team is a skill that can be learned, although some people are **natural** team players anyway.

Employers consider your being able to work effectively as part of a team as important as your being able to work independently.

When working as part of a team it is important to remember that the role you play is only a part of the overall process. You will be expected to **contribute** to the project or task in hand, **share ideas** with other members of your team and **compromise** on a possible solution or a range of solutions. You will need to be able to treat the ideas of others with **respect**, be able to **collaborate** and be prepared to **share** the **responsibility** for the overall outcome with other members of the team. It is possible, however, that when you are completing your allocated task you may well be working individually.

An example of **collaborative teamwork** is software development. It is very unlikely that if you develop your skills and are employed as a programmer that you will ever write a program from scratch in isolation. In fact, it is more likely that you (and other team members) will be asked to individually code sections from a larger program that will ultimately be put together once all the parts have been completed. For more on software development see **Unit 18** – Principles of Software Design and Development and **Unit 20** – Event Driven Programming.

Verbal and written communication skills

Most employers use GCSE English as an indicator of your achievement in this subject, although the key skill **Communications** completed at Level 2 is an accepted equivalent.

For the purposes of this book, these skills will be covered in significant depth later in this chapter.

Numeric skills

From an employer's perspective, they will want to be reassured that you are relatively numerate: that you can **add** numbers together, do simple **multiplication, division** and **subtraction**, and that you can work confidently with **percentages** (for example value added tax (VAT) is calculated at 17.5 per cent in addition to the cost price of items).

Unit Link

GCSE Mathematics is used as a national benchmark for achievement in this area, although the key skill **Application of Number** completed at Level 2 is considered an equivalent. This qualification also contains a maths unit that you can study as one of the optional units (**Unit 17** – Mathematics for IT Practitioners).

Often, if other more technical number ability is required by a post or job, the employer will seek **to test this skill** prior to (or during) the interview.

If you have any doubts about your maths skills, you should take any opportunities you are offered for basic support, to ensure that when you finish your National Diploma, your number skills will be as strong as your IT skills.

Other skills, such as creativity

Creativity is a much harder transferable skill to evidence when it comes to ICT. With art-related subjects (for example fine art or photography), it is not uncommon for students to create a **portfolio** of their work, which they will offer as evidence to a university or to an employer.

During this course (and dependent on the unit choices made by your centre), you will have an opportunity to create **websites** and **computer programs**, and work with **digital graphics**. All of these can be evidenced with **screenshots** and included in a personal portfolio that you can use during the applications process.

In general

In terms of key skills/core skills or wider key skills, UCAS offer points for achievement of these on the UCAS Tariff. For example, each key skill achieved at Level 2 is worth 10 UCAS points, and each key skill achieved at Level 3 is worth 20 UCAS points (this information was correct as at 14 November 2006 and is taken from the UCAS website – www.UCAS.com on the Information tab, under Tariff Calculator, and should be checked prior to using this information to form part of your university or college application).

As such, achievement of these skills is useful, both to evidence your abilities and achievements to a potential employer and also to improve your UCAS points score.

1.3 Attitudes

In terms of attitudes, employers are looking for you to show that you possess a **variety** of **positive traits**. These are a few examples.

Determined

This is your **determination** to **achieve** or **succeed** in a particular environment or with a project. You should, at this stage, be determined to complete your BTEC National Diploma, Certificate or Award.

Independent

Employers need to be reassured that their employees can **work without supervision**. Although you will obviously have a supervisor or line manager, it is likely that this person will also have a number of other employees to look after. As such, your ability to get on and do what you have been asked to do will be invaluable.

Integrity

In simple terms, integrity is a measure of your **honesty** and your **sense of duty** and **respect**. Employers will want to **trust** you – that you will arrive at work on time, even if there is no one there, that you will not steal from the organisation (on any level), that you will always strive to do your best and that you will be respectful to your colleagues and others within the organisation.

Tolerant

Working with other people is likely to have its difficulties. Particularly, you may well find yourself working with people you do not like or who treat you with less respect than you feel you would treat them with. At these times you will need to be tolerant. You will need to show that you **respect other people's views, practices** and **opinions**, even if you do not necessarily agree with them.

A lack of tolerance is often what causes **conflict** between colleagues.

Dependable

Trustworthy and **consistent** are two more usual descriptors of the word dependable. As already suggested, you will need to show that you can work with a minimum of supervision and not knowingly take advantage of the organisation. In addition, dependability also means that you will be **consistent**, for example in the **quality** of your work, your **timeliness** and your **willingness** to help the organisation meet its objectives etc.

Problem solving

Your ability to think laterally will need to be evidenced here. This means that you can **creatively** find ways **around issues**, or you can find new and **innovative** ways of doing something which is already taking place.

The wider key skill **problem solving** can be studied alongside your National Diploma to help you improve your skills in this area. Alongside good problem-solving skills, you will need to develop your **time management** and **team-working** skills as your ability to manage your time, and your ability to work with others, will be paramount to helping you solve problems.

Other traits (e.g. leadership, confidence, self-motivation)

Whether or not you are a good leader is often **difficult** to assess. Many people think that if you can take charge of a group of people (for example as part of a project) you must be a good leader. In fact, quite the opposite may be true – you might be an awful leader, particularly if all you are is effectively bossy and controlling. Good leaders know how to **support** the people below them and **get the best** out of them, without having to boss them about!

Many people believe that aggression is a characteristic of confidence. In fact confidence, is about being **self-assured, believing in yourself** and having **faith** in your own abilities.

Self-motivation is an important attribute because if you are self-motivated, it means that you do not constantly need to be kept on track by others (e.g. a line manager or supervisor). You will be happy to be in **control of your own work**, you will move **confidently** between tasks, work to a high **quality** and meet **deadlines**, simply **because you want to**.

1.4 Organisational aims and objectives

All organisations, regardless of whether they are profit- or non-profit-making organisations, will have **aims** and **objectives** that they are working towards meeting through their activities. Possible aims could be to:

◆ provide 2000 employment opportunities to the general community
◆ make 20 per cent profit each year
◆ make charitable contributions to causes in the local community each year
◆ cut CO_2 emissions by 5 per cent each year.

Most organisations will have a **mission statement**.

This statement is designed to communicate the organisation's vision.

The Vodaphone® mission statement as of 2006 was:

The Vodafone Group Foundation is driven by a Passion for the World Around Us. The Foundation makes social investments that help the people of the world to have fuller lives by:

◆ Sharing the benefits of developments in mobile communications technology as widely as possible;

◆ Protecting the natural environment; and

◆ Supporting the local communities in which Vodafone's customers, employees, investors and suppliers live.

Statement used with permission of Vodaphone.

The Nike® mission statement is:

To bring inspiration and innovation to every athlete* in the world.

   * If you have a body, you are an athlete.

Statement used with permission of Nike.

In both cases the mission statement says something about the organisation and its positive corporate identity.

As relevant to the role of individuals

While all employees are working towards **helping the organisation meet** its aims and objectives, your role in this as an employee will be through **supporting** whichever aim you have the power to change. For example, if you work in the production department of a factory you might able to help them reduce their CO_2 emissions, or if you are a manager you might be able to organise the charitable contributions made each year. The one aim to which ALL employees can contribute will be the 'make 20 per cent profit each year'. This is because employees can help the organisation to save money, buy goods more cheaply and work more efficiently etc.

Responsibilities of the individual in promoting organisational brand or image

When you were at school you may well have been expected to wear school uniform. During this period in your life, you will have been asked by your teachers to make sure that you always looked smart when leaving or arriving at school, or just in general if you were wearing the school's uniform, because while wearing the uniform you would effectively be **representing** the school.

In the same way, when you are in employment you will be asked to be considerate and conscientious about helping the organisation promote a **positive image** through the way you dress, talk and interact with customers and other organisations. This is often called being an organisation's **ambassador**.

Braincheck

1 Define **attribute** and give an example.
2 Define **skill** and give an example.
3 What is a **PS**?
4 What is **flexi-time**?
5 Name two of your three responsibilities in terms of **health and safety** in the workplace.
6 What is **collaboration**?
7 What does **tolerance** mean?
8 What is **integrity**?
9 What is a **mission statement**?
10 What is an **attitude**?

How well did you do? See answers on page 421!

Activity

In preparation for a job or university application you have been asked to undertake a skills audit. Using a grid similar to that which often records a PS, you have been asked to consider your own strengths and weaknesses. Complete the following grid and discuss with your personal tutor or learning mentor.

Attributes	Strenths	Weaknesses
Experience		
Qualifications & Training		
Abilities		
Job Circumstances (e.g. mobility/late/early working)		

2 Understanding the principles of effective communication

2.1 General communication skills

Effective communication has a number of common elements, which will be briefly considered here. When communicating:

◆ Use **terminology** that will be understood by all those involved in the communication.

◆ Ensure that communication is **unambiguous**, be as **clear** as possible.

◆ As only a small percentage of a communication is accounted for by the words used, you should ensure that non-verbal communication is also used appropriately.

◆ Ensure that those involved can seek **clarification** if necessary.

◆ **Repeat** aspects of the communication as and when necessary to make sure that it has been **correctly received**.

◆ Encourage the **recipient** to **feed back** to you, so that you can check that they have fully understood.

Cultural differences

While you may well already appreciate that cultural differences exist between people from different nationalities, you might not be aware that there are regional variations within the UK as well.

A simple misunderstanding can occur when a physical gesture which in one country means 'wonderful', 'excellent' or 'first class', is interpreted as something exceedingly rude and derogatory in another country.

Figure 1.4 Child's footwear

Even the English language has some regional differences: for example, children at primary school wear the following items of footwear:

But what are they called? Regional variations include:

◆ daps
◆ plimsolls
◆ pumps
◆ canvas pumps
◆ deck shoes
◆ gym shoes.

Similarly, sausages in parts of Scotland are known as **links**. This is a word which in other areas of the UK means something completely different, for example links in a chain, links between websites. It is no wonder that at times communication can be misunderstood, particularly if the two individuals communicating have a different understanding of some of the words used.

Adapting content and style to audience (e.g. modulating voice, terminology, format)

A useful tool in ensuring that you have adapted communication to suit a particular age group for example is applying a **readability test**. Although a number of techniques exist, the commonly used one is known as the **Flesch-Kincaid** test. By applying a mathematical formula, the text is given a **score**. The score can then be compared to a list of accepted scores for the reading ability of different age groups.

An alternative **readability test** is the SMOG test (where SMOG means Simple Measure of Gobbledygook), which was developed by G. Harry McLaughlin in 1969 (taken from the following website):

http://webpages.charter. net/ghal/SMOG.html

To use the SMOG calculator, you simply key in your text. Click to calculate the grade for the text (as with the Flesch-Kincaid test, a mathematical formula is applied).

When compared against the list of educational levels, this score falls in the following category:

Type document title here (optional)

Similarly, sausages in parts of Scotland are known as links. This is a word which in other areas of the UK means something completely different, for example links in a chain, links between websites. It is no wonder that at times communication can be misunderstood, particularly if the two individuals communicating have a different understanding of some of the words used.

Calculate SMOG grade   Reset Form

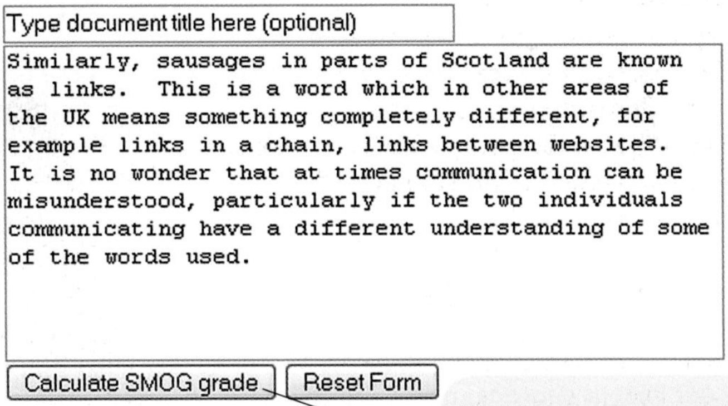

Figure 1.5 Using the test software

When the user then clicks on calculate SMOG grade a grade profile appears. The SMOG grade for this sample of text is 14.4.

    13 – 15   Some college

and where

    12 is high-school graduate and 16 is university degree

As such, this paragraph is considered suitably written for learners on a course like the National Diploma.

An alternative example would be the telling of the fairy story of the three bears. The following text was keyed into the SMOG software:

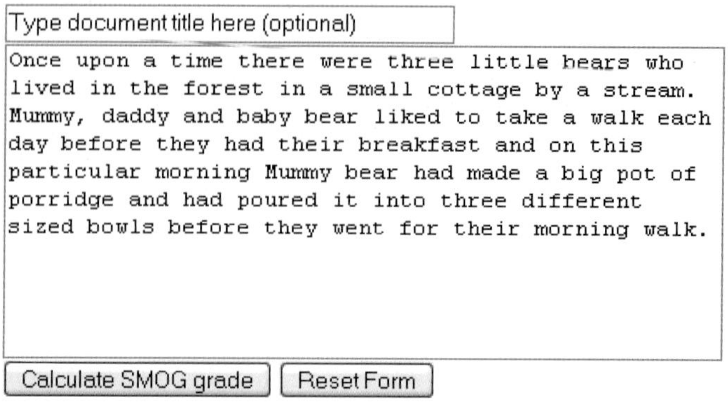

The calculated SMOG grade was 8.45 which would still be considered too high for very young readers where a SMOG grade of 0 to 6 would be considered ideal. Let's see if we can simplify the language.

This simplified version of the beginning of the story has now scored 3.0 and would be considered of an appropriate difficulty level for small children.

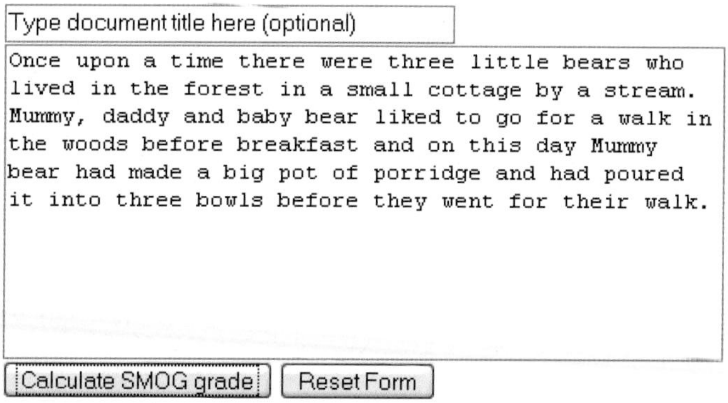

As such, terminology is clearly an important consideration when adapting the style of a communication to suit a particular type of audience.

Another adaptation technique will be to consider the format of a communication, whereby you decide how best to communicate your message to your audience. Might a Microsoft PowerPoint® presentation be the most appropriate format or would a report be more suitable? Will a series of carefully annotated diagrams and charts be more successful in getting the message across? The communicator needs to make these decisions and be able to justify their choices.

Figure 1.6 Fairy story

Figure 1.7 Simplified English

Providing accurate information

While it goes without saying that information that is being provided should be completely accurate, it is easy to make mistakes in generating this information because you might make assumptions about what someone does or does not know.

Take the following example.

What, exactly, is the purpose of the line graph shown in Figure 1.8? It is clear that the values are 4, 2, 7, 4.5, 5.5, 6, 8, 9, 3 (and these values are in fact correct), but there is no indication about what the graph is trying to convey. There is no title. The X-axis (X – across), contains numbers, but what do they mean? What does the Y-axis detail convey?

Would the revised chart in Figure 1.9 be better?

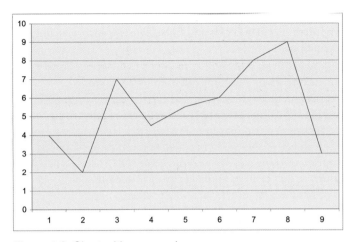

Figure 1.8 Chart with no meaning

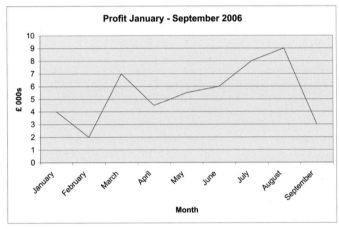

Figure 1.9 Chart with titles

Even now this graph can be further improved (better use of colours, possibly use a bar or column chart instead, name of the organisation)!

Differentiating between facts and feeling

While it is fair and valid (as long as your employer considers it appropriate) to give **your opinion** as part of the information you convey, you should ensure that your recipient knows whether the information you are providing is indeed **factual**, or is an **assumption** made by you based on **previous experience** or **gut instinct**. Sadly, if we fail to make this clear, **feeling** can very quickly become **established fact** and if the detail is incorrect, significant **time, money** and **resources** may be wasted in trying to recover from having acted on incorrect information.

Many entrepreneurs say that they are successful partly because they have a good **gut instinct**. This largely comes from their previous experience and their willingness and ability to take risks. This is fine if the risk is theirs – your employer might not be so forgiving and understanding if your misinformation puts the organisation at risk.

Techniques for engaging audience interest (e.g. changing intonation, use of multimedia, question and answer sessions, use of animation in presentations)

Think about what you like about lessons you attend. Do you like sitting and listening as someone goes through a Microsoft PowerPoint® presentation? Or do you prefer to be working practically, asking questions, using multimedia and the Internet? Most learners would say the latter. If you like your classes to be interesting, with a mix of techniques, animated presentations and lots of interaction, then surely you should expect your audience to want the same from you. Here are some suggestions:

◆ Changing intonation – this means changing the **pitch** of your **voice** when speaking.

- Use of multimedia – this means using facilities on the computer to help you maintain the interest of your audience. Modern multimedia computers also **play DVDs** and **CDs**. Consider incorporating moving images or sound into your presentations.
- Question and answer sessions – give your audience an opportunity to interact with you. Allowing them to **ask you questions** or indeed you **asking them** questions can liven up a session.
- Use of animation in presentations – in education today there is a growth in the use of information learning technology (ILT) in the classroom. Your college or school may well have an **electronic whiteboard** and **LCD projector** in your classroom – you may be able to use it at times, particularly when you are giving presentations. The advantage of this medium is that you can display moving images, rather than that old-fashioned option of using an overhead projector (OHP) and an acetate. An OHP is simply a bulb and series of mirrors that displays an image from an **acetate** (plastic sheet often containing hand-drawn diagrams or handwritten notes) on a white screen.

The best way to ensure that you keep an audience engaged with any type of communication is to use varied techniques to ensure that the audience stays interested.

2.2 Interpersonal skills

Your interpersonal skills are how you interact with others – they are about your ability to relate to others. How this can be done successfully is explained in the next section.

Methods for communicating interpersonally (e.g. verbal exchanges, signing, lip reading)

There are a number of ways in which we physically communicate. The most common way is to enter into verbal exchanges with each other. This is all very well for those individuals who can speak and/or hear. But for those who can not there are two alternatives.

Signing is a familiar method of communicating with those who have hearing difficulties. There are, however, multiple standards for this method of communicating.

Figures 1.10 and 1.11 show examples.

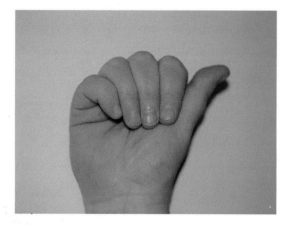

Figure 1.10 American Sign Language 'A' (American one-handed alphabet)

Figure 1.11 British Sign Language 'A' (British two-handed alphabet)

Both the examples mean the letter A. The obvious difference is that the American alphabet has been developed for one hand only, while the British version clearly uses two hands. That would tend to suggest that as a reader you would know automatically **which alphabet** you were looking at.

To confuse things further, Chinese sign language is based on American Sign Language (ASL) and has similarities, but it also has differences!

Another common technique for those with hearing difficulties is **lip reading.** Here the recipient literally watches the mouth of the communicator. It is something that often people are not aware they can do until they try it. With lip reading you are able to recognise letters by the way that they are formed with the mouth and lips. See the examples in Figures 1.12 and 1.13.

Figure 1.12 The 'th' sound

It is quite clear that some letters are easy to identify, while with others you might need to see the rest of the word to make sense of a **missing** letter. For example jar, shar and char would all look the same. But in a sentence you would assume that the person would not be asking for a shar of honey or a char of honey! Thus, you would need to contextualise the word in order for it to make sense.

Lip reading can be a very useful technique if you are trying to **hear** what someone is saying when you are not close enough to hear the sounds!

Techniques and cues (e.g. body language, use of intonation, use of 'smileys', capitalisation of text in emails)

In addition to the words used in communication there are a number of other cues that a recipient can **read** that come from the communicator. Here are some examples.

Figure 1.13 The 'o' sound

Body language

Most people would agree that the person in Figure 1.14 looks unhappy. Folded arms, a down-turned mouth and a frown are pretty obvious indicators that things are not as they should be!

Figure 1.14 Body language

Figure 1.16 Facial expression 2

What emotion is being experienced in the figure 1.15?

Figure 1.15 Facial expression 1

In this image the person is **sad**. The head is tilted and slightly down, the eyebrows are furrowed and the mouth shows no real expression.

And finally – what is the person in Figure 1.16 feeling?

She's clearly very happy!

Intonation

Your vocal **intonation** (as suggested earlier in this chapter) can give the recipient **clues** about the way you are feeling. Changes in intonation are actually quite difficult to describe in writing, so for the benefit of this book, here are only a few examples:

◆ Speaking **s-l-o-w-l-y** and **deliberately** – this often shows frustration on the part of the communicator.
◆ **SHOUTING** – is a clear indicator that the communicator is angry.

- **Raising** your voice in pitch on the last syllable of a sentence, leaves the recipient knowing that you are actually asking a **question**! Say the following out loud:
  - I am hungry – are **you**?

You will notice as you say the last word, your voice will rise!

Using smileys

As chatting on the Internet has become more prolific, closely followed by texting using mobile phones, a whole new language has developed. This has been necessary to **help** readers **interpret** messages sent to them.

For example:

- You looked really silly today.

If you received the above comment via either a mobile phone text or an email, you might be **offended**. If, however, you received the text like this you would probably see that the sender was actually **teasing you** and laughing with you:

- You looked really silly today. ☺

These **smileys** (known technically as **emoticons** – an abbreviation of emotions and icons) are now so common that some key combinations on a standard keyboard will result in the keystrokes being replaced by an image. The key is to ensure that the relevant keystrokes are pressed one immediately after the other. Here are some examples.

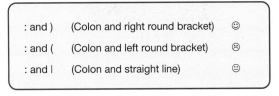

: and)	(Colon and right round bracket)	☺
: and (	(Colon and left round bracket)	☹
: and l	(Colon and straight line)	☺

Other key shortcuts are:

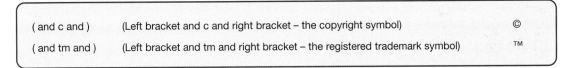

| (and c and) | (Left bracket and c and right bracket – the copyright symbol) | © |
| (and tm and) | (Left bracket and tm and right bracket – the registered trademark symbol) | ™ |

There are many other emoticons on the Internet, some of them are even animated, that can be used in emails. For more information search the Internet using the key word 'emoticon'.

Capitalisation of text in emails

Prior to the development of emoticons, the only ways to stress information in writing would have been to underline it, **embolden it**, or *put it in italics*. To stress a point it was not unusual to see ***all three used simultaneously***.

USING CAPITALISATION AS PART OF YOUR TEXT IN AN EMAIL is considered today to be **bad netiquette** (internet etiquette), as you will be interpreted to be **shouting** at the recipient!

Paying attention

No-one would disagree that trying to have a conversation with someone who doesn't appear to be listening is both **irritating** and **frustrating**. It is a common courtesy to actually **pay attention** to someone when they are talking to you – stand still, give eye contact and the occasional nod of the head. This will show the speaker that you are interested in what they have to say.

Positive and negative language

There are many ways to say negative things without them sounding quite so critical or rude. Here are some examples:

◆ 'John, that painting is awful – you should have used better colour combinations.'

Replaced with:

◆ 'John, that's an interesting painting that might have been even better if you had considered your colour combinations.'

Both of the above statements are critical of John, but the second one is not as aggressive or negative as the first – in fact the second statement could be mistaken for guidance! Here is another example:

◆ 'You don't appear to be particularly committed to your job.'
◆ 'At present Sam, you are possibly not as dedicated to your job as I know you could be.'

Again, the first statement is very direct. The second statement is actually saying the same thing but leaves the recipient on a positive note.

Active engagement (e.g. nodding, summarising, paraphrasing)

There are times when it is useful if you can actually show that you are engaged in a particular discussion. Nodding is a useful tool to show that you are actively participating. It lets the speaker know that you are listening. Summarising (where you repeat the main points of an exchange) or paraphrasing (where you use other words to relay the same information to aid understanding and clarification) are also useful when used to show active participation, although these should be used carefully. Imagine you are talking to someone else and every time you stop, the other person immediately repeats everything you said back to you! You would obviously wonder what was going on! Equally, if the person you are talking to is **constantly nodding** or **shaking their head**, it can be equally **disconcerting**. Each technique should be used when appropriate and not excessively.

Barriers (e.g. background noise, distractions, lack of concentration)

To improve interpersonal communication, one of the key factors is to begin by removing any barriers to the communication. Examples of this could be:

◆ **Moving away from an area where there is significant background noise** – this can be very irritating, particularly if it also means that you have to shout to be heard.
◆ **Moving away from distractions** – these distractions could include the television or be as simple as another person. You are more likely to be able to have a discussion with someone if there is no one else there!

Both excessive background noises and distractions will ensure that you and/or the recipient will not be able to fully concentrate.

Consider also whether the person you wish to communicate with might be preoccupied with other tasks. This is particularly true if you suddenly decide to have a conversation *now* and the person you want to speak to is very busy or has an important deadline to meet. This kind of stress is not conducive to a good discussion.

The person might have other priorities – it might be late in the afternoon and they want to go home, or close to their lunch break.

In general, to make discussions and communications more likely to be successful, you should ensure that you consider as many potential barriers as possible and try to eradicate them.

Types of questions (e.g. open, closed, probing)

The type of question you ask will also have a bearing on how responsive the other party is in a communication. You will tend to mix the type of questions you use, depending on the situation. For this reason, you should understand different questioning techniques and the responses you are likely to receive:

Open questions

An open question is one where the question is structured in such a way as to allow the responder some control over how much they say in their response. For example:

◆ 'How are you today?'

The responder might say 'Very well, thank you!', or could begin by saying 'You know, I've had an awful day. I overslept this morning, got into work late and it meant that I spent hours trying to catch up with my work.'

Closed questions

A closed question is one where the question is structured in such a way as to limit the possible responses:

◆ 'Are you over 18 or under 18?'

Here it would be likely that the response would be 'I am over 18' or 'I am under 18'. In some circumstances the responder might add 'I am 17' or 'I am 23' to further clarify their answer, but what else is there to say? Closed questions often result in a 'yes' or 'no' response.

Probing questions

A probing question is one which is likely to encourage the responder to say more than they might have intended to. Quite often this is done intentionally, to make the responder believe that they are giving the information voluntarily, whereas the questioner was actually clever in the construction of the question in that a fuller response was always the intention:

◆ 'Is that everything or is there anything else that you can think of?'

Or:

◆ 'Is there anything else you can tell me about the accident?'

Carefully selecting your questions prior to a meeting or discussion can be useful to a) ensure that the meeting moves at the pace you want it to and b) to ensure that you ask everything you need to, and receive the right level of detail.

Appropriate speeds of response

There is a great debate about the appropriateness of response speeds and what that says about the recipient.

A quick response could be interpreted in two ways:

The responder is needy and over eager.

The responder is enthusiastic and interested.

A slow response could also be interpreted in two ways:

The responder does not care and could not be bothered to respond more quickly.

The responder has taken a great deal of care and considered their response.

In most cases, a measured response is the most appropriate. In other words – do not respond too quickly or too slowly – try and aim for somewhere in the middle!

2.3 Communicating in writing

Following organisational guidelines and procedures

When it comes to written communication, most organisations have procedures and guidelines that they themselves predefine and that they expect all employees to observe.

Most commonly, this will be known as a house *style*. The style will include guidelines on layout – for example:

Left margin	3 cm
Right margin	2.5 cm
Top margin	4 cm (this is often to accommodate the organisation's own letter-headed paper)
Bottom margin	2.5 cm
Justification	Full
Indentation	Blocked style
Line spacing	1.5 (except in an address)

Key Terms

Justification defines whether the edges of the page are consistent and in a straight line or not. See the following paragraphs (the borders have been added so that you can see where the margin actually is).

This paragraph is right justified – this means that the right edge of the text is always aligned and the left side of the page will probably have sentences which are of different lengths. For obvious reasons this is called **ragged left**, which is another term for **right justified**. This style is particularly used when including a sender's address at the top of a letter.

This paragraph is **fully justified** – which means that both sides of the text are always aligned. What the computer does is even out the gaps between the words so that it is not obvious that the gaps on each line are of a slightly different width. If you look at a newspaper you are likely to see all the columns printed in full justification.

Key Terms

Indentation identifies whether a paragraph starts at the edge of a page or whether it begins a number of spaces in. The two main options are blocked or indented.

This paragraph begins at the edge of the page. The writer immediately keys in text without pressing the space or tab bar to show where the paragraph begins.

In this case, when a subsequent paragraph begins, a clear line must be left between the old and new paragraphs to make it clear where one paragraph ends and another starts. This is known as blocked style.

Alternatively, you could use what is called **indentation**.

Here the first line of the paragraph is indented (moved in), with all subsequent text aligned to the left-hand margin. Getting the space or gap is easy – it can be achieved either by pressing the tab button or simply by pressing the space bar a set number of times.
When a new paragraph begins, it begins on the line below the end of the previous paragraph, with the first line indented as previously.

Whichever style is used, you should ensure that the entire document is consistent!

Some organisations also predefine the **line spacing** for documents. Some rules do exist in general – for example, if you go on to university it is likely that you will be asked to submit all your assignments in double line spacing. This is so that your tutor or lecturer can write comments between lines of your text.

According to Demszcinsky, et al (1994), the main reason for submitting this kind of
why Mary?
evidence is to ensure that the process has quality. Without quality the whole point of the
You have not said how!
exercise will be lost and there is a risk of misinterpretation.

Figure 1.17 Double line spacing

In the above example, the text has been written in **double line spacing**, which has allowed the tutor to write in-between. The text in this book generally is in single line spacing (each line follows the line written above, with no gap). In addition to single or double line spacing, you can set the spacing to be 1.5, or allow a user to define a particular spacing. It would be unusual to type the name and address on a letter in anything other than single line spacing, as it would be unlikely that you would be able to see all of the name and address in the **envelope window** unless it was typed in this type of spacing. Some envelopes have a clear plastic panel on the front – this allows companies to print **names** and **addresses** directly onto the letter or circular in the knowledge that when the item is folded, the name and address will still be **fully visible**.

Each organisation will set its own **house style**. This is usually felt to be a good representation of the company's professionalism.

Identifying and conveying key messages in writing (e.g. letter, fax, email)

Figure 1.18 Envelopes

In a fast-paced world where everyone is always busy, it is essential that when you are communicating you convey your message as quickly, efficiently and as simply as possible. Long and drawn-out sentences and paragraphs are difficult to read and are time consuming for the reader. To ensure that your letters, faxes or emails are efficient, it is best to plan ahead:

1 Identify the key issues without which the communication will be deemed to have failed.
2 Identify what it is you want to say about these issues.
3 Decide how you want to say it (tone, etc.).

Certainly in these days of word processing, rather than the days where letters had to be typed and changing a word would potentially require the whole letter to be retyped, there is no excuse for sending out poorly worded or incorrect correspondence. This is because the written word is now very easy to check, correct and reprint if necessary.

Using correct grammar and spelling

When you consider that most word-processing software now has spellchecking, grammar checking and thesaurus capabilities, there is really no reason why correspondence should be sent out unchecked and uncorrected. However, there is no substitute for **proofreading**, as can be seen in Figure 1.19a.

Some Peploe say " it dnso' et mtetar how txet is wittren as lnog as the frsit and lsat ltteres are in the rhgit oerdr and rghit psoitnios, bacusee the hmaun bairn can srot out the maennig aynawy" .

Can you read the above? Most people can. It should say:

Some people say " it doesn' t matter how text is written as long as the first and last letters are in the right order and right positions, because the human brain can sort out the meaning anyway" .

Figure 1.19a Proofreading

Research has been undertaken which suggests that the brain has the capacity to interpret badly written English (see **http://www.languagehat.com/archives/000840.php** for further information).

However, the incorrectly written paragraph does not exactly look very professional does it? Poor spelling and grammar usually suggest that the writer did not take particular care in the presentation of their work. This is paramount, particularly if you are writing to individuals outside an organisation, as through the communication you will be considered to be representing the organisation!

Key Terms

Spellchecking facilities are often written into software packages to help the user to ensure that documents are correct. Often the software will highlight words that it has assessed as being incorrectly spelled.

In the example in Figure 1.19b, the incorrectly spelled words have been highlighted with a red underscore.

Some Peploe say "it dnso'et mtetar how txet is wittren as lnog as the frsit and lsat ltteres are in the rhgit oerdr and rghit psoitnios, bacusee the hmaun bairn can srot out the maennig aynawy".

Figure 1.19b Proofreading

Unfortunately, the system can not identify correctly spelled words that are used in an incorrect context. For example, which is correct?

a) I will not go their or b) I will not go there

In this case **b** is correct because the word **their** in sentence **a** means their in the sense of belonging to them. There are a number of common words that are often incorrectly interchanged. Here are some examples to watch out for.

Word	Meaning
There	In that place
Their	Belonging to them
Where	In what place? – used in a question
Wear	To be dressed in
Pair	Two identical items
Pear	Fruit
Whether	Often used to introduce a number of alternatives, for example, 'whether good or bad, we will proceed with the sale'
Weather	Sunshine, rain etc.
Fair	A place you go with dodgems and rides
Fare	The cost of getting from a to b

In each case, the word in the table would not throw up a spelling error. Only proofreading and an understanding of the word in its correct context will ensure that these errors are not made in written text.

Key Terms

As with spellchecking functionality, a **grammar check** is also built in to many software packages.

This time, the system will check whether the sentences have been constructed correctly. Unfortunately, this does not identify whether words have been used in an incorrect context – and again will not help you to decide which version of **pair** you need to include in your sentence. In the event that the grammar checker finds sentences that are deemed to have problems, the software will highlight the words involved using a green line, much like the red line you saw in Figures 1.19a and 1.19b for the spellchecker.

Key Terms

The final tool is the **thesaurus**. This is an extremely useful tool because when activated, it offers the user a selection of alternative words which more or less have the same meaning. Here's an example:

> *Actually, he was wrong when it came to his description of the actual man he had seen.*

In this example, the word **actual** has been used **twice** (once as **actual** and the second time as the basis of the word **actually**). Why is the word used in the first place? To try and stress the point being made. Using the thesaurus we can change both (or just one) of the occurrences of the word actual.

Here are some alternative words that the thesaurus suggests for the word **actually**:

In fact	**Really**
In point of fact	**In reality**
Truly	**Essentially**

The following words are the thesaurus' suggestions as alternatives for the word **actual**:

Real	**Definite**
Genuine	**Authentic**
Concrete	**Tangible**

Now let's rewrite the sentence again using some of the alternative words:

> *In fact, he was wrong when it came to his description of the actual man he had seen.*

Interestingly, in this example, we decided to keep the word actual and replace the word actually. Why? Because the words offered by the thesaurus to replace the word actual did not seem to quite fit the sentence.

As such, while the thesaurus is an extremely useful tool, the decision has been made on this occasion to change the one instance and leave the other.

Knowing when it is appropriate to make changes, and when it might be more suitable to leave words as they are, is part of your skill as a communicator.

Structuring writing into a logical framework

Even though it is ultimately up to you what you put in a letter (although, as suggested earlier, your employer will also have ideas about what should and should not be included in letters, faxes or emails), using a formal structure or framework for a written communication is important.

Most letters have a format similar to that in Figure 1.20.

Firstly, please note that we have closed with **Yours sincerely** because we began the letter with **Dear Mr Smith**. Had we started with **Dear Sir** we would have closed with **Yours faithfully**.

The advantage of using a logical structure, such as the one shown, is a little bit like using a recipe to make a cake – if you follow the recipe you will have a useable product! In addition, if all organisations use a similar basic structure for their business documents (with organisational variations of course), then you will always know what information should be available in a document because you understand what the document is, how it works and what is usually included. For example, any business documentation associated with money (sales

```
        Name of organisation sending the letter
                  Address of organisation
                              Post Code
              Telephone Number (if appropriate)

Date of letter
Reference (some organisations include  information
that they ask you to quote when responding)

Name of person/organisation the letter is going to
Address of person
Post Code of person


Dear Sir or Dear Mr Smith (known as the salutation)

Subject of the letter is often written here

This will be where the main content of the letter is
typed. A sample of a completed letter from Lee
Office Supplies follows this example.

Yours faithfully (if you wrote Dear Sir), or Yours
sincerely (If you wrote Dear Mr Smith)


                          ┌──────────────────────┐
                          │ Room is left here to  │
                          │ ensure that the person│
                          │ sending the letter has │
                          │ space to sign it.      │
Name of sender            └──────────────────────┘
Job in organisation
```

Figure 1.20 A sample letter template

invoices, purchase invoices etc.) will have a VAT number on it, if the company is registered for VAT. A company is not allowed to charge VAT on an invoice unless it a) is registered and b) has displayed its number on the documentation. Clearly, as a letter is not the same as a purchase or sales invoice, it does not need to have the VAT number shown on it.

Particular documentation standards, which have been used by businesses for many years, have now provided the structure for many of the templates you will see within the software you use. Letters, memos, business cards, invoices, orders, delivery notes, greetings cards and many more have a similar format, with artistic variations to suit an organisation or individual.

```
                              Lee Office Supplies
                                 21 Golden Road
                                        Mytown
                                      MY10 1BF
                                    01166 878216

15 November 2006

Reference: BF/ja


Mr S Smith
Greenacres
Mytown
MY11 1MF

Dear Mr Smith

Order Number: 126552

We are delighted to inform you that the special
envelopes and photographic paper you ordered
are now in stock, a week earlier than anticipated.
Furthermore, we were able to secure additional
discount and we will be reducing the cost of your
order by a further 5 per cent.

Please call in at our offices at your earliest
convenience to collect your order.

Yours sincerely



Bernie Fishpool
Sales Manager
```

Figure 1.21 The template in use

Identifying relevant information in written communications

In order to explain this concept, it is probably better to give you an example. You have received the correspondence shown in Figure 1.22.

Review this letter and decide what the relevant (and thus important) information actually is! The answer is as follows:

◆ Your dental appointment is now on Monday 2 April at 2.45 pm.
◆ Please let us know if the new date or time is inconvenient.

Did you really need to know **why** the appointment had been postponed? Does your knowledge of this fact have **any** influence on what you **think** about this? Probably **not**!

As such, the adaptation of the letter shown in Figure 1.23 would have been wholly appropriate.

Being able **to extract relevant information** from writing is a **skill**. You have to decide which parts of the communication contain information you might want to use again or refer to at a later date. Here is an overview on how to do this:

◆ Read the document through so that you understand in general what it is about.
◆ Read again and make notes about the important aspects of the text.

Dear Mrs Fishpool

We regret to inform you that your dental appointment has been postponed and will now be on Monday 2 April at 2.45 pm.

This is because the dentist has been asked to speak at a charity function and while this is actually a lunchtime appointment, we were concerned that he might be late and thus would keep you waiting. So we thought it better to change the time.

If this new date or time is inconvenient, please call and let us know as soon as possible.

Yours sincerely

Dental Practice

Figure 1.22 What information is truly necessary?

Dear Mrs Fishpool

We regret to inform you that your dental appointment has been postponed and will now be on Monday 2 April at 2.45 pm.

If this new date or time is inconvenient, please call and let us know as soon as possible.

Yours sincerely

Dental Practice

Figure 1.23 Amended letter

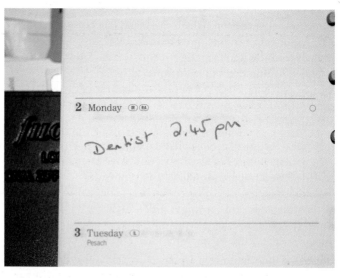

Figure 1.24 A diary extract

- Highlight the key points.
- Write the relevant information down in your own words!

If we use the dental appointment as an example, it would now be likely that we would find our diaries, cross through the original entry for the dental appointment and write the new details on the appropriate date (as shown in Figure 1.24).

With experience you will soon be able to tell what information is likely to be important and which information can be ignored. Similarly, you will learn to write letters that are to the point without waffling on about things that have no relevance.

Activity

You have been given the following **typed record** of a **telephone message**:

> Mrs Jones rang about the missing items from the last order. She says that she really isn't very happy about the way that our organisation has dealt with this issue. She says that when she dealt with Smethurst Office Supplies she never had these kinds of problems. If something was missing from an order they would courier it to her immediately. She also said that she was always given goods on account and 30 days' credit, and they didn't even chase her for an additional 15 days after the account was due. Her number is 01234 567891. She will be on this number from 3 to 4.30 pm today.

Extract the important information from this message. Answer on page 436.

Reviewing and proofreading own written work

It is absolutely essential that you learn to review and proofread your own written work. The more important a document is the more carefully the document should have been reviewed and proofread.

Key Terms

Reviewing – is where you look at the factual content and check it is correct. Again using the dental appointment example, the letter writer should check that the appointment has been correctly entered in the appointments book for the date and time specified in the letter!

Proofreading – is where the spelling and grammar of the document is checked. If you are concerned about your proofreading skills, ask someone else to proofread for you or with you. You should, however, endeavour to be able to do this yourself in the long term. As suggested earlier in this chapter, if you are using software to create your documents, you will be able to make use of the software tools available. You should never rely on this – you should always read the document through again yourself to be absolutely sure that it is correct.

Conveying alternative viewpoints

One of the most important aspects of writing is that the writer has to be able to convey alternative viewpoints – viewpoints with which they might not actually agree! Consider the following.

The event – an election was being held to select a new local councillor. Martha Hargreaves is the Conservative candidate. Elena Malowski is a Labour candidate and Justin Newman is standing for the Independents. They were each asked to speak about the state of the county's roads! This is how the event was written up in two local papers.

Paper A	Paper B
Martha Hargreaves highlighted the dreadful state of the roads, particularly since the last election when the Independents took control of the council. 'There are increasingly potholes in the streets, causing a trip hazard to the elderly and small children, and causing unnecessary stress on the suspensions of local car drivers.' She said 'something needs to be done'. Elena Malowski and Justin Newman agreed.	After a debate the councillors agreed that something should be done about local roads in the county as potholes are increasingly a hazard for all road users.

It is clear that Paper A has focused on Martha Hargreaves and has only mentioned the other candidates at the end, almost dismissively. In addition, it makes Martha appear proactive and strong, and the other candidates weak because they simply agreed with her and did not appear to have had any original thoughts of their own!

In the second account, no one councillor is quoted, just the summary of what was said. This does not emphasise a contribution from any one councillor and thus is more balanced! Obviously, when there is really an election, it is in a political party's interest to get as much coverage for its own candidates as possible!

Reviewing and editing documents created by others

There will be instances where you are asked to review and edit documents that have been created by other people.

Firstly, you should review the document. Read it through to ensure that you understand what it means. If you have any doubts about any aspect of what is written, consider (if you can) asking the person who originally wrote the text what they meant. Clearly it would not be possible to ask Shakespeare to explain exactly what he meant in a line of dialogue from Romeo and Juliet, but with works such as these there are plenty of books available that will explain the text to you. Under normal circumstances it is likely to be something a colleague or a member of your family has written.

When editing a document you should ensure that when you make your changes, you do not change the sense of what the writer was trying to say in the first place unless, of course, the writer is happy for you to make these changes. For this book there are a number of individuals who will have an editing role for each chapter. In the first instance, the writers are largely taking responsibility for specific units, and the other member of the writing team is acting as an editor – reading through the content to make sure that it is accurate and makes sense. Once the chapters are sent to the publisher, another editor will look through the text. They will not change the content in any way (it is unlikely that they will be a computing specialist in the first place) but will check spelling and grammar. This is not the last time the script will be checked. It is likely that the writers will also see it again before it goes to print and that desk editors at Hodder Educational will look it over.

The key with editing is that the originator (person who wrote the document to begin with) must be happy about the changes that have been made.

Note taking

This is a very useful skill, particularly if you need to make a paper record of a meeting. Prior to the development of voice recognition software such as Dragon NaturallySpeaking®, which allows the user to dictate the text verbally rather than using a keyboard to facilitate the input, notes had to be taken in longhand (written word for word, slowly by a note taker) or in shorthand. Shorthand is a written language that uses symbols that are quick to write as abbreviations for common words.

'**We have**' for example looks like this, in Pitman 2000® shorthand:

The hook and upstroke mean **we** and the down curve is a visual representation of a **V sound**. The position of this image in relation to a line is also important, as this position determines which vowel sound is intended.

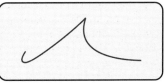

Figure 1.25 Shorthand

Shorthand is still used by secretarial staff and journalists, although in both cases tape recorders are also very often used and are practical alternatives.

The third option is using a medium such as Speedwriting®. With this technique, the words written down are abbreviations of the original words, symbols used to denote a particular common word, or are phonetic spellings (when a word is written as it actually sounds).

For example:

◆ **Few**   would be   **fu**   phonetic spelling
◆ **The**   would be   **.**   symbol
◆ **Could**   would be   **cud**   abbreviation

One very important facet about taking notes is that you should always write up the notes as soon as possible, otherwise you might no longer be able to remember what you meant, particularly if you made errors!

Braincheck

Match the following terms with their correct explanation.

Term	Explanation
Spellchecking	Where text is written in capital letters or emboldened
Yours faithfully	Assessing the suitability of a piece of text for a specific age range
Indented paragraph	Where both sides of text are aligned (straight)
A closed question	Where the first line is set in from the subsequent lines in a paragraph
Proofreading	Offers a selection of alternative words that can be used to replace the word highlighted that have an identical or similar meaning
Shouting in emails	Closes a letter that began with Dear Mr Smith
Full justification	Using software to check the accuracy of a piece of text
Thesaurus	Checking the correctness of spelling and grammar in written text
Readability test	Closes a letter that began with Dear Sir
Yours sincerely	Where the answer can only be one of a limited number of options

See answers on page 421.

3 Ability to exploit ICT to communicate effectively

Your ability to use ICT to communicate effectively is dependent on your having the **relevant software skills** and **your understanding** of the **nature** of communication.

3.1 Communications channels

There are a number of common ways in which we communicate information today – some of which will be examined here.

Word-processed documents

Word processing has revolutionised the way in which organisations communicate, particularly with the outside world. It has seen many organisations produce more professional and complex documents than they might have done in the days of typewriters!

Thus, it has become easier and cheaper to create mail-merge letters, leaflets, flyers, posters etc. Most software also has a range of templates that can be used and the facility for organisations and individuals to create their own templates. In addition, more and more design styles can be downloaded and incorporated within existing software as and when they are created by the manufacturers.

As suggested earlier in the chapter, grammar and spellchecking facilities have ensured that written documentation looks more professional.

Presentations

Businesses frequently use this technique for passing a significant amount of information to a number of individuals simultaneously. You may well be asked to present some of your coursework in this format.

It usually requires that the presenter speaks formally to the audience, using any one of a range of visual aids to help them get the message across. Slide shows, DVDs, leaflets and handouts may all be created to be used during the presentation.

Web pages

Web pages can be created and uploaded to the **World Wide Web** (the **Internet**) or they can be included on an organisation's own internal website, usually called an **intranet**.

One distinct advantage of web pages is that they can include **hyperlinks** to other web pages, thereby reducing the amount of information that an organisation might have to include because the information can be accessed on someone else's website!

Some web pages are **interactive** (for example where you can order and pay for goods or services); other pages act as **online brochures** (for example a tourist information website for your town might have **lists of attractions** or **accommodation** that a visitor might like know about before coming to your town or village).

> **Activity**
>
> Using a search engine such as **Google**™ or **Yahoo!**®, have a look at the tourist information website for your own town or area.
>
> **Key Words:** Your town name + tourist information

Email

Increasingly used in preference to letters, email has become the main method of communication, particularly within organisations where less formal communication is required. It has all but replaced the concept of an **interoffice memorandum** (which was laid out similarly to an email and was usually sent via an internal mail system).

The main advantage of email is that it is extremely quick and is a cheap method of communication! In addition, if you use a **read receipt** you can be advised when the recipient (person receiving your email) has read it! This can be very useful in helping to get things done quickly, as someone could always say 'I didn't receive your memo', but would be less likely to claim that they had not received an email.

Specialist channels (e.g. blogs, vlogs, podcasts, video conferencing)

Blog is an abbreviation for weblog. This is a newsletter or information website (sometimes in diary form). It tends to be updated on a regular basis and is intended to be used by anyone who wishes to see it!

Vlog is principally the same as a blog but uses video as part of its format.

The term **podcast** is derived from the Apple product the **iPod**® and the concept of the **broadcast**. Essentially a podcast is a **media file** that can be **downloaded** to an individual's own computer or mobile device to be played back. Depending on the originator, these files might be free or the receiver might have to pay some sort of subscription.

Video conferencing has significantly modernised the way in which businesses can communicate over distances. Where in earlier years executives would have had to travel to another office or a client's premises for a meeting, the advent of this technology has ensured that many people in different locations can come together for a meeting without actually having to travel anywhere. Using simple webcams or even fully integrated systems, users can see each other during the discussion. As such, they can also see demonstrations of products, drawings etc.

Benefits and disadvantages

This is an overview of communication channels.

Channel	Benefit	Disadvantage
Word-processed documents	Permanent record that can also be easily edited	Users need reasonable word-processing skills otherwise creating the documents can be laborious and time consuming
Presentations	An interactive way of presenting information to a large number of individuals simultaneously	They can be nerve-racking for those who are shy or who are not used to giving them
Web pages	Can be interesting and interactive, and can reach many people across multiple time zones and continents	Need to be updated regularly and checked for accuracy, particularly taking into account any legal issues between countries
Email	Quick and efficient	They can be intrusive and extensive SPAM email (unsolicited

▶

Channel	Benefit	Disadvantage
Email *cont.*		email from companies trying to sell you things) can be irritating
Blogs/vlogs/podcasts	These tools have ensured that there is now information on more or less anything on the Internet!	Some might not be suitable for some age groups and as they are difficult to police, some might cause offence
Video conferencing	Being able to communicate visually with others without having to travel	

3.2 Software

Word processing

Using products such as **Microsoft Word**, **Microsoft Works** or **Corel WordPerfect**®, has **transformed** business communication. For Linux-based systems, Open Office® has become one of the most commonly used software packages for this function.

These products contain additional tools and templates that can help the less able user to create professional documentation with little effort.

Presentation packages

As with word-processing opportunities, there is a range of software that can be purchased for both Microsoft Windows®- and Linux®-controlled systems.

This software works by allowing users to create slide shows. Each slide will usually contain text, images, graphs and charts (or a combination of these), with the advantage that the slide show can be printed in the form of a handout to be taken away by delegates as a permanent record of the presentation.

Using this type of technique will also ensure that if you have to give the same presentation to a number of groups (possibly even over a number of weeks or days), the content of each presentation is likely to be more or less the same as the first occasion.

Other (e.g. email software, specialist software for the visually impaired)

As with all applications, there will be a variety of useable software for every eventuality. Many internet service providers (**ISPs**) (such as Blueyonder®, Yahoo!®, AOL®) have their own software interface for email. Alternatively, if you are using a product such as Microsoft Office you can use Outlook® and set it up to receive and display your emails from one or more providers.

Some organisations have messaging software built in to their intranet to cut down on the number of internal phone calls made between people in different departments.

There are a number of Braille software products available for the visually impaired, such as **Braille n' Speak**® and **Braille Lite**®. In addition, there is a Braille email package available called **Pine**® that was developed by the Computing and Communications Group at the University of Washington, USA. For more information see **http://www.washington.edu/pine/tutorial/index.html**.

3.3 Software Tools

It is not possible to provide you with a definitive list of software tools because each software manufacturer has its **own suite of functionality** that it adds to its own software. However, there are a number of basic tools which tend to be common across the range of available applications. These will be briefly mentioned here, although they are described in more detail earlier in the chapter.

Proofing tools (e.g. thesaurus, spell checkers)

Spell checkers check the spelling of individual words. They are able to identify if letters in a word are missing or if they have been transposed (switched around). However, this tool is unable to understand the sense of a word and thus is no substitute for reading the document yourself. It can not differentiate between words that sound the same but have different spellings. In addition, the spell checker must be compatible with the language in which you are writing. While this may sound silly, it would not be very helpful to use a spell checker that has been set on American spelling if you are writing documents in the UK for UK recipients. This is because some common words are simply spelt differently in the USA. For example:

Colour	is	color	(the u can thus be omitted with some words)
Organisation	is	organization	(the s is substituted with a z in the USA)

The thesaurus is a very useful tool if you are unable to think of an alternative word. By keying in a word, highlighting it and activating the thesaurus, you will be offered a number of alternatives from which you can choose. Most have the same or very similar meaning to the word you highlighted. You should be cautious, however, that your choice of a substitute word does not change the sense of what you are trying to say.

As available within software packages (e.g. conversion of tabular information to graphics, text readers)

Inside some packages there are additional converters. For example, some word-processing software will take a table that contains numbers and allow you to create a chart or graph from it.

Some packages allow you to **print to a file**. This means that instead of printing the document using a conventional printer, the tool converts the content of your word-processing file into a different file format (for example, making a .pdf file which stands for **portable document format**) which can not be altered by a reader.

Quite often it is simply useful to experiment with software to find out what it does. Alternatively, you can read the manual, as most software packages have online help systems.

Activity

Pick a typical computer room at your school, college or institution and identify the following:

1 types of common software installed (excluding the operating system)
2 types of specialist software installed.

Using this information, complete the following grid.

Software name (e.g. Microsoft Word)	Function (e.g. word processing)

You should retain this list to act as an **aide memoire** (aid to memory).

4 Identifying your personal development needs and addressing them

In order to be an effective individual (not just an effective employee) you will constantly need to review your own situation as you move through your personal and working life. Others will help you to identify your own training and developmental needs along the way but, primarily, you should be prepared to self-evaluate from time to time, to ensure that you are getting the best out of your life and your situation. Here are some examples of how needs are identified.

4.1 Identification of need

Self-assessment

In section 1 of this chapter you were asked to undertake an activity in which you identified your own strengths and weaknesses. This is known as **self-assessment**. In this type of activity you highlight **what you feel** you are good at and **what you think** you are bad at. In most cases, the **what you think you are bad at** list is what is used to identify training and development needs. However, the list of **what you feel you are good at** also needs to be explored, because human nature dictates that we will sometimes think we are better at things than we really are.

An example might be: 'I have always considered myself to be very well organised – and in many ways I am. If I were doing a self-assessment activity I would probably list this as one of my positive attributes. Lately, however, I have forgotten many birthdays. As such, I am clearly not as well organised as I used to be. Putting this right is relatively straightforward, I just need to keep a diary and refer to it on a regular basis! If I make this modification to my behaviour, I will correctly be able to claim being well organised as a positive personal trait.'

Formal reports (e.g. following appraisal meetings)

Key Terms

Appraisal When you are in **employment** you will have **regular appraisals** with your line manager. Usually taking the form of a **meeting**, you will be asked to **self-assess** and you will discuss your **positive** and **negative attributes** and **attitudes** with your manager or supervisor.

However, it is likely that your manager or supervisor will also have their **own ideas** about your good and bad traits! The appraisal is usually written up as a **formal document** and an **action plan** is established to help you to develop.

This plan could list a number of courses that might be useful to you. Alternatively, it might contain a personal attitude target, for example 'think before you speak', or 'arrive at work on time'. Targets that are set should be **s**pecific, **m**easurable, **a**ppropriate, **r**ealistic and **t**imed (**SMART**).

Other (e.g. customer feedback, performance data)

Some organisations also use other information to help identify your developmental needs. It is not uncommon for organisations to ask customers for feedback. As part of your course your college or school will receive a visit from an Edexcel external verifier (EV). This person is employed by Edexcel to check that the standards of assessment being applied at your institution are the same as the standards being applied over the rest of the country. The EV will be in contact with your teachers/lecturers and you may not be aware that this process is taking place.

However, after the EV has completed their duties with your institution, your teachers/lecturers will be asked to feed back to Edexcel on the EV as well. If the report is good (i.e. the EV was pleasant, courteous, efficient) then the verifier will receive more work. If the report is negative, then Edexcel would be unlikely to offer that person any more work as a verifier. This is an example of customer feedback, where Edexcel is the provider and the institution (your teachers and lecturers) are in fact the customers!

In some environments there is what is called performance data, which can help managers to assess the needs of their employees. For example, the sales records for a given area can be used to establish whether a sales representative is performing adequately. If they are over their target sales, they might get a bonus. If under the sales target, questions will be asked and the representative will be asked to explain.

Similarly, how you and your classmates performed in your school SATs tests will have had an influence on where your school or college came in a local league table of education providers. If your institution was low down the list, the board of governors may well have asked the management team to explain the performance of the students or pupils at the institution. Individual teachers or lecturers might also have been called to account.

While this might all sound extreme, in the current information age all this data is readily available and as such it is often used as part of the assessment process.

From your perspective, you will probably be having tutorials with a tutor or learning mentor where you will be discussing your progress and achievement, and you will be highlighting any areas where you feel you need additional support.

4.2 Records

Personal development plans including target setting

As suggested in the previous section, an action plan is often created as part of the appraisal process. This is formalised so that it can be used in a subsequent review (where your work towards meeting these targets is discussed). Targets that have been set are usually formalised with a **by when** notation, so that your development is not left open-ended but is tied to specific dates in the calendar.

Other (e.g. appraisal records)

Most institutions will have their own version of an appraisal record. Figure 1.26, shows a typical example.

Appraisal Form

Name of Employee:	Department:
Position:	Name of Manager:

Please define your job role:

How has the period since the last appraisal been? Good/ satisfactory/bad (Please delete as appropriate and state why:

What have you achieved in the last year?

What do you find difficult about your job?

What do you like most about your job?

What can be done to help you improve?

What would you like to be doing in 3 years' time?

Figure 1.26 An appraisal form

This form is usually filled in by the employee prior to the appraisal. It is given to the manager so that they are aware of the issues that the employee has identified.

During the subsequent appraisal meeting (sometimes also known as an interview), the second part of the appraisal record is filled in. In this section, the manager and the employee discuss the answers given by the employee to the questions, and the main points of the discussion are noted.

At the end of the session, an action plan will be completed, something like this.

Action point	How/By whom?	By when?
Improve timekeeping	Employee	1 month
Further Microsoft Excel® training required	External training course	July 2007
First aid training	External training course	December 2007
X would like to work in reception	Reception training	3 months

The action plan will be signed by both the employee and the line manager, both of whom will get a copy.

4.3 Methods of addressing needs

How personal development for the employee will be facilitated is dependent on a number factors, but particularly on the following:

a) how much money the organisation has for staff development
b) the time needed for training.

Clearly an organisation will want to spend as little as possible on training its employees. Here are some methods of training that organisations use:

Job shadowing

It was suggested in the example action plan that the employee would like to do some work in Reception. To this end it might be possible for the employee to **shadow** (observe and help) the receptionist over a given period. The advantage to the employee of this activity would be that they would get **first-hand experience** of the job. The advantage to the employer of this would be that there would be another member of staff trained to cover this important business function. The main disadvantage for both the employee and the employer is that while the employee is shadowing the receptionist, their usual job might not be getting done.

Formal courses or training (external, internal)

If an organisation has the budget, there is no substitute for formal training courses. Many organisations, to save money, pay for one employee to do a particular course and, if possible, they use that employee to **cascade** the training to others who might need it.

Courses organised by schools, colleges and other training providers would be considered **external training**, because while the organisation might have some input on what is covered by the training provider, an external agency is paid and ultimately has control of the process.

Internal training courses are obviously much cheaper to run (this is often where the cascade training comes in), and are equally as enjoyable. However, there is a possibility that if you are doing an internal course **on site** (where you would normally work), you might be called out of the training course to deal with a problem, and as such you might miss important parts of the training. Clearly if you are on an external course, and not on site, it is unlikely that this would occur!

Other (e.g. team meetings, attending events)

In addition to formal training or job shadowing, you could be asked to attend team meetings. These might be for your own team or for teams from other areas – for example, if you work in sales, you might be asked to attend a production meeting so that you can understand what that area does.

Alternatively, you might be offered an opportunity to attend a trade show (a computer fair or another exhibition relevant to your job). Here you would be able to gather information about products and services, or even just about ways of doing things that will impact on how you do your own job.

4.4 Learning styles

When your teachers and lecturers learned their profession, one of the most important things they had to learn was about the concept of individual learners having different learning styles. In principle, this means that because we are all different, the way we learn will be different too. Some of us will be able to learn something merely because we read it in a book. This does not work for others who will only learn something if they do it practically. You may not be aware that someone at your own institution has probably carried out a learning styles test on you, and your teachers generally know how you learn best.

Examples of systems (e.g. active/reflective, sensing/intuitive, visual/verbal, sequential/global)

There are many examples of educational theories or systems which can be used to help you and your teachers identify how you like to learn. The example listed in the content for this unit is explored here, although there are other equally acceptable theories that you could explore and would be asked to explore if you later decided to train as a teacher.

Active/reflective

Physical activity and reflection on your learning are what is suggested here. If you like to learn with your hands, you like to make or build things and experiment then think about what you have done, this would be your preferred learning style.

Sensing/intuitive

Our five senses are at work all the time (these are hearing, sight, smell, touch and taste), although these are not necessarily all working at the **same** time! Someone who has a sensing/intuitive learning style will enjoy learning through sights, audio stimuli or physical sensations such as touch, and they will enjoy working with ideas, particularly where they can use personal memories to help them have insights into what they are learning.

Visual/verbal

The visual leaner likes to learn through diagrams, demonstrations, images, charts and graphs, or through the written or spoken word. This type of learner will like to use their eyes and ears to gather information that they can process into learning.

Sequential/global

A sequential learner likes to progress in stages – usually taking small steps and learning a subject a little at a time. Global learners, on the other hand, want to see the bigger picture; particularly they want to understand how what they are learning fits into the context of their own previous experiences.

Learning style	Learning activities
Aural	You learn best through music and sound
Visual	You like to see images, pictures, demonstrations – for example you particularly like the use of interactive whiteboards
Physical (kinaesthetic)	Practical activities such as model making, using a computer, making finished products
Logical	Mathematical reasoning, following steps like in a recipe
Verbal	You learn through hearing or reading words
Solitary	You prefer to learn on your own
Social	You prefer to learn with others

A variation on this model is the simplified concept that we are all predominantly one of the types of learner shown in the table.

Identification of preferred style

To identify your own learning style you can do a free online test on the following website:
http://www.learning-styles-online.com/inventory/

By answering a series of questions, the system will calculate your **own** learning style profile. This will not give you a single learning style (e.g. kinaesthetic) but will tell you how much of each of the learning styles you have. You might find you are a logical, kinaesthetic, social learner, which will mean that you like practical activities where you can apply mathematical reasoning and you like to do this with a group of people. This is only one example.

Once you have done a test like this (and there are many others online to choose from), you should not assume that your learning style is now set in stone, because your learning style can **change** over the years.

How we benefit from knowing your learning style

One of the main benefits of knowing your own learning style is that you can make sure that you are on courses, or that you are using learning materials, from which you know in advance you will ultimately learn. What you will probably have experienced in your own classroom is that the teacher or lecturer uses a variety of different activities to help you learn a subject. You might watch a presentation, listen to the teacher talking, do some research on the Internet and build a model. From your perspective this is a good example of the teacher having variety in the classroom. In actual fact the teacher is teaching the subject in ways that will appeal to different learners in your group. That way everyone has a better chance of learning! Think about it – if the whole class was asked to read a chapter from a book for 30 minutes, how many would actually do it, and would learn from it, compared with those who would get agitated and frustrated after a reasonably short space of time and would possibly be hard to motivate!

Understanding how other people's learning styles impact on team working

Because we all have a different preferred learning style, we need to **accommodate** these in **other** people when we are trying to do group work. If you know that your colleague is a physical learner, it would not be very valuable to send them to watch a video or DVD.

 Activity

Discuss your **preferred learning style** with your **teacher** or a **tutor**.

It is highly possible that they will already have formed their own ideas about how you learn best, and it might be interesting to **compare** what you think with what a professional sees in you!

 Activity

Find out about **your own** preferred learning style using the following website, or one of the many **alternatives** available:
http://www.learning-styles-online.com/inventory/

Case Study

In this unit you have already been introduced to **Lee Office Supplies**, which is a small stationery and office equipment supplier trading with our other two organisations, **Frankoni T-shirts Limited** and **KAM (Kris Arts & Media) Limited**.

Frankoni T-shirts Limited is a national company with outlets in larger towns. They specialise in producing personalised t-shirts on demand, using iron-on designs that they buy in from other companies, but particularly from KAM Limited.

The t-shirts themselves can be purchased from a range of alternative suppliers.

KAM (Kris Arts & Media) Limited is primarily a graphic design company. The company specialises in taking photographic images for use in advertising and other artistic pursuits, along with hand-drawn and computer-generated images, particularly used in t-shirt design. Trading only from one location, Kris' artistic reputation has seen a vast increase in his customer base.

The three companies seen here will be used throughout this text to underpin activities and to provide a contextual framework for some of the concepts you will meet.

Links

The content of this unit has conceptual links to **all** other units on this course, which is why it is a compulsory unit regardless of which qualification you are doing (BTEC National Diploma, BTEC National Certificate or BTEC National Award) or within which pathway you are studying (IT and Business, Software Development, System Support or Networking).

In addition, this unit has direct links with:

Unit 18 – Principles of Software Design and Development and **Unit 20** – Event Driven Programming for software development.

Unit 17 – Mathematics for IT Practitioners, for working with numbers.

Achieving success

In order to achieve each unit you will complete a series of coursework activities. Each time you hand in work, your tutor will return this to you with a record of your achievement.

This particular unit has 13 criteria to meet: 7 pass, 4 merit and 2 distinction.

For a **pass**:

>   You must achieve **all** 7 pass criteria.

For a **merit**:

>   You must achieve **all** 7 pass and **all** 4 merit criteria.

For a **distinction**:

>   You must achieve **all** 7 pass, **all** 4 merit **and both** distinction criteria.

So that you can monitor your own progress and achievement in each unit, a recording grid has been provided (see next page). The full version of this grid is also included on the companion CD.

Assignment	Assignments in this unit			
	U1.01	U1.02	U1.03	U1.04
Referral				
Pass				
1				
2				
3				
4				
5				
6				
7				
Merit				
1				
2				
3				
4				
Distinction				
1				
2				

Help with assessment

The key issue with this unit is to ensure that you can **evidence your professionalism** and **your commitment to your studies** and to your **own professional development**.

It is likely that you will **create** a **range of documents** to evidence your ICT skills, that your **interpersonal skills** will be **explored** and **assessed** and that a portfolio of evidence might well be created, drawing evidence not only from coursework undertaken within the unit but through coursework undertaken for other units also.

The **merit criteria** focus on **your effectiveness**, your **professionalism** and evidence that **your understanding of your own abilities** can **help you improve** your efficiency as an **individual** and as an **employee**.

For a **distinction** you need to show that you can place your learning in the **context of a working environment** and that you **understand** how to recognise your own skill needs, finding **appropriate ways** to **identify** mediums to improve.

Online resources on the CD

Electronic glossary for this unit

Key fact sheets

Electronic slide show of key points

Sample document templates

Multiple choice self-test quizzes

 ## Further reading

Maggio, R., 2005, *The Art of Talking to Anyone: Essential People Skills for Success in Any Situation*, McGraw Hill Higher Education, ISBN 007145229X.

NCCER, 2005, *Employability Skills: Trainee Guide 00108-04*, Prentice Hall, ISBN 0131600125.

Computer Systems

Capsule view

Computer Systems is a 60-hour unit which is designed to introduce you to the **hardware components** that exist inside a typical computer. In addition, it also helps you to learn about important **software** such as the **operating system** and crucial **utilities** such anti-virus suites and firewalls.

Practical tasks are also covered; as part of your studies you will be required to perform both important **hardware** and **software maintenance** and use **file management tools** to keep the system running **smoothly**.

This unit provides a critical platform for your success in other units.

1 Understanding the hardware components of computer systems

Learning aims

1 Understand the hardware components of computer systems.
2 Understand the software components of computer systems.
3 Be able to undertake routine computer maintenance.

1.1 System unit components

A typical computer system (see Figure 2.1) consists of a tower (or base unit), monitor, keyboard and mouse.

Inside the base unit, a number of **standardised components** are used to create a number of different connected **subsystems**. Components and subsystems built using **industry-standard designs,** which ensure they are **compatible and interoperable** worldwide. Figure 2.2 illustrates a typical computer subsystem.

Figure 2.1 PC system (including tower, keyboard and mouse)

Motherboard

The motherboard is perhaps the **most important hardware component** located inside the computer system's **case**.

The reason is simple: the motherboard is where other key components are **plugged in** or **connected**.

Most modern motherboards are based on a particular **form factor** (describing its **dimensions** and **features**) called Advanced Technology Extended (**ATX**). **Standardised form factors ensure build compatibility** between different motherboards, cases and components.

Figure 2.2 is a typical motherboard.

Figure 2.2 ATX Motherboard

Key	Component
1	The motherboard backpane which demonstrates its external connectivity. See Common Connection types later in this unit for more details.
2	Processor socket – where the CPU is fitted. The socket has to have the same number of pin holes and pin configuration as the processor. Typically a socket's name reflects the number of pins, e.g. Socket 478, Socket 754 and Socket 939.
3	Ram slots – where DDR DIMM memory is fitted. Usually 2 or 4 slots.
4	ATX connection for connecting the power supply unit.
5	Primary (Integrated Drive Electronics) connector – connects to Hard Disk, CD-ROM, DVD etc. In addition this board supports SATA drives but has no Secondary IDE slot.
6	SATA drive connections, superseding older IDE connections.
7	The BIOS (Basic Input Output System) chip.
8	Southbridge chip – manages data traffic between slower components on the motherboard.
9	Northbridge chip – manages data traffic between faster motherboard components (RAM, CPU and graphics subsystem).
10	PCI Express (×16) slot for a graphics card, superseding the older AGP (Accelerated Graphics Port) slot.
11	Older PCI (Peripheral Component Interconnect) expansion slots; the newest, faster standard with a different form factor is PCI Express.
12	PCI Express (×1) slot.

The motherboard **chipset** is the combination of the **Northbridge** and **Southbridge processors**. Some chipsets are **more popular** with system builders because they are **more reliable** or **perform quicker** in **benchmarked tests**. A Southbridge may **not** be present on all motherboards; some manufacturers prefer to **delegate** its role to separate subprocessors.

Figure 2.3 BIOS chip

BIOS

The **b**asic **i**nput **o**utput **s**ystem (**BIOS**) is a small collection of programs that are stored in **r**ead **o**nly **m**emory (**ROM**), **p**rogrammable **r**ead **o**nly **m**emory (**PROM**), **e**rasable **p**rogrammable **r**ead **o**nly **m**emory (**EPROM**) or most commonly these days, **flash memory**.

Existing as a small chip, the BIOS is fitted onto the motherboard of a typical PC system.

On a typical PC system, the BIOS chip contains all the code required to

control the keyboard, display, disk drives, serial communications and other critical functions. It can also **monitor hardware** (temperature, hard drive status etc.) and **take action** (i.e. shut down the PC) to prevent any damage occurring to the hardware.

In addition, it has a **BIOS setup program** (typically accessed by pressing a designated key on power-up, usually **F2** or the **Delete key**) which lets the user **configure** the **basic operation** of the hardware.

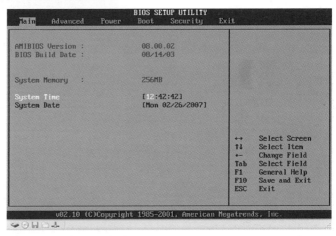

Figure 2.4 A typical BIOS setup screen

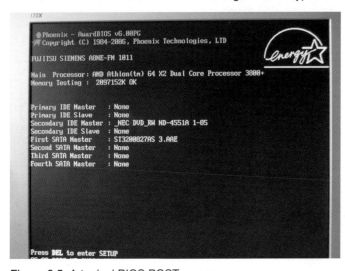

Figure 2.5 A typical BIOS POST screen

Another function of the BIOS is the **P**ower **o**n, **s**elf **t**est (**POST**) procedure that checks to see that all connected peripherals (e.g. **keyboard**) and components (**CMOS, BIOS, RAM** and the **input/output controller**) are functioning correctly.

Malfunctioning devices are often reported via short on-screen messages or, quite commonly, as a series of **beep codes**. Unfortunately beep codes tend to be specific to different BIOS manufacturers.

An **unsuccessful POST** will usually cause the computer system to **halt**.

Since BIOS is stored in flash memory, it is possible to update it by downloading new BIOS images from the Internet. The process of **updating** the BIOS is called 'flashing'. It is possible that flashing can go wrong and this can often kill the BIOS chip permanently, effectively rendering the motherboard **useless**.

BIOS updates are often used to add **new functionality** or **fix existing bugs** (problems) with the original BIOS **firmware**. Checking the motherboard manufacturer's website is usually the best way of finding out if new BIOS updates are available.

The final job of the BIOS is to **seek an operating system** on an available **drive** (floppy, hard disk or CD/DVD, USB pen drive) or via a **network**

Accessing the BIOS

Using an available PC, **switch it on** and **access its BIOS** using the designated key.

Explore its menu system using the cursor keys and Enter key.

Make a list which details:

◆ the name of the company who produced the BIOS
◆ the BIOS version number
◆ the 'top row' menu options
◆ the types of hardware monitoring the BIOS can perform.

connection. Once found, control is passed to the operating system as it is loaded into **r**andom **a**ccess **m**emory (**RAM**). This is called the **boot process** (from the expression 'pulling oneself up by one's own bootstraps').

If the BIOS is unable to find an **operating system**, the boot process will also **halt**.

CMOS

Complementary **m**etal **o**xide semiconductor (**CMOS**) is a special type of **battery-backed memory** that **stores** the **settings** made by the **BIOS setup program**.

If problems occur (usually when a PC refuses to boot after settings have been changed) the settings may be reset by either **removing** the 3V lithium **battery** or by using the '**clear CMOS' jumper** that is usually located near to the battery or BIOS chip on the motherboard.

This jumper is often **coloured differently** (usually red) to emphasise its importance.

Figure 2.6 CMOS battery

CPU

In simple terms the **c**entral **p**rocessing **u**nit (**CPU**) is the brain of the computer system. In reality the **processor** (as it is often called) is a lot more complex.

Sitting at the heart of the computer system, the processor's job is to process **data** and **instructions**.

The instructions are specific to the CPU in question; we call this **'machine' code**. Machine code from one type of processor will not traditionally work on another unless they belong to the **same family** (they are then said to be **code compatible**).

For many years **Intel®** have developed an **x86 family of processors** including the 486, Pentium®, Pentium 2®, Pentium 3®, Pentium 4® etc.; these were all **backwardly compatible** with each other. Other manufacturers such as Advanced

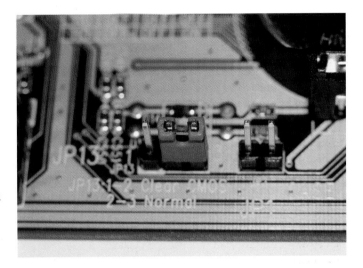

Figure 2.7 Clear CMOS jumper

Micro Designs (**AMD**) created processors which were machine-code **compatible**; these included the K5, K6, Athlon™, Duron™, Sempron™ etc.

Processor speed

Processor speed is measured in **megahertz** (**MHz**) or **gigahertz** (**GHz**).

The speed is actually the **clock frequency** of the processor. **Accepted wisdom** is that a faster processor will execute a program's instructions faster. **This is not necessarily true.**

Some processors have more **efficient designs** or have **multiple cores** (e.g. dual core with two processor units within the same package). In addition, processors either handle **32-bit** or **64-bit chunks of data**; at the **same clock speed**, a processor that **digests** 64-bit parcels of data will do so **more efficiently**.

The only downside to processor innovations is that software has to be written to **take advantage** of their efficient **architecture**. For example, a **64-bit processor** would require a **64-bit operating system**; Microsoft Windows® XP Professional is available in both 32-bit and 64-bit implementations.

Processor bus

This is also called the front **s**ide **b**us (**FSB**).

It is the **bidirectional link** between the **motherboard** and the **processor** itself. Like the processor it operates at a certain clock speed, usually measured in MHz.

Multiplier

A bus multiplier is a value used to calculate the **maximum processor speed**.

The general equation for working this out is:

Maximum processor speed = processor bus speed × maximum multiplier

e.g. 1992 MHz (2 GHz) = 166 MHz × 12

Overclocking and underclocking

Overclocking is the act of running a processor **beyond** its maximum **rated performance**.

In theory, if a processor can be kept **cool** (and other components, e.g. RAM, can **keep up**) it can be pushed beyond its theoretical speed limit by **manipulation** of the **multiplier**. Overclocking has the reputation of **shortening the lifespan** of a processor. Some processors are **locked** (they have their speeds fixed) by their manufacturers.

Underclocking is the opposite act; deliberately **throttling a processor** to keep it **cool**, save **electrical power** and **perform more reliably**. Servers often have the ability to be underclocked when they are idle.

Cache memory

Cache is high-speed memory that is used as a temporary store for recently processed instructions and data, or those which the CPU predicts will be processed very soon (i.e. by anticipating the program's logical flow).

It is much quicker to access instructions and data from cache memory than requesting it from normal RAM as data transmission speeds reduce once the data has left the CPU and starts to travel across the motherboard (see 1.3).

Modern PC PSUs – what you need to know

The most common PSU types are:

◆ **AT** power supply – used in older PCs
◆ **ATX** power supply – most commonly used today
◆ **ATX-2** power supply – a newly introduced standard.

ATX PSUs introduced software-based **power management** (including **standby mode**) and the lower 3.3V supply needed for newer processors.

Two types of cache exist, Level 2 (L2) and Level 1 (L1). L2 cache can be on the motherboard, located between the CPU and RAM, L1 cache is part of the CPU itself. Cache memory is typically very expensive and so would be prohibitive to use in great quantities.

Power supply unit

A **p**ower **s**upply **u**nit (**PSU**) converts the incoming **110V** or **220V** **a**lternating **c**urrent (**AC**) into various **d**irect **c**urrent (**DC**) voltages suitable for the computer's internal components.

A power supply's output is measured in **watts**; **400 watts** is a typical PSU power output in 2007.

Most PSUs come **already fitted** inside the computer system's case; however they may be purchased **separately** when a replacement is needed. As they contain **lethal voltages**, they should **never** – <u>under any</u>

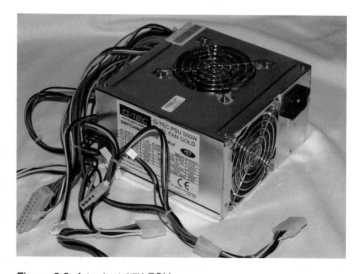

Figure 2.8 A typical ATX PSU

circumstances – be dismantled, <u>even after</u> the power has been removed.

A number of PSU connectors are commonly found.

Floppy drive (FD) connector

This is also known as a 4-pin Berg connector

These are used to connect the PSU to small form factor devices, such as 3.5 inch floppy drives, or even supply supplementary power to a graphics card.

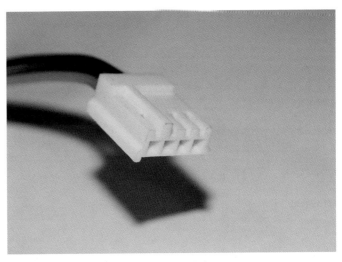

Figure 2.9 Floppy drive connector

They may also be used to power additional universal serial bus (USB) hubs.

Common on: **AT**, **ATX** and **ATX-2**.

4-pin 'Molex' connector

This is used to power various components, including hard drives, optical drives and system fans.

Figure 2.10 4-pin Molex connector

Molex is actually the name of the company that created this type of plastic in the 1930s.

Common on: **AT, ATX** and **ATX-2**.

20-pin ATX power connector

This is used to provide the main power to the motherboard in ATX systems.

ATX power supplies can be controlled by the BIOS and the OS.

Common on: **ATX (ATX-2 has 24 pins)**.

Figure 2.11 20-pin ATX power connector

4-pin auxiliary 12V power connector

These are very common on Pentium® 4 processor motherboards.

Common on: **ATX** (it was **integrated** into the power connector in ATX-2, hence **24** pins).

Figure 2.12 4-pin auxiliary 12V power connector

6-pin auxiliary connector

This provides +5V DC, and two connections of +3.3V.

Common on: **ATX/ATX-2**.

Figure 2.13 6-pin auxiliary connector

Fan and heat sink

During operation, a CPU generates a lot of **heat**. Although a CPU can operate at higher temperatures (well above 80 degrees Celsius), it is thought to shorten its lifespan.

In order to keep the processor cool, the simplest approach taken is to use a **heat sink** and **fan** combination.

Figure 2.14 Heat sink, fan and thermal paste syringe

Figure 2.15 CPU fan header on the motherboard

The heat sink, traditionally made from **aluminium** or **copper** (which is better), **draws the radiated heat away** from the top of the processor through a process called **conduction**.

This process is made easier through the use of **thermal compound**. This is typically a white paste, traditionally containing **aluminium oxide** or **silver**, which is **spread thinly** between the top of the CPU and the **underneath** of the heat sink.

A fan, usually revolving between 2000 and 4000 **revolutions per minute** (**rpm**) will **draw the hot air away** from the top of the heat sink through the process called **convection**.

This fan draws its **12V** power from a **CPU 3-pin fan header** located near the processor socket on the motherboard. The **red** wire contains the 12V supply, the **black** wire is ground while the **yellow** is used by the BIOS to **monitor** the CPU fan **speed**.

It is through this monitoring that the **BIOS health check program** can **switch off** the system if the fan speed **drops below** a certain **rotational speed**. This is set in the BIOS setup program (as previously described). Similar settings may exist for 80mm case ('**system**') **fans** present.

Liquid cooling

```
           Phoenix - AwardBIOS CMOS Setup Utility
              Power

             HardWare Monitor                    Select Menu

   CPU Temperature            78°C          Item Specific Help▶▶
   M/B Temperature            41°C
   5Usb                       4.99U         Enable/Disable the
   Uccp                       1.41U         control of the
   5U                         5.89U         system/CPU fan speed
   12U                        12.15U        by changing the fan
   CPU Fan Speed              943 RPM       voltage.
   System Fan Speed           2526 RPM

   Fan Control                [Enabled]
   Fan Low Temp               [78°C]
   Temperature Range          [2°C]
   Set CPUFAN RAMP RATE       [7 secs]
   CPU Fan Low Voltage        [ 4.7 U]
   System Fan Low Voltage     [12.0 U]


   F1:Help    ↑↓:Select Item   -/+: Change Value    F5:Setup Defaults
```

Figure 2.16 Health check settings for the CPU fan in the BIOS setup program

An alternative to traditional cooling is the use of **liquids**; water is approximately **25 times** more effective at conducting heat than air.

Scorecard

+ **Quieter** than traditional fans
+ **More effective** than traditional cooling techniques
− Can be **difficult to install**
− Can be **dangerous** if not installed **properly**

Hard-drive configuration

Hard-drive mechanisms are controlled by their integrated **d**rive **e**lectronics (IDE) (a printed circuit board located **underneath** the drive mechanism) and the **IDE controllers** located on the **motherboard**.

Enhanced IDE supports **four devices**; **two devices** on a **primary channel** and **two device**s on a **secondary channel**.

Each channel has a **master** and a **slave** drive. Typically, the master drive is the **faster** of the two.

Each channel's cable has **two drive connections** (**master** and **slave**); the master is connected to the **end of the chain**, the slave in the **middle**. The drive also has similar jumpers for the 'master'/'slave' or 'cable select' settings.

Ports – USB, parallel, serial

Modern computer systems use a number of different **ports** to enable a user to connect **peripherals** such as **keyboards**, **mice**, **printers**, **scanners**, **cameras**, **graphic tablets** and **MP3 players** etc.

Although **USB** is by far the most common method, other types of port exist.

The image right and table below give an overview of common ports found on a computer system.

Liquid cooling – what you need to know

Uses water or special coolant solution.

Key components of the system are:

◆ **reservoir** – to store the coolant
◆ **pump** – to circulate the coolant
◆ **water blocks** – to snap onto components needing cooling (e.g. CPU)
◆ **radiator** – to transfer heat from water to the air
◆ **power input** – needs around 12V power supply (from typically 4-pin Molex from the PSU).

Figure 2.17 Motherboard backplane with common connectors

Picture key	Type	Data transfer speed
1	6-pin PS/2 (green) mouse	
2	6-pin PS/2 (purple) keyboard	
3	USB 1.1	1.5 Mbps (low) 12 Mbps (full)
	USB 2.0	480 Mbps (hi-speed)
4	25-pin parallel port (IEEE 1284)	2 Mbps (practically)
		4 Mbps (theoretically)
5	9-pin serial port	115 Kbps (maximum)

Common connection types

Older devices such as serial, parallel and PS/2 are called **legacy** ports. Some newer motherboards **do not** have these types of connector, preferring to use **USB** and **Firewire**® instead.

Figure 2.18 Audio ports

Additional connections may be present which represent the computer system's **audio** input/output through either a **sound card** or **integrated sound chip**.

Picture key	Type
1	Blue line-in socket for 3.5mm jack. Used for connecting sound card from an external sound source.
2	Pink microphone socket for 3.5mm jack.
3	Green headphones socket for 3.5mm jack.
4	Yellow musical instrument digital interface (MIDI) or gameport.

Peripherals

A peripheral is often defined as any device that is connected externally to the CPU and main memory. In reality, this is revised to mean 'connected outside the case', i.e. using one of the backplane connectors.

Common types of peripheral include:

◆ printer (laser or inkjet)
◆ plotter (drum or flatbed)
◆ digital camera or video camera
◆ scanner
◆ gamepad or joystick.

Most modern peripherals use a simple **USB connection** with most users now being **familiar** with USB devices and their '**plug and play**' (**PnP**) approach to loading the correct **drivers**. A **driver** is a small program which **tells** the **operating system how to talk** to the **hardware**.

Internal memory

We have already talked about **ROM** during the overview of the **BIOS**. Although ROM is important, **RAM** is **absolutely critical** to the successful operation of the computer system.

RAM is the type of memory used to store the **operating system**, **programs** being run and, most importantly, the **data** being processed. It is also faster than ROM, which is why the BIOS is often **shadowed** (copied) to RAM and executed from there.

Another important thing to remember is that RAM is **volatile**. This means that the **contents** of RAM are **completely lost** when electrical power is removed.

When looking into RAM it is useful to think about memory **size**. In computing, memory has traditionally been **grouped** into collections of **bits** (**b**inary dig**its**) and **bytes** (eight bits make one byte). You may have encountered **larger multiples** of these before e.g. **kilobyte**, **megabyte** etc.

Memory sizes – what you need to know

The following table lists **common memory sizes** for you so that you can reference them easily in the future.

Unit size	= Bits	= Bytes	= Kilobytes
Bit	1	–	–
Byte	8	1	–
Kilobyte	8192	1024	1
Megabyte	8,388,608	1,048,576	1024
Gigabyte	8,589,934,592	1,073,741,824	1,048,576
Terabyte	8,796,093,022,208	1,099,511,627,776	1,073,741,824

As memory needs increase, larger units of storage are created. The following exist but are not yet in everyday usage (in ascending order):

◆ petabyte (**PB**)
◆ exabyte (**EB**)
◆ zettabyte (**ZB**)
◆ yottabyte (**YB**)

Memory unit summary

RAM exists in many different package **formats**. Double **d**ata **r**ate (**DDR**) and DDR2 are the most popular RAM package formats at the moment, offering **enhanced data throughput** by reading data on both the **leading** and **failing** edge of a clock 'tick'. The following images show common memory packages.

An SDRAM DIMM has **168 pins**.

Figure 2.19 PC133 SDRAM DIMM

Figure 2.20 PC3200 DDR DIMM

A DDR DIMM has **184 pins**.

Modern motherboard designs group RAM slots by the CPU. In the following figure you can see four empty DDR slots on a motherboard.

The white clips are used to secure each memory rail in place.

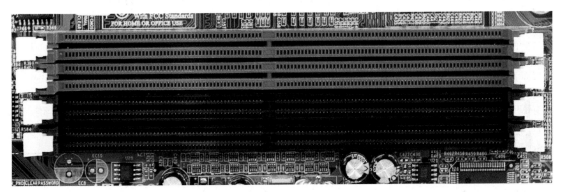

Figure 2.21 RAM slots on a typical motherboard

Modern PC memory modules – what you need to know

These come in a variation of different forms. The table below gives you a **basic comparison guide** of the most popular modules.

Module name	Module type and format	Clock frequency	Transfer rate
PC100	SDRAM DIMM	100 MHz	800 MBps
PC133	SDRAM DIMM	133 MHz	1066 MBps
PC1600	DDR200 DIMM	100 MHz	1600 MBps
PC2100	DDR266 DIMM	133 MHz	2133 MBps per channel
PC2700	DDR333 DIMM	166 MHz	2666 MBps per channel
PC3200	DDR400 DIMM	200 MHz	3200 MBps per channel

Module name	Module type and format	Clock frequency	Transfer rate
PC2-3200	DDR2-400 DIMM	100 MHz × 2	3200 MBps per channel
PC2-4200	DDR2-533 DIMM	133 MHz × 2	4264 MBps per channel
PC2-5300	DDR2-667 DIMM	166 MHz × 2	5336 MBps per channel
PC2-6400	DDR2-800 DIMM	200 MHz × 2	6400 MBps per channel

You will also note (I'm sure) that early modules were named after their **frequency** while later ones after their **transfer rate** (or **bandwidth**).

Activity

Activity 1

Use the BIOS to identify the amount of RAM installed on an available PC. Write this down using the correct units.

Activity 2

Use the operating system (e.g. Microsoft Windows®) to display the amount of RAM installed on an available PC. Does this agree with the figure reported in the BIOS?

Activity 3

With supervision as needed, safely disassemble the same PC to examine the RAM physically.

What type and quantity of memory modules did you find?

Specialist cards

The key to a computer system is **expansion**.

Motherboard slots such as **PCI**, **AGP** and **PCI-Express** offer both expansion and, in doing so, **upgrade opportunities**.

In order for an expansion or upgrade to be compatible, the correct type of card needs to be selected; this is because any particular type of card (e.g. a video or graphics card) could be available in PCI, AGP or PCI-Express formats. You must match the card to the available motherboard expansion slot.

Graphics cards

Unless the motherboard has an integrated graphics processor (**IGP**), also known as onboard graphics, the PC system will need a graphics card in order to **translate data** into **video signals** which will be sent to a **monitor** or **TFT** (Thin Film Transistor).

IGPs are typically present if the motherboard's **backplane** has a blue VGA (or HD-15) female connector.

Figure 2.22 Blue VGA or HD-15 female connector (also known as the 'VGA' connector)

Common terms associated with graphic cards include the following.

Refresh rate

The refresh rate is a simply how **many times per second** an image is **redrawn** on a screen by the graphics card.

The refresh rate is given in **hertz** – a measurement of **frequency**.

It is sometimes called the 'vertical refresh rate' or 'vertical scan rate'. It is a particular feature of older **c**athode **r**ay **t**ube (**CRT**) displays. A standard-definition television set usually uses **50 Hz** or **100 Hz**.

Refresh rates for computer displays less than 60 Hz tend to irritate the viewer as they usually notice the flicker caused by the image being rescanned (updated). Viewers with 17-inch or 19-inch monitors often prefer refresh rates of 85 Hz or more for this reason.

Refresh rates are usually set in the operating system, effectively controlling the graphic card's output to the display device.

If a refresh rate is set too high – and the display device cannot support it – the display device may go 'out of synch(ronisation)' and the image may be temporarily lost, often signified by a flashing or red/orange light-emitting diode (LED) on the monitor.

Resolution

The display resolution is given in **pixels** (**pic**ture **cel**ls or **el**ements). These are the miniscule dots that make up display images.

The resolution is expressed **pixels X** (across) **by pixels Y** (down), e.g. **1024 × 768.**

Higher-resolution images (which appear **more realistic** to the viewer) require more video **RAM** (**VRAM**) to display and are often limited by the maximum resolution of both the graphics card in use and the actual display device.

Again, the resolution is controlled by the operating system, as shown in Figure 2.24.

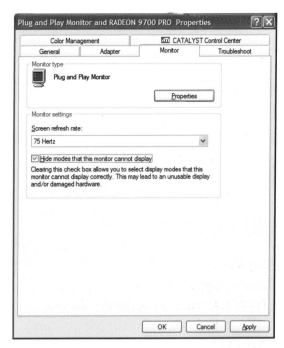

Figure 2.23 Changing the refresh rate in Microsoft Windows XP®

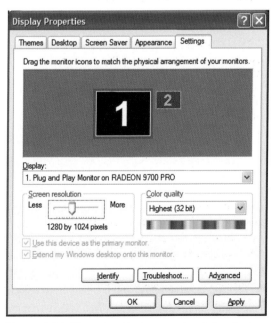

Figure 2.24 Changing the screen resolution in Microsoft Windows XP®

In the example shown in Figure 2.24 the resolution has been set to 1280 × 960 pixels.

The amount of VRAM required to generate such a display cannot be calculated by resolution alone. In order to accurately calculate the VRAM requirement it is also necessary to factor in the colour depth.

Let's take a look at this now.

Colour depth

This is a term used to describe **the number of colours available** in a particular graphics **mode**.

Help with assessment

Colour depth works on a **binary** (base 2) principle.

For example **4-bit colour** would provide **16 different binary patterns** that each represent a different colour. Any pixel's colour would be described by a **4-bit binary code**.

For example:

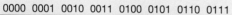

Given a **resolution of 320 × 200 pixels** with **4-bit colour** would require **31.25** kilobytes.

So how is this worked out?

320 × 200 pixels = **64,000 pixels**

Each pixel = **4 bits**

64,000 × 4 = **256,000 bits**

256,000 bits / 8 (bits per byte) = **32,000 bytes**

32,000 bytes / 1024 (bytes per kilobyte) = **31.25 Kb**

Both the **colour depth** and **resolution** are needed in order to **quantify** the amount of VRAM required to generate a display image.

Other colour depths are far more common, for example:

◆ **8-bit** (256 colours)
◆ **16-bit** (65,536 colours, often called 'high colour' or 'hi-color')
◆ **24-bit** (16,777,216 colours, often called 'true colour').

True colour is a combination of 24 bits (8 bits for **red**, 8 bits for **green** and 8 bits for **blue**) used to describe the **r**ed, **g**reen and **b**lue (**RGB**) components of any particular shade.

Scientists believe that the **human eye** is only actually capable of distinguishing between approximately **ten million different colour**

Activity

How much VRAM is required to support a video mode with resolution 1024 × 768 pixels and 16-bit colour depth?

shades. In reality, this means that true colour displays are demonstrating ranges of colours which we cannot actually fully tell apart.

In addition, a number of **different types of video signal** may be generated.

Figure 2.25 Digital visual interface

DVI

Replacing VGA connectors, especially for connecting to digital devices such as liquid crystal display (**LCD**) panels.

Composite

A lower quality image where brightness and colour information are combined together to form a video signal.

HDMI

Used to connect LCD flat panels, plasma televisions etc.

S-Video

A better-quality video signal where brightness and colour information are separated.

Component

High-quality output with separated red, green and blue signals.

Figure 2.26 Composite video

Figure 2.27 High definition multimedia interface (HDMI)

Figure 2.28 S-Video

Figure 2.29 Component output

Activity

Find out about your sample PC's **graphics card**.

Using the operating system discover:

◆ whether the display is generated by an IGP or dedicated graphics card
◆ the manufacturer of the graphics card
◆ the model of the graphics card
◆ the maximum display resolution
◆ the maximum colour depth
◆ the maximum refresh rate
◆ what type of video signal is being generated.

Write down your findings.

Network cards

A network card, or more correctly, a **n**etwork **i**nterface **c**ard (**NIC**) is a device which typically connects a computer system to a network. These cards may be **wired** (i.e. use **cables**) or be **wireless**.

Again, it is common for network functionality to be built into modern motherboards.

Network cards can transmit and receive data at:

◆ **10 Mbps** (**m**egabits **p**er **s**econd)
◆ **100 Mbps** or
◆ **1000 Mbps** (often called **Gigabit Ethernet**).

Figure 2.30 shows a typical wired Ethernet NIC.

Wireless solutions are also available (though less secure). Figure 2.31 shows a PCI Wi-Fi card. Again, it uses a PCI bus edge connector to plug into the motherboard.

Case Study

Kris Arts & Media (KAM) Ltd is currently investigating the purchase of a new graphics card to support the editing of video they have recorded.

Research and recommend a suitable graphics card for this situation.

Video card technology – what you need to know...

Onboard graphics **scorecard**

+ saves money
+ drivers will come with motherboard
+ upgrading is optional; usually will be acceptable for business use
− average performance only
− unlikely to support latest operating system features

Figure 2.30 Wired network interface card (PCI adaptor)

Network cards are very important in modern computer systems as users increasingly rely on **internet** online services and products. Network cards are used in conjunction with **routers** and **broadband modems** to supply broadband connections (whether via **cable** providers or ADSL).

Unit Link

You can find out more about networking in Unit 8 – Communication Technologies.

Figure 2.31 Wireless network card with antenna (PCI adaptor)

Network interface card technology – what you need to know...

Popular network card **manufacturers** include: 3Com, Belkin, Cisco, D-Link and Linksys.

Every network device has its own **unique physical address**. This is also called its media **a**ccess **c**ontrol (**MAC**) address.

A typical MAC address looks like a string of **6 hexadecimal** (base 16) **paired-digits**, in fact, a bit like this:

00-50-70-92-02-AB

Activity

Find your network card's manufacturer.

In Microsoft **Windows XP**® click:

Start → **Run** → **cmd** < **enter** >

Type **ipconfig / all** and press < **enter** >

Find the '**Physical Address**' among the displayed information.

Use a web browser to visit this online resource:

http://www.curreedy.com/stu/nic/

Type the physical address found on your sample PC and click the '**Find Manufacturer**' button.

The web site should respond with the name of your network card's manufacturer.

Internal modem

Modem stands for **mo**dulation **dem**odulation.

This is a term which describes the process of converting the **digital signals** used by a computer system to the **analogue sound waves** which travel over a standard telephone line. At the receiving end another modem reverses this process. This forms a **point-to-point** connection between two computers.

Modems are typically used in **narrowband dial-up connections** where broadband services such as cable and digital subscriber line (DSL) are not available.

Modems are **not fast**, the fastest connections being around just **56 Kbps**. The sluggishness of dial-up connections became more apparent as websites increasingly became more graphically intensive. The end result was that a dial-up user could wait many, many minutes for a page to load.

The gradual shift to cheaper, 'one-monthly payment, always on' broadband connections has further reduced the modem's appeal.

Whether the modem is integrated onto the motherboard or exists as a separate expansion card, the type of connection it uses is called an **RJ11** – similar, but smaller, to the RJ45 used with a wired NIC.

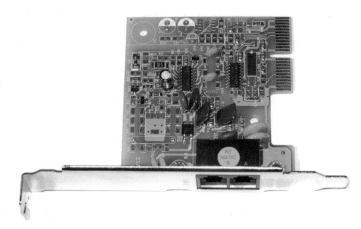

Figure 2.32 An internal PCI modem card

Figure 2.33 A modem's RJ11 connector

Braincheck

1 Which **four basic components** comprise a typical computer system?
2 What is the **BIOS**?
3 What is a motherboard's **form factor**?
4 What function does the **PSU** perform?
5 What is the purpose of the **CPU fan** and **heat sink**?
6 How does **parallel** and **serial** data transmission **differ**?

 7 Each **IDE** channel has a _____ and _____ connection.
 8 What is a **USB**?
 9 What does **IDE** mean?
10 What is the difference between **ROM** and **RAM**?
11 What is the difference between **DIMM** and **DDR RAM**?
12 What is the **clock frequency** of PC3200 RAM?
13 What is the **transfer rate** of DDR2-667?
14 What role does **cache memory** perform?
15 Name four **peripherals** used for **input**.
16 Name four **peripherals** used for **output**.

How well did you do? See page 421 for the answers!

1.2 Backing store

As we have seen, a computer system's main memory (RAM) is typically **volatile**. This simply means that it **loses its data** once its electrical power is removed. In order to store data (and programs) more **permanently**, non-volatile storage must be used. This is called its **backing store** (or backing storage).

There are a number of different types, usually grouped by their storage **mechanisms**. The three most common storage mechanisms are as follows.

Magnetic

Replacing older punched cards and paper tape, magnetic storage has been the primary backing storage technology since the mid-1970s. Magnetic media tends to be either **fixed** (a hard disk) or **removable** (a floppy diskette).

The 3" **floppy disk** (as it is commonly known) in its current form has been around since being created by Sony back in 1985. Although still reasonably popular, its **small capacity** (when used with modern, complex programs) has tended to reduce its **usefulness**; as many desktop and notebook PCs **do not have** an **internal floppy drive** fitted **as standard** any more (although **external floppy drives** can be connected via USB).

Hard disk technology has embraced three standards. The oldest technology, advanced technology attachment (**ATA** – now known as **p**arallel **ATA** or just **PATA**) – connects **IDE** hard

Figure 2.34 External USB floppy drive

drives to a motherboard via **40-** or **80-** wire cables.

The most recent ATA standard is **ATA133**.

Another hard disk **technology**, **s**mall **c**omputer **s**ystems **i**nterface (**SCSI**) and pronounced 'scuz-zy', has long been favoured for server systems, having a combination of **large capacity, fast rotation speeds** and **superior transfer rates** (when compared to ATA/IDE).

Improvements in ATA/IDE technology have reduced the SCSI market somewhat in recent years.

A more recent development, **s**erial **ATA** (**SATA**), has been introduced and is quickly becoming **popular** with hardware manufacturers. External **SATA** drives (**eSATA**) are also available.

Figure 2.35 ATA/IDE hard drive exposed to show platters and read/write heads

Figure 2.36 Floppy (with twist), SATA and PATA cables connect drives to the motherboard

SATA vs. PATA – what you need to know

SATA has three **primary advantages** over the older PATA technology:

1 It is **hot-pluggable** – drives can be connected/disconnected while the PC is still running.
2 **Thinner cables** reduce footprint inside the case, are easier to fit and help air-flow and cooling.
3 Uses **tagged command queuing** (**TCQ**) – a way of **reordering** a CPU's data access requests inside the drive so that data in neighbouring physical locations can be accessed sequentially, saving time.

The major **disadvantage** to SATA is that SATA drives are generally **10 per cent more expensive** than their PATA equivalents.

Magnetic disks have **platters** (**glass** or **aluminium**) which are **evenly coated** in a **ferrous material** which has **magnetic properties**. The disk drive's head can **read** the **magnetic fields** on the surface of the disk, **converting them** to **electrical impulses** (and then to **data**).

Writing data to the disk requires **creating** a **minute magnetic field** from **electrical impulses**. The effect of this is to change the magnetic alignment of the surface of the disk and hence the data being stored there.

Optical

Optical backing storage devices use **laser-generated light** instead of magnetic fields to 'read' and 'write' data. In comparison it is typically **slower** than magnetic mechanisms.

The most common optical storage devices are **c**ompact **d**isc (**CD**) and **d**igital **v**ersatile **d**isc (**DVD**); they seem physically similar and both have the same **diameter** of **120 mm** and are approximately **12 mm** thick.

Figure 2.37 A typical DVD-ROM drive

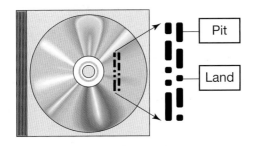

Figure 2.38 Magnified section of CD showing pits and lands

The majority of optical devices use removable media; you are certainly familiar with **CD**-**d**igital **a**udio (CD-DA) discs used for music and **DVD**-**r**ead **o**nly **m**emory (DVD-ROM) discs that hold popular films, television series and concerts.

CD-**r**ead **o**nly **m**emory (**CD-ROM**) discs are manufactured with data literally 'pressed' into them in the form of **pits** (small indentations) and **lands** (the flat area between the pits). These pits

and lands exist in a **long spiral starting** at the **centre** of the disc and working to the **outer edge**. If the spiral was straightened it would stretch approximately 6.5 kilometres!

As you can see in the **cross-section** in Figure 2.39, when the CD-ROM's laser is fired at the surface of the disc, light hitting a land is mostly **reflected** back to the drive's lens.

Whereas light hitting a pit (see Figure 2.40) is **scattered**.

The amount of light received by the lens tells it whether it is located over a pit **or** a land. The **change** from **pit-to-land** or

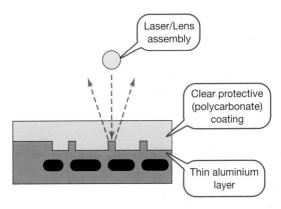

Figure 2.39 CD cross-section with laser light bouncing off a land

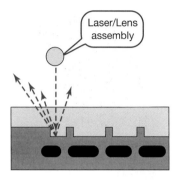

Figure 2.40 CD cross-section with laser light scattering off a pit

land-to-pit represents a **binary 1**, everything thing else is a **binary 0**, e.g.

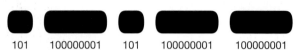

101   100000001   101   100000001   100000001

These codes are then translated using a mechanism called **e**ight to **f**ourteen **m**odulation (**EFM**) into standard binary for the computer system to use as data.

A **CD-r**ecordable (**CD-R**) uses a **radiation-sensitive dye** to record data sent by the CPU; the dye's **colour** can only be changed once. A CD-rewriteable (CD-RW) uses a more **chemically complex dye** to record and erase data; the dye is **reusable**. A more powerful recording laser is used to create the pit sequences using the changed dye colour.

A number of different recordable formats exist for both CD and DVD and they are often **not interchangeable**. Care should be taken when building a computer system to ensure that the **optical drive** and **media used** are **compatible**. Many systems include 'combo' (combination) drives which include **both CD-RW** and **DVD-ROM** functionality for flexibility.

Flash (electronically alterable)

Apart from the BIOS chip inside the computer system itself, flash memory is commonly used in two types of devices:

Pen drives (also known as USB flash drives or UFDs)

Introduced in the late 1990s, pen drives are an increasingly popular form of backing storage due to their **portability**, **ease of use** and **value for money**. Based on NAND-flash architecture developed by Toshiba in the late 1980s, a pen drive consists of a male **USB** connector, a printed circuit **b**oard (**PCB**) containing **flash memory** and a **clock crystal** (for synchronisation).

These components are typically housed in **toughened plastic packaging** which includes a **removable** (or swivel) **cap** to protect the sensitive contents from **e**lectro **s**tatic **d**ischarge (**ESD**).

Some pen drives might also have LEDs to indicate read/write status, a **write-protect switch** and a hoop for connecting a **keychain** or **lanyard**.

Optical drive speeds... what you need to know

Optical drives are often given using the following convention:

8x 16x 32x or 8/16/32

In the case of a sample CD-rewriter, this would mean:

8x – 8-speed for 'burning' CD-RW discs
16x – 16-speed for 'burning' CD-R discs
32x – 32-speed for reading discs into the computer system's RAM.

1x is approximately 150 Kbps.

Pen drives are compatible with the majority of modern operating systems including Microsoft Windows® (2000 onwards), Mac OS (9.x onwards) and various Linux distributions.

Flash memory cards

There are many different formats of flash memory cards currently available and in use.

Most flash cards use the same NAND-flash architecture as pen drives but come in a number of different **form factors**. Common varieties include:

◆ **CompactFlash®** (**CF**) created by SanDisk in 1994
◆ **MultiMediaCard®** (**MMC**) created by SanDisk and Siemens AG in 1997
◆ **Memory Stick®** (**MS**) created by Sony in 1998; varieties include Pro, Duo and micro
◆ **Secure Digital®** (**SD**) created by Panasonic, Toshiba and SanDisk in 1999
◆ **xD-Picture Card®** (**xD**) created by Olympus and Fujifilm in 2002.

It is becoming increasingly common for computer systems (especially PCs) to have **front bezels** which contain **multi-format card-reading slots**.

External card readers are also available and relatively inexpensive, connecting to the system via a standard USB port.

Figure 2.41 Inside a USB pen drive

Figure 2.42 Various flash memory cards and flash card reader

Although commonly used in **p**ersonal **d**ata **a**ssistants (**PDAs**), mobile cellular telephones and portable game consoles, its most important application is undoubtedly in **digital photography**.

Performance factors for backing storage mainly concern three main aspects:

◆ **Capacity – how much data** it can store
◆ **Data access time** (**DAT**) – **how quickly** specific data can be **found**.
◆ **Data transfer rate** (**DTR**) – **how quickly** data **moves** from the device into the computer.

The following table shows comparison of performance factors for common devices:

Backing store name	Storage mechanism	Typical capacity	Typical DTR	Removable or fixed media
3.5 inch floppy diskette (FD)	Magnetic	1.44 MB	500 Kbps	Removable
PATA IDE hard disk (HD)	Magnetic	60 ~ 500 GB	133 Mbps (ATA133)	Fixed
SCSI hard disk (HD)	Magnetic	30 ~ 300 GB	320 Mbps (Ultra320)	Fixed
SATA hard disk (HD)	Magnetic	60 ~ 500 GB	150 Mbps (SATA150) 300 Mbps (SATA300)	Fixed
CD-R	Optical	650 ~ 700 MB	150 Kbps (x1)	Removable
CD-RW	Optical	650 ~ 700 MB	150 Kbps (x1)	Removable
DVD-R	Optical	4.7 ~ 16 GB	1.3 Mbps (x1)	Removable
DVD-RW	Optical	4.7 ~ 16 GB	1.3 Mbps (x1)	Removable
USB pen drive	Flash	Up to 64 GB	1 ~ 25 Mbps	Removable
Flash memory card (e.g. Magic Stick Pro®)	Flash	Up to 128 GB (theoretically)	20 Mbps	Removable

Activity

Examine the backing storage options that exist in a selected computer system.

Which mechanisms do they use?

What capacities of data storage do they theoretically provide?

Who manufactured the various backing storage devices in the selected computer systems?

Does the system provide direct support for flash memory cards?

Braincheck

1 Why is backing storage **necessary** for a computer system?
2 Name **three different** backing storage **mechanisms**.
3 What is a floppy disk's **main disadvantage**?
4 Name **three different** hard disk **technologies**.
5 A CD's **surface** contains …?
6 What is the **storage capacity** of a typical CD-ROM?
7 Name three components typically found inside a pen drive.
8 Name **three different types** of commercially available **flash card**.
9 What is **DAT**?
10 What is **DTR**?

How well did you do? See page 421 for the answers!

1.3 Data transmission

Transmission rates vary greatly in a computer system.

Generally, any device which is **mechanical** by **nature** (e.g. hard disk, optical drive etc.) is **relatively slow** when compared to a **solid-state electronic device** (e.g. CPU, RAM etc.).

Figure 2.43, courtesy of Apple, demonstrates the **various buses** which connect different components and subsystems together in an iMac.

1.4 Considerations for selection

In order to assemble a new computer system, a **number of factors** have to be taken into **consideration**.

These should include:

◆ **cost of hardware, software and delivery**
◆ **user requirements**.

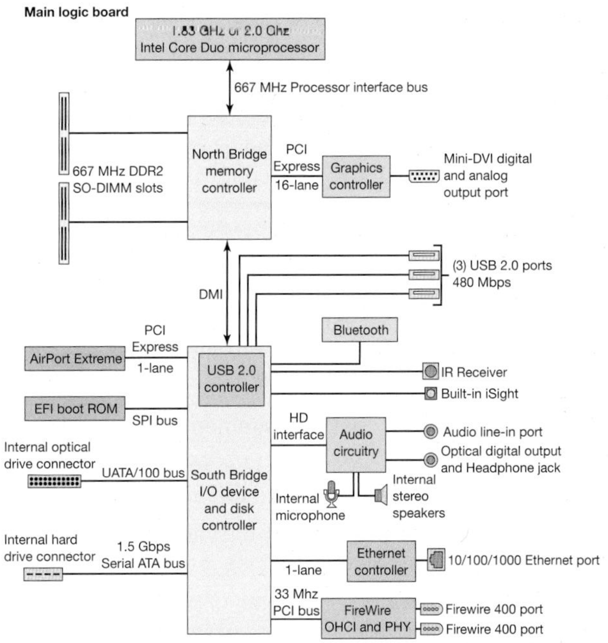

Of the two, **user requirements** are the most demanding **factors** to **quantify** as there are many different **aspects** which must be satisfied.

Main logic board

Generally speaking, data travels **fastest** while **inside** the CPU.

Once data travels across the **front side bus** onto the motherboard it **slows down**.

Northbridge components tend to have **faster buses** (for RAM and video) than the **Southbridge components**.

Figure 2.43 iMac block diagram

User requirement	Details
Software to be used	Fact: operating systems **do not** sell computer systems. Application software does!
	The choice of operating system (OS) is **less likely** to do with **budgetary concerns** and more connected to the **OS required** to run a **particular application** (be it a business application such as a database or a leisure application such as a recording and mixing suite).
	The first user requirement to fulfil is: **what kind** of computer system do I need to **install** and run **this** program (whatever it may be) **successfully**?
Maintenance	Fact: computer systems go wrong from time to time.
	Although building a new computer system is possible, enjoyable and a worthwhile practical challenge, there is little backup when things go wrong (apart from manufacturer guarantees on individual components).
	Buying a new system will often give the user:
	◆ a period of **RTB** (return to base) if problems occur ◆ an **extended warranty** covering replacement parts and **labour charges**.
	Although this can significantly **add to the cost** of the computer system, it will provide **peace of mind**.

User requirement	Details
Need for integration and connectivity	Modern computer systems are often bought as a part of a **larger solution**, e.g. a **home-entertainment system**. Thought must be given to how this new system will **integrate** with **existing systems**. This could also include **network connectivity**.
Processing power	Modern programs are **resource hungry**. Processing power is a **vital tool** in achieving **good system performance**. This usually means investment in a **quality motherboard, processor, RAM** and **video card**. Again, software will have **minimum** and **recommended hardware requirements**. Optimum performance **always** requires an **excess** of processing power – always **meet** or **exceed** the **recommended requirements**.
Storage capacity	User **data requirements** are **increasing** every year. As users move over to **digital libraries (music – MP3s, MP4s** etc., **pictures** and **video**), the need for **larger hard-drive capacity** increases too. In addition, any critical storage will need backup, effectively doubling the **storage capacities** required. Fortunately, **costs** of **hard disks** and **flash memory** continue to fall.
Accessibility and ease of use	Modern users are concerned with **functionality** and **ease of use**. Any computer system has to be as **intuitive** as possible with a friendly **graphical user interface** and informative feedback (which avoids technical jargon in its description). In addition, **regular maintenance tasks** should either be fully **automated** (and **invisible**) or be **simple** for a **novice** to **operate** safely. In addition, **accessibility** for **less able users** is also **crucial**. Modern computer systems should integrate **voice commands** (through speech recognition), support **innovative human interface devices, high-contrast displays** for **visually impaired people** and **narration** for **onscreen events**.
Sustainability	Computer systems should **last** or at least provide the **maximum amount of usage** before components need **replacing** or **upgrading**. Options should also exist for **ecologically friendly options** (e.g. **low emissions**, **refillable ink, safe disposal of toxic motherboard components**, encouraging the use of **electronic documents** where possible etc.).

 Activity

Kris Arts & Media KAM Ltd is currently investigating the purchase of a new computer system for use in its graphic design.

The software they wish to use is: **Adobe Photoshop® CS2**

1 **Investigate** the **minimum requirements** for this package at
   http://www.adobe.com/products/photoshop/systemreqs.html
2 Give details of **two possible computer systems** that could be **purchased** by **KAM** to run this software **successfully**.

2 Understanding the software components of computer systems

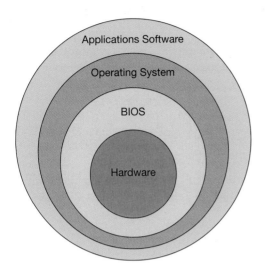

Figure 2.44 Computer system layers

Core interlocking components of an OS

Let's examine these in a little more detail:

Resource management

Resources found on a modern computer system are:

◆ **physical memory** (RAM)
◆ **virtual memory** (disk space used as **RAM**)
◆ **disk cache** (**RAM** storing the **most recently accessed data** from the disk)
◆ **CPU** (the processor, particularly the **balance** between OS 'time' and application 'time')
◆ **bandwidth** (networking, video, bus etc.).

It is the operating system's job to **juggle** these resources to keep the computer system running **smoothly** (avoiding too **many peaks of activity** where there is no **free capacity**).

User interface

As detailed later in the 'Command line and GUIs' section, an operating system has to have some form of user interface.

The interface is responsible for:

◆ **accepting** user commands
◆ **parsing** user commands (working out what the command actually is)

2.1 Operating systems

An operating system (often abbreviated to 'OS') is the essential **layer** that exists **between** the **BIOS** and **applications software** (e.g. word processing, spreadsheet, graphics, database, web browsers etc.).

The suggestion here is that when a user **opens a spreadsheet file** (in Microsoft Excel®) the **correct instruction** needs to travel **through** the **OS** and **BIOS levels** before the appropriate **electronic signals** are **generated** which **tell** the disk drive's **reading heads** to **find** and **transfer** the **required data** into **RAM**.

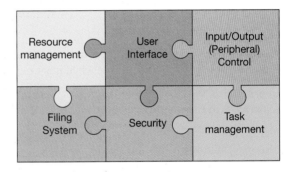

Figure 2.45 An OS's Interlocking components

- ◆ **displaying error** or **warning messages** when **processes** or **devices fail**
- ◆ **informing** users of **critical system** events (e.g. system is about to shut down)
- ◆ **confirming** that a command has been **successfully completed**.

As we will see, there **are two basic types** of user interface – the **command line** and the **graphical user interface**. The trend towards graphical user interfaces has made computer systems much more **user-friendly** and thus **approachable** for novice users.

Input/output (peripheral control)

Modern OSs are **PnP compatible** so tend to **recognise** new devices when they are **first connected**. Through the use of a **driver**, the OS can **communicate** with the hardware.

In addition, it is the operating system's job to **control the amount of CPU attention** that an input/output device **receives**. An OS is also vital in **scheduling input** and **output operations** so that the CPU **is not idly** awaiting data.

Filing system

A modern OS must be able to **create** and **maintain** a **robust** and **reliable** filing system (usually one which uses magnetic and optical disks).

The filing system's job is to **store** and **organise data** and **program files** on a backing storage device. It must also be able to **retrieve t**he file when it is needed **again**.

In order to do this, the filing system must create some kind of **logical index** or **table of contents** which **maps parts of files** to **physical locations** (e.g. a disk's tracks and sectors) of the backing storage media.

FAT32 (file allocation table) and **NTFS** (**n**ew **t**echnology filing **s**ystem) are popular filing systems used in **Microsoft Windows XP®** and **Vista®**.

A popular filing system used by Linux distributions is **ext2** (**second extended file system**). However, ext2 **cannot** be **natively read** by Windows® OSs.

Modern **Apple Mac®** computer systems use **HFS+** (**h**ierarchical **f**ile **s**ystem).

Backing storage such as **hard disk drives** need to be **partitioned** (the act of splitting large physical drives into numerous, smaller logical volumes) and then **formatted** for the appropriate filing system before they can be used. It is typically the operating system's **responsibility** to perform these acts.

Security

Security is a **critical component** of modern OSs, especially as **increasing numbers** of users are **connected to other systems** via the **Internet**.

Security should encompass: **user data, connectivity, access to applications software, access to system configuration** and **access to the filing system**.

Task management

One of the principal jobs of an OS is **task management**; the job of **running other applications**.

There are many different ways that this can be achieved. Perhaps the most common method is **pre-emptive multitasking** as it is used by OSs such as **Windows XP®**, **Linux** and **MAC OS X**. Pre-emptive multitasking is the ability for an OS to **divide its resources** between a **number of processes**. These resources include **RAM, i**nput/output and **CPU processing time**.

In pre-emptive multitasking, the OS takes responsibility for **starting** and **stopping** different processes (**each application** that is running may consist of **many different processes**). In addition it also allocates RAM and CPU time for **each task**. If a process is more **critical** it may give it a **higher priority** (more CPU time) to accomplish its task.

In the example above, **process 3** has been given a **higher priority** than processes 1 and 2.

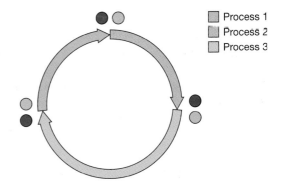

Figure 2.46 Pre-emptive multitasking

When a process is **stopped**, its **state** (where it was, what was happening **inside** the CPU) is **frozen**. This happens when each task is **suspended**. When each process is **restarted** their states are **unfrozen** and the processes **recommence** as if they had **never** been paused.

Because this process switching happens **so very quickly**, it appears that a **single processor** is running **multiple tasks simultaneously**. The **pre-emptive description** reflects the fact that it is **the OS** that **decides when** processes **should halt**, not the processes **themselves**. The allocated CPU period assigned to a process is sometimes called a **time slice**.

Operating system examples

Although it is referred to as a 'piece of software', in reality an OS is **not** a single program; it is a collection of hundreds of **smaller modules**, with each module responsible for fulfilling a **specific** task.

Building an OS in a **modular** fashion ensures that it can be easily updated or **'patched'** (its errors are fixed) in a more manageable way. An OS may receive many online patches via a live internet connection, typically to **resolve security issues** or mend 'bugs' that have been reported.

There are many different **commercial** OSs.

Most home users are familiar with **Microsoft® OSs**, particularly the older **MS-DOS** line and newer **Windows** family. The newest Microsoft OS is **Microsoft Vista®**, released to businesses in November 2006, which will supersede the older Microsoft **Windows XP®**. It is likely that this is the OS you use at home, school or college.

Figure 2.47 Microsoft Windows Vista® logo

Linux

Linux was initially created as a **hobby project** by a young student, **Linus Torvalds**, while studying at the University of Helsinki in Finland. Linus had a keen interest in a small **Unix system** called **Minix**; his goal quickly became to create an OS that **exceeded** the Minix functionality. Although he started work on this in 1991, it would not be until **1994** when the 1.0 version of the **Linux Kernel** (the core part of the OS) was **publicly** released.

The Linux kernel is **developed** and **released** under the **GNU general public licence** and as such its **source code** is **freely available** to everyone.

These days other hands guide Linux's ongoing development, and there are literally **hundreds** of different **Linux distributions** ('distros') which are **freely available** for download. Each is geared for a particular purpose (e.g. scientific research, education etc.); some even fit onto a single floppy diskette!

Common distributions include:

◆ **Ubuntu** (www.ubuntu.com)
◆ **Fedora** (fedora.redhat.com)
◆ **OpenSuse** (en.opensuse.org)

Tux the Penguin is the official **mascot** of the Linux OS, as created by **Larry Ewing**.

Figure 2.48 Tux the Penguin

Command line and GUIs

OS user interfaces come in two different varieties:

1 command **l**ine **i**nterface (**CLI**)
2 **g**raphical **u**ser **i**nterface (**GUI**)

The **CLI** is the oldest form of user interface, being present in early OSs such as **Unix**, **CPM** (**c**ontrol **p**rogram monitor) and **MS-DOS**® Microsoft **d**isk **o**perating **s**ystem).

It typically features:

◆ text-only output
◆ keyboard-only input
◆ basic command names
◆ limited user help for commands
◆ very basic error messages.

The most well known CLI is that represented by **MS-DOS**; even today it still exists as a '**command prompt**' in modern versions of Microsoft Windows® OSs.

In Microsoft Windows the CLI is accessed using **Start** → **Run** → **Cmd** then click the **OK** button.

Figure 2.50 is a typical view of a **CLI** in **Microsoft Windows**®.

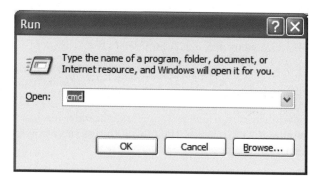

Figure 2.49 Microsoft Windows® run dialog

In Linux distributions, the GUI is **optional**; in theory all system functions can be controlled from the CLI.

As such it is more powerful and has better user support in the form of **online manuals** ('MAN' files), which tell the user in detail how a command may be used.

The Linux command prompt is called the **Terminal**.

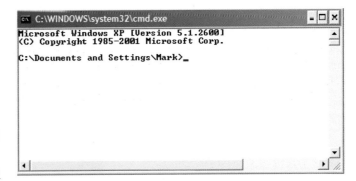

Figure 2.50 Microsoft Windows® command prompt

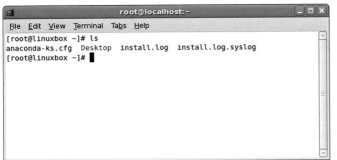

Figure 2.51 Linux command prompt

A **GUI** (pronounced 'goo-ey') is based on **WIMP** (**w**indows, **i**con, **m**enus and **p**ointing device) systems as developed in the early 1970s by the famous innovators at **Xerox PARC** (**P**alo **A**lto **R**esearch **C**enter).

A GUI creates a user-friendly media-rich environment for users to explore, work and play in using a combination of **moveable** and **resizable windows**, **representative icons** and **intuitive point-and-click mouse control**.

Perhaps the most familiar GUI is the one presented by **Microsoft Windows**®.

Command line interfaces ...what you need to know

The CLI is used to input basic OS commands which the computer system typically executes when the **Enter key** is pressed.

Bad commands generate a brief **error message** which the user must understand in order to try again.

The CLI is often seen as an **unfriendly environment** (compared to a GUI) where complex commands **have to be remembered** by the user

Scorecard

– Not very user-friendly
– Not very aesthetically pleasing
– Help may be limited
– Relies on good keyboard skills
– Error messages are generally not helpful
+ Provides a quick response, even on slower equipment
+ Proficient users can perform complex tasks very quickly
+ Commands can be joined to form scripts which automate regular jobs

The Apple Mac OS also has an intuitive and attractive GUI.

Figure 2.52 Microsoft Vista® 'Aero' interface

Linux desktop managers are also becoming more intuitive, robust and aesthetically pleasing.

GUIs are popular as they represent a good levelling tool; users of any age and IT experience can quickly feel at

Figure 2.53 Apple Mac OS X Leopard interface

home, performing a combination of both simple and complex tasks with equal ease. Figures 2.59 and 2.60 demonstrate formatting a disk through the GUI and CLI.

Figure 2.54 Linux Fedora Core 6 – Gnome interface

Graphical user interfaces ...what you need to know

These are now the standard interface for modern OSs. Although they generally rely on mouse and keyboard, some have **voice recognition** software which allows the OS to respond to vocal commands. This is particularly useful to those with **limited mobility**. In addition, **narrator** software is also present to describe events and options on screen for those **visually impaired**. Both aim to improve **equal opportunities** among users.

Scorecard

- − Graphically intensive GUIs require faster processing.
- − This can make them slow to respond on less powerful hardware.
- − Newer OSs require more hard disk space to install.
- − And they need greater system resources (processor, memory etc.) to run.
- + They are very user-friendly.
- + They are easy to configure to suit different user's preferences.
- + They provide comprehensive input device support.
- + There is no need to remember complex CLI instructions.
- + Basic operations can take longer than when using the CLI.

Braincheck!

1 Which two layers does the OS sit between?
2 Name any four core functions of the OS.
3 Where is an OS typically stored?
4 Which two types of OS user interface are available?
5 What is the process of updating part of an OS called?
6 What is multitasking?
7 What is virtual memory?
8 Complete the following CLI commands for Windows and Linux. (If you get stuck, help can be found on the companion CD.)

Objective	Windows	Linux
List files in a directory		
Create a new directory		
Delete a file		
Change to the 'root' directory		
Examine the computer's network adaptor information		

Describe three differences between Microsoft Windows XP® and a typical Linux distribution (e.g. Fedora, Ubuntu etc.).
Name five pieces of information that a filing system knows about a file.

How well did you do? See page 421 for the answers!

2.2 Software utilities

Virus protection

A virus is a **malicious program** that **infects** a computer system. Viruses can **spy** on users and cause **irreparable damage** to **personal** or **business** data.

Initially, virus spreading was limited by relying on physical transport through **removable media** such as **floppy disks**. However, growth in **internet downloads** and **email attachments** has made virus infection a very real threat to most users: An unprotected computer system could be infected with a virus within one minute of venturing online.

Virus **authors** typically target **Microsoft Windows®** OSs (which account for the majority of users), but **Linux** and **Mac** OSs are starting to come under pressure.

Antivirus software (usually third-party, i.e. not written by the OSs developers) is freely available, although **regular updates** are usually required to keep **virus definition files** (**see 3.1**) or virus '**signatures**' up to date.

AVG Anti-Virus from Grisoft (**http://free.grisoft.com**) is a good all-round utility.

Antispyware

Spyware is a type of malicious software that **monitors the actions** of a computer user.

Sometimes the software has been **legitimately installed**, perhaps to keep an eye on an employee (e.g. for security or **workplace monitoring**); at other times it has been installed **without** the **knowledge** or **permission** of the user.

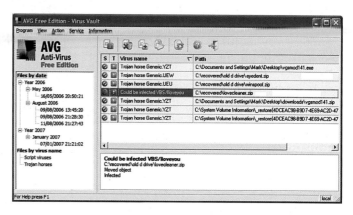

Figure 2.55 AVG Anti-Virus shows its virus vault of quarantined files

The use of such monitoring tools is varied. A typical use is to **collect marketing data**, showing users websites which may have goods related to searches they have carried out. In most case spyware is an **annoyance** rather than a **threat** (like a virus).

More intrusive software might **report on user activities**, permit their machine to be **remotely controlled** (a 'zombie') or create a security loophole which will allow a 'rogue user' to **harvest personal information** (e.g. **passwords**, **credit card** information, **account details** etc.) in a bid to perform **identity theft**.

Antispyware is a piece of software that can **identify**, **disable** and **remove** such software.

Microsoft Defender® is a typical antispyware product.

Firewalls

A **firewall** is a **program** which runs on a computer system (client or dedicated) that **filters network traffic**. In addition it can also specify which **programs** are **allowed** to access the network.

Typically, a firewall is placed **between** a **trusted**, **private network** and an **unprotected public network** (such as the Internet), often built into a **router** or **gateway**.

Defragmentation

Most OSs have **disk filing systems** which create **fragmentation** over a period of time.

Fragmentation occurs when **space reclaimed** after a file is **deleted** is used to **store parts** of a **larger file**. The end result is that a file **does not exist** in **contiguous** (i.e. adjacent) **disk locations** (Microsoft Windows® calls these '**clusters**').

Figure 2.56 Microsoft Defender® explores programs loading at start-up

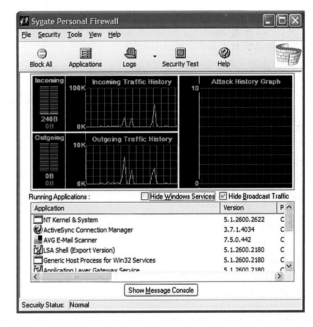

Figure 2.57 Sygate firewall watches network traffic and applications using the network

For example:

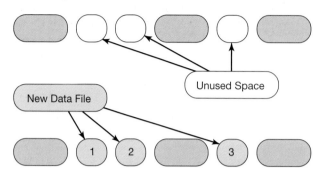

Fragmented files are **slower to load into RAM**, simply because the hard-disk drive has to **work harder** to **physically locate** and **read** the various clusters which form the file.

Most OSs have a utility to **defragment** a file system. This utility may be run as an **ad hoc** (i.e. unplanned, whenever needed) **process** or on a **regular schedule**.

It is often recommended that a fragmentation of 10 per cent or more should be fixed.

Drive formatting

Before a magnetic disk can be used, it must be **prepared** for use.

This process is called **formatting**. Formatting theoretically **erases all data** previously stored on a disk.

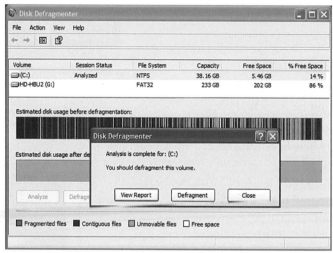

Figure 2.58 Microsoft Windows Defragmenter® utility finds a problem

Formats are **specific** to the disk operating system in question, for example a disk formatted for use on a Microsoft Windows system will not read **natively** on an Apple Mac (special **drivers** are required).

Operating systems such as Microsoft Windows® have GUI format utilities but can also perform the same process from the CLI.

A disk format:

◆ prepares the **physical locations** ready for recording
◆ sets up a **filing system** (e.g. **FAT**) on the disk
◆ checks the disk for **physical** or **magnetic errors.**

In reality, formatting a disk **clears** the filing system's '**table of contents**'; the **data** is **still there** but the OS will have **no idea where** the various files are **physically stored**. This means that data may still be **recoverable** using **specialist data recovery**

Figure 2.59 Microsoft Windows® disk format (GUI)

Figure 2.60 Microsoft Windows® disk format (CLI)

software. **Sensitive** data (i.e. **personal** or **business**) should be safely deleted using **data shredding software**. Of course, the surest way to erase data is to **physically destroy** the disk itself!

Clean-up tools

Modern OSs keep a detailed account of user activity.

There are times when such accounts are **not required**.

In order to manage such activity, most OSs and applications have **options** to **clear personal data** from the system.

In the **Internet age**, possibly the two most common 'footprints' to erase are:

◆ **internet history** (which websites have been visited by whom – and when)
◆ **cookies** (small text files stored on your machine containing personal data used by websites to recognise the user)
◆ **passwords**
◆ **information entered** into **online forms**.

Such options may be located and set in the OS or internet **client software**.

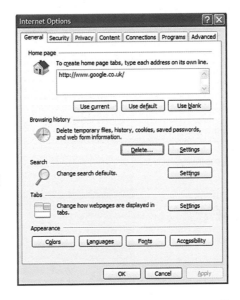

Figure 2.61 Microsoft Internet Explorer® 7's options

Of course, there may be **situations** where such **user activity logs** are **important** and should be **kept intact**; for example, students in a college and employees in the workplace may have to **obey** their organisation's **communication policy**.

3 Be able to undertake routine computer maintenance

3.1 Software maintenance

The most common software maintenance tasks for an IT practitioner are as follows.

Upgrade software

Software often has to be upgraded in order to **fix identified bugs**, **improve performance** or **add new functionality**.

A popular example of this would be **updating virus definition** files (virus **signatures**) in an antivirus suite.

Scheduling maintenance tasks

The majority of OSs have **automatic scheduling facilities**. These allow the practitioner to set **routine operations** to **run** at **set times** and **dates**.

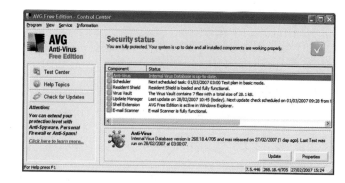

Figure 2.62 AVG update option for virus definition file

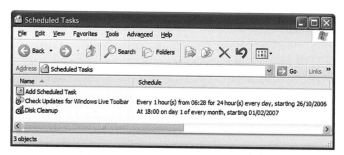

Figure 2.63 Scheduled maintenance tasks

◆ **disk defragmentation**
◆ **update** of virus definitions
◆ **checking** for new versions of software or patches.

Installation of patches

Patches represent a **fix** made to software that involves **overwriting** an **existing section** of **program code** with a **new sequence** of instructions.

Although all software can be patched, the most common type of patch is that made to **OSs** in order to **close security vulnerabilities** that have been identified. Some OS patches are so critical that they are **automatically downloaded** (via the Internet).

A typical example of this would be to set a full antivirus scan to run while the computer system **is not being used**. This could be on shut-down or at a time when the system is idle (i.e. late at night or very early in the morning).

Scheduled tasks could include such operations as:

◆ **backup** of user data
◆ antivirus or spyware **scan**

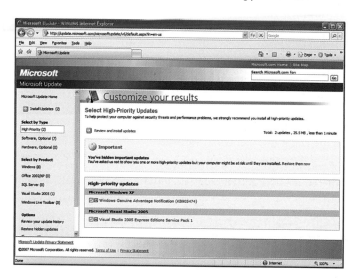

Figure 2.64 Microsoft Update® for MS Windows-related products

Utility software

OSs often have a collection of **utilities** – **supplementary programs** designed to carry out a **specific function**, usually performing regular **housekeeping tasks**.

Common utilities include:

◆ **defragmentation tools** (see 2.2. for more details)
◆ **disk 'clean-up' tools** – for getting rid of unnecessary files which may accumulate
◆ **disk scan tools** – for checking the integrity of backing storage and fixing errors found
◆ **system profiler** – a tool for creating an **inventory** of **hardware components** and **installed software**. In an organisation, system profilers are often used for **auditing software licences** and calculating the total cost of ownership (**TCO**) of the current IT systems.

Compression utilities

Utilities which **compress data** (e.g. **WinZip** and **WinRar**) are also **popular** even though most modern OSs have **transparent** (it is there but you do not see it) **compression support**. Most third-party compression utilities have **additional options** which make the process much less time consuming (e.g. batch file operations).

Spyware and antivirus removal

These were covered in **2.2**. An IT practitioner should be **fully conversant** with these types of utility as they are **critical** to the **smooth running** of a **modern computer system**.

3.2 Hardware maintenance

In addition, **hardware maintenance** is **equally** important.

The most common hardware maintenance jobs are the following.

Cleaning equipment

Typical devices to clean are: **keyboards**, **mice** and **screen displays**.

Keyboards and mice get especially **dirty** after prolonged use and screen displays (particularly CRT monitors) are often **smeared** with **greasy fingerprints**.

It is also possible that **exhaust vents** (used for **cooling**) may be **blasted** with **compressed air** to **displace dust** which may **clog up** fans.

Standard tools for this type of maintenance include:

◆ **dry cloth** or duster
◆ recommended **cleaning fluid**
◆ **cotton buds**
◆ a can of **compressed air** or a **vacuum cleaner**.

Cleaning equipment is seen as a **laborious task** but is important to **extend equipment lifespan** and **contribute** to good standards of **health and safety**.

Install and configure new peripherals

You will be expected to install and configure new peripherals e.g. scanners, printers etc.

Modern peripherals are **PnP** and as long as the **BIOS** and **OS** support PnP too, the correct device should be **correctly identified** and **drivers loaded** from:

◆ the accompanying **CD**
◆ via the **Internet**
◆ from **default drivers** stored in the OS.

Care should be taken to **follow the installation instructions** of any new piece of hardware; this can be particularly important if the drivers are to be loaded **before** the device is connected. In addition, peripherals should be **registered** with the **manufacturers** so that **additional support** (**including free driver updates** etc.) can be obtained.

Install and configure new internal devices

In addition to installing and configuring new peripherals, the IT practitioner often has to open the system's case and safely install **new internal components** and **devices**.

Perhaps the most common installations are to:

◆ add additional RAM
◆ add new hard drive (or change existing one)
◆ add new optical drive (or change existing one)
◆ upgrade CPU
◆ replace CPU or case fan
◆ change PSU
◆ upgrade specialist card (e.g. graphics card, sound card or network interface card).

Working with an open case provides extra challenges, for example components are often difficult to remove or replace due to cramped space inside the case. Also, there are many sharp metal edges which often cause cuts and abrasions.

In addition, it is possible to damage electrical components through **electrostatic discharge** (**ESD**). In order to prevent this happening, the IT practitioner should be **adequately grounded** by wearing an antistatic wrist strap and by **placing** all of the **components** (including the case) on an **antistatic workbench mat**.

Figure 2.65 A practitioner wearing antistatic wrist strap

Some articles recommend using the **ground pin of the plug** (i.e. keeping the computer system **plugged in** but **not switched on**). This is **not** recommended.

3.3 File management

Practical file management is a **key skill** when using computer systems.

A **proficient user** should be able to perform the following **file management** tasks:

◆ **create a new folder (subdirectory)**
◆ **perform a backup**
◆ **rename files**
◆ **delete files**
◆ **change a file attributes**.

Links

Unit 2 is a **core unit** on the BTEC National Award for IT Practitioners.

Owing to its underpinning concepts, it is also a **core unit** on **all four routes** of the Certificate and BTEC National Diploma for IT Practitioners (**IT and Business, Networking, Software Development and Systems Support**).

There are particular links, however, to the following:

Unit 4 – IT Project

Unit 15 – Organisational Systems Security

Unit 16 – Maintaining Computer Systems

Unit 23 – Installing and Upgrading Software

Unit 28 – IT Technical Support

Unit 29 – IT Systems Troubleshooting and Repair

Unit 36 – Supporting Users and Troubleshooting Desktop Applications on the XP Operating System (Microsoft)

Unit 37 – Supporting Users and Troubleshooting the XP Operating System (Microsoft)

Unit 38 – Client Operating Systems (Microsoft 70-270)

Unit 39 – Server Operating Systems (Microsoft 70-290)

Unit 40 – Server Infrastructure (Microsoft 70-291)

Unit 48 – A+ 220-602 (part of CompTIA A+)

Unit 49 – IT Essentials (part of CompTIA A+)

A link has also been made with:

Unit 8 – Communication Technologies (for Networking Hardware)

Flash tutorials for completing these operations are available for Microsoft **Windows®** and **Linux OSs** on the **companion CD**.

So that you can monitor your own progress and achievement in each unit, a recording grid has been provided (see on next page). The full version of this grid is also included on the companion CD.

Achieving success

This particular unit has 13 criteria to meet: 5 pass, 3 merit and 2 distinction.

For a **pass**:

You must achieve **all** 5 pass criteria

For a **merit**:

You must achieve **all** 5 pass and **all** 3 merit criteria

For a **distinction**:

You must achieve **all** 5 pass, **all** 3 merit **and both** distinction criteria.

Assignment	Assignments in this unit			
	U2.01	U2.02	U2.03	U2.04
Referral				
Pass				
1				
2				
3				
4				
5				
Merit				
1				
2				
3				
Distinction				
1				
2				

Help with assessment

This unit is fundamental to all four routes as it covers a number of underpinning knowledge areas.

In order to **pass** this unit you will need to have an understanding of the various components inside a typical computer system, have experience of at least two operating systems and be able to use software utilities and perform routine maintenance tasks. These are baseline performance indicators.

Merit grades ask more from you, principally being able to safely perform hardware replacement and judge the effects of software maintenance on the performance of a computer system. In addition, you will be asked to compare the functions of the two different operating systems you have used.

Distinction criteria generally ask you to critique and evaluate. In this case it is necessary to be able to competently examine three different computers systems and judge (and qualify) which one is best in a given scenario (typically some form of business requirement). Additionally, you will be asked to justify a particular upgrade (could be software or hardware) to an existing system.

 Online resources on the CD

Electronic glossary for this unit
Key fact sheets
Electronic slide show of key points
Flash animated tutorials

 Further reading

Anderson, H., and Yull, S., 2002, *BTEC Nationals IT Practitioners: Core Units for Computing and IT*, Newnes, ISBN 0750656840.

Dick, D., 2001, *The PC Support Handbook: Configuring and Systems Guide*, Dumbreck Publishing, ISBN 0952148471.

Knott, G., and Waites, N., 2002, *BTEC Nationals for IT Practitioners*, Brancepeth Computer Publications, ISBN 0953884821.

Unit 3

Information Systems

Capsule view

Information Systems is a 60-hour unit that helps you to develop an understanding of how **computers** and **information technologies** are used **within business**.

You will be introduced to the concepts of **business information** and you will learn how **information generated** through **business activities** is used to **support** the **performance** of organisations.

Learning aims

1 Know the source and characteristics of business information.
2 Understand how organisations use business information.
3 Understand the issues and constraints in relation to the use of information in organisations.
4 Know the features and functions of information systems.

Key Terms

Data is a collection of raw facts and/or figures that have not yet been processed, manipulated or interpreted into useful information. Once the data has been processed, it can be considered to be information, e.g. times, weights, measurements, sales.

Information is therefore data that has been manipulated so that some meaning can be derived from it, e.g. TV listing, bus timetable, top 40 singles download chart.

1 Know the source and characteristics of business information

1.1 Characteristics

When considering this type of topic it is sometimes useful to begin with a series of definitions (see key terms)!

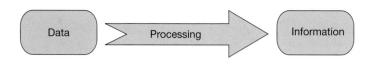

Figure 3.1 Data becomes information

Figure 3.1 represents this as an image.

Look at the data given in the table below.

Name	Height in metres
Aimee	1.64
Josie	1.58
Katie	1.60
Sophie	1.65
Alice	1.57

The table gives you a list of facts, as it lists the name and height of each of five girls. As such, it is merely data. We now manipulate (or process) the table.

Name	Height in metres
Sophie	1.65
Aimee	1.64
Katie	1.60
Josie	1.58
Alice	1.57

What we now have is a degree of knowledge about the group. Sophie at 1.65 metres is the tallest; Alice at 1.57 is the shortest.

In addition, we can use the data to find the mean average height (1.608 metres) and we can now see that Katie is the one closest to the average height for the group.

So we have learned about the group by manipulating the data in a number of ways.

Key Terms

Qualitative data – involves data/information that cannot be measured in the usual way. As such, it is usually in some sort of narrative form (spoken or written). An example might be 'customers generally feel product X represents good value for money'.

Quantitative data – is data or information that can be measured numerically and can be proven as fact. For example, the girls' height information included previously would be an example of quantitative data – each girl's height would have been measured to provide the actual figure. If we take the qualitative data example and revise it to be an example of quantitative data we would say '76 per cent of customers said that they believed product X to be good value for money'. In this instance, the percentage can be proven (assuming that the raw data was available).

Key Terms

Primary data is data that you (or your organisation) gathers and interprets yourself. An example of this might be that you do a survey among your customers about the quality of the service your organisation offers.

Secondary data would be where another organisation uses the data you have collected and interprets it for other purposes (for example in a comparison of customer satisfaction for a number of organisations offering the same type of service).

Characteristics of good information (e.g. valid, reliable, timely, fit for purpose, accessible, cost-effective, sufficiently accurate, relevant, having the right level of detail, from a source in which the user has confidence, understandable by the user)

Information is clearly of little use or value unless it is fit for the purpose for which it was intended. The list above provides a range of characteristics which will be explained here:

Valid

Data being valid is the most fundamental characteristic of good data/information. This means that the data must be completely **accurate**. It is the responsibility of the data or information gatherer to make sure that all aspects of the information are correct. This means that the information should have been **properly checked** before being used.

Reliable

The worst situation when using information or data would be to find out after you had finished using it that the data was **inaccurate**.

Firstly the data should have come from a **source** which you feel you can **trust**. In general you should feel that you can trust books and publications, as these will largely have been checked for you. In addition this would apply to organisational websites. However, there are likely to be some websites that would **not** be considered reliable. This is because the website originator might not be keeping the data and information on the website **up to date**. They might not have fully checked the validity of the data or information when it was put on the website and, ultimately, no one has queried it.

Another way to check that information is reliable is to check the data a number of times, ensuring that the result is the same. Here is an example.

Three salesmen work in the same geographical area. Their monthly sales have been represented in the table shown below and then the computer and a calculator have been used to find the average monthly total. These are the results.

	January	February	March
Chris	1653.25	1958.47	1744.23
Matthew	1954.77	1362.38	1659.48
John	1083.42	1124.61	1367.14
Average (calculated by computer)	1563.81	1481.82	1590.28
Average (calculated with calculator)	1563.81	1481.82	1590.28

According to the computer, the average for January is 1563.81. The calculator also averages the result at 1563.81.

Having used the calculator to check the result we can now consider the result as reliable. It has been checked using **alternative means** and if the calculation was done again and again, using the same data, the result would still be the same. As such, we can say that the data is **reliable**.

Timely

The concept of timely information is a simple one. Timely information is information that was prepared and ready at the point where it needed to be used. In most organisations, managers hold **regular meetings** where information is checked and shared with other managers. As an example, we will use the idea of a quarterly sales meeting. The first meeting for this year will be on 15 April 2007. At this meeting all the **sales statistics** and **corresponding information** for the months of January to March 2007 (inclusive) will be discussed. If the information is ready and is used at the 15 April meeting, the information will be said to have been **timely**. If, however, only information for January and February is prepared, then clearly the meeting will not have had the intended opportunities for discussion, because the purpose of that meeting on 15 April was to discuss **all** sales information for the first three months of the year.

Fit for purpose

In order to establish whether information is fit for purpose, we first need to set criteria against which this can be measured! These **criteria** will obviously vary from situation to situation but here are some generalisations.

The following chart has been created using the same sales data as provided earlier in this chapter.

Average weekly wage	260.1	295.875	304.8756
Average house price	75246	65324	71599
Weekly wage as percentage of house price	0.345666215	0.452934603	0.42580986

Average weekly wage	£260.10	£295.88	£304.88
Average house price	£75,246.00	£65,324.00	£71,599.00
Weekly wage as percentage of house price	34.57%	45.29%	42.58%

Average weekly wage	£260.10	£295.88	£304.88
Average house price	£75,246	£65,324	£71,599
Weekly wage as percentage of house price	35%	45%	43%

Figure 3.2 Sales performance chart

We are now going to ask the question 'how fit for purpose is this?' Firstly we need to decide what the chart is trying to display:

Sales Performance for the months from January to March 2007 inclusive

If you look at this chart, can you get the required information? No!

What is wrong with the above chart?

No chart **title**. The X-axis has **no title**. The Y-axis has **no title** and has a scale top value that is unnecessary (the figures do not go above 2000; in which case, why have a top value of 2500?).

The columns cannot be identified (e.g. you **cannot** identify which column reflects the sales of which representative.

Although there is a legend (a key to the different column colours), it does not provide any useful information!

The chart needs to be modified to make it fit for purpose.

Is the modified version better?

Average weekly wage	260.1	295.875	304.8756
Average house price	75246	65324	71599
Weekly wage as percentage of house price	0.345666215	0.452934603	0.42580986

Average weekly wage	£260.10	£295.88	£304.88
Average house price	£75,246.00	£65,324.00	£71,599.00
Weekly wage as percentage of house price	34.57%	45.29%	42.58%

Average weekly wage	£260.10	£295.88	£304.88
Average house price	£75,246	£65,324	£71,599
Weekly wage as percentage of house price	35%	45%	43%

Figure 3.3 Annotated sales performance chart

The second version of the column chart is clearly much more useable than the first attempt.

In terms of information being fit for purpose, here is an example from **KAM (Kris Arts & Media) Limited** which is intended to show their agents' **sales commission** based on **recorded sales**.

Category	Amount 2003	Amount 2005	Amount 2007
Average weekly commission based on average sales	260.1	295.875	304.8756
Average sales per week	5600.34	6780.34	12,002.25
Weekly commission as percentage of sales	0.046443609	0.043637192	0.025401537

In this instance, there are various numbers which are all accurate but which are **difficult to read** because of they way they have been **formatted**. Let's see if we can improve the table.

Category	Amount 2003	Amount 2005	Amount 2007
Average weekly commission based on average sales	£ 260.10	£ 295.88	£ 304.88
Average sales per week	£ 5600.34	£ 6780.34	£ 12,002.25
Weekly commission as percentage of sales	5%	4%	3%

This should now be easier to read. The **currency figures** have been formatted to **two decimal places** which forces the **decimal points** to **align**. In addition, rather than just stating that the weekly commission is being represented as a 'percentage of the sales', the figure has been **formatted** as a **percentage**.

In this version it is easier to see that the weekly commission has significantly **reduced** over the last four years. Should KAM's agents be worried?

The second table would be considered fit for purpose, depending on the importance of some of the other criteria in this section (such as **having the right level of detail** or **sufficiently accurate** which follow).

Accessible

We would all agree that it would be pointless for a functional area of an organisation to **generate data** and information that it would then be **unwilling to share** with other areas, particularly when you consider that all parts of an organisation should ultimately be working together towards a common goal.

Each department will need to take responsibility for preparing its data in such a way that it will be useable by other parts of the organisation.

Cost-effective

There are times when **costs** of gathering data are **too high** in comparison to the advantages to be gained from having the data available. Let's look at an example.

An organisation wants to find out how many males and females there are in the UK and where they live, broken down by country.

While there are a number of ways to gather this data, there are two obvious avenues to explore:

1 Pay a consultancy or data agency to gather the information for you (which will cost a significant amount of money).
2 Look up the population information on **http://www.statistics.gov.uk/**.

This page, from the government's own statistics website, would be considered a reliable source of secondary data, and from the writer's perspective, gathering this information was very easy and cost-effective. To have gathered this information **first hand** (primary data, through questionnaires etc.) would have been **time-consuming** and extremely **costly**.

There are times, however, when first-hand research is an absolute necessity because the information does not already exist or is in a format which is inappropriate for the uses to which it is going to be put. Sometimes the cost is not in physical money but in the time it will take to gather the information required.

Sufficiently accurate

It is possible that there will be occasions when you will be able to use data that is not 100 per cent accurate but is almost accurate. It will then be up to you to decide how useable a piece of data is.

The following is an example:

You have a bank savings account that contains £130.76.

When you use this information, how accurate you need to be about it will depend on what you are using the information for:

a) You want to buy an item that costs £130.76; clearly the whole value is very important (if you had less you would not be able to buy the item).

You are telling a friend about your savings account – you could say 'I have just over £130', which is

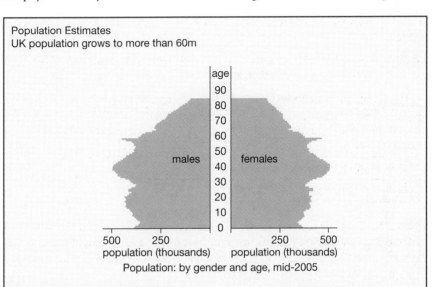

Population Estimates
UK population grows to more than 60m

Population: by gender and age, mid-2005

In mid-2005 the UK was home to 60.2 million people, of which 50.4 million lived in England. The average age was 38.8 years, an increase on 1971 when it was 34.1 years. In mid-2005 approximately one in five people in the UK were aged under 16 and one in six people were aged 65 or over.

The UK has a growing population. It grew by 375,100 people in the year to mid-2005 (0.6 per cent). The UK population increased by 7.7 per cent 1971, from 55.9 million. Growth has been faster in more recent years. Between mid-1991 and mid-2004 the population grew by an annual rate of 0.3 per cent and the average growth per year since mid-2001 has been 0.5 per cent.

The mid-2005 population of the constituent countries of the United Kingdom is estimated as follows:

	Population	Percentage of total UK population
England	50,431,700	83.8
Wales	2,958,600	4.9
Scotland	5,094,800	8.5
Northen Ireland	1,752,400	2.9
United Kingdom	60,209,500	

Figure 3.4 Government statistics

still **relatively accurate**. Or you could say 'I have over £100'; after all, does the friend really have to know **how much** you have in the account to the penny? Ultimately, all these statements are true, they are just increasingly inaccurate!

You have secured a job working five hours per week. Would you like to know exactly how much you get paid for each hour you work (e.g. £4.75), or would you be satisfied to know that you will earn approximately £5? In this case, you would want the information to be exact.

How accurate information is will depend on what it is going to be used for. That is a decision that will be made by the person who is going to **use** the information.

Activity – relevance

The concept of **relevance** in information is relatively easy to understand, and it is probably **best explained** using a series of **questions** and **answers** – in each case, read the question and decide which information would be **most relevant**.

1 You are looking at the price of an item you wish to purchase in the next few days. Which of these is likely to be the most relevant?
   a) the price of the item last week
   b) the price of the item next month
   c) the price of the item today.

2 Sales information for the first quarter of this year – which figures would be **most relevant**?
   a) January to March 2007 information
   b) April to June 2007 information
   c) January to March 2006 information.

3 You are going to travel in Europe – which of the following would be **relevant**?
   a) the US dollar to £ exchange rate
   b) the Euro to US dollar exchange rate
   c) the £ to Euro exchange rate.

4 You are travelling to America – which of the following would be **relevant**?
   a) weather report for Kingston
   b) weather report for New York
   c) weather report for New Delhi.

5 Production information for widgets – which of the following would be **relevant**?
   a) number of widgets being produced each month
   b) when current widget was designed
   c) colour of the widgets in the workplace.

Answers on p436.

So – relevant information is information that is needed to investigate an issue or answer a particular question. Irrelevant information is, in effect, useless in its contribution to the investigation or search for an answer.

Having the right level of detail

Certainly, in some situations, having a level of detail down to thousands of a millimetre may be appropriate. An example of this would be in engineering where measurements have to be incredibly accurate.

Take the following number: 5.81333333cm

An engineer might need to work with the figure 5.8133cm, while a salesman might well say that the item is 5.81cm.

There is another perspective on this and to explain, we will once again refer to the monthly sales results.

It might well be sufficient to give the monthly results, without giving the individual figures for each week. It will very much depend on how the information will be used and why.

From a source in which the user has confidence

While we can be relatively confident about the content of books, journals and newspapers (because the activities of publishers are policed and checked), the same is not true of internet sites. For this reason, users should be careful about trusting the reliability of websites unless they feel sure that their content is up to date and accurate.

Take the following websites as an example:

www.bigjimscomputerhardwarewebsite.com/
www.microsoft.com/

Which of the two websites is likely to be **more reliable**? We would clearly say Microsoft® because the organisation polices its website and ensures it stays up to date. The reason it does this is that it wants to present a **professional image**. Ultimately its reputation is at stake. This will be the same for any organisation. However, **bigjim** might actually be an anonymous person who just happens to like computers. They might well believe that the information they have on their site is accurate. It might not, however, be the case. As such, it is unreliable.

Understandable by the user

Part of the reason why we include titles and legends on graphs and charts is to make information more understandable by the user. Clearly, if information cannot be understood, then it cannot be considered information in the first place. When developing information, ensure that it is what your user ultimately wants.

Transformation of data into information (e.g. collection, storage, processing and manipulation, retrieval, presentation)

We have already considered what is often called the data processing cycle.

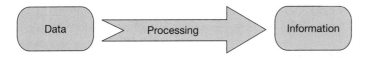

Figure 3.5 Data processing cycle

This diagram represents this activity and shows how data collected or gathered will need to be **processed** into information.

In reality, however, this is really much more complex as we need to take additional features into consideration.

Collection

Data can be collected in many ways. It can be collected physically, as in paper forms, or electronically, through a computer. The following are data collection techniques:

◆ **application form** (could be for a job or even for a library card)
◆ **registration form** (for this course your organisation will have completed a registration form for you that will have ensured that you are registered with Edexcel, the awarding body for this qualification)
◆ **questionnaire** (you might create one or you might be asked to complete one)
◆ **interview** (this could be recorded on paper or using an electronic device such as a tape recorder)
◆ **observation** (this will be where you watch something to gain information)
◆ **discussion**
◆ **online** website **form**.

Storage

Once data has been collected or gathered, it will need to be organised in some way so that it can be stored. Failure to **organise** data **successfully** will possibly make the data more difficult to **process** and **manipulate**.

Data can be stored electronically in files, in paper archives such as A4 files or on video tape or cassette. How the data is stored is important not only in terms of how it will subsequently be used but how it will be protected. The main advantage of data stored electronically is that it can be copied and stored elsewhere. It is difficult to achieve this with A4 paper files, video tapes or cassettes.

Processing and manipulation

How data is **processed** will depend on what the data is and **what** it will be **used for**.

Data containing numbers may well be subjected to a variety of **calculations**. The data can be categorised, sorted and manipulated. While there is still significant argument over where this saying originated, 'lies, damned lies and statistics' is a suggestion that you can make numbers say just about anything you want them to. At the end of the twentieth century, during a period of high unemployment, the statistics suddenly changed as 'young people in training' disappeared from the national figure. You must always take care to be honest with your number manipulation.

Textual information can be processed by, for example, categorising or sorting it. This is usually done with records, particularly in a database.

Retrieval

Once the data has been manipulated, it needs to be **retrieved**. Database information is retrieved using **filters** and **queries**. Information will be searched using **key words** and the relevant information copied and pasted into relevant documents. If the data moves outside its original source (a paragraph from a book, for example), the source should be **attributed**. This means that as the data user you are responsible for saying **where** the original data or information **came from**.

Presentation

Ultimately, all information that has been retrieved from systems will need to be presented.

There is significant presentation software on the market today. What follows is a small range of the software you can use to help you to effectively present information you have gathered.

Software manufacturer	Application purpose
Microsoft Word®	Word-processing package for presenting text
Corel WordPerfect®	Word-processing package for presenting text
Microsoft Excel®	Spreadsheet package for working with and presenting numbers, and with functionality to help users create graphical representations such as charts and graphs
Trius Inc As Easy As®	Similar to Microsoft Excel®, but requires an MS-DOS operating system
IBM Lotus 1-2-3®	A third spreadsheet package
Microsoft Publisher®	Presentation package which can be used to create leaflets, newsletters, advertisements, menus, business cards etc.
Microsoft PowerPoint®	Presentation software that creates slide shows which can be used when presenting information to large groups of people
Harvard Graphics Advanced Presentations®	An alternative package to prepare slide shows
OpenOffice®	A multi-platform open-source free product that has some of the functionality of Microsoft Office®

Whichever software is used to present information, the user should endeavour to make the information as professional as possible.

Braincheck

Crossword puzzle
Try the following crossword based on what we have covered so far. The **grid** and **clues** are provided, along with the **answers on page 421** (if you get stuck).

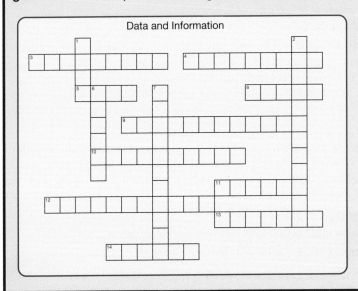

Data and Information

1.2 Sources of information

To complete the topic of sources and characteristics of information, we need to consider where data and information can be drawn from by an organisation.

Internal information (e.g. finance, personnel, marketing, purchasing, sales, manufacturing, administration)

Internal information is information that is generated through the **normal business activities** of an organisation. This information tends to be generated by a specific **functional area** within the organisation but can often be used by more than one other business function. This list of functional areas of an organisation is not exhaustive, and in some companies these functional areas might have different titles.

Finance

This area of an organisation deals with all aspects of the company's monetary activities. It will include the **accounting** department, which will be responsible for recording the business' activities such as purchase invoices and sales invoices, will monitor creditors (those to whom the organisation owes money) and debtors (those who owe the organisation money), and will handle VAT payments. Based on the activities of this area, other departments will be given working budgets (amounts of money that the managers of functional areas can use as they see fit, to support their own area of the organisation).

The **payroll** functional area is responsible for administrating the salaries (money usually paid monthly) and wages (money usually paid weekly) of all employees. Payroll will calculate how much is to be paid, it will make deductions for tax, National Insurance (NI) and pensions contributions, and will pay these amounts to the Inland Revenue when required to do so.

Both of the areas defined within the **financial** operating area will be using information generated by other departments and will be providing information to those departments in return.

Internal information inside this function will include:

◆ invoices
◆ debtors and creditors lists

- VAT returns
- purchase and sales ledgers
- budgetary information
- wage records
- National Insurance and tax contribution information
- Inland Revenue returns.

Personnel

The **personnel** function of an organisation is concerned with the general **recruitment** and **selection of employees**. They will help managers to write job specifications, organise interviews, generate letters offering employment and, ultimately, will **administrate** the employee's records while the employee remains in service. This is usually a reactive function which jumps into action when a department's needs have been identified (for example, when someone has resigned).

The **human resource** (**HR**) functional part of this area is concerned with helping the organisation to plan its people needs. Usually proactive (involved in planning and in the decision-making process), HR managers assist the organisation at a strategic level, defining recruitment strategies to meet the organisation's long-term goals, or suggesting training schemes for existing employees (whichever is more cost-effective and appropriate).

Internal information inside these functions will include:

- job specifications
- interview lists
- training records
- sickness and holiday records
- disciplinary records.

Marketing

As with **finance** and **personnel**, the **marketing** function also has two strands: **marketing** and **advertising**, although sometimes you will hear the terms used interchangeably. In actual fact, the roles are very different!

The **marketing** function of an organisation is responsible for devising a strategy to make customers aware of the organisation and its products. It is about researching the market (gathering information about potential customers and their buying habits), planning how and when to advertise and, in some cases, marketing executives will get involved with product design as they may well have information about what features customers want from products.

Advertising is more about the physical promotion of the service or product. Specialists in this field will design the posters, leaflets, radio jingles etc. that will help to bring the product or service into the public arena. They will find the best deals to get the most exposure for the company's money, might organise slots on TV or radio, could purchase newspaper or magazine **space**, and might well find distributors for the leaflets and posters.

In a nutshell, **marketing** is about **planning** and **strategy**, **advertising** is about **doing**.

Internal information inside this function will include:

- market research information
- strategic plans
- advertising costs and comparisons

Purchasing

The **purchasing** department is responsible for **buying goods** and **services** on behalf of the whole organisation. For example, the purchasing staff will find the best deals on raw materials used in production, they will **negotiate contracts** with distributors (such as couriers) and they will monitor their buying strategies to ensure that they always buy at the best price. This might mean that the company will need to buy materials in bulk (more than they require to reduce the price), or that there is an opportunity for a composite purchasing strategy (where making up a large combined order for a number of products will bring down the price of the individual items because costs such as transportation can be reduced).

Where appropriate, they will raise purchase orders and, liaising with the relevant departments, will set delivery deadlines for suppliers.

Internal information inside this function will include:

◆ purchase orders
◆ manufacturing schedules
◆ composite or bulk deal information.

Sales and customer services

Firstly, it is important to be aware that not all organisations have a **sales** department. Some have **customer services** instead and other companies have both!

The **sales** function is usually the **face** of the organisation and is made up of individuals with an excellent product knowledge and a good understanding of customers and their needs. Sometimes this **face** is actually a **voice** as increasing numbers of companies invest in **telesales** staff. These staff usually make first contact with prospective customers, which is often followed up by a sales representative.

The function of the sales team is to **secure actual business**, selling the organisation's products and services to customers, but also they are responsible for **expanding** the organisation's **existing** customer base.

Institutions such as the **National Health Service** (**NHS**), however, do not have a **sales** function in the traditional sense. This is because customers (as patients) tend to come directly to them, or because they have been referred by their **general practitioner** (**GP**) or **doctor**. On the other hand, the individual parts of the NHS will want to know what their customers think about the services they provide and, as such, they have a **customer services** function. Staff in this area will handle **enquiries**, offer **advice** and deal with any **complaints** or **criticisms** that are made of the service.

Internal information inside this function will include:

◆ products lists, price lists and brochures
◆ customer questionnaires
◆ sales targets.

Manufacturing (also known as the production department)

Only companies that make a product will have a **manufacturing** department. Manufacturing by definition is a function that changes **raw materials** into **products** which might be used in the manufacture of other products, or into customer-ready finished goods.

Internal information inside this function will include:

◆ product plans/recipes/designs
◆ production schedules

- staff rotas (particularly important if the organisation operates a 24/7 manufacturing operation
- machine maintenance records
- production records (including batch numbering information where relevant).

Distribution (also known as the dispatch department)

The **distribution** function of an organisation is responsible for ensuring that the **products** and **services** supplied by the company get to its customers when intended. It will organise the physical transport, whether this is using the company's own vehicles or using transport companies or courier services. It will also take the responsibility for any export issues that may arise if goods are to be sent overseas.

Internal information inside this function will include:

- any hazard information that will affect either the transportation or handling of the products
- emergency details for alternative transport should any issues arise that prevent the company working in the usual way.

It is not unusual for the **stock** or **warehouse** functions to be included under the **distribution** umbrella. Whether the items that need to be distributed have been manufactured by the organisation or have been purchased by the organisation for resale, they will need to be stored prior to dispatch. Goods are then removed as and when sold, and delivery notes are raised that accompany the goods to their destination. These delivery notes are often then used by companies to generate invoices. However, sometimes goods are sold **cash on delivery** (**COD**), which means that the customer has to pay for the goods when they are delivered.

Administration

Considering **administration** as a discreet function can be a bit misleading. In some organisations administration is undertaken by clerical staff who work **within** each functional area (purchasing clerks or sales clerks for example). In other organisations the administration activity is more **centralised**, where the clerks will undertake any administration tasks, as and when required. In this situation, whoever is free will undertake the task. Sometimes this functional area will also have a responsibility for the company's estate (buildings, car-parking arrangements, security). It will depend very much on the individual organisation as to what the administration function will do.

Research and development

Where organisations work with physical products, they may very well have a **research and development** department, whose job it is to **develop new products** and **find enhancements** for existing ones. Working with customer feedback, the staff in this area will try and estimate what we, as consumers, will want to buy in the future. For obvious reasons, this functional area will work very closely with the marketing and sales departments in trying to establish what customers may want in the future.

Internal information inside this function will include:

- strategic plans
- product design information
- customer feedback.

Ultimately, as suggested much earlier in this chapter, it is likely that most departments will share information, or will generate information that must be passed between them to support the business' activities.

Some of the information, however, will need to be sent outside the organisation, while other information from outside will need to be brought in.

Braincheck

Matching exercise
Match the **departments** to their **key functions**.

Letter	Department	Number	Functions
A	Purchasing	1	Recruitment and selection of employees
B	Human resources	2	Recording business activities, monitoring debtors and creditors
C	Manufacturing or production	3	Making contact with customers and presenting the company's portfolio of products and services
D	Marketing	4	Physical promotion of goods and services with campaigns
E	Distribution	5	Developing new products and improving current ones
F	Finance	6	Handle enquiries, offer advice and support, and deal with complaints
G	Sales	7	Buying goods and services from suppliers and negotiating contracts for stock or materials
H	Research and development	8	Ensuring products and services get to customers
I	Personnel	9	Making the products that the company will sell
J	Customer services	10	Planning the use of staff
K	Advertising	11	Strategic planning based on market research, product redesign

Answers on p421.

External information (e.g. government, trade groupings, commercially provided, databases, research)

Most organisations also interact with external agencies (those outside the company), receiving and providing information as required. Some of these external organisations are investigated here.

Government

All companies, whether they are limited companies, partnerships, sole traders or charities, **must** pass information to the **government**. Equally, some information will be passed in.

The organisation must supply the following:

◆ VAT information
◆ tax and National Insurance information about amounts deducted from employees
◆ pension information
◆ information about the company's turnover (for company tax purposes, as companies are taxed as well as their employees).

The organisation must receive and respond to the following:

◆ legislation
◆ gathering and paying of VAT.

Trade groupings

There are some industrial and service sectors which have **trade groupings**. These groupings are usually made up of companies operating in the same sector, where they come together to raise standards, set prices and develop policies.

A more extreme example of a trade grouping is the Organisation of the Petroleum Exporting Countries (OPEC). Formed in 1960, OPEC was intended to make the petrol companies fairer in their dealings with the oil-consuming countries. This was partly because there are obviously going to be countries in the world that do not have oil resources but who will need the oil and petroleum products to fuel their cars and other associated services. OPEC was designed to ensure that the oil rich nations would not treat oil-poor nations unfavourably, charging them high prices because they did not have any alternatives.

More recent developments have seen the creation of the OPEC Fund for International Development (OFID) – an OPEC-led organisation that is investing some of OPEC's revenues in health and social concerns across the world.

Commercially provided

If an organisation is not able to generate its own information (for example, customer feedback on its products), it may well need to buy in such information from outside agencies. There are agencies, for example, who **gather information** and **sell it** to **anyone** who wants to **purchase it**. Other agencies are specialists and will help an organisation to secure the information by helping them to devise a data gathering and analysis strategy. Clearly this is done for a fee.

Databases

It is well known that information about us is stored by many organisations and institutions for various purposes. In order to store such data, these organisations need to comply with the legislation set out in the Data Protection Act 1998 and the Freedom of Information Act 2000 (both of which will be covered later in this chapter).

There was a time, however, when it was not uncommon for one organisation to sell its customer list to another organisation that was not in direct competition. For example, a sports company could sell its customer list to a CD outlet. While this does still happen, many organisations are more reluctant to pass this information on, particularly because, in some cases, there has been negative feedback from customers for organisations that have done so.

Research

While in the real world there is significant ongoing research in many areas, one spin-off from these activities is that sometimes other information, not necessarily required as part of the research aims, can be collected along the way. It would thus make sense if this data were to be sold on to other organisations that might find it useful, thereby recovering some of the cost for the originator of the research.

2 Understand how organisations use business information

2.1 Purposes

It is essential that organisations have access to business information in order for them to be able to function. This section discusses some of the ways in which information can be used to sustain ongoing business activities.

Operational support (e.g. monitoring and controlling activity)

To support its daily activities, all organisations need to have access to information. Operational information can be divided into two subcategories: monitoring and controlling.

The types of information that an organisation will use in order to help it monitor its activities could include:

◆ how much stock of each product it has to sell
◆ how many hours overtime were needed to complete a particular order.

Control information is much more obvious and may well include:

◆ production schedules (what the organisation will be making today)
◆ what deliveries need to be made.

Without the records of day-to-day activities, an organisation will find it very difficult to function normally. It needs to constantly monitor its own performance and control its activities so that precious resources are not wasted.

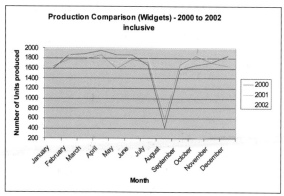

Figure 3.6 Trend analysis with predictable event

Analysis (e.g. to identify patterns or trends)

To be effective, managers must understand their own data. They must be able to look at tables or charts of performance data and be able to explain any anomalous values (these are values that are unusual and not expected). Take the line chart in Figure 3.6 as an example (note that the lowest value is 200, not 0, so that the lines are better emphasised).

It is clear that there is something unusual about August, where widget production has been repetitively low. The production manager would probably be able to explain this with relative ease because it is a recurring event. The possible explanations are:

a) significant staff are on annual leave and so production is affected
b) the company always closes down for two weeks in August, so no widgets are produced.

Look at the graph in Figure 3.7.

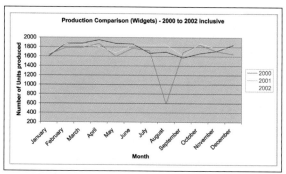

Figure 3.7 Trend analysis with exceptional event

In this case the production figure only dropped in 2001 and was more or less **normal** in August 2000 and August 2002. Now the event is even more puzzling. What could have happened in August 2001? Here are some possible explanations:

a) The organisation was let down by its suppliers and did not have the raw materials to produce the widgets.
b) There were major problems with machinery – significant breakdowns caused a delay in production.
c) There were major problems with machinery – the organisation could not get spares when one of the primary machines developed a fault and needed a new part.

Clearly there will be other possible explanations.

What should be noted here is that the data has been presented visually as a chart. Here is the raw data on which the chart was based.

Would it have been quite as easy to identify the anomaly if the data had been presented in this way? Probably not, other than the fact that the number 587 has only three figures and the rest of the numbers have four! What would have happened if the anomaly had been 1001? It would not have stood out!

Analysing data is a complex subject area and people who do this type of work have traditionally had to be highly trained. Today, however, there is software that can monitor your data and can **flag unusual events** (known as **exception reporting**) as and when they occur. This has made it much easier for organisations to monitor their activities.

	2000	2001	2002
January	1601	1636	1654
February	1872	1784	1871
March	1877	1789	1843
April	1952	1871	1799
May	1874	1598	1671
June	1863	1774	1844
July	1667	1721	1838
August	1694	587	1844
September	1572	1686	1610
October	1662	1845	1872
November	1711	1706	1766
December	1842	1648	1791

Decision making (operational, tactical, strategic)

Information gained from the organisation's usual activities, together with information that can be projected (estimated based on previous trends), will be used to help the organisation make decisions. Each type of decision has different characteristics, which will be explained here.

Operational decisions

These are decisions about the establishment's activities now and within the next 6 to 12 months. For example:

1 A number of production employees are off sick – what do you do in the short term to ensure that production is not affected?
2 What raw materials will we need today?
3 Can we organise ourselves differently and speed up operations?

To enable it to make these decisions, it needs the following sorts of information:

1 Who has called in sick today and how long they are likely to be away from work.
2 What is going to be produced today (we will assume that the raw materials stock was checked a few days prior to **today** – assurance that the raw materials have been moved to the production area.

3 A floor plan and production flow information (looking at how the goods move through the production line).

Tactical decisions

These are decisions about what will happen within the organisation in the next five years or so. These decisions are often informed by market research, to ensure that the company remains safe in the medium term. For example:

1 Are there any new products that we should be making?
2 Are there any existing products that we should stop making?
3 Do we need to make any capital investment to meet the organisation's longer-term strategy?
4 Do our staff need any training to enable us to meet our longer-term goals?

To enable it to make these decisions, it needs the following sorts of information:

1 Information about what competitors are making. Information about what customers' changing wants are.
2 Stock information on existing products and information about stock movement (if the stock is not moving then it is not selling, in which case it might well be selected as a product that should be discontinued)
3 What our current capital reserves are. If there is insufficient finance available, should we be taking out a business loan to finance future strategies?
4 What training does our staff have? Will this training be sufficient and suitable to enable us to meet our mid-term goals or do we need to have some staff trained? What training courses are available?

Strategic decisions

These are decisions that have a long time frame and require organisations to look well into the future (in excess of about five years). For example:

1 Should we expand?
2 Should we buy larger premises?
3 How should the organisation be structured?

To enable them to make these decisions they need the following sorts of information:

1 Estimates of how our organisation will develop over the next five to ten years.
2 The costs of larger premises, including the anticipated overheads on such properties (such as council tax, average heating and lighting costs), so that they can be compared with current expenditure on these items.
3 The current organisational structure should be identified and written down, so that managers can discuss whether changes in the hierarchy could be achieved and how they see these changes being implemented

Clearly in all three cases the lists are not extensive, or definitive, but the lists are representative of the types of decisions that the management of organisations needs to make at various points. They should give you a flavour of business decision-making issues.

Gaining commercial advantage

Clearly it is in an organisation's interests to find ways of gaining an advantage over its competitors. To this end, those individuals working for the company who have marketing responsibilities will be closely monitoring what competitors are doing. They will be watching pricing strategies, looking at what products competitors are offering for sale and what they have withdrawn. They can gain operational information about companies by looking at a competitor's accounts. This is only possible if the company is a **Public Limited Company** (**PLC**) – a company whose shares are offered for general sale on the stock exchange – or a **Limited Company** (one owned by shareholders but not floated on the stock exchange, where shareholders are usually invited to purchase shares as an investment in the organisation's future). These types of companies have to register their operational accounts at the end of each financial year with Companies House. These can be accessed by any individual who is interested.

Charities also publish their accounts, to assure the public that the monies they donate are being used properly for the purpose for which they were intended.

Case Study

Paul Lee, the Chief Executive of Lee Business Supplies, has been on holiday for a few weeks and he has returned to discover that a number of **decisions** need to be **made**. Clearly the company has been busy in his absence!

In order to help Paul, he has given you a **list of problems** and issues and asked you to **prioritise** them for him. To do this, you have been asked to identify whether these problems or issues are **operational** (require immediate resolution), **tactical** (could wait, but need to be done relatively soon), or **strategic** (need to be done in the longer term).

Clearly the growth of information technology has given many companies information at their fingertips that they might have struggled to gather and interpret five years ago. However, as a note of caution, organisations must remember that while they can now gain information about their competitors more easily, their competitors can equally gain information more easily about the organisation too!

Braincheck

Complete the following grid. In each case, say whether the issue is operational, strategic or tactical.

Number	Issue or problem	Operational? Strategic? Tactical?
1	One of your managers has heard that a competitor is dropping prices on their main stock items next month.	
2	You seem to have a large amount of stock of product X that does not appear to be selling very well – should you continue to stock the product or maybe delete it?	
3	Most staff in the distribution area (primarily drivers) have all called in sick with stomach upsets (suspected food poisoning) which means that out of a team of six staff, only two people are in.	

Number	Issue or problem	Operational? Strategic? Tactical?
4	Our vehicle fleet is old and in need of significant investment. Do we want to replace the vehicles or maybe outsource this part of the organisation to a courier?	
5	A supplier was not paid at the end of last month and is refusing to provide any more stock.	
6	A supplier has told you that they will be bringing in a whole new range of business products in about 18 months' time and has asked you whether you think your customers might be interested.	
7	The distribution manager has said that we are increasingly running out of storage space in the warehouse. As there is no opportunity for physical expansion at our current premises, should we consider moving operations elsewhere?	

Answers on p421.

2.2 Functional areas

Functional business areas (e.g. sales, purchasing, manufacturing, marketing, finance, personnel, administration)

This topic has been covered extensively in section 1.1 of this unit. As such, this table will provide a brief overview of each functional area (for a more in-depth explanation, please see earlier in this unit).

Department/ functional area	Description
Accounts (finance)	The functional area concerned with recording the financial transactions of the organisation, both income and expenditure (payments in and out). This area will chase debtors (those who owe the company money) for late payments and ensure that sufficient funds are available to pay staff and creditors (those to whom the company owes money).
Payroll (finance)	Coming under the accounts or finance umbrella, the payroll function is solely responsible for ensuring that employees are correctly paid for their services. Payroll employees will calculate gross wage (the total amount you earn), and will take off any deductions for tax, National Insurance or pension contributions as appropriate. The employee will then be given a payslip reflecting this information and the net pay due (calculated as the gross salary less any deductions).

Personnel	This area is responsible for recruiting staff and, in some cases, terminating employment contracts. They will undertake the general administration of staff records, including sickness records and holiday entitlement, and will monitor training expiry dates to ensure that recertification is achieved in good time. An example of this would be forklift truck (FLT) drivers. Each FLT driver has to have a specialist licence, which needs to be renewed on a regular basis. If the licence is allowed to expire, then the employee will not be able to drive a forklift truck until such time as they resit the test successfully. This is also true of first-aid officers, who must also renew their practising licences on a regular basis.
HR (human resources)	Looking at staff as a resource like any other organisational resource, the HR function will help managers plan how the resource will be used most effectively.
Marketing	Employees who work in marketing will be gathering and analysing information that includes customer feedback, product information and development information, to enable them to design strategies for promoting new products in the marketplace.
Advertising	As suggested previously, advertising is about the physical promotion of the service or product provided by the organisations. Employees in this functional area will be creating the leaflets, posters etc. that we see each day.
Purchasing	This area is responsible for buying the products and services that the organisation will use to support its activities.
Sales	Staff in this functional area secure business for the organisation by selling its goods or services to customers. In addition, sales representatives are responsible for growing (expanding) the organisation's customer base.
Customer services	Customer services generally handle complaints and concerns that are being directed at the organisation. But this area also has a positive side – staff in customer services will also provide product support or advice and guidance.
Manufacturing or production	This is the functional area that is responsible for physically making the products sold by the company.
Distribution or dispatch	The distribution function ensures that the goods and services provided to customers arrive at their destination. In some organisations this department also has a responsibility for stock.
Administration	An administrative department will be very different within each organisation in terms of what it actually does. Administration will include many different types of clerical work but can also include responsibility for the estate of the organisation (buildings, maintenance, security etc.).
Research and development	Research and development is an important functional area as it is the 'think tank' for new products and services that the company might want to sell in the future. In addition, this department will constantly revisit existing products to see if they can be improved.

2.3 Information flows

To fully understand how functional areas within an organisation interact and exchange information, it is necessary to analyse the types of information that flow between them. It is clear from content earlier in the unit that information is generated by functional areas, is shared with other functional areas within the organisation (**internal information flow**), or passed to agencies outside the organisation (**external information flow**).

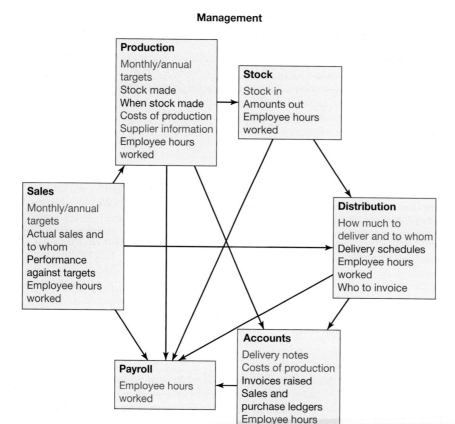

Figure 3.8 Flow of data between departments

It is becoming increasingly common for departments in an organisation to share information – it is now considered that a company's information belongs to the whole company, not to a particular department. Look at the following simple diagram that represents some company information, broken down by departments.

All information shown in purple is **generated by the department and passed to another area**.

All information shown in blue is **passed into the department from outside**.

All information in black is generated **within the section** but might not be used by any other area.

Notice that the management function is over <u>**all**</u> other areas – this implies that managers will have access to all information generated by the organisation.

Internal information flows

Even as late as the 1980s, it was more common for departments in an organisation to communicate using internal phone systems or memos if they needed to have a paper copy of a communication. These days, however, it is more common for employees to communicate via **email** or, in some cases, an organisational messaging system (a little bit like a company chat program). Many organisations also have an **intranet**, which is a **website** created and **managed internally** for the benefit of the employees, usually containing links to **organisational policies**, **news** and **important events**. Clearly there are now multiple ways of communicating that do not necessarily require moving paper between departments!

Having focused largely on communication between departments, we also need to consider that the information also flows vertically (up and down) within the organisation. Managers will set targets for departments and will provide instructions about how various activities should be undertaken. The employees will then carry out the tasks and send back relevant information to the managers that confirms that targets have been met or that instructions have been followed.

Information flows to external bodies

There are a number of important external agencies or bodies with which organisations will need to communicate. Sometimes the communication can be **unidirectional** (one way), while on other occasions it will be **bidirectional** (both ways).

The common agencies with which most organisations will communicate are listed below, together with examples of the sorts of information that are exchanged.

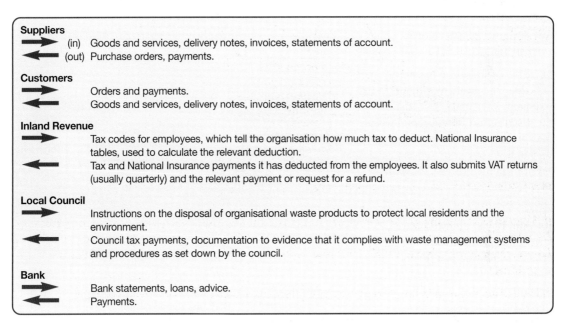

Suppliers
(in) Goods and services, delivery notes, invoices, statements of account.
(out) Purchase orders, payments.

Customers
Orders and payments.
Goods and services, delivery notes, invoices, statements of account.

Inland Revenue
Tax codes for employees, which tell the organisation how much tax to deduct. National Insurance tables, used to calculate the relevant deduction.
Tax and National Insurance payments it has deducted from the employees. It also submits VAT returns (usually quarterly) and the relevant payment or request for a refund.

Local Council
Instructions on the disposal of organisational waste products to protect local residents and the environment.
Council tax payments, documentation to evidence that it complies with waste management systems and procedures as set down by the council.

Bank
Bank statements, loans, advice.
Payments.

Information flow diagrams

When it comes to drawing diagrams to represent an organisation's information flows you will find many different diagram styles in the books you read and on the websites you visit. There are no hard and fast rules as to which technique is best, or which technique you **should** use.

What you should remember is that whatever diagramming style you apply, you need to do it **consistently**! What follows here is a diagram that represents an e-business organisation like **Amazon.com** or **Play.com** (both of whom trade solely online).

The diagram will include representations for both **internal functions** or **departments**, and external agencies with which the organisation will communicate. In each case, the arrow showing the information being passed also shows the direction of the information flow (the originator and the recipient).

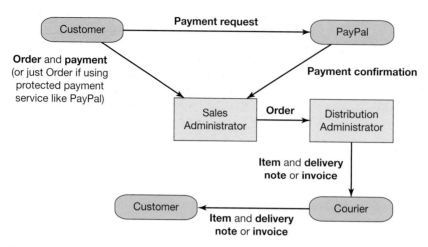

Figure 3.9 Customer order information flow

In general this is a very straightforward process:

The customer **places an order** – they could **pay** the company **directly** or alternatively could instruct an **intermediary** such as PayPal to pay the organisation.

Once the organisation has **both** the **order** and **confirmation of payment**, it will **pass** the **order** to the **distribution function** that will **pack** it and **prepare** it for **dispatch**. A courier or delivery service will then **receive** the **item** and **documentation**, and the item will be **delivered** to the **customer**.

It would be very unusual to attempt to represent every aspect of an organisation in a single diagram. It is much more likely that you will be asked to draw a diagram that represents the information flows in a particular functional area, or for a specified process.

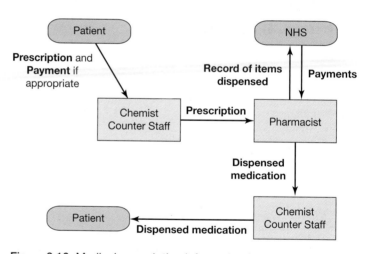

Figure 3.10 Medical prescription information flow

Here is another example.

In this example the patient gives a prescription to the counter staff in a chemist. If they have to pay for their prescriptions, they will also provide payment. The prescription goes to the pharmacist who dispenses the medication. The medication is the given to the counter staff, who hand it to the patient.

If the patient does not pay for prescriptions, the items dispensed are recorded and the money is claimed from the NHS.

The most important factor about drawing information flow diagrams is that both the originator and the reader can both fully understand what is being communicated.

Case Study

Rington College is a sixth-form college that offers a range of Level 2 and 3 vocational courses in ICT, engineering, health and social care, hair and beauty, and land-based studies.

In order to properly advise prospective students about these courses, the **course teams** in each area provide course information to the **academic advisors**. This information is then passed to **schools** in the area or directly to prospective **students** on request.

Activity

Draw an information flow diagram

Using the case study for Rington College, draw a **simple information flow diagram** that represents the **processes** as described.

Answers on p436.

3 Understand the issues and constraints in relation to the use of information in organisations

3.1 Legal issues

In general it is fair to say that there is significant legislation with which an organisation must comply. Some legislation not only applies to individuals as employees, but also to individuals in the population at large – this includes the following (although there are many more):

◆ Sex Discrimination Act 1975
◆ Race Relations Act 1976
◆ Disability Discrimination Act 1995.

Owing to the growth in computing technology, there have been a number of Acts which have been directed specifically at information and how it is used by organisations. This is in addition to Codes of Practice that many organisations may wish to impose on their staff, but which are not enforceable in law (in other words, you will not go to prison for breaching a Code of Practice, but you may well have your employment terminated). Codes of Practice will be covered later in this unit.

At this point we will consider the relevant legislation.

Relevant data protection legislation (e.g. Data Protection Act 1998, Freedom of Information Act 2000)

The first two Acts we will consider are the **Data Protection Act** and the **Freedom of Information Act**. Both of these acts are designed to **protect individuals** and **organisations** by setting out **guidelines** that must be strictly adhered to. Failure to do so can result in **prosecution** (and **imprisonment**), because breaching these Acts is a criminal offence.

Data Protection Act 1998

Both individuals and organisations that are holding **personal information about individuals** must inform the **Office of the Information Commissioner** that they are in **possession** of such data. In other words, organisations must register the fact that they are holding personal data and they must pay a **small annual fee**. According to the British Computer Society:

The eight principles require personal data to be:

- fairly and lawfully obtained;
- held only for specific and lawful purposes and not processed in any manner incompatible with those purposes;
- adequate, relevant and not excessive for those purposes;
- accurate and where necessary kept up to date, not kept for longer than necessary;
- processed in accordance with the rights of the person to whom the data refers;
- kept securely to ensure data is not lost, disposed of or misused;
- not transferred out of the European Economic Area unless the destination has an adequate level of data protection.

Source: http://www.bcs.org

There are also a number of direct **offences** for which organisations and individuals can be fined – for example, **selling data** is against the law.

Freedom of Information Act 2000 (FOIA)

Although the Freedom of Information Act was passed in the autumn of 2000, it was not fully implemented until January 2005. With the knowledge and understanding that more and more data was being held about us as individuals, the government passed this Act to give us improved access to our individual records.

In order to gain such access, individuals need to make a direct request to the organisation holding the information. The Act actually stipulates how such requests should be made. Again drawing on information gained from the British Computer Society:

The act sets out that public requests must be managed as follows:

- Requests must be written; no set format or justification is defined.
- The request must be processed within 20 days of receipt.
- The body must inform the requester if the information is not available or cannot be supplied with full justification.
- The body must contact the requester and discuss the requirement, if the request for information is vague or complex, so that the request can be met.
- The requester can appeal if the information is not made available.

Source: http://www.bcs.org

As long as individuals comply with the request guidance, the organisation is obligated to provide the relevant evidence.

There are, even so, a number of exceptions where the Freedom of Information Act **does not** apply:

FOIA does not authorise the disclosure of the following:

- information more than 50 years old;

- commercial secrets;
- national security information;
- information that would prejudice commercial and/or public affairs;
- court records;
- personal data, as this is regulated by the Data Protection Act 1998.

Source: http://www.bcs.org

This provides an overview – for more detail on the Freedom of Information Act 2000 or the Data Protection Act 1998, see the British Computer Society website (as above).

Other relevant legislation (e.g. Computer Misuse Act 1990)

The following legislation does not apply directly to data, but to the use of computers in general.

Computer Misuse Act 1990

The Computer Misuse Act came into being to attempt to resolve a **surge in criminal activity** surrounding **computers** and **their use** – primarily the increase in instances of **computer hacking**. Hacking is the intentional accessing of computer systems to **illegally gain access to data** (for the purposes of theft) or with other **malicious** (and sometimes quite serious) **intent**. The legislation covers activities such as the denial of service (DOS) attack.

A DOS attack, for example, is where the intention is to prevent legitimate users from using their systems by disabling ports or dramatically increasing network traffic to slow down or simply prevent access.

According to the Department for Education and Skills, the Computer Misuse Act recognises three key offences:

- Unauthorised access to computer material.
- Unauthorised access with intent to commit or facilitate commission of further offences.
- Unauthorised modification of computer material.

Source: http://stagesafety.ngfl.gov.uk/

Terrorism Act 2000

The Terrorism Act 2000 also has implications for computing and ICT in that it is now an offence to use computers to intimidate individuals and groups, particularly from a political perspective or hack or block any websites for political reasons. For further information see http://www.homeoffice.gov.uk.

There are other Acts such as the **Privacy and Electronic Communications (EC Directive) Regulations 2003**.

The Directive primarily required the EU Member States to introduce new laws regulating the use of:

- unsolicited commercial communications (spam);
- cookies;
- location and traffic data; and
- publicly available directories.

Source: http://www.junk-mail.org

Activity

Match the Act to its correct description

Act	Description
Data Protection Act 1998	An Act intended to reduce the instances of unsolicited communication using electronic means.
Freedom of Information Act 2000	This Act is designed to prevent groups and individuals from intimidating others for political ends.
Computer Misuse Act 1990	This Act gives us the right to know what data is being kept about us.
Terrorism Act 2000	The principles in this Act define how data about us is captured, used and stored.
Privacy and Electronic Communications Regulations 2003	An Act designed to discourage individuals from using computers to support criminal activities.

Answers on p436.

3.2 Ethical issues

In the previous section you were introduced to legislation that can be enforced by law. In addition to this legislation, organisations and institutions can develop their own policies with which employees or service users must comply. Failure to do so will not result in criminal prosecution, but the outcome will probably be a sanction of some sort that is imposed by the organisation. Some of these sanctions will be more serious than other sanctions. These issues are ethical rather than criminal, where the term **ethical** means a **generally accepted type of behaviour**.

Ethical behaviour requirements are usually set through **Codes of Practice** or **Organisational Policies** set by organisations. While these terms are frequently used interchangeably, general consensus is that Codes of Practice are usually set by external bodies (for example the British Computer Society has developed a suite of behavioural codes including the **Code of Good Conduct** and the **Code of Good Practice** when applied to ICT). Many **trade bodies** develop Codes of Practice designed to be used and adhered to by members of their industry. In some cases, failure to comply with these codes may well see the organisation or individual excluded from the trade body.

These are frequently adopted by organisations as a basis for expected behaviour, with policies added which are designed around the needs of the organisation. It should also be remembered that codes and policies you have to observe with one employer will probably be different with a subsequent employer.

Some examples of codes and policies will be investigated here.

Use of email and the Internet

Generally, employers expect employees to use **email** and the **Internet** for business purposes only. This will include emailing colleagues about business-related issues, emailing suppliers and customers and other external agencies. Employers do not usually allow employees to use email to send personal correspondence or to surf the internet during the working day. Why is this? This is largely because if employees are sending personal mail or surfing the net, they cannot possibly be working! However, many employers will accept limited use of these services during work breaks.

Whistle-blowing

When applied to ICT, whistle-blowing is about employees having a responsibility to their employers for reporting their colleagues for any inappropriate behaviour that they witness in relation to the use of the organisation's systems. While in most cases employees are more likely to report their colleagues for **serious misuse** (such as hacking into the organisation's systems, data theft), most will not report others for **excessive email** and **inappropriate internet use**. Ethically they should, particularly if it is part of the organisation's policy or code of practice. Failure to do so could be seen by the employer as **complicity** (you will effectively be considered an accomplice to the offence).

Information ownership

The interesting part about the concept of information ownership is that morally, if you own something you should take responsibility for looking after it. Certainly some organisations have an information ownership policy or a set of guidelines for employees. Hampshire County Council, for example, set out their own information ownership policy on their website, where they state that 'every web page' on their website:

has to be owned by a nominated person. They are responsible for:

◆ the accuracy and currency of the information provided
◆ ensuring that if the information has come from another source, the source is clearly identified
◆ providing the name (or job title/team name), along with an email address (or preferably an online form) and a telephone number, to whom a visitor can address any queries.

Source: http://www3.hants.gov.uk/webstandards/web-information-ownership.htm

This is an example of **responsible** information ownership.

We have also previously suggested that organisational departments should take responsibility for the information they generate and distribute. This means that they are particularly responsible for the accuracy of its content.

When it comes to the ownership of information stored by organisations about individuals, many organisations will require employees to sign **non-disclosure agreements**, which means that the staff member will promise not to pass on any information belonging to the organisation to a third party. This includes information about the organisation's activities in general, not just information about individuals.

3.3 Operational issues

From an operational perspective, the company initially needs to ensure that its data and information are secure and can be recovered in the event of a disaster. It also needs to be aware that there will be additional costs incurred in working with data, and ensure that employees working with ever more complex systems are suitably trained.

Security of information

Computer security is a very important issue for any organisation that uses ICT to support their business activities. The physical loss of the computer system or its data can be damaging for organisations and for this reason there should always be systems in place to protect both the **data** and the **systems** as far as possible. What are the potential security threats to the data?

◆ theft of data
◆ damage to data.

Theft of data

This includes the intentional removal of data using physical means such as floppy disks, data sticks or copies burned on to CD or DVD, or electronic transfer of all or parts of the data using email.

Clearly, theft is an intentional act and as such it is a criminal offence. Individuals who take part in such activity may not only lose their employment but could well lose their liberty.

Data that can be targeted by thieves includes personal information to be used in identity theft, research information, diagrams of products under development and ideas for new products and services. These might be offered for sale to competitors.

Damage to data

Data can be damaged in two ways:

Firstly a **physical** part of the system could be damaged. In extreme circumstances, intentional damage can be done to physical aspects of the system (intentional damage is known as **malicious** damage). This could include the insertion of foreign objects into open parts of the machine (say into the cooling fan or into the DVD or CD drives), or this can happen accidentally, for example because the machine gets wet. If parts of the physical system become damaged, the data could also become damaged. In addition, parts of the machine could simply break down (such as hard-drive failure).

Alternatively, the **data files** themselves could become **damaged**. Again this could be done **intentionally** or **accidentally**, for example **viruses** introduced through external media such as USB devices or as attachments to emails.

Data can also be damaged due to simple **human error!**

To reduce the **likelihood** of data becoming **damaged** there are a number of **software solutions** that organisations can consider **installing**.

The most common ones are as follows.

Destruction can occur in two ways – the virus-infected file can simply be **deleted** from the system or, alternatively, the virus can be **healed**. In the event that the software is unable to heal the virus, it

> **Key Terms**
>
> **Antivirus software** can be installed on a network or on individual PCs and is intended to screen the system regularly, while monitoring the file content of any input devices. Commercial software is available such as Norton, McAfee, Sophos and Grisoft AVG (a free antivirus solution for home and individual use). This software serves two purposes: detection and destruction.

can isolate it by putting it into a **virus vault**. The vault essentially separates the virus from the remainder of the system, to prevent it from doing any damage (or any further damage).

Antivirus software has to be updated regularly to ensure that it stays up to date. New viruses are being written all the time and, as such, **antivirus signatures** (identification and destruction protocols) need to be downloaded to tackle these new viruses. Usually, if you have purchased antivirus software, these updates are free.

Firewall software can **take time** to **configure** as, when first installed, every communication will be questioned by the software and the user has to make one of the following choices **each time** they are asked:

◆ Yes, always allow.
◆ Yes, allow just this once.
◆ No, never allow.
◆ No, deny just this once.

Any firewall settings can be **modified** at a later date. For this reason it is better to deny rather than allow any communications you are unsure of.

The following products are examples of software designed to handle **spyware** and **adware**:

◆ XoftSpySe®
◆ Spyware Nuker®
◆ NoAdware®
◆ Adware Alert®
◆ Microsoft Defender®

Popular forms of **encryption** include:

◆ **PGP®** (**P**retty **G**ood **P**rivacy) – invented by Phil Zimmermann – which is popular for encrypting data files and email. It is often described as a **military-grade** encryption algorithm because of its complexity.
◆ **RSA** (named after the inventors – **R**ivest, **S**hamir and **A**dleman) which is often used in **electronic commerce**.
◆ **WEP** (**W**ired **E**quivalent **P**rivacy) and **WPA** (**W**i-**F**i **P**rotected **A**ccess) for encrypting **wireless communications**.

> **Key Terms**
>
> A **firewall** is a program that **monitors** a computer's data communications (both **incoming** and **outgoing**). This software can **reject** data transfer based on the fact that the destination has a particular **IP address**, that a **specific port** is being used or because a **program** is trying to transmit data to the outside world. Alternatively, if the user wishes this transfer to take place, the user can **allow** the transmission.

> **Key Terms**
>
> **Spyware** and **adware protection**
>
> Spyware programs **covertly gather information** about a system and send the information to a **third party** via an **internet connection**, usually **without** the **knowledge** of the user. Adware programs are designed to constantly **display advertisements** whether a user **wishes** them to be displayed or not.

> **Key Terms**
>
> **Data encryption** is where the data will be scrambled in some way so that it makes it unusable, even if it is intercepted. In order to read the data, it will need to be **decrypted** using some sort of **algorithmic process** – a little bit like a **key**. Loss of the key or the ability to **decrypt** the data will make the data useless.

Unit Link

The whole concept of system security is now so important that an entire unit has been dedicated to it (**Unit 15** – Organisational Systems Security).

In addition, WEP and WPA are examined in greater detail in **Unit 8** – Communication Technologies.

Whether attempting to counteract potential data loss through **physical** or **logical** means, one recommended solution is for the organisation to keep **regular backups** of the data. This will be considered in the next section.

Backups

There is now a range of options available to enable organisations to make backups of their data.

Storage media include the following.

Removable **zip drives** remain a popular option.

If backup files are made, they should be stored **off-site**, or in a secure medium such as a **fire-proof safe**, otherwise there will be little point in having the backup (it would potentially be destroyed along with the original).

Figure 3.12 Removable backup storage devices, such as DVD multi-recorder drives

Figure 3.13 Zip drive

Some organisations that have multiple branches use a round-robin style approach to data backup. The diagram in Figure 3.14 represents a group of four outlets that are using each other's systems to keep their data safe.

In this diagram, the data is backed up to another branch or outlet:

◆ Bristol's data is copied to Birmingham.
◆ Birmingham's data is copied to Manchester.
◆ Manchester's data is copied to London.
◆ London's data is copied to Bristol.

Figure 3.14 Backup strategy between branches of the same organisation

In the event that any of the outlets lose their data, it can be recovered by being copied back from the second location.

How often should backups be taken? That will depend very much on the **volume** of **transactions** that would be lost in the event that the data was lost. With some companies once a week will be sufficient, with other organisations it might need to be two or three times a week. In some instances it might be at the end of **each day** – or in truly high-volume situations, particularly where systems are running in real time (transactions are processed instantly), this could be done **hourly**, or even after each transaction!

Health and safety

When considering this topic area, we need to look at the subject matter from two perspectives – firstly in terms of **using** systems within the workplace and secondly from the perspective of **responsibility** for monitoring and maintaining the working environment in situations where computers are used.

Using computers

There is now increasing legislation on the use of computers in the workplace, including specific guidance on what individuals can do (in addition to what employers can do) to ensure that risks are minimised.

Common conditions that can develop as a result of computer use are eye-related conditions such as headaches, visual fatigue and blurred or watery vision. Musculoskeletal problems can also become exacerbated including stiffness, aching joints and muscles from sitting in the same position for extended periods of time and **r**epetitive **s**train **i**njury (**RSI**) which is usually experienced in the wrists or hands.

The following websites give extensive guidance on health and safety issues when working with computers:

◆ **http://icthubknowledgebase.org.uk/healthandsafety** (general guidance on working with computers and associated technologies)
◆ **http://www.hse.gov.uk/pubns/indg36.pdf** (guidance on working with VDUs)

What should be mentioned here, however, is that this guidance is based on current legislation surrounding computers and their use. As such legislation can change, this information was correct at the time of printing.

The main laws associated with this issue are:

◆ Health and Safety (Display Screen Equipment) Regulations 1992
◆ Management of Health and Safety at Work Regulations 1992
◆ Provision and Use of Work Equipment Regulations 1992
◆ Workplace (Health, Safety and Welfare) Regulations 1992

To enable employees to work as safely as possible, **employers** should:

◆ ensure that employees can have breaks or change their activities to vary what they do
◆ ensure that employees have up-to-date health and safety information (and training if required)
◆ arrange for eye tests for those employees whose job requires them to have prolonged contact with computer systems
◆ analyse and monitor an individual user's requirements in terms of the workstation they are using (including furniture and equipment considerations, special chairs if appropriate)
◆ ensure that the workstation that the employee is using meets the minimum requirements, which include considerations such as suitable lighting, screen type and positioning, keyboards, desks, chairs and footrests (if required).

Employees should also attempt to work safely by:

◆ ensuring firstly that there is sufficient space to work
◆ adjusting any equipment where positions and heights, for example, can be altered, until the user feels fully at ease (of example the chair height and back support)
◆ positioning VDU equipment where glare is reduced, away from bright light, adjusting contrast and brightness of the display as required
◆ experimenting with the layout of the keyboard, mouse, screen and documents to find the most suitable positions for these items

- taking regular breaks (frequent short breaks are better than longer, less frequent breaks)
- trying to change their seating position rather than sitting in the same position for extended periods of time.

Responsibility

As you can see, working safely is today considered to be a shared responsibility for both employer and employee. An **employer** must:

- keep up to date with legislation
- comply with legislation
- ensure that the working environment is monitored
- resolve any problems identified either by staff in general or employees designated to monitor the health and safety of the working environment
- respond to employee needs (and accept that these may change)
- provide relevant equipment.

The **employee** must:

- comply with legislation
- help the employer by monitoring their own working environment and reporting any problems
- be generally aware of the working environment and report any issues identified
- be realistic and give employers sufficient warning to allow them time to respond
- work safely.

Ultimately, if the employer fails in their responsibilities, this might result in the employee being able to take **legal action**. If, however, the employee fails to monitor their own environment and report any safety issues then really the employee has no grounds for complaint!

Organisational policies

As suggested earlier in this unit, organisations may well create policies in line with external agency **Codes of Practice** or to reflect **legislative requirements**. In addition, they may well create policies that dictate how data will be accessed, used and managed.

In terms of accessing the data, for example, some organisations dictate that screens must be positioned in a way that unauthorised users will have limited visibility. This is to promote confidentiality.

In addition, some organisations make employees sign **non-disclosure** agreements which will prevent staff from discussing any information gained from within the organisation, outside. This will usually cover all types of information, from information about suppliers, customers and employees to information about products and services.

Other policies have been covered earlier in this unit.

Business continuance plans

When you consider that many organisations today are heavily reliant on computer technology, any organisation that does not plan a strategy for overcoming a catastrophic event could well be destroyed by such an occurrence. The incident could be man-made (for example an arson attack), or could be the result of a natural disaster such as a flood.

Help

The key to **successful business continuance planning** is:

- identifying potential risks
- fully **understanding** how the organisation will be **affected**
- **identifying factors** and **implementing resolutions** as far as possible to **minimise** the **risks** in the first place
- implementing **safety strategies** (such as **backing up** data regularly)
- **testing** the plan by **simulating** a **disaster** and seeing whether the organisation can recover (if not, why not, and what can be done)
- ensuring **staff understand** the **role** they will play in the recovery process (ensuring that they receive any appropriate training)
- **reviewing** the **plan** at regular intervals, to ensure that it is still current when you consider that the organisation and its needs may have changed over time.

Apart from anything else, formalising such a plan will ensure that, should there be a disruptive incident, the organisation and staff will have a well-defined plan to follow.

As this is such an important facet of business, there are many companies that specialise in helping organisations plan for disaster recovery.

Costs (e.g. additional resources required, cost of development)

In order to respond to every eventuality, whether it be the need for change within the organisation, or business continuance strategies, organisations need to understand that they will need to invest in the resources that will facilitate these needs.

Disaster planning, for example, takes time which in itself is an **indirect** cost of developing such a strategy. Usually teams made up of key personnel **meet regularly** to monitor the organisation's situation and advise if appropriate. Clearly, if staff are involved in such activities, they will not be doing their own jobs! However, from a company perspective, this type of investment is important to ensure the longevity of the organisation. Many companies will spend hundreds of thousands of pounds over the years developing strategies to overcome catastrophe, when in fact catastrophe never strikes. Some would argue that this was a waste of money – why worry because it probably will not happen.

Think about it in these terms – why pay any type of insurance (because essentially that is what business continuance planning really is)? Because one day, it could be them!

Impact of increasing sophistication of systems (e.g. more trained personnel, more complex software)

As ICT systems develop, many are becoming more **integrated** (working together and reliant on each other). This in turn means that, in general, systems and software are becoming increasingly complex. In order to work with the systems:

- More staff with the right skills will be required, and these may well need to be brought in from outside the organisation.
- Existing staff may need to receive further training to ensure that they understand and can confidently and competently work with more of the system.

Again, this is an investment issue for most organisations – but their failure to seriously consider these issues may see systems that they have purchased at great expense, not used as efficiently as they should or could be.

Activity

Operational issues word search

Find the words listed right in the grid shown.

Answers on p436.

```
R N F I R E W A L L C D S H V
R E O P P E U M T O T E P T G
N E S I O U Z Q N A P S Y L Z
H X C P T L K T O I D T W A Y
H I Z O O P I C Z U L R A E T
T T S E V N Y C A X T U R H I
H U U N U E S R Y B Q C E Z R
E V V A T X R I C S O T Q G U
F O N L U K S Y B E N I E W C
T C T I N O U T P I D O Q E E
E S U R I V T F E Z L N J D S
N O I T P Y R C N E R I C O T
E G A M A D S A F E T Y T C F
N L R L L K W S B J T G M Y I
F W R U Y L Q B D J W W M E B
```

CONTINUANCE
DECRYPTION
FIREWALL
RECOVERY
SECURITY
VIRUS
CODE
DATA
ENCRYPTION
POLICY
SAFETY
THEFT
BACKUP
DAMAGE
DESTRUCTION
HEALTH
RESPONSIBILITY
SPYWARE
ZIP

4 Know the features and functions of information systems

4.1 Tools

What is the difference between a **computer with data** and an **information system**? The distinction is much as it would be if we defined the difference between data and information.

In reality, information systems are made up of a number of components. Which components a particular information system has will depend on what the system is supposed to do.

Many information systems are built on **databases**. This is because in order to have data to analyse to convert into information, you need to have it stored **electronically**. In most cases this will be in a database, although on occasions you will see a spreadsheet used instead (because spreadsheets also have limited database functionality).

Activity

Definition of data and information

Can you remember and write down the definition of data and information?

Answers on p436.

Key Terms

A **database** is a collection of records that have been organised in a logical way.

From the example in Figure 3.15, you will see that each **column** of information (known as a **field**) will hold a different piece of **like** information for a number of students. Each **row** will hold a **different** record.

In Figuer 3.15, if we were to add a subsequent record, the (AutoNumber) in the first field would **increment** (increase) to 2.

Databases that are structured in this way form the basis for most information systems, and other software can be used to manipulate, interrogate or make judgements about this data. This is essentially what an information system does.

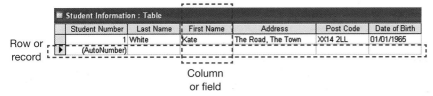

Student Information : Table					
Student Number	Last Name	First Name	Address	Post Code	Date of Birth
1	White	Kate	The Road, The Town	XX14 2LL	01/01/1965
(AutoNumber)					

Row or record ▸

Column or field

Figure 3.15 Database table

There are a number of examples of information systems – these will be explored here.

Artificial intelligence and expert systems

Artificial intelligence is a huge **developmental area** at present, where scientists attempt to program machines that can **mimic human thought processes**, and react accordingly. Robots that can learn are a good example.

Let's think about this in real terms. The **RoboMow Robotic Lawnmower®** is an **intelligent** lawnmower that, once set up, can cut your grass without any human intervention.

In this instance the sensors help the machine to **mimic** thought processes and react accordingly and so the lawnmower will only mow the grass where there is in fact grass, staying away from objects such as bushes and borders.

Another example of an expert system is **NHS Direct**. This service is designed as a first port of call for patients and their families when they have urgent queries regarding medical conditions. It is a **medical diagnosis** tool. This is how it works.

1. The patient, or a member of the family, calls the designated phone number.
2. The phone is answered by a trained nurse who runs through a series of set questions.
3. Depending on each answer that the caller gives, the next question is activated. Figure 3.18 shows an example.

Figure 3.16 Robomow

The robomow in action!

How does it work?
Robomow requires a one time simple set-up, which can be easily done by the consumer himself. A standard electric wire is laid around the outer edges of the lawn, and attached to the surface of the lawn with pegs every few meters. The wire and pegs are supplied with the unit in the same box. The wire is connected to a small battery powered current source called Perimeter Switch (also supplied in the box). Typically the wire will be covered by grass and become unnoticeable in a matter of 2-3 weeks. Robomow recognizes the wire using a special sensor, and makes sure it always stays inside.

Figure 3.17 How the Robomow works

The expert system is effectively rule based (forming a **decision 'tree'**), and it depends on how each condition is resolved as to the action the system then takes.

Other professionals will also use industry-related expert systems – for example engineers, geologists and chemists will use such software.

The main advantage of these systems is firstly they can be easily updated and secondly that relatively inexperienced professionals can use them effectively. Expert systems, particularly, will be based on the concepts of a database.

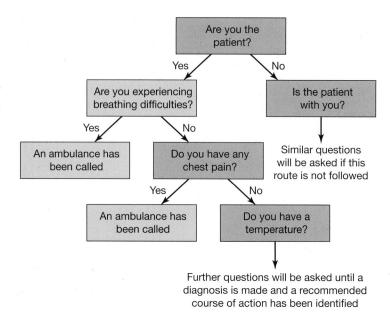

Figure 3.18 NHS Direct

Internet

With the significant growth in recent years of e-commerce (doing business online), many organisations rely on websites, supported by databases, to manage and record their business transactions. In fact, some organisations trade solely online. Many companies with **high-street** outlets have created websites as an additional means of selling their goods and services. The following company, however, began with a website and now has a shop as well.

Images used with the kind permission of The Spice of Life (**www.thespiceoflife.co.uk**).

This is a small business that trades in the herbs and spices used in traditional curries and other associated dishes.

Once the user selects a category, all products available are listed. Customers can browse the various **categories** and **choose to buy products**.

If the user wishes to buy, for example, a Bengal Balti mix, they will key in the quantity they require and then click on the buy button. When they have selected all the items they want to buy, the checkout button will then take them to their **shopping cart** where they can arrange for payment and delivery.

Essentially, all the products that the company stocks are recorded in a database. The data stored is manipulated by server-side software

Figure 3.19 The Spice of Life

so that it can be **accessed** and **displayed** via the **internet**.

Once input, customer details will usually be stored in another part of the database. Some websites also store **payment information**, so that the customer has less to key in on subsequent visits to the site.

Subsequently, the database content can be used by the business to provide management information on, for example, stock movement and customer buying trends, and may well enable the organisation to predict times of high sales turnover (which will in itself assist in the planning of manufacturing).

Figure 3.20 Choosing your items

Others (e.g. data-mining systems)

In order to enable organisations to use their data effectively, possibly even after a trading year has ended, software has been developed to enable them to do this. Two examples of such software are:

◆ Data-mining systems such as Statistica® created by StatSoft (**www.statsoft.com**) or RandomForests® developed and released by Salford Systems (**www.salford-systems.com/ randomforests.php**)
◆ Data-warehousing systems such as Enterprise Data Warehousing® from Kalido (**www.kalido. com**) or Master Data Management® from the SAS Institute Inc. (**www.sas.com**).

But what does this software do?

Data-mining

Data-mining software provides specific types of functionality that are not usually available in regular software, without intervention and activity from the user. Earlier in this unit we looked at the line graph now shown in Figure 3.21.

In order to identify that there was a problem with the data, it required the user firstly to make the chart, then to interpret whether there was anything **exceptional** about it.

Data-mining software can not only identify unusual events, but has **drill down** functionality so that the data can be investigated at lower and lower levels until the exception is found and can be understood.

Typical data-mining software has:

◆ number crunching and statistical functionality not usually found in software like Microsoft Access®
◆ ability to analyse sublevels in the data
◆ report-writing functionality
◆ the ability to be used with most database software.

Data-warehousing

In order that historical data is available after the trading year has finished, data can be deposited into data-warehousing software.

The data must be:

◆ well organised (often by subject or theme)
◆ stored in a way that it is non-volatile (cannot be deleted or overwritten by mistake).

Once the data is stored in the warehousing software, **data-mining** or other **analytical tools** can be used to **interrogate** the data and make comparisons.

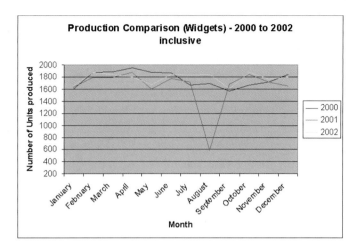

Figure 3.21 Exception report

4.2 Information systems examples

In general terms, the information produced by information systems is used in the following activities:

◆ planning
◆ decision making
◆ controlling operations
◆ forecasting the future.

Realistically, these activities will be undertaken in **all functional areas** of an organisation. Here are some examples of the sorts of information that can be extracted from a good information system. Also shown is the business reason why an organisation would want the information.

Other types of information and how it is used can be found earlier in this unit.

Type of information	Functional area	Business use
Sales performance (e.g. comparing one sales area against another, comparing one year's sales against another, comparing the sales of particular products across a number of years or financial quarters)	Marketing	Being able to react to business opportunities and threats will be dependent on the ability of an organisation to fully understand the environment in which it operates – when information is compared, any anomalies will be highlighted and investigated so that the company can understand why a particular event occurred.
Competitors (e.g. prices, delivery, terms and conditions)	Marketing	Knowing the pricing information of competitors will help an organisation to set its own prices.
Development (e.g. new products or services)	Marketing	Information about the technological developments in the real world will help an organisation plan its own developmental strategies.

Financial costs (e.g. budgets and targets)	Financial	Setting budgets is essential to ensure that no area of the organisation spends more money than it should.
		Similarly, setting targets enables functional areas of a business to know what is expected of them.
Investment returns	Financial	Any money invested by the organisation should be monitored – for example, an organisation could have invested in new production machinery and it needs to establish whether the investment was worthwhile (has production throughput increased?).
Financial performance (e.g. profit and loss)	Financial	The organisation overall needs to know how profitable it is – this will help it to plan its expenditure, expansion and possible investment.
Staffing (records)	Human resources	The organisation must hold extensive information on its employees – in addition to standard information such as personal details, next of kin, bank details.
		They must know which functional area individual staff belong to and how many staff overall work in each part of the organisation.
Professional development	Human resources	The needs of each area must be met by the staff that work in that area – if those needs change, then the organisation must endeavour to develop the staff accordingly through training programmes.

4.3 Management information systems (MISs)

Essentially, an MIS is a system that is designed to help executives to manage an organisation, by giving them sufficient information to help them **control** the **overall direction** and the **day-to-day activities**.

Features

While the **key elements** of an MIS can be seen in the next section of this unit, it might be appropriate at this stage to explain that all information systems are said to have a behaviour – this behaviour is defined by the level of predictability the system is said to have.

Lucey (2000: 38) defines a series of information system **behaviours**, of which the following are the most notable.

Deterministic

This is where the exact outputs of the system can be predicted because the inputs are known in advance: e.g. a manufacturing process where a number of predetermined inputs go into the system so that a particular product can be output.

Probabilistic

By using prior knowledge about the system, the likely outputs can be predicted: e.g. the overall number of hours of downtime on a piece of production machinery can be estimated based on previous breakdown history, but the actual hours that will be experienced (it could be higher or lower than previously) will not be known in advance.

Self-organising

These systems are by nature reactive – the inputs are unknown and unpredictable and the potential outputs will be variable and also unpredictable: e.g. a social work department may have a series of 'routine responses' for given situations, but the response actually taken will need to be adapted to accommodate factors not necessarily known in advance.

Benefits

The business benefits of information systems have already been stated repeatedly through this unit – but as an overview, these systems provide information that is:

◆ up to date
◆ timely
◆ accurate
◆ reliable
◆ valid
◆ fit for purpose
◆ accessible
◆ cost-effective.

The additional benefit is that the information can be backed up with relative ease to ensure that recovery from organisational disaster is more likely.

Effectiveness criteria (e.g. accuracy, sustainability, timelines, confidence)

How **effective** any information system is will be determined by a number of factors, some of which are measurable and others which are subjective. The same system could be used by two competing companies and one might say the system is effective while another might disagree.

Measurable criteria include:

◆ **Accuracy** – this is easy to measure – where the outputs are **correct** or **incorrect**. It is not unusual for organisations to have checked the outputs of systems by other means, such as using a calculator!
◆ **Sustainability** – the system is said to be sustainable if the quality of the outputs from the system can be maintained on an **ongoing basis**.
◆ **Timeliners** – the system needs to be able to respond with appropriate outputs **at the right time** (information that is produced too late is clearly not very useful).

Subjective criteria include:

◆ **Confidence** – this is difficult to measure and will largely depend on the **personal judgements** of the individuals **using the information** output by the system – if the users' experiences have been largely positive, they will be said to have confidence in the system.

4.4 Key elements of information systems

In order to be an effective information system, the following key elements should be in place:

◆ **Data** – data must firstly be introduced to the system as inputs, before it can be processed and output as useful information. This data will be generated by all functional parts of an organisation, as well as being received into the system from outside the company.
◆ **People** – staff must have the right skills to enable them to get the best out of an information system.
◆ **Hardware** – the computer hardware must be capable of running the software and handling the volumes of data that are put through the system. Large volumes of data being interrogated (searched through) by a computer system that is old and slow will cause significant frustration to users.
◆ **Software** – the software that is installed must have the features and functionality to produce the information required by the organisation. In some instances staff using the software must have relevant training.
◆ **Telecommunications** – if information output from systems is required in multiple locations, the telecommunications infrastructure must be in place to enable the data to be distributed.

4.5 Information systems functions

In basic terms, the functions of an information system are simple:

◆ Capture and store inputs.
◆ Process them.
◆ Output them.

Input and storage, processing and output

The Figure 3.22 is a good representation of the nature and source of inputs, typical processing functions and potential outputs:

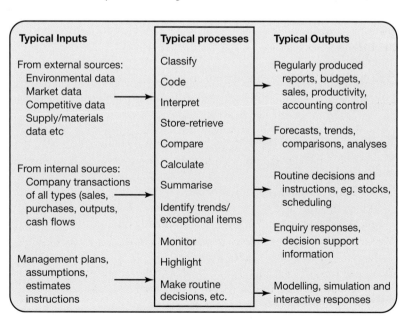

Figure 3.22 A typical information-processing system
Source: (Lucey 2000: 39)

Control and feedback loops and closed and open systems

The functionality of information systems can be defined as being **closed** or **open**.

The definition will reflect how the system interacts with the environment in which it exists.

A **closed** system:

◆ is largely **isolated** from its environment
◆ any interaction will be **totally predictable** and probably **automated**
◆ **does not** influence the external environment in any way.

Examples:

A refrigerator or central heating system is an example of a closed system.

The refrigerator cools when triggered to do so by a sensor. When the correct temperature has been reached, the machine switches off.

A central heating system is triggered by a thermostat and timer. The timer ensures that the system becomes active at specific times each day, and that the radiators are heated if the temperature is lower than a set value.

In actual fact, this is an example of a **control and feedback loop**. The system constantly repeats the same sequences, activated by the same triggers.

An **open** system:

◆ **fully capable** if interacting with its environment
◆ will receive inputs and other influences from the environment
◆ will pass back outputs and influences to its environment
◆ is capable of handling unexpected events because it is constantly monitoring and anticipating the environment.

Example:

Most functional areas of organisations are effectively open systems, because they interact with the other functional areas around them, and also with factors even outside the organisation. Take the example of the marketing function in an organisation:

◆ They **investigate** the market, having contact with the public and/or other organisations.
◆ They have to **react** to legislative changes.
◆ They must **respond** to changes in user needs.
◆ They must **respond** to developments in technology.

Achieving success

This particular unit has 11 criteria to meet: 6 pass, 3 merit and 2 distinction.

For a **pass**:

You must achieve **all** 6 pass criteria

For a **merit**:

You must achieve **all** 6 pass and **all** 3 merit criteria

For a **distinction**:

You must achieve **all** 6 pass, **all** 3 merit **and both** distinction criteria.

Help with assessment

This unit is fundamental to your understanding of ICT in the real world. You will need to demonstrate a familiarity with the information needs of organisations, and explain how the information is generated and used to support its activities.

The **merit** criteria see these concepts developed, with you being asked to give real examples of information needs and the importance of quality information. In addition, you will be required to explain a number of data analysis tools currently available.

For a **distinction** you must show that you can evaluate the effectiveness of information systems tools in supporting the decisions that are made within organisations on an ongoing basis.

Links

The content of this unit has links to **all** other units on this course, primarily because the infrastructure of most organisations is built on information.

Unit 3 is a **core unit** on the BTEC National Certificate and BTEC National Diploma for IT Practitioners (**IT and Business, Software Development and System Support routes**).

Unit 3 is also a **specialist unit** on the following BTEC National route:

Networking

There are particular links, however, to the following:

Unit 1 – Communication and Employability Skills in IT

Unit 7 – IT Systems Analysis and Design

Unit 15 – Organisational Systems Security

Unit 35 – Impact of the Use of IT on Business Systems

In addition this unit has identified direct links with:

Unit 8 – Communication Technologies

Online resources on the CD

Electronic glossary for this unit
Key fact sheets
Electronic slide show of key points

So that you can monitor your own progress and achievement in each unit, a recording grid has been provided (see below). The full version of this grid is also included on the companion CD.

Assignment	Assignments in this unit			
	U3.01	U3.02	U3.03	U3.04
Referral				
Pass				
1				
2				
3				
4				
5				
6				
Merit				
1				
2				
3				
Distinction				
1				
2				

 Further reading

Anderson, H., and Yull, S., 2002, *BTEC Nationals IT Practitioners: Core Units for Computing and IT*, Newnes, ISBN 0750656840.

Bocij, P., Cheffey, D., Greasley, A., and Hickie, S., 2000, *Business Information Systems: Technology Development and Management*, FT Prentice Hall, ISBN 027388146.

French, C., 2002, *Computer Science*, Thomson Learning, ISBN 082646761X.

Knott, G., and Waites, N., 2002, *BTEC Nationals for IT Practitioners*, Brancepeth Computer Publications, ISBN 0953884821.

Lucey, T., 2000, *Management Information Systems*, 8th edn, London:Continuum Press, ISBN 0826454070.

IT Systems Analysis and Design

Capsule view

IT Systems Analysis and Design is a 60-hour unit that focuses on **how** new systems are developed.

Understanding the principles of analysis and design, the **role** of the **analyst** is to **investigate** user requirements, offer **advice** on **alternative solutions**, and **create** a **design** for the **chosen solution**.

At the end of this process, the solution design will be passed on to system developers (either programmers, network specialists, database designers, or even all three) for the **physical solution** to be **built** and **installed**.

The last job of the analyst is to design a **test plan** for the implemented solution. This is because it is the analyst who will probably know the organisation best, and who will be able to select the **best test data**, based on their **knowledge** and **understanding** of the organisation. In this unit you will **investigate** and **design** a **system solution** for an **organisation** to solve a business **need**.

1 Understand the principles of systems analysis and design

1.1 Development life-cycle models

Every system, whether it is computerised or not, has a **life cycle**; this means that in order to have been developed the system will have been:

◆ defined
◆ investigated
◆ designed
◆ implemented and tested
◆ maintained and reviewed.

Ultimately, over time, the system will decay (become less useable and useful as the needs of the users change).

Learning aims

1 Understand the principles of systems analysis and design.
2 Be able to investigate, analyse and document requirements.
3 Be able to create a system design.
4 Be able to design a test plan.

If you look in systems analysis theory books, or on the Internet, you will find a huge selection of analysis methodologies, each with their own variation of the life-cycle model.

Firstly we will investigate a number of alternative life-cycle models.

Waterfall model

The system life cycle that belongs to the waterfall methodology looks something like Figure 7.1.

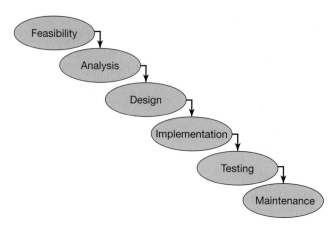

Figure 7.1 System life cycle (waterfall)

Each ellipse (oval) represents a different part or stage of the life cycle and the diagram suggests that you start at the beginning of the process, carrying out each level of the process one after the other, returning to the beginning of the process once you have reached the end. In effect, when the system starts to decay during the end of the life cycle, you may be looking at the feasibility of modifying the system or doing something completely different, thereby starting the process again. This will be considered later in this unit.

The key point with this life cycle is that, like a waterfall, the process falls from the top to the bottom. As we all know, water cannot flow **upwards**. Thus, this diagram implies that each level or stage will be undertaken **after** the previous one is **finished**, with no possibility for going back and revisiting an earlier stage if anything goes wrong.

V-shaped model

Similar to the waterfall model, and containing most of the same stages or levels (even if slightly differently expressed), this model places a heavy emphasis on the need for testing for the outcomes of the various stages of the development, with tests planned and then executed after implementation. As a diagram, the V-shaped model is as shown in Figure 7.2.

If we were to express this whole life cycle as text, we would say the following:

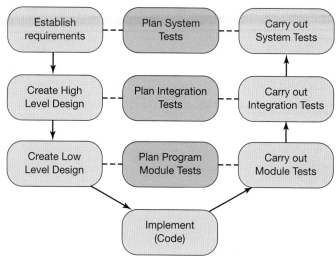

Figure 7.2 System life cycle (V-shaped)

◆ Establish the requirements of the system (and plan tests to check whether, after implementation of the system, these requirements have been met).

◆ Create a logical design of the system in the context of the other systems around it (and plan tests to check whether the system does fully integrate into its context, after implementation).

- Create a logical design of the system itself (and plan to test each functional part to make sure it does what it is meant to).
- Implement (or code) the solution.
- Test the functional parts to ensure they do what they are supposed to.
- Test the whole product alongside systems with which it must integrate – does it do so successfully?
- Test the whole system and check that the users' original requirements have been met.

Effectively, when using this model, we go down the left-hand side of the diagram, through implementation, which is at the bottom, then up the other side.

Rapid applications development (RAD)

RAD has a much simpler life-cycle model.

Made up of four basic stages, steps 2 to 4 inclusive are repeated as many times as required until the user (or users) are satisfied that the problem has been solved. Clearly, this model is reliant on the users being heavily involved in the development process, and this would be an unrealistic model if there were a large number of potential system users – it is difficult to please everyone, opinions can vary too much.

Benefits

What are the benefits of following any of these life-cycle models?

Quite simply, choosing not to adopt a recognised development model when designing and implementing a business system is a little like attempting to build flat-pack furniture without any instructions.

It is extremely difficult, and could potentially go wrong many times along the way.

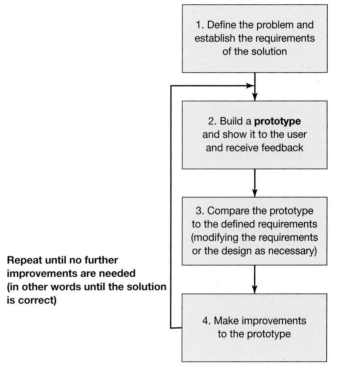

Repeat until no further improvements are needed (in other words until the solution is correct)

Figure 7.3 System life cycle (RAD)

These models provide a blueprint which, if followed, should result in a satisfactory system being built. They provide guidance and support for the process.

Considered specifically from the perspective that these are theoretical models, each one has a particular focus, which, if identified and understood, might help users to choose appropriately when developing a solution.

The **waterfall** model essentially places **equal emphasis** on **each stage**, and it recognises that when the process is finished it may well **begin again** to ensure that the system **continues** to meet the needs of the organisation.

The **V-shaped** model places a great deal of importance on **testing** and requires the analyst to plan a series of **rigorous tests** from various **angles**: testing that the required functionality is in place, testing that the product fits into the context of all the systems inside the organisation and testing that the system meets the needs of the users as defined at the beginning of the process.

Adopting the **RAD** approach is ideal if the developer has open access to the intended users of the system and can get **feedback** easily. With this in place, the product will be developed quickly. The only real danger is that the developer could get side-tracked as the users add functionality that they might just have thought of, but which was not in the original proposal.

Stages (e.g. initiation and feasibility, investigation, requirements analysis and specification, design (logical and physical), build systems, testing, implementation, maintenance)

With the exception of the **RAD** model, you will have seen that the life-cycle diagrams essentially contain the same basic elements. We now need to explore the principles of these elements, although you should understand that there will be some slight differences when they are applied to specific models and methodologies. We will begin by considering a **generic** life-cycle model.

The generic life-cycle model is also very similar to the software development life-cycle model, which consists of the following elements:

◆ determining the problem scope
◆ gathering requirements
◆ writing the specification
◆ designing a solution
◆ coding the design
◆ testing the program code
◆ writing documentation
◆ reviewing and maintaining the solution.

Unit Link

For more on this model see **Unit 18** – Principles of Software Design and Development.

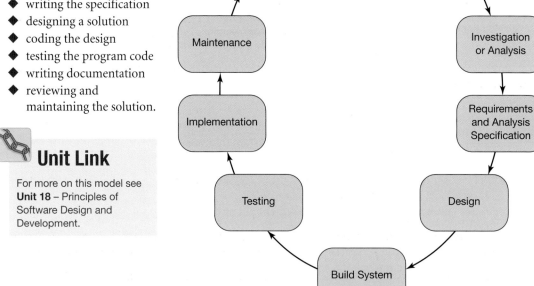

Figure 7.4 Generic life-cycle model

Initiation or problem definition

The life cycle has to have a beginning. At this point the project is said to be **initiated** or **defined**. How does this happen? Usually one of two ways:

1 A **user** or **group of users identifies something that the system needs to do** and cannot (or can, but does so slowly).
2 The system needs **change** for one of the following reasons:
    a) **Speed** and **efficiency** can be improved if a manual system is updated to a computerised one (the manual methods are effectively just too slow).
    b) The organisation identifies that functions within it need to **process large volumes** of similar **data** (e.g. invoices, payroll, mail-order transactions).
    c) It becomes necessary for the same **data** or information to be **shared** in various locations.
    d) It becomes necessary for the **data** or information to be constantly **updated.**
    e) There is obvious **duplication of effort** by a number of users of the system.
    f) More **control** over activities is needed.
    g) **More** (or **missing**) **management information** is required.

The process may well begin as a result of informal discussions between individuals inside the organisation. Before any formal activity begins, however, it is important that the problem, as understood by all, has been agreed and written down, as this will form a record and provide boundaries for subsequent activity. Although this might be modified during the life cycle of a project, if this is not done formally there is a potential for misunderstanding between users, analysts and developers about **what** was identified as being needed and **what** has subsequently been **developed.**

Feasibility study

Initially, a feasibility study is undertaken. This study usually looks at the problem from three perspectives: **economic**, **technical** and **social**.

Economic – will any investment in new system be cost-effective? We should remember here that the costs of a system can be split into **two** categories – **development costs** (the expenditure to purchase and implement the system) and **running costs** (the ongoing expenses that will have to be met once the system is up and running, for example the purchase of consumables such as printer paper and cartridges, or the need for a maintenance contract).

These costs will need to be measured against the potential benefits the system will provide:

◆ **Indirect benefits** – improved customer service, better access to information.
◆ **Direct benefits** – reduced costs (less labour expense for example).

Technical – will a new system work in the context of the organisation? If it is to be integrated with other systems, will this be successful?

Technical feasibility issues are possibly the easiest to resolve, as it is likely that any discrepancies or technical problems can be overcome with a little more money. Providing that this still remains within the organisation's overall budget, technical issues are unlikely to prevent a project from moving forward.

Social – this involves consideration of how developing a system may **affect** those that will need to interact with it, e.g. staff and customers. One ramification of changing a system from a manual to an electronic one might be that the organisation will probably require **fewer staff** to do the same work that is currently undertaken by a larger group. How will the surplus human resource be resolved? Will there need to be **redundancies**? Will the organisation wish to **retain** these staff and **retrain them** or **relocate them** to other parts of the organisation? Will those staff who continue to work with the system be able to be effective, or will they need **training** to use it? Will the service to customers be affected in any way?

Ultimately, in a project such as this, the cooperation of staff will be paramount. Understanding how the proposals will affect them will be essential in securing their assistance.

Once the feasibility study has been undertaken, it will be written up formally in report format, where ultimately the conclusion will be that it is feasible to move forward with such a project, or the project should be halted immediately.

The report will contain a **cost-benefit analysis** which will itemise the physical **costs** of a solution, will draw the organisation's attention to **indirect costs** of the project, and will list the **benefits** the organisation should receive once the project is implemented.

Finally, any constraints on the project that have been identified will be itemised and recorded. Usually these will include:

◆ the **budget** for the project?
◆ any **organisational policies** that must be considered?
◆ the **timescale** for the project (when the solution is expected to be fully up and running
◆ whether the system will have to incorporate any **legacy systems** (the existing systems)
◆ whether the solution will need to be developed to incorporate any current hardware or software (particularly in terms of compatibility).

In the event that the recommendation is to move forward, the life cycle will move to the **investigation** or **analysis** stage.

Investigation or analysis

Before deciding exactly what an organisation needs in terms of a new system, the analyst or team will need to undertake a **detailed investigation** of the **present system**. This is so that there will be a full understanding of how the system **currently works**, and how it could **change**. Each of the following aspects of the existing system needs to be investigated and recorded.

Data
◆ What data exists?
◆ How it is used?
◆ The volume of the data.
◆ The number of transactions.
◆ The characteristics of the data.

Procedures
◆ What processes and procedures are carried out?
◆ Where they are carried out?
◆ When?
◆ How are errors or exceptions intercepted and dealt with?

Future needs
◆ Does the company have any medium-term plans that might have a bearing on a new system?
◆ Is the company going to expand?

◆ Does the organisation expect growth in any areas, for example the number of anticipated users, volumes of data etc?

Management needs
◆ What sorts of outputs do managers receive from the existing system?
◆ What do these outputs contain?
◆ How often are they required?

Problems with the existing system
◆ Are there any specific problems that have already been identified by users with any of the above?

In order to carry out an investigation into all the areas highlighted above, the analyst will have to be familiar with and able to use a variety of fact-finding methods. These techniques, which will include **observation**, looking at existing **documentation**, **interviews**, **questionnaires** etc., will be investigated in detail later in this unit.

Once the full analysis has been undertaken, the findings are presented to the organisation in report format, supported by diagrams and charts (if appropriate).

Requirements analysis and specification

Having now done sufficient research to understand what the system currently **does**, a **requirements analysis** and **specification** are developed.

The requirements analysis focuses on what the new system will **need to do** to enable users to carry out their individual tasks from a **functional perspective**. Once the functionality of the system has been established, the necessary inputs can be identified, the processing requirements can be established, and the outputs predicted.

At this stage, however, there are no suggestions on how the functionality will be achieved. In other words, you might have established that a Microsoft Access® or Visual C#® solution is required, but you will **not** make any attempt to design it.

The specification will contain a list of any identified hardware or software requirements, or anything else that will be needed to facilitate the solution (for example network cabling, desks and chairs, four PCs with wireless connections and a wireless router, security software for these machines etc.).

As with previous phases or stages of the life cycle, the analysis and specification must be recorded, often through a report.

Design (logical and physical)

The design phase begins with the analyst creating a logical representation of the new system, using diagrams and supporting text. This is usually achieved through a series of diagrams. The type of diagram will depend on the solution that has been identified.

Entity relationship models (ERM) and **data flow diagrams** (DFD) are used to express the **logical** design of systems that contain data.

The **ERM** will provide a design for the tables that will be storing the system's data in a Microsoft Access® database, for example. This design tool will be explored later in this unit.

In addition, a series of **DFD**s will be developed that will represent the functional areas of the organisation and which will show how the data is **used**, **processed** and ultimately **output** by the system.

These diagrams will probably have been in one of the supporting documents in the system investigation because they can just as easily represent a current system as a future one.

In the event that the solution is (or requires) a network, a **network diagram** will be created that represents the various aspects of the network.

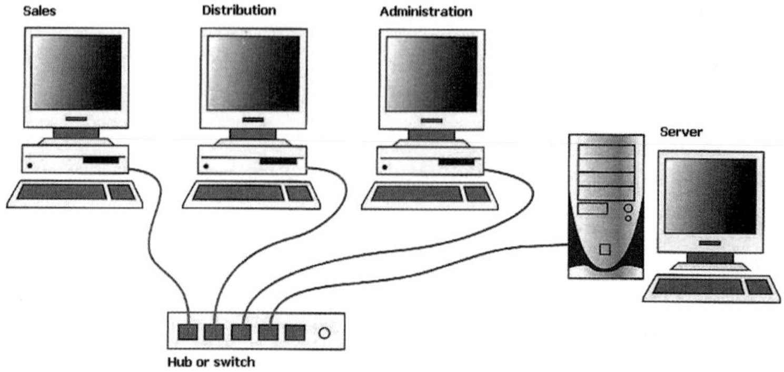

The **logical** design will then be supported by the **physical** design that will include the following information.

For data-intensive systems:

Figure 7.5 Proposed network

◆ a data table (or data catalogue) containing the names and data types of each piece of data and showing how data items link together
◆ details of how the data will be sorted or indexed
◆ explanations of how columns will be ordered
◆ how each output will be designed (for example a management report – the title, data included and any calculations required will be identified and recorded)
◆ drawings of the user interface.

Where computer programming is involved, there is a range of techniques that may be used to support the design of a programmed solution:

◆ **Jackson structured diagrams** (**JSD**) are used to represent solutions that will be coded using a procedural language such as Pascal or C (for more on JSD, see **Unit 18** – Principles of Software Design and Development).
◆ **Pseudocode**, which is based on structured English and laid out like programming code, can be used, again to support procedural languages (for more on pseudocode, see **Unit 18** – Principles of Software Design and Development).
◆ **Storyboards** are used to represent programs that will be written in visual languages such as Microsoft Visual C++® or Visual Basic®.

For network-based solutions:

◆ proposed locations of equipment
◆ lengths of cabling
◆ network connectivity
◆ IP addresses
◆ security proposals.

Bearing in mind that the developers of the solution might not be the same as the analysts, the analysts' last job will be to develop **test plans** for the finished product as it is the analyst and their team that will have the best understanding of what the system is supposed to do, and they will also know where test data can be obtained and what format it will take. They will establish **what data** will be available to test the system and they will dictate **how** the system will be fully **tested**.

Build the system

This is where the system developers enter the process, although in some organisations the same team can be responsible for the whole project.

If the previous stages of the project have been correctly and successfully executed, it should be entirely possible for the developers of the system to be able to use the design documentation of a system to produce the actual solution.

As the build process nears completion, the team will also write any **documentation** that will be required for the system. This will usually include **technical documentation** and a **user guide**. However, some theorists believe that this should not be undertaken until after the system testing is fully completed, as the testing itself should also be formalised and included as part of the technical documentation.

In real terms, most systems will be built by a development team rather than an individual person and where this occurs, the team should have regular meetings to ensure that there are no surprises when they finally attempt to integrate all of the developmental work into the final solution!

With a Microsoft C#® or Visual Basic® solution, for example, a number of programmers might be involved in writing the code. As they will all be writing their own parts, they will need to have established some basic elements prior to starting work:

◆ names of variables
◆ data types
◆ data sizes (if text).

The following example illustrates this.

Two programmers are developing code using the same variable – **customer name**. Prior to starting the code, they agreed that the customer name would be identified in the code as **tCustomer**.

	Programmer 1	**Programmer 2**
Names it	tCustomer	tCustomer
Data type and size	Text (40)	Text (10)
Outcome	If the data handled by the code is passed at any point to code created by programmer 2, it will be truncated because programmer 2's variable is smaller than the one created by programmer 1	There will be no problem if the data is passed to programmer 1, because the tCustomer variable is bigger

It is essential, therefore, that the programmers have **agreed** not only the identifier or variable name, but also the **data type** and **size**.

Once the system is fully complete, the formal testing will begin. It should be understood, however, that during development there will be ongoing testing – programming code will be **checked**, as will **validation routines** or **input masking** in databases.

Testing

Using the test plan developed by the analysts, the development team will now test the product on all levels. In some cases the developers will have access to **live test data** belonging to the organisation. Alternatively, the team will need to develop **dummy** test data. This is data that is similar to the actual data that will be used in the system, but which is not real.

Ultimately, once all aspects have been tested and the results of testing have been documented, the solution will be uploaded to the client's system for live testing, where the users will make use of the system as if they were using it in their usual activities.

Usually, at this stage, the organisation will continue to use the old system as well, so that if any problems in the new system are found, the organisation will be able to continue to function until the problems are resolved.

Implementation

When the system has been tested and is believed to be fully functional, it needs to be formally implemented. Users will need to change from the **old system** to the **new**. Depending on the situation, one (or a combination) of four possible **changeover** strategies will be used.

Direct changeover

This is where on a given date the old system will cease to be used and the new one will begin. A common strategy, this would see the old system used up until the close of business on a Friday, for example, and the users come in and begin using the new system on the following Monday. This is often referred to as the '**big bang**'.

One of the advantages of this is that it is an extremely fast and efficient way to change systems, and the weekend could be used to create the master files. Let's use the example of a stock system.

Prior to changeover, master records would have been created about the stock. These will have included:

◆ **part numbers**
◆ **item descriptions**
◆ **item cost**
◆ **item price**

Now, over the weekend between the old system closing down and the new one beginning, the **quantity in stock** would have had to be added for each item. This would ensure that the system could be used live on the following Monday.

The main weakness with this strategy is that in the event that users then experience problems when they use the system, the old system will no longer be useable because the data will quickly have become out of date.

Even so, many organisations take this risk and use a direct changeover strategy.

Parallel conversion (or parallel running)

If using a parallel conversion strategy, the old and new systems will be allowed to run alongside each other for a period of time. This could be a few days, a few weeks or even months. **Cautious** organisations will tend to use this strategy, particularly if they feel that the time frame for parallel system use will be relatively short.

The main advantage of this conversion strategy is that the new system can constantly be **checked** against the old system to **ensure** its **accuracy**. Any problems experienced by the user can be addressed as soon as they occur, without having a detrimental effect on the organisation.

The main disadvantage, however, is that this clearly requires **duplication in effort** if every transaction needs to be executed twice. This can put excessive strain on staff and should, for this reason, not be used as a strategy for anything more than a few days, unless the organisation is willing to recruit some temporary workers to help out.

Once the system is seen to be functioning correctly, the old system will be discontinued.

Phased conversion

A phased strategy is where the system will initially be introduced to **one part** of the organisation and if the system is then seen to work well, the **next part** of the system will be **added**. This will allow the organisation to see how the system works, and provide opportunities for resolving any problems before the system is fully rolled out.

A phased changeover can be achieved using parallel or direct principles.

Pilot conversion

This strategy is common if an organisation has multiple outlets or sites. For example, a large chain of restaurants wishes to implement a booking system for all outlets where the system will provide managers with statistical analysis on table usage, average customer spend etc.

It is likely that the product, once developed, will be initially implemented in a single restaurant, with others added once the system is seen to function correctly.

As with a phased conversion strategy, a pilot strategy can be achieved using parallel or direct principles.

Maintenance

Once the system is in place, maintenance activities will begin – usually in the order shown.

Corrective

As problems with the installed system arise, they will need to be dealt with. This could be for any of the following reasons (although this is not an exhaustive list):

1 Something does not happen when it should.
2 Totals are missing from reports.
3 The sequence of columns in a report may not be accurate.

While errors 1 and 2 should have been identified and resolved during development, errors can clearly slip through. If this was not the case then software manufacturers would not have to release **beta** versions of their software where bugs are identified by their clients and then eradicated.

Error 3 may not have been seen as a problem by the developer, but the organisation might have a particular reason why the content of two data columns should be reversed (it might be an aesthetic preference).

Corrective maintenance is usually required instantly, or certainly within a few days.

Perfective

Perfective maintenance is usually undertaken where a system does actually run as expected, but it is felt by the organisation that a few aspects could be done **better**. For example:

◆ Additional management information could be **available** if a few of the new reports were modified.
◆ Queries on files or database tables **run slowly** – modifying parts of the system may improve the speed.
◆ The **tab order** (order in which input boxes are accessed) is slightly incorrect – changing the tab order will speed up input.

Clearly perfective maintenance is about making the system work **more efficiently** and **effectively**. As such, activities as part of perfective maintenance are **not as urgent** as those required for **corrective maintenance** and as such these fixes are a **lower priority**. There is no fixed time frame, although it is likely that the organisation (or individual users) will be keen to have some aspects resolved more **quickly**. As a general rule, however, it is anticipated that these issues will be addressed within weeks, or maybe a few months (depending on the quantity of modifications involved).

Adaptive

Adaptive maintenance is a much more long-term concern. This is because the organisation is unlikely to stay still. Its needs will change, sometimes quickly, sometimes more slowly. Either way, the system will need to adapt to these needs. Some possible triggers for adaptive maintenance could include:

◆ organisational **expansion**
◆ **more** potential users
◆ **larger volumes** of data
◆ **technological advances** (better hardware or software becomes available)
◆ activities of **competitors** might mean that the system needs to be upgraded to ensure that the organisation can maintain a **competitive advantage**.

The time frame usually involved in adaptive maintenance is very long term and it is often **proactive** as the organisation defines its future strategies and identifies that its information needs may have to change to support new activities. In some instances, however, it will be **reactive**; it will need to react to technological development and the activities of competitors.

Review

The final stage of the life cycle is the review, where all those individuals who were involved in the development of the system will sit down together and evaluate the project, the process and the outcome! This means that each stage of the life cycle will be discussed, and good and bad experiences will be explored. It is through this process that analysts, developers and project managers learn. When undertaking the next project they will feel more confident about what went well and will try and anticipate and avoid anything that went badly.

Eventually, through review activities, a new project may be defined and the whole process will begin again (hence the term 'life **cycle**').

1.2 Developmental methodologies

We have already explored some of the developmental methodologies in the previous section by looking at their respective life cycles, and we will fully investigate **structured systems analysis design methodology** (**SSADM**) (one of the most commonly used developmental methodologies) later in this section. To provide an overview of some of the methods we have already considered, what follows is a comparison table that compares the methodologies by commenting on common elements:

◆ **Required level of user involvement** – some methodologies require a high level of user involvement in order to allow the project to progress. This is particularly true of RAD, which requires constant input from users, as there is likely to be very little design documentation to work with.

◆ **System size** – some methodologies are best used for investigating and developing a solution for a particular size of system.

◆ **Tools and techniques** – this is a brief comparison of tools and techniques used by each methodology.

◆ **Additional facts.**

	RAD	Spiral	Information engineering	Yourdon structured method	Soft systems/ multiview	SSADM
Required level of user involvement	Very high	Medium	Medium	Low to medium	Medium to high	Medium
System size	Small	Medium	Large	Any size	Small	Large
Tools and techniques						
Prototyping	Yes	Yes	Yes	Yes	Yes	Yes
ERM	Possibly	Yes	Yes	Yes	Yes	Yes
Normalisation	Possibly	Yes	Yes	Yes	Yes	Yes
Structure diagrams	No	No	No	Yes	No	Yes
Low level diagrams	No	No	Yes	Yes	No	Yes
Additional facts	Good for developing **non-critical systems** such as accounting, graphics or word-processing solutions.	Good for looking at a **potential system** in the **wider context.**	Good for **complex systems** and is proactive as it expects analysts and developers to be included in **strategic planning**, so that **future information needs** can be established early.	This is one of the methodologies that only considers the **feasibility, analysis** and **design** stages of the life cycle and does not concern itself with build, implementation or maintenance.	The smallest methodology as it is only concerned with the analysis and design stages of the life cycle.	The most commonly used methodology. Even though it has many tools and techniques, it is accepted that only those that are **appropriate** will be used during an investigation.

There are many more methodologies than those that have been listed and described here. Clearly, attempting to cover them all in depth would require at least one book in its own right. For this reason, the only methodology that will be covered at this stage will be SSADM.

SSADM

At first glance this methodology can be quite overwhelming, particular to a new analyst. This is because as a **structured** methodology it is quite prescriptive. The defined steps are known as stages and it is recommended that each stage is followed to guarantee a successful outcome to the project.

You should notice immediately that the process does not continue on to build, implementation, maintenance and review.

Stage 0	Feasibility study
Stage 1	Investigation of current requirements
Stage 2	Business systems options
Stage 3	Definition of requirements
Stage 4	Technical systems options
Stage 5	Logical design
Stage 6	Physical design

With the exception of stages 2 and 4, these stages are as described earlier in this unit.

Business systems options (**BSO**s) are relatively easy to explain – they are the alternative solutions that could be created, viewed from a business perspective. The BSOs are intended to offer business solutions without getting involved in defining specifics about the technical environment. For example, a solution could be an **application**, purchased complete, which just requires data to be input for it to function (e.g. **Sage Accounting**®). The alternative would be a **tailored** solution using a base program like Microsoft Access® or Microsoft Excel®, which needs to be modified and **set up** before data can be input.

The final business option will be a **bespoke** solution – one that is programmed from scratch using a programming language such as Microsoft Visual Basic®, C or Java.

Ultimately, a single BSO will be chosen with which the project will move forward.

Technical systems options (**TSO**s) are the physical media on which the business solution will ultimately be installed. Sometimes, particular hardware or software will need to be used because of functional aspects of the proposed system – at other times there will be much more flexibility. Often a series of TSOs will be developed that consider different hardware and software configurations, levels of technical support and cost.

As with the BSOs, a single TSO will be chosen and the project will move forward.

Bearing in mind that SSADM is a structured methodology, in most circumstances all of the steps will be undertaken (in some form), although the method does accept that inappropriate steps can be missed, or techniques ignored or replaced by suitable alternatives. One example would be the use of **data flow diagrams**. SSADM uses these at both the investigation and design stages of the life cycle. However, if your system is a website, your solution might not have any data in the conventional sense. As such, using data flow diagramming or normalisation, just because they are available techniques in the methodology, would seem to make very little sense.

 Unit Link

Normalisation is covered in depth in database design in **Unit 5** – Advanced Database Skills and **Unit 11** – Data Analysis and Design.

Typical tools and techniques (e.g. activity diagrams, dataflow diagrams, computer-aided software engineering (CASE) tools)

The text of an analytical report will usually be supported by one or more of a series of diagrams.

Activity diagrams essentially represent the actions of a process, without getting bogged down with data. For example, the production manager asks a purchasing administrator to place an order for a large amount of raw materials.

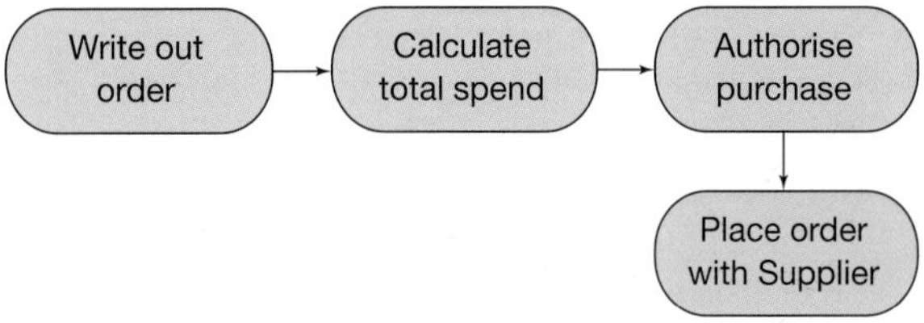

Notice that the following are **not** specified on this diagram:

◆ What the order is written on.
◆ How the total spend is calculated (or what formula to use).
◆ How the purchase becomes authorised, or by whom.

The **same** basic process as described in the activity diagram will now be redrawn as a **DFD**.

This diagram represents the same process, but has different elements.

Figure 7.6 Basic activity diagram for purchase order

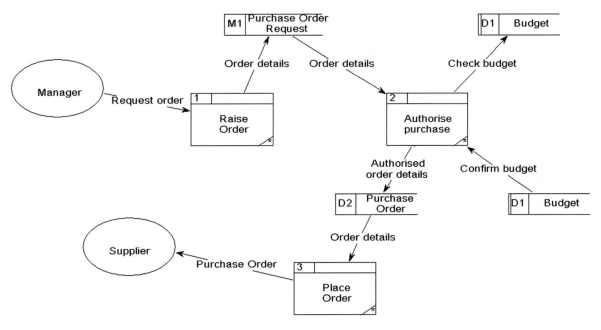

Figure 7.7 Level 1 DFD for purchase order

The first difference is that the **calculate total spend** activity is missing. This does not imply that it will not be done, it just does not need to be represented on this diagram.

The originator of the activity is identified, as is the final recipient.

Physical data stores are identified:

◆ **Purchase order request** – this could be something as simple as a **note** on a **piece of paper**, detailing what the manager has requested, or it could be something as **formal** as an **official form** which is passed on to be authorised before an actual purchase order is raised.
◆ **Budget** – the chances are that the manager and their department will have a budget. This will need to be checked to see whether their department has **enough money** to pay for the goods they are about to order. The **budget file** is checked.
◆ **Purchase order** – once authorised the purchase order is created and is finally sent to the supplier.

Each data store is **numbered**. You will notice that the **purchase order request** data store is marked M1, while the **budget** and the **purchase order** stores have identifiers that begin with a D – D1 and D2 respectively.

The **M** is the annotation for a **manual** data store. This will be a physical piece of paper. The **D** data stores are **digital**. This means that the information is stored in **electronic files**. It is likely that the budget will be stored in a spreadsheet (D1) and that the purchase order will be stored as a record in a database (D2).

Finally, each line (known as a **data flow**) must be **annotated**. The data flow could, however, be made up of verbal data. For example, when the manager requests the administrator to raise an order, they are likely to have made that request verbally. Similarly, the final part of the process, the purchase order flowing to the **supplier,** will probably be as a document or email.

What is particularly interesting about this diagram is not the content itself, but the tool that was used to create the diagram. Figure 7.7 was created using a **CASE tool**. **CASE** stands for computer-aided software engineering and it is a piece of software that is used to assist developers in the creation of software solutions. The software used in this instance (**Select SSADM Professional**®) is a tool that can easily create the diagrams needed in systems analysis and solution design. Without this tool, developers would need to use tools such as Basic Shapes and Text Boxes linked as groups, created in Microsoft Word®. This can be time-consuming to say the least!

Some CASE tools not only create these diagrams but also have functionality to create the **skeleton program code** at the touch of a button, based on the diagram created by the user. This code really does only have the basic functionality and will need to be heavily modified by the developer.

1.3 Key drivers

We have already considered a number of **possible triggers** for the need to develop a new system including users identifying a need or an organisation needing to keep up with competitors. A few more drivers are considered here.

Business need (e.g. need for growth, company acquisition, need to increase productivity, legal requirements)

Need for growth

Sometimes businesses can become **stagnant**. This means that they are **not growing** (gaining new business and exploring new opportunities), or **shrinking** (losing business). Eventually, businesses that do not have any movement or change will begin to decline, although this can take some time.

Most organisations want to advance – they want to expand, become involved in **new markets** and **increase profits**. They need to **grow** to survive and for this they need to have a **strategic plan**. This is where the company decides what it **wants to do**, and what **direction** it wants to take. As part of this process, its systems will be examined to ensure that they are capable of supporting the proposed growth. If this is not the case, then the organisation has time to address the issues.

Company acquisition

It is not unusual for one company to buy out another. For example, the media company **Telewest** was purchased by the larger group **NTL** in the last few years. Since then, it has been sold again – this time to the **Virgin Media Group**.

An organisation may well buy another company for any one or combination of the following reasons:

◆ **To access new markets** – a company selling sports equipment, for example, buys a sports clothing company so that it can add products and services to its portfolio that it feels will interest its existing customers. Alternatively, an organisation might purchase a company that is active in a completely different market sector so that it can get involved in new and completely different activities.
◆ **To increase market share of existing business** – one supermarket chain buys out another supermarket chain, thus having more outlets and business overall.
◆ **To acquire particular assets** – sometimes the acquisition is because one company needs to purchase the **assets** of another company so that it can use them itself. An example might be a car manufacturer buying an advertising company so that it can reduce its **marketing** and **advertising** costs.

If one organisation acquires another, it can do one of two things:

a) Allow the systems to continue running separately for each company.
b) Find ways of integrating systems so that organisations can work together.

Which route is taken will depend very much on what managers intended when they purchased the company. If the acquiring company does not intend to keep its acquisition, for example, there would be little point in integrating the systems.

Need to increase productivity

When systems have been in place for a period of time, they are said to decay. This means that they become increasingly less useful to the organisation. Consider Figure 7.8.

What causes system decay? These are a few examples:

◆ **New technology** becomes available which would help increase productivity by improving efficiency.
◆ **Capacity** needs to increase because sales have improved and productivity output does not match demand.
◆ The **activities** of competitors **demand** that the organisation improves its **ability to respond**.

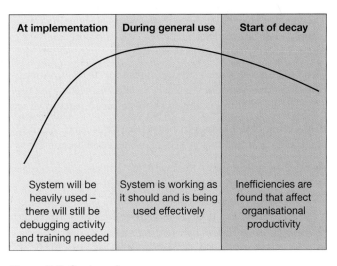

At implementation	During general use	Start of decay
System will be heavily used – there will still be debugging activity and training needed	System is working as it should and is being used effectively	Inefficiencies are found that affect organisational productivity

Figure 7.8 System decay

◆ More **users working** on the system can slow it down, thereby making the system less productive overall.

At times an organisation has no other option but to respond to changes in the law. Responding to and implementing required changes in health and safety legislation is essential if an organisation is going to continue to operate within the law.

The one advantage of changes in legal requirements is that they are usually anticipated. It would not be fair if changes needed to be made immediately, which would disadvantage one company over another. When new laws, or changes in existing laws, occur, companies usually have a **grace** period of time to prepare prior to the law coming into force.

1.4 Benefits of effective systems analysis procedures (e.g. reduced risk of projects running over budget or over time, good quality software that meets requirements, manageable projects, maintainable systems and code, resilient systems)

The main benefit of using any prescribed process is that carefully following a series of steps that have been tried and tested is more likely to produce a successful outcome or end product than merely guessing your way through the process!

Some of the other benefits are:

Reduced risk of projects running over budget – if projects are not completed within the anticipated budget, it is possible that the project may not be completed at all, even if significant work has already been done. The company may simply not have the money to complete it. As such, meeting deadlines is a priority.

Reduced risk of projects running over time – if projects run over the anticipated time frame, developers might simply run out of time and the project could be shelved. More importantly, with some projects, developers might be expected to pay a **fine** for late completion (a little bit like paying a library fine for not returning a book on time). This means that the development team will effectively **earn less** for the completed project than they were expecting to because they will end up **repaying** some of the money. The **penalties** can be very severe, particularly if the organisation receiving the system is relying on the completion of the system on a given date and other activities will be heavily affected by its non-delivery. Again, meeting deadlines is a priority.

Good quality software is produced **that meets requirements** – if each of the steps in the project has been **fully** and **accurately** completed, it should ensure that the users receive a **good quality product**. It suggests here that this is largely about software, but in real terms it applies to any type of system.

Projects are better managed – formalised deadlines should be agreed at the beginning of a project. These are usually recorded in a project plan that should contain:

◆ **Specific milestones** – these will be points in the process where tasks should have been completed.
◆ **Team meetings** – regular team meetings where progress is reviewed should also be planned, as an opportunity for members of the team to **get together** and **discuss** any issues that are arising. However, this can become **unproductive** unless the meetings are kept short and to the point.
◆ **Interim review dates** – where the team and the client get together to review progress and discuss any issues.
◆ The **final handover date** – this should reflect the date previously agreed with the client.

All methodologies accept that a **poorly managed project** will ultimately **result** in a **poor outcome**.

Maintainable systems and code are produced that produce more **resilient systems** – the requirement to document completed systems is part of most methodologies. Good technical documentation will ensure that systems are easy to maintain, because information is available to those whose role it is to carry out the relevant **maintenance**:

◆ **Data tables** (used for any system that contains data) should be produced that include information about input masking or validation routines.
◆ **Programming code** should be fully commented to explain what particular lines of code, functions or procedures do. Variables should be explained.
◆ **Network and cabling diagrams** will explain how systems are wired. IP addresses for machines will have been logged.

Project planning – useful things to remember

When planning a project, ensure that you allow **sufficient time** to undertake **all aspects** of the project, from analysis, through design to building, testing, implementation and review.

A **novice analyst** is likely to **underestimate** the **time** it **actually** takes to **build** and **test** the system. In reality, **testing alone** can take as much as **50 per cent** of the **total development time**.

Ultimately a system that is well maintained is one that will fail rarely – hence the term 'robustness'. Everything is known and documented in a way that makes the information accessible and complete.

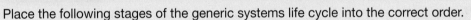

Braincheck

Place the following stages of the generic systems life cycle into the correct order.

A) Review	B) Feasibility	C) Build system	D) Design	E) Testing
F) Implementation	G) Investigation or analysis	H) Requirements analysis and specification	I) Initiation or problem definition	J) Maintenance

See answers on p421.

Braincheck

Methodologies crossword puzzle
Try the following crossword based on what we have covered **so far**. The **grid** and **clues** are provided, along with the **answers on page 421** (if you get stuck).

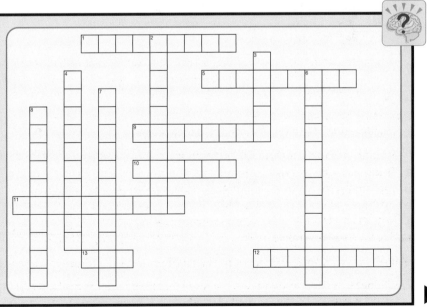

Clues:

ACROSS	DOWN
1. What a methodology brings to the process of analysis	2. The type of maintenance undertaken to eradicate system bugs
5. The life-cycle model that only flows down?	3. When the system begins to become inefficient
9. A type of diagram used to represent only the actions of a process	4. Delivery dates for tasks in the development process
10. The changeover strategy where one system finishes and another starts	6. The A in RAD
11. The scope of a project has these	7. A type of testing undertaken to establish whether the system will work alongside existing systems
12. One of the three perspectives in a feasibility study	8. The structured English design tool for programmers
13. Physical and L.......... design	

Answers can be found on p421.

2 Be able to investigate, analyse and document requirements

2.1 Investigate techniques

There are a variety of investigation techniques at the analyst's disposal. In any situation one or more of these might be used to ensure that ultimately sufficient information about the current system is obtained. These techniques include:

◆ interview
◆ questionnaire
◆ data analysis – examination of records
◆ meeting
◆ document analysis – examination of existing documents
◆ observation.

Each method has very different uses, and consequently has advantages and disadvantages when applied to analysis activities. How appropriate a specific technique will be will be dependent on a number of factors:

◆ size of the organisation
◆ number of staff employed (and who could be potential users of the system)
◆ location
◆ distribution.

What now follows is a review of these techniques.

Interview

An interview is a process where the analyst and user discuss the **user's functional role**. This is usually **prearranged** at a **convenient time**. In order to ensure that the user will supply the correct information when interviewed, a **checklist** of **points** and **questions** should be created in advance. At times, this questionnaire will be given to the user prior to the interview, so that the user can think about answers that they might need to give.

To ensure that this technique will have a successful outcome, the interviewer should ideally have received extensive training in interview techniques. They will need to be able to build a rapport with the interviewee to ensure that the interviewee will feel at ease and able to give responses that will be of benefit to the design of the new system.

Questions must be carefully written to ensure that they are **unambiguous**, as the questions could otherwise be misunderstood by the interviewee and the response might not be what was expected.

If the analyst is in any doubt about the validity of questions that have been asked as part of the interview process, they should find another method of validating the response (by using another technique for example).

Interview scorecard

+ Interviewing is useful as it will allow the analyst to gather **facts** and **information** from those who have **experience** of the **system**.
+ Having this level of contact with a user will enable the interviewer to ask **additional questions** if further information is required.
+ This can have the advantage of **highlighting issues** that the analyst might **not** have **considered** (and not prepared questions for).
- This process can be very **time-consuming** and **expensive** as significant time will need to be allocated to interview each user, so it is **unlikely** that this technique would be used where there is a **large body** of **system users**.
- Some users are **suspicious** of this type of interview and they could be **uncooperative**. This could be illustrated through a refusal to answer questions, changing the subject, getting side-tracked by irrelevant information, or just not providing enough detail for the response to be of any use. In extreme cases, the interviewee could intentionally provide incorrect information in an attempt to sabotage the process.

Questionnaire

While lists of relevant questions, formatted as a questionnaire, are an exceedingly useful investigation tool, the success rate in acquiring the right information is lower than for most other techniques. This is because with most other techniques there is either an element of face-to-face contact, or physical documents or records will be used, which will ensure that information gained will be reliable.

Questionnaire scorecard

+ Questionnaires are extremely useful when you want to gather **small amounts** of information from a **large number** of **users**, particularly if they are also in multiple locations.
+ Every user will be asked **identical** questions – which will make the **analysis** of the responses much **easier** to facilitate.
+ As there is **little personal contact** involved, it is likely that the users will be happy to provide responses, particularly if they are reassured that their forms will be anonymous.
+ Questionnaires are good for gathering **factual information** that can be **measured** (so is quantifiable). On average, how many records do you think you have to create each week? How many edits are you likely to do? These sorts of questions will help analysts establish volumes of data, for example.
− If a questionnaire has been **poorly written** then it will effectively be **useless**. The users might not have interpreted questions correctly and may have given incorrect or inappropriate answers.
− Sometimes a response might be interesting and it may highlight new, as yet unconsidered, issues. The analyst may want to talk to the user to discuss the issue further. However, if the responses were **anonymous**, the analyst has no way of **tracing** the **originator**.
− It can be useful to see a system **in action** and words on a questionnaire might not adequately explain aspects that the analyst really needs to see to fully understand – it can all be a little **remote**.
− With this technique the analyst can never be sure whether or not the user is being **honest**. As with interviews, the analyst could intentionally be given incorrect information.

With this technique **preparation** is the key.

Data analysis

What is required with this technique is that the analyst will **examine** the organisation's **existing records**, from a **data** rather than a **document perspective**. These records could be in many forms. If the organisation currently has a manual system it will be likely that they will be **ledgers, record cards, files of invoices, statements** and **orders**.

If the system is already computerised, even in part, there will be **electronic data** to consider – possibly using software that is unfamiliar to you.

Data analysis scorecard

+ The main advantage of **examining** current **records** is that the **types** of **data** stored can be physically seen and, to some extent, the **volume** of data can be **estimated**.
+ Particular **transactions** can be **traced** back through the records to establish the types of **processes** that are **applied** to a specific item of data.

- The main disadvantage of this technique is that analysts can sometimes feel **overwhelmed** by the **quantity** of data they are given to look at.
- It is sometimes **difficult** to be sure that you have all the **relevant records**.
- It can be **difficult** trying to decide where to **stop**!
- Some of the records might be **out of date** and may not be used any more.

This really is one of the essential techniques that can be used when developing data-driven systems. It does not require any input from the users unless the analyst wants to ask particular questions.

Meeting

Meetings are a useful way of **effectively** interviewing a **large number of people simultaneously.** As with the one-to-one interview, this will usually take place at a **prearranged time** that is **convenient** for **all** those attending.

Meeting scorecard

+ Meetings are useful for gathering **facts** in an environment where attendees might be able to add useful information, or **introduce valuable** and **constructive** new lines of **investigation**.
+ The personal contact will also enable the analyst to ask **additional questions** if further information is required.
+ **Less time-consuming** and **expensive** than the one-to-one interview, this technique would be used where there is a **larger** (but not excessively large) **body** of **system users** who can be consulted together.
- Some individuals might be **reluctant** to voice **opinions** and give too much away about what they do with others present.

To ensure that this technique will have a successful outcome, the meeting should have some structure (particularly an agenda and a prescribed time frame), otherwise useful time could be wasted as those attending get bogged down with irrelevancies.

It would still be useful if the analyst had prepared some specific questions in advance to guide the meeting.

Document analysis

This requires the physical examination of the organisation's documents. If current procedures and processes are well-documented then these will provide a convenient source of useful information. The types of source documents that the analyst might be offered include:

◆ sales invoices
◆ delivery notes
◆ purchase orders
◆ statements

- purchase and sales ledgers
- customer record cards
- supplier record cards
- HR (human resource) documents
- production documents.

Document analysis scorecard

+ As **documents** could be considered to be some of the **outputs** of the system, the analyst should initially ascertain whether the document does actually fulfil some **useful purpose**.
+ This activity can highlight **redundant** and **repetitive activities** the organisation might not have been aware of.
- The difficulty here is that the document may need to subsequently be **redesigned**.
- As with the examination of records, the analyst can be **inundated** with documentation that needs to be **sorted** and **analysed**.

The analysis of these documents can help the analyst to develop an understanding of how the information flows throughout the organisation, and ultimately to the external entities that interact with the system.

Observation

Like interviews, observations can be extremely informative. One of the main reasons is that during an interview, or even on a questionnaire, a system user will probably have no difficulty recalling and describing activities that they do on a regular basis. What is likely, however, is that irregular tasks may be forgotten.

Observation scorecard

+ Aspects of the current system that would be difficult to document could be **experienced** by the analyst – for example, the office layout, the positioning of electrical points, the condition of desks, ventilation, temperature, lighting etc. which could all have an effect on the **productivity** and **efficiency** of both the staff and the current system.
+ The analyst will be able to **formally observe** the **workload** that the system user undertakes, comparing it with the estimates of **volume**, and, more importantly, will be able to identify whether there are any **peaks** or **troughs** in the activity, or whether the processes are evenly spaced over the period.
+ **Bottlenecks** in particular **processes** will be identified (which the user might not even have been aware of), especially if the user is normally busy!
- Individuals are often **sceptical** about being observed and **distrustful** of the usefulness of this technique.
- Yet again, this technique is **time-consuming** as it requires the analyst to spend a reasonable amount of time with users. This would be inappropriate for systems where there are a larger number of users.

To ensure that this technique is used **transparently** (there is nothing hidden about the process) it can be useful if the analyst and user discuss the analyst's findings after the observation, so that the person being observed can **feel reassured** about the process.

The key with observations is to ensure that all staff being observed should be **advised in advance**, and any **concerns** they might have should be dealt with **prior** to the observation taking place.

Sensitivity in collecting information and observing individuals at work

One of the most difficult aspects of impending change is that most employees will **fear** the process. This is largely because they **do not really understand the procedure**, and often have no real comprehension of **how** the **change** will affect them on a **personal level**. In some cases employees will be worried that their **jobs** could actually be at risk.

As an analyst, you should be **sensitive** to this kind of **insecurity**, particularly when you are collecting information about them and what they do, or when you are observing them in their own working environments. Usually, if the organisation has properly prepared the workforce for such an investigation by fully explaining the process, the organisation's intentions and how staff will be affected, then most system users will be **cooperative**, even if you find some will be more **reluctant** than others.

The analyst and the development team really should ensure that they build up a **good rapport** with system users.

Cost-benefit analysis

The cost-benefit analysis initially itemises the costs of the project in monetary terms. It will break these costs down in a logical way, so that the organisation is left in no doubt about how much it will need to spend. This breakdown is also useful as, if the project is running close to budget, managers and developers can use this information to possibly find some savings:

◆ **Development** – how much it will cost just to develop the solution.
◆ **Installation** – the costs of implementation, for example the costs for installing new cabling.
◆ **Equipment** – hardware costs (including peripherals such as printers, routers etc.).
◆ **Personnel** – training costs for example.
◆ Projected **operating costs** – how much the system will cost to run.
◆ **Indirect costs** – the costs of staff time when they are involved in meetings or one-to-one interviews, taking part in training and other developmental activities, and are thus not doing their normal job.

The **benefits** that the organisation will see are then also listed, for example:

◆ **reduction** in staff **costs**
◆ **savings** in other operating costs that the organisation experiences such as consumables
◆ **better** sales as marketing information and data analysis improves
◆ **improved** cash flow position because invoices and statements go out faster
◆ **better** stock control
◆ **enhanced** customer service
◆ **happier** staff
◆ **better quality** and **quantities** of information for managers.

Through the cost-benefit analysis, the client should be able to see that the project will be worthwhile, even if some of the benefits are also indirect, such as better staff morale.

2.2 Requirements specification

Scope

Defining the scope of the project by writing the requirements specification will ensure that all those involved in the project will have no doubts about what the system will and will not do.

Initially, the **system boundaries** will be specified. This is a description of the functionality the finished system is intended to have, described in very general terms, which will specify any **limitations** that are known in advance. The functionality is broken down into the **inputs**, **outputs** and **processing** it requires.

Inputs

Inputs are what goes **into** the system. At this stage, the types of information that will be input and stored in the system will be described in general terms. It is also useful to specify how the data will be **captured** (input into the system), for example:

◆ customer records – keyboard and mouse
◆ supplier details – keyboard and mouse
◆ stock – keyboard and mouse
◆ sales – barcode reader.

Ultimately, data that goes into the system will be processed and will provide the outputs.

Outputs

The specified **outputs** of the system will be a combination of **on-screen displays** and reports necessary to produce the required functionality of the system. At the requirements specification stage, what the analyst will produce will be a list of **proposed outputs** (the reports and displays will be formally designed later in the process).

Using the example of a stock system, the list might look something like this:

1 On-screen displays:
    ◆ single stock item
    ◆ all items in a category
    ◆ all items for one supplier.

2 Reports:
    ◆ items at or below minimum stock level
    ◆ items not sold in last three months
    ◆ all products with cost and resale price
    ◆ all products with resale price only (for price list).

Clearly this is not a **full list** but it does provide a good **sample**. These outputs will have been chosen through discussions with the users and through looking at the documentation the organisation currently has.

Processes

In order to specify processing, we need to decide how the information that is input will be **transformed** into the outputs, but still in general terms. In the design section that follows, we will look at processing in more detail.

So – how will we process the inputs we have obtained above, to provide the outputs? Let's take the on-screen display outputs one by one:

◆ Single stock item – a query allowing the user to search for a single item based on the item code or name.
◆ All items in a category – a query allowing the user to search for all items in a single category (identified by the category input by the user).
◆ All items for one supplier – a query where all products will be listed for a particular supplier (identified by the supplier code).

Notice that at this stage we have not listed or described what will be physically output (which bits of the records). For example, with the single stock item we have not identified that we will display the stock code, description, cost price, resale price, supplier code(s). That level of detail will be recorded in the design stage.

Alternative solutions

The final investigative aspect that must be recorded is evidence that alternative solutions were considered by analysts before a single one was recommended to the organisation.

In terms of IT, there are four main alternatives in any situation – three of these solutions are electronic and the remaining one is a manual solution:

1 **bespoke**
2 **off-the-shelf application**
3 **tailored**
4 **improved manual system**.

Each of the above solutions has **advantages** and **disadvantages** for the organisation and the development team.

Bespoke

A bespoke solution is one that is created **from scratch** and which is developed using a programming language such as Microsoft Visual C#®, Microsoft Visual Basic®, Microsoft C®, Microsoft C++® or Java.

Advantage

The organisation will get a system which completely meets its needs.

Disadvantages

This is likely to be an expensive solution, in which case it might be outside the financial scope of some organisations.

It will take a significant amount of time to develop, so the organisation will have to wait.

The developer will need the right level of programming skill in all the relevant areas.

At times there is no option other than to create a bespoke solution, usually because **no current** off-the-shelf application exists, and a tailored solution might still **not provide** all the functionality that is required by the system users.

Off-the-shelf application

Over the years, many applications solutions have been developed that have specific functionality. Many of these can be purchased as complete solutions, which require only data to be added as all of the functionality is pre-programmed.

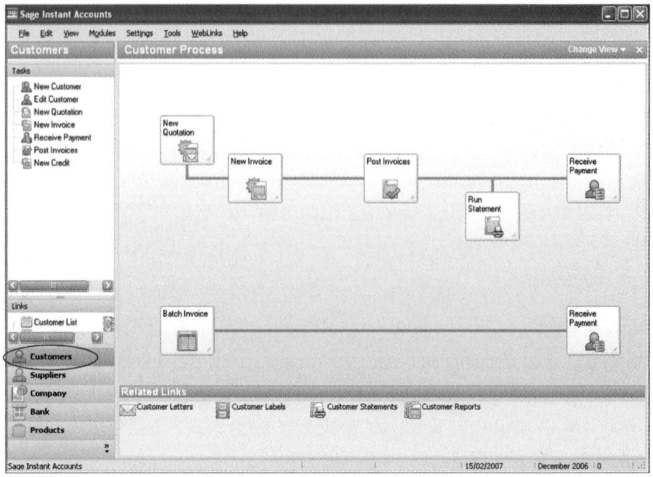

The following is an example of an off-the-shelf application – **Sage Instant Accounts**® is an accounting package designed with all the functionality required to run most businesses.

The functionality has been organised into a series of categories. With the **Customers** category highlighted, the list of possible activities or tasks is as shown in Figure 7.10.

Figure 7.9 Sage Instant Accounts®

On the customers menu, the usual functionality such as adding and editing customer records is present, along with the ability to create quotations and new invoices, process payments as they are received, and manage credit levels on customer accounts.

In addition, there are **related links** with other optional functionality, including creating statements, customer letters, mailing labels and reports.

The **Company** category would clearly require different functionality.

Here, for example, VAT returns are managed and monthly statistics are generated.

Figure 7.10 Customer tasks

Off-the-shelf applications are ideal in most situations, where a specific type of application is required. This software, for example, also has a simple stock system. However, it does not have any distribution management facilities.

Advantage

No development time needed (this really is an instant solution!). All that is required is that the master data is input, and the system can be used.

Figure 7.11 Company tasks

Disadvantages

It can be expensive, particularly if the software requires organisations to buy and maintain **site licences**.

It might not have **all** the functionality needed.

It will require unfamiliar users to be **trained**.

If the organisation requires functionality that is not included in a solution, they might need to purchase further software. In these circumstances, there could be a compatibility issue between systems and, as a result, problems sharing their information.

Tailored

A tailored solution uses a generic package or combination of generic packages to build a solution. The Microsoft Office® suite, for example, has spreadsheet, database, word-processing and presentation capabilities. However, it is not quite as straightforward as it is with off-the-shelf solutions because when using a database package like Microsoft Access®, the database itself has no **structure**.

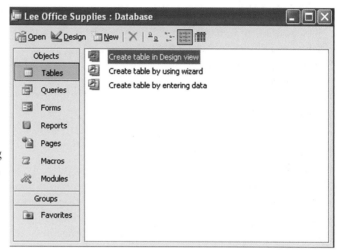

The database shown in Figure 7.12 has been created for Lee Office Supplies. However, at this stage it is empty – the tables need to be created, data types declared, links between tables established, queries designed, reports developed. Only then will the system users be able to key in the data and begin using the system.

Figure 7.12 An empty database

A tailored solution, therefore, is always developed from an existing piece of software that is modified or tweaked to provide the necessary functionality.

Improved manual system

Analysts and developers should always remember that **computerisation is not** necessarily going to be the **appropriate solution** for **every situation**. There are instances, for example, where it might simply not be cost-effective. In the first example below we are considering a solution for a small business.

From the scenario below the following should be clear:

> Tony Drogan is a painter and decorator.
> He has his company, but as a sole trader he has no employees.
> His business is that he subcontracts his services and expertise to larger companies building houses, offices and factories. As such, they provide his materials.
> Contracts are usually a minimum of two weeks, but can be for up to six months.
> He is asked to invoice monthly.

◆ Tony only pays his own wages.
◆ He will not raise more than two invoices at most in a month.
◆ He does not have to handle any purchase invoices.

As such, a computerised system would probably be considered

excessive. Tony is much more likely to maintain a simple record system because he is effectively only charging out his labour.

Consider this second scenario:

> Oldbridge Squash Centre is a five-court squash facility on the outskirts of a medium-sized town. It currently has a manual-facilities booking system which it has been using successfully since the centre opened five years ago. A few months ago this system began to become unreliable. There were increased instances of double bookings and the centre lost members. The centre manager is considering implementing a computerised system to eliminate these kinds of problems. During the investigation, however, the analyst discovers that the problem is largely down to Millie, the new receptionist, who curiously started working at the centre around the time that the problems first developed! Millie came straight from school, has received no training since joining the centre and is often left alone at peak periods when the most members are using the centre. She is trying to maintain bookings while handling payments and membership enquiries.

Is a computerised system required? Possibly not – what may well be required is one of the following solutions:

a) Train Millie to better manage the tasks.
b) Double the reception staff for the peak periods.

As can be seen, there may be occasions when investing in an electronic system might **not** be necessary and, as such, improvement of the existing manual system should **always** be considered as an option. However, in the case of the Oldbridge Squash Centre, it is possible that once Millie is trained, and even with reception staff doubled at peak times, the problem might continue or reoccur at a later date. This could be because the volume of transactions that must be dealt with increases as the centre becomes more popular. If this occurs, then the original solutions of training Millie and doubling the staff might simply have delayed the inevitable – that a computerised system ultimately is required!

For the purposes of an analysis, there should be documented evidence that alternative solutions were at least **considered** as part of the development process. This will reassure the client that the solution that was ultimately recommended was the right one for the situation.

2.3 Analysis tools

We have already briefly considered **DFDs** and **activity diagrams** earlier in this section. However, in reality, there are other tools at the analyst's disposal that can be equally useful in supporting analysis activities.

The DFD shown in Figure 7.7, for example, serves two purposes. Firstly it can be used as the basis for a discussion: the analyst and user discuss a process or series of processes – the analyst draws the diagram based on their **understanding** of **what** the user explained – both parties then discuss the diagram to confirm its accuracy. In other words, it can be used to **document an existing system**.

DFDs are equally useful for **documenting** the **design** of **new systems**. In a real project, it would not be unusual to see a DFD created during analysis, merely modified to show **how** the system is changed by the design process.

DFDs, flow charts and entity relationship diagrams can all be used both in **analysis** and **design** activities. These tools will all be covered in depth in the next section of this unit. However, you should understand that not all methodologies make use of all of these tools. It depends on which methodology is chosen.

It is only after the existing system has been **fully analysed**, and the **specification** for the **new system** has been **created** that the **actual design** of the new system can be **attempted**.

3 Be able to create a system design

3.1 Documentation

Inputs and outputs (e.g. screens and report design)

At this stage, decisions would have to be made about these inputs – firstly, we need to show specifically what **data types** individual inputs will be. The chosen data type will be dependent on the extreme values that the input is expected to contain. Let's take the example of integers. The following table provides a view of the integer data types available in C#.

Integer type	Description	Min. value	Max. value
sbyte	8-bit signed integer	–128	127
short	16-bit signed integer	–32,768	32,767
int	32-bit signed integer	–2,147,483,648	2,147,483,647
long	64-bit signed integer	–9,223,372,036,854,775,808	9,223,372,036,854,775,807
byte	8-bit unsigned integer	0	255
ushort	16-bit unsigned integer	0	65,535
uint	32-bit unsigned integer	0	4,294,967,295
ulong	64-bit unsigned integer	0	18,446,744,073,709,551,615

How will the analyst make the decision about which integer data type to use? This decision will be based on what the analyst has found out about this particular piece of data from users, existing documents etc.

Similar decisions will need to be made about all other pieces of data that the system is expected to hold. While this will seem like a long-winded process, these decisions are quick and easy to make if you are an experienced analyst.

The **input screens** themselves will need to be designed. The one advantage of this part of the design activity is that the analyst usually has something to work from or to use as a template.

If an input screen will be an electronic representation of a form that the organisation intends to continue using, it would make sense that the layout of the **online version** will be similar to the **manual form**. This is because it will be easier for the user to key in the information if the two forms have **inputs** in more or less the same places.

Key Terms

Signed integers – a signed integer can have a value that is **positive** or **negative**, e.g. a bank account balance.

Unsigned integers – unsigned integers only represent a **magnitude**, e.g. age is an unsigned integer.

Unit Link

The following table shows the different integer data types available in the programming language Microsoft C#®.

A similar table for the Java programming language can be found in **Unit 18** – Principles of Software Design and Development, section 1.4.

Library Membership Request Card

Last Name: _____ First Name: _____

Address: _____

Post Code: _____ Date of Birth:

Telephone: _____

Sex (please tick as appropriate): Male ☐   Female ☐

Age group (please tick as appropriate): Under 5 ☐
5–13 ☐
14–17 ☐
18–59 ☐
60+ ☐

Let's look at the membership card in Figure 7.13 which new library members are asked to complete when they join their local library.

Figure 7.13 Membership card, completed by hand

The design for the onscreen version can be done in many ways.

It could be hand-drawn, see Figure 7.14.

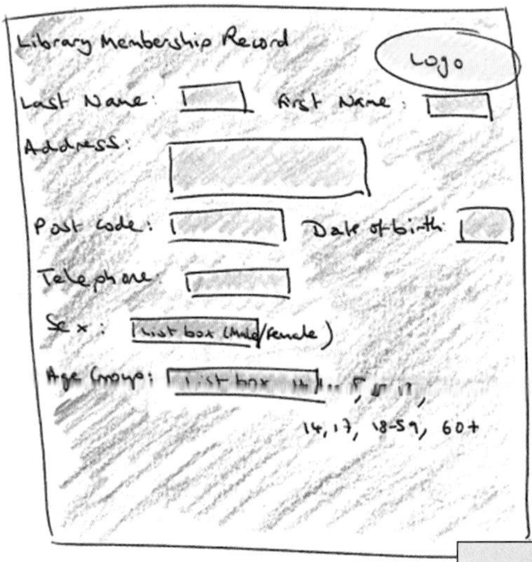

Figure 7.14 Hand-drawn representation of input form

Or it could be created using a software package, see Figure 7.15.

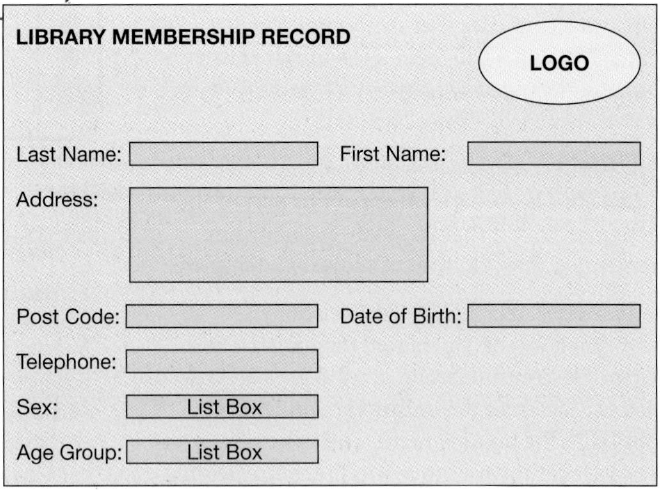

LIBRARY MEMBERSHIP RECORD   LOGO

Last Name: [   ]   First Name: [   ]

Address: [   ]

Post Code: [   ]   Date of Birth: [   ]

Telephone: [   ]

Sex: [List Box   ]

Age Group: [List Box   ]

Figure 7.15 The input form reproduced as an electronic design

Tab order and logical flow

Ensure that the **flow** of movement from box to box in an electronic form is identical to the **flow** on the manual form. This will vastly increase the input speeds achievable by the user. If, however, it is essential for data items to be placed differently in the electronic version of the form, then ensure that the **tab order** remains the same. The tab order is the order in which the input boxes are accessed as the user presses the tab key on completing an input.

Most experienced users will not look at the screen as they input the data, they will merely use the tab key to navigate and key in while looking at the original manual form (this is often called **copy typing**). As such, as long as the order in which the boxes are accessed remains the same, the actual position of the boxes on the screen might not be as critical.

Similarly the **outputs** of the system will need to be designed. This will be achieved in a similar way (through hand-drawings or computer-generated samples). However, there are likely to be many more outputs designed than there were inputs. This is because the system will give users the opportunity to manipulate and view the data in different ways. While there will usually be some examples of reports which the organisation has that were generated in other ways, many of the outputs defined at this stage will be new. Also, unlike the inputs (which will mostly be computer-based, because sometimes organisations take this type of activity as an opportunity to modify their paper-based forms also), the outputs could be either **screen reports** or **paper-based reports**.

What will need to be defined, in addition to the layout of the form, is what data will actually be output. Which columns will be used and what titles will be included will need to be decided.

The outputs of the system will need to be justified – the **business purpose** of the report will need to be established. This is to ensure that developers do not create reports which the organisation **does not really** need!

Dataflow diagrams

The dataflow diagrams created at the analysis stage will now be modified and new ones may be drawn. These diagrams can be drawn at different **levels**. **Context** (or Level 0) and **Level 1** are the most common (although further levels can be drawn if appropriate).

Fundamentally, dataflow diagrams are made up of four components.

Figure 7.16 is a **process box**, used to represent a procedure undertaken within a system. If the process consists of a single action (for example, *place order*), then the process will be considered to have been defined at its **lowest** level. The inclusion of the / and * symbols in the bottom right of the box indicates that this is the case. If these symbols are not present, an analyst will know that the process is made up of a series of actions, which might need to be explained on a lower-level diagram (Level 2 for example).

Figure 7.16 Process box

Process boxes are numbered, although it should be noted that the numbers do not bear any relevance in the flow of the diagram; they are merely numbered for recording purposes. A process box is **never repeated** within a diagram.

Figure 7.17 represents an **entity**. An **entity** is something that interacts with a process, and it may or may not be external to the organisation. As long as it is not part of the process itself, it will be considered an entity. It can put something into a process, trigger a process or receive something from a

Figure 7.17 Entity

process. A customer making an enquiry could trigger a process. The organisation invoicing the customer could be another process from which the customer would receive an invoice. Entities are shown within an ellipse (the oval shape), and these **can be** repeated within a diagram.

Figure 7.18 A repeated entity

Figure 7.19 Data store

Figure 7.20 A repeated data store

If this occurs, the symbol is modified (including the original instance of the entity).

You should bear in mind, however, that if an entity is repeated a third time or more, the symbol does not change.

Figure 7.19 is a **data store**. A data store represents a file (held in any format). It could be a customer file on a computer or supplier record held in a card system. Annotating whether a data store is electronic or manual is as simple as changing the letter at the beginning of the data store identifier. A **D** represents a digital (or electronic) store and an **M** a manual store (we discussed this earlier in this unit). As with entities, data stores can be repeated within a diagram. In that eventuality, the notation is modified by adding an extra bar to the beginning of the box.

As with repeated entities, you do not add extra bars if you subsequently repeat the data store a third or fourth time.

The main reason why entities and data stores have to be duplicated is because the diagram has become so well **populated** (or full) that in order to link a data store or entity with another process you would have to cross the data flow lines. **This is not allowed.**

⟶ A **data flow** denotes the data that is moving between processes, entities and processes, or data stores and processes.

Now that we have considered the notation used in data flow diagrams, we will consider the two types and you will be given examples of both.

Context (Level 0) diagram

A context diagram represents the whole system as a single process. If you consider our library example as a **whole system** then the diagram might look something like Figure 7.21.

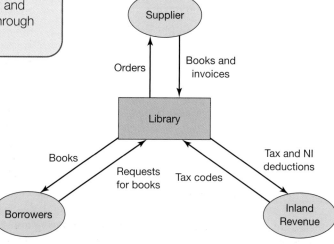

Figure 7.21 A context diagram for the whole library

The first thing to notice is that all the **entities** that are shown here are going to be truly **external** to the organisation. **Suppliers**, the **borrowers** (effectively the customers of the library) and the **government department** known as the **Inland Revenue** will all be interacting with the system. There will be many more that we could have included here.

In the subsequent diagram, we have refined the system to be concerned only with the book and loan system. As the Inland Revenue has no connection to either the loan of books or their purchase, the Inland Revenue entity **disappears** in this diagram. However, if we were going to include the payroll function of the library (those paying the wages of library staff), the function would have to appear as an external entity as it would be outside the book and loan process.

Level 1 data flow diagram

The Level 1 diagram for Figure 7.22 would now show all the activities that create or use these data flows, and it would also include information about how the data is stored (in what files for example).

When developing diagrams at lower levels you would not expect any entities to be added, although data stores and processes may well be.

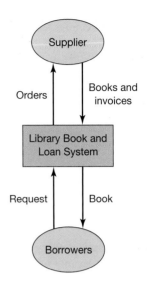

Figure 7.22 Context diagram for the book and loan system

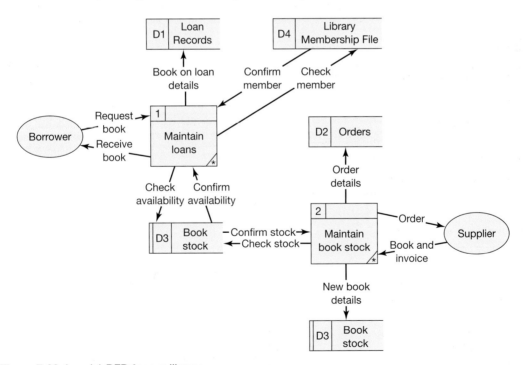

Figure 7.23 Level 1 DFD for our library

This diagram, while correct in terms of what we were trying to record, does not cover **all the possible processes** that might exist in a book and loans system. What **other functionality** could there be?

- ◆ book reservations
- ◆ overdue book reminders
- ◆ fines for overdue books
- ◆ paying suppliers for the books.

Whether or not these aspects would be included in the diagram would be dependent on whether the system being designed was going to include that functionality or not.

During the design phase of the lifecycle, one or more diagrams like Figure 7.23 will be created that will represent **what the system will be like** and **how the data will be processed** and used. It is extremely useful for defining what data will be stored, although at this stage **nothing else** about the data is defined.

Entity relationship diagrams (ERD)

Another, complementary method of documenting the design of a system will be to create an **ERD**. This is particularly relevant for database systems, although in that particular environment you will probably see the diagram referred to as an **entity relationship model** (ERM)), as it is one of the major database modelling tools currently used in industry.

From a more generic systems design perspective, the basic concept remains the same:

> In an ERD, we investigate the relationship between the **data items** and any **relevant entities**, ignoring the process! This will help us to define what actual data will be held, and how that will be structured.

An **entity**

A **relationship**

ERDs are made up of two components; entities and relationships.

The point of an ERD is ultimately to show how all of the **data items** in a system **relate to each other** and to establish how the different parts of the data will link together in a logical way.

In concept, a relationship will be **one** of **three** types.

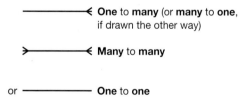

One to **many** (or **many** to **one**, if drawn the other way)

Many to **many**

or ─────── One to one

Key Terms

What are **entities**? Entities are **things** about which we want to **store information** or **data** inside a **system**.

Entities are said to have **relationships** with **each other**.

But what is a **relationship**? The relationship is the **definition** of **how** the entities are linked. For example:

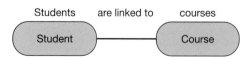

Students   are linked to   courses

Student   Course

However:

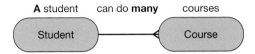

Equally:

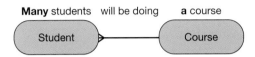

The resulting relationship would look like this!

Ultimately, for this particular model we need to **resolve** the many-to-many relationship, as the diagram should ultimately contain **only one-to-many** or **many-to-one** relationships. **Many-to-many** and **one-to-one** relationships **should not exist** in a well-structured system (although there are exceptions).

So how can we break down the relationship between the student and the course? One possibility might be to consider that students must enrol (register) to attend a course.

This diagram now reads as follows:

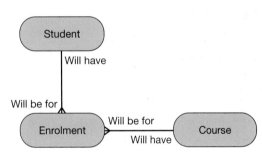

◆ A student will have one or many enrolments.
◆ An enrolment will be for one student.
◆ An enrolment will be for one course.
◆ A course will have one or many enrolments.

In its simplest form:

An enrolment will be for one student on one course!

Using the library as an example – we would first consider the following question:

What do libraries need to hold information about?

Two things are immediately obvious: **Borrowers** and **Books**.

So we begin our diagram.

What is the relationship?

Or – a borrower will have a loan of one or many books and a book can be loaned by one or many borrowers! This is a **many-to-many** relationship that we now have to go on and resolve.

What is the nature of that relationship? The actual loan of the book. We will obviously want to store data about that!

So, we need to **modify** the diagram.

Now we can read the diagram as follows:

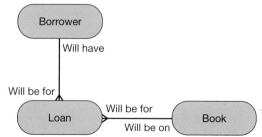

- ◆ A borrower will have one or many books on loan.
- ◆ A loan will be for a single borrower.
- ◆ A loan will be for one book.
- ◆ A book will be on loan one or many times.

We have now resolved this, but we still have more data to store. Clearly, as it is the major part of a library's activities, we might want to store information about the suppliers we get our books from.

We need to add the **supplier** to the diagram. But what are we going to link the new entity to?

Can we link it to the borrower? No, the borrower will not have **any interest** in who supplied the book!

Can we link it to the loan? No because there is **no connection** between the **supplier of a book** and **who** it was loaned to.

Can we link the supplier to the book entity? **Yes**, because the book will have originally come from a supplier!

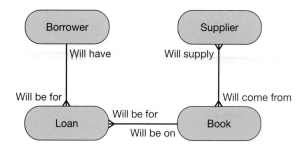

Oh dear! We have another many-to-many relationship. What links a book to a supplier? The order which was placed to get the book in the first place!

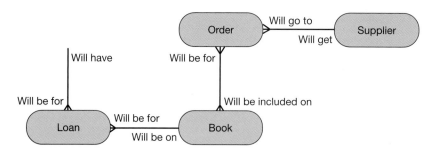

We still do not seem to have fully resolved the problem, because even though we have added an entity, when we think through the relationships logically, the relationship between the book and the order is still many-to-many, even though the one between supplier and order is now fine.

Why is there still a problem? Because a book can be ordered many times and an order can be for many books.

So, how do we take the final step? Let's consider what the order might look like.

Where does the book title go on the order? Well, the book title being ordered will be one of one or many books on that particular order. These are listed in the item lines on the order. That is the missing entity!

PURCHASE ORDER

Order Date:

Supplier Details

Delivery Address

Quantity	Title	Author	Price per book	Total

Special Instructions: The books listed are required by Friday 19th January 2007.

Figure 7.24 Library purchase order form

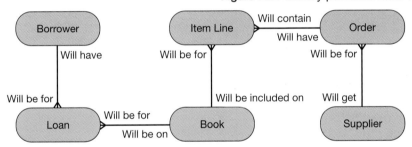

And finally:

◆ A borrower will have one or many books on loan.
◆ A loan will be for a single borrower.
◆ A loan will be for one book.
◆ A book will be on loan one or many times.
◆ A book will be included on one or many item lines (for an order).
◆ An item line will only ever be for one book.
◆ An item line will only ever exist on one order.
◆ An order will have one or many item lines.
◆ An order will only ever go to one supplier.
◆ A supplier could get one or many orders.

From this model we now know we need to store information on:

◆ **borrowers**
◆ **loans**
◆ **books**
◆ item lines (which are part of **orders**)
◆ **suppliers** .

Having now created a Level 1 DFD and an ERD for the library problem, you should now be able to compare these two diagrams and identify the fact that you have arrived at the same point. The diagrams should ultimately match, and these do, even though the ERD has the additional **item lines** entity, which is needed to help define the actual file structure.

Entity	Present on DFD?	Present on ERD?
Borrower	Yes (as an entity and a data store)	Yes
Loans	Yes (as a data store)	Yes
Books	Yes (as a data store)	Yes
Orders	Yes (as a data store)	Yes, but further defined to resolve many-to-many relationship
Suppliers	Yes (as an entity)	Yes

The ERD is now used to develop a **data dictionary**.

Data dictionaries

The data dictionary is a formal record of what **attributes** will be created to hold the data within each entity.

It is the job of the data dictionary to record the attributes for each entity in a structured way. At this point, the data types, lengths and any input masking or validation that might be applied will also be listed.

Data Dictionary

Attribute Name	Entity	Data Type	Description	Format or Length	Validation/ Input Mask
Book Title	Book	Text	Title of book	50 characters	Upper case
Edition Number	Book	Integer	Edition number if appropriate		
Genre	Book	Text	Book category eg. Children	25 characters	
Author(s)	Book	Text	Names of all authors	100 characters	
Publisher	Book	Text	Name of publisher	25 characters	
Year of Publication	Book	Integer	Year only, eg. 2007		> 1980

Figure 7.25 Data dictionary example, completed for the book entity

Although there are many variations on the subject of data dictionaries, a common template would look something like Figure 7.25.

Sometimes a single data dictionary is created with all attributes for all entities included in a single document (hence the inclusion of the entity column). The alternative would be to develop a data dictionary for each entity individually. This is also fully acceptable.

You will also see variations on what columns should be included in a data dictionary.

Process descriptors (e.g. decision tables, flow charts, structured English)

The final parts of the system that will need to be designed and defined are the processes themselves. What does the system do to make **input A** become **output X**?

The usual methods of demonstrating the intended design of processes are decision tables, flow charts and the use of structured English.

Decision tables

In simple terms, a decision table is used to concisely represent a process where a number of **different actions** may be taken, **dependent** on a **range of conditions**. It allows the analyst to record all of the possible conditions that might occur, and define a suitable action or response. It may be easier to look at a documented example.

The conditions themselves are listed at the top of the table, with the actions listed below.

Staying with our library example, let us look at a decision table that records all the conditions that need to be tested and the actions that could be taken when a borrower requests a book.

		A	B	C	D
Condition	Is a library member?	Y	Y	N	N
Condition	Book is in stock?	Y	N	Y	N
Action	Loan book	Y	N	N	N
Action	Record loan	Y	N	N	N
Action	Refuse loan	N	Y	Y	Y

Had this tool not been available, we would have had to use either a flow chart or text to represent this process. As text it would have been explained as follows.

Scenario A
- The borrower is a library member.
- The book is in stock.
- Loan the book to the borrower.
- Record the loan.

Scenario B
- The borrower is a library member.
- The book is not in stock.
- Refuse the loan.

Scenario C
- The borrower is not a library member.
- The book is in stock.
- Refuse the loan.

Scenario D

- The borrower is not a library member.
- The book is not in stock.
- Refuse the loan.

Realistically we know that with scenario B we would have offered to put a reservation on the book when it was returned and notify the borrower at that time.

For scenario C we would have offered the prospective borrower library membership, then loaned the book and recorded it.

For scenario D we would have offered the prospective borrower library membership, then we would have put a reservation on the book when it was returned and notified the borrower.

However, these additional actions were **not required** in this particular decision table because there is nothing in the ERD or the DFD to suggest that we have a reservations process or data store, create new member process, or notification process.

Flow charts

To give you an example here, however, we again use the **maintain loans** process defined in the DFD in Figure 7.23, and the decision table recorded in the previous section.

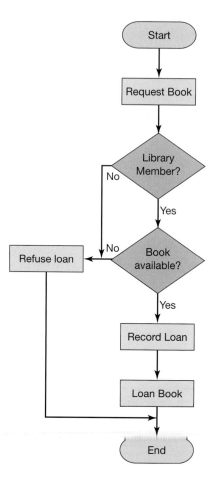

Figure 7.26 Flow chart for maintain loans process

This flow chart explains the process, showing how the system should react, but interestingly further explains the decisions. In the decision table, it is implied that if the potential borrower is not available and the book is in stock, we refuse the loan. In reality, if the potential borrower was not a member, we would not check the book's availability in the first place! This diagram makes this clear.

Unit Link

Using flow charts to represent how a process works is also an extremely useful design tool. Flow chart components and further examples can be found in **Unit 18** – Principles of Software Design and Development.

Use of structured English

As a final design tool, using **structured English** to describe processes is the closest an analyst can come to writing the actual program code because the process is described and laid out in the way it will ultimately appear in code, but without using any compiler syntax (terminology). This is often also called **pseudocode**. Using the process defined in the flow chart in Figure 7.26, the description would look like this.

Maintain loans process

```
1  Write: Is a member?
2  Check: If Yes
3     Write: Is book available?
4     Check: If Yes
5        Record Loan
6     Else
7        Write: Refuse loan
8  Else
9     Write: Refuse loan
```

For the purposes of the design, the processes will individually be defined in this way. It is then up to the programmer or developer to interpret this into program-specific code.

The absolute key with good solution design is that ultimately all diagrams created, explanations written and decisions made are **consistent**. Inconsistencies between any of these will cause difficulties when the system is developed, because they will cause developmental errors.

3.2 Constraints (e.g. costs, organisational policies, timescale, legacy systems, available hardware platforms)

From the design perspective, you will take the constraints placed on the development of the system earlier in the system's life cycle and explain how your design has accommodated these constraints – you will explain how you have worked around them. Sometimes it can be useful to represent this in a table, where all the constraints can be listed, together with the description of how the constraint has been managed.

Constraint	Accommodation
Costs	Solution will be within budget providing there are no unforeseen issues.
Organisational Policies	All organisational procedures and policies have been accommodated as required.
Timescale	Development plan includes 6 weeks of recovery time to accommodate the unforeseen. If these weeks are not required the project will finish ahead of schedule.
Legacy Systems	Existing data files can be converted to provide master data for the new system. Conversion time planned into main schedule.
Hardware Platforms	Existing hardware will be fully upgraded. New equipment should be ordered to ensure that it is available for week 34.

Case Study

The management at **Frankoni T-Shirts** have asked you to design a new **sales** and **stock system** for them, to replace their current **manual system**

which is becoming increasingly **unreliable**. What follows here is a write-up of the notes from an interview that one of your colleagues carried out with the main users of the system.

Customers usually place orders as a result of visiting the shop, phoning through an order, or placing an order online using Frankoni's website.

When the order is received, two stocks are checked:

a) t-shirt stock
b) designs stock (the stock of iron-on designs supplied by KAM Limited (Kris Arts & Media).

An order is then raised and is placed in an order file. This file is then used by the production department to get the information to make up the t-shirts. The order is then stamped as completed and placed in a completed order file. Once a day, the completed order file is accessed by the accounts department who will then use that information to create an invoice.

Once the invoice has been raised, it is sent, along with the relevant order items, to the customer who will then return the payment.

Activity

Create the following diagrams based on the scenario described:

◆ Level 1 DFD
◆ ERD that represents the data.

Answers on p436.

4 Be able to design a test plan

You might actually wonder why, if as an analyst you will not be creating the physical solution, you should be concerned with testing. A good question! The answer is actually very simple. If the development team and programmers are going to enter the life cycle at the implementation stage, they will effectively not have been involved in the analysis and, as such, they will not have seen the actual system the client currently has, or the data within that system. Therefore it makes sense that you will define how the system you analysed and designed will ultimately be tested.

4.1 Testing strategies

Black box

Black box testing is where the system is tested based on what it is supposed to do – on its functionality, and so when black box testing is carried out, the tester will need to check that the solution is capable of doing everything it was expected to do (compared to the requirements specification).

Continuity testing is also a function of a black box testing process. Here calls to and returns from modules, functions and procedures are checked.

The simplest way to plan black box testing is for the analyst to create a table that includes a full list of all the functionality that the system must have (taken from the specification), which the developer will then use as a checklist.

It is important that you remember the term **functionality** also includes:

◆ **checking calculations** (having first worked out what that result should be using alternative means such as pen and paper, a calculator or a spreadsheet)
◆ **checking** the **query results**
◆ **checking report outputs.**

Black box testing can be recorded using any effective recording mechanisms.

Unit Link

Trace tables are often used (for further information see **Unit 18** – Principles of Software Design and Development), as are test plans like the one shown in Figure 7.29.

The columns shown with a ⬤ are completed during the design phase of the life cycle. The remaining columns are then completed by the developer during or after system building.

Test #	Purpose of test	Test values (or data source)	Expected results of test	Actual results of test	Actions required
⬤	⬤	⬤	⬤		

Figure 7.29 Sample test plan

White box

When it comes to white box testing, the plan must be developed from the flow charts, decision tables and pseudocode. This is because white box testing is not concerned with checking for functionality or presence of functionality, but is concerned with ensuring that all logic within the system works.

Maintain loans process

```
1 Write: Is a member?
2 Check: If Yes
3    Write: Is book available?
4    Check: If Yes
5       Record Loan
6    Else
7       Write: Refuse loan
8 Else
9    Write: Refuse loan
```

A test plan would now be written and the values defined to test each possible **path** through this code. There would be two variables: **member** and **book**.

On the first run through we would give **member** a value of N (for No):

Lines 2, 8 and 9 should execute.

On the second run through we would give **member** a value of Y (for Yes) and **book** a value of N:

Lines 2, 3, 4, 6 and 7 should execute.

On the final run through we would give **member** a value of Y and **book** a value of Y:

Lines 2, 3, 4 and 5 should execute.

So in our plan, to carry out white box testing on the maintain loans process, we would run the code three times with the following test values:

Test # (or number)	Value of member	Value of book	Expected result	Actual result	Comment
1	N		Refuse Loan		
2	Y	N	Refuse Loan		
3	Y	Y	Record Loan		

Trace tables can also be very successfully used as part of the white box testing process.

V-model

Planning testing around the V-model requires the analyst to plan testing to accommodate the right side of the diagram in Figure 7.2 at the beginning of this unit.

The plan must:

◆ Test the functional parts to ensure they do what they are supposed to.
◆ Test the whole product alongside systems with which it must integrate – does it do so successfully?
◆ Test the whole system and check that the users' original requirements have been met.

As with the other strategies, clear documentation that contains sufficient evidence of testing is essential as this also forms part of the technical documentation for the solution.

4.2 Testing purposes

There are two main purposes for testing:

a) To confirm the functionality meets the original system specification.
b) To confirm the user is happy with the end product (acceptance testing).

Confirm functionality meets specification

Confirming that the functionality meets the specification is a good way to validate the success or failure of a project. A solution that does not fully meet the original specification cannot be said to have succeeded.

For user acceptance

Once the system is fully functional and has been installed, acceptance of the system by its users will be sought. This can be done through a round of interviews (if the system is relatively small), but with medium or larger systems it is more likely that a user questionnaire will be developed that will be distributed to users and which they will complete with their feedback.

The questionnaire concept is a good one as if there are any problems; the developers will have a formal record of problems found, which will make perfective maintenance easier to achieve.

4.3 Components of a test plan

Firstly it is important to note that if the client already has data that can be used as part of the testing process, this should be used in preference over any fictitious data as far as possible.

Collecting suitable test data is important both in the **quantity** and **quality** of **spread**.

Inputs

Inputs should be defined that will cover a suitable test range, and should be of sufficient quantity to adequately test each part of the system.

Expected outputs

The anticipated outputs from using the range of inputs described in the previous section should be defined.

The outputs expected from running a query should be predicted. The outputs from reports should also be predicted, including the values of any totals that will be visible.

Actual outputs

During and after system development, these values will all be used to test the functionality and logic of the system. The fact that the test plan was defined by the analyst or system designer, and the test data selected by the same individual, should ensure that the process will be robust.

Test data

Data selected for testing purposes should cover the following range:

◆ **Normal data** – the program needs to be tested with data that is **within** a **sensible range**. This is the data that is expected to be input when the system is being used normally.
◆ **Extreme data** – the program should also be tested with data which while still within a sensible range, is **less likely** to be input. For example, an age over 115 is not impossible, it is just unlikely!
◆ **Erroneous data** – this is data that is neither normal nor sensible! It is data that is blatantly incorrect. The data will contain **values outside valid ranges** and **incorrect types of values** (e.g. characters where numbers are expected and vice versa).

Activity

Complete the following test plan to reflect testing for **normal**, **extreme** and **erroneous** data. In each case, suggest at least two values!

Test	Normal data	Extreme data	Erroneous data
Age is between 18 and 21			
Height is between 1.5 and 2.2 metres			
Quantity (must not be 0)			
Price (must be more than 0, but less than £20.00)			
Choice must be A, B, C, D or E			
Hours worked (must be greater than 0, but less than 50)			

Achieving success

This particular unit has 11 criteria to meet: 6 pass, 3 merit and 2 distinction.

For a **pass**:

You must achieve **all** 6 pass criteria

For a **merit**:

You must achieve **all** 6 pass and **all** 3 merit criteria

For a **distinction**:

You must achieve **all** 6 pass, **all** 3 merit **and both** distinction criteria.

So that you can monitor your own progress and achievement in each unit, a recording grid has been provided (see below). The full version of this grid is also included on the companion CD.

 Unit Link

Unit 7 is a **core unit** on the BTEC National Diploma for IT Practitioners (**Software Development route**).

It also a **specialist** unit on the following BTEC National routes:

IT and Business

Networking

Systems Support

For more on **trace tables and JSD** see **Unit 18** – Principles of Software Design and Development.

For more on **flow charts** see **Unit 18** – Principles of Software Design and Development.

For more on **normalisation** and **ERDs** see **Unit 5** – Advanced Database Skills and **Unit 11** – Data Analysis and Design (in the companion book).

This unit also has conceptual links to:

Unit 20 – Event-Driven Programming

	Assignments in this unit			
Assignment	**U7.01**	**U7.02**	**U7.03**	**U7.04**
Referral				
Pass				
1				
2				
3				
4				
5				
6				
Merit				
1				
2				
3				
Distinction				
1				
2				

Help with assessment

To **pass** the unit you will need to show that you are competent as an analyst and designer. You will need to show an understanding of methodologies and analytical process, as well as applying the theory to a live or simulated scenario.

For a **merit** you will need to show that you can undertake an investigation with the minimum of supervision and input from your assessor, as well as being able to justify your strategy choices.

For the higher grade (**distinction**), you will need to show that you can successfully evaluate your experiences of the process and be able to explain how risks that could be faced within such a project could be eliminated or at least minimised.

Online resources on the CD

Electronic glossary for this unit
Key fact sheets
Worked case studies
Electronic slide show of key points

Further reading

Howard, A., and Yull, S., 2002, *BTEC Nationals – IT Practitioners: Core Units for Computing and IT*, Elsevier Science and Technology, ISBN 0750656840.

Lawson, J., Jarvis, A., Reid, K., and Soomary, N., 2003, *BTEC Nationals for IT Practitioners: General*, Heinemann Educational Secondary Division, ISBN 0435456695.

Reid, K., Jarvis, A., Blundell, P., Lawson, J., and Soomary, N., 2004, *BTEC National for IT Practitioners: Software Development*, Heinemann Educational Secondary Division, ISBN 0435456679.

Reid, K., Jarvis, A., Soomary, N., Smith, A., and Lawson, J. (ed.), 2003, *BTEC Nationals for IT Practitioners: ICT Systems Support* Heinemann Educational Secondary Division, ISBN 0435456687.

Communication Technologies

Capsule view

Communication Technologies is a 60-hour unit which is designed to introduce the learner to the **theoretical** and **practical challenges** of planning and using **emerging communication technology** to **improve** business **productivity** and **performance**.

The unit focuses on both the **underlying** communication technology and the **principles** which make it work and **interoperate seamlessly** with **different systems worldwide**.

1 Know the main elements of data communications systems

1.1 Communication devices

Communication devices are often grouped into **categories** which either describe their **purpose** or their **underlying technology**.

Learning aims

1 Know the main elements of data communications systems.
2 Understand the communication principles of computer networks.
3 Understand transmission protocols and models.
4 Understand internet communications.

Data terminal equipment

Data terminal equipment (**DTE**) is any device that **generates data** (as a **sender**) or is (as the **receiver**) the **final destination**.

Example DTE includes: a computer system acting as a **terminal**.

The DTE is normally seen as the **end point** in a data communication link.

The terminal's job as a DTE is to **convert incoming data** into **information** for the **end user** and convert **information** provided by the user **back into data for transport** (achieved by a **DCE**).

Data communications equipment

Data communications equipment (DCE) (or, in some sources, **d**ata **c**ircuit-terminating **e**quipment) is a term that is used to describe **devices that provide a communications link for a DTE**.

An example of a DCE would be a **modem** (**mo**dulator **dem**odulator), a device which can convert a computer's **digital signals** into **analogue signals** for use over a **telephone line** (and **back again** when **receiving**).

Originally these terms were exclusively used with **serial data transmission** as part of the **RS-232 standard** (see 1.4). In more recent years the definitions are much more loosely used.

Traditionally, **DTE** and **DCE** devices are **wired**. More modern technologies such as the **cellular telephones**, **PDAs** and **notebooks** use **wireless** connections, relying on various **radio frequencies** to make connections.

1.2 Signal theory

Data is represented in a **digital format** based on binary (base 2) principles.

Digital signals are said to be **discrete** – they offer **no continuous graduation** between values; the values are **stepped**.

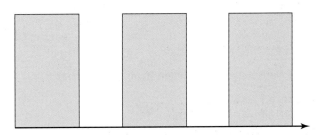

Data

The smallest element of data is the **bit** or binary dig**it**.

This can represent either a **1** or a **0**.

When bits are **grouped together** they form more useful units of data, e.g. **8 bits** form a **byte**.

Concept of a packet

In networking, data has to be **encapsulated** into a suitable 'package' for transport.

The actual format of this package changes between different types of network, however the term **data packet** is generically used to describe this package.

A **data packet** should minimally contain the source and destination addresses, data and error control.

The **source address** is sent so that the recipient knows **who** has sent the data. The **destination address** is used to **find the right recipient**. Data is the actual '**message**' being sent. **Error control** is added to the packet to help **identify problems** with the data **once it has been received**.

A common error control method is the concept of a **checksum**. You will read more about these in 1.3.

Asynchronous vs. synchronous transmission

Asynchronous transmission means that device two must **acknowledge receipt** of data **before** device one will send **more**.

This is because there is **no attempt** by **either** device to synchronise **before** data transfer starts. They rely on the receiving device recognising that a stream of data is beginning or ending. This is usually achieved with **start** and **stop bits** (see 1.4)

In **synchronous transmission**, both devices will **synchronise** with **each other before any data is sent.** When no transmissions are being sent, the two devices will transmit **special characters** to each other to keep each other 'in synch'.

Bandwidth

This is generally defined as the quantity of data that can be sent through a data transmission medium over a specified period of time.

Bandwidth is usually quoted in (from slow to fast):

◆ **bits per** second (bps)
◆ **kilo bits per** second (Kbps)
◆ **mega bits per** second (Mbps)
◆ **giga bits per** second (Gbps)

Data compression

Data compression is the process of **removing unnecessary padding** from data so that it takes up less **physical** or **electronic** 'space'. Compressing data makes more efficient use of available bandwidth.

1.3 Data elements

Checksum

Part of the **error control** mechanism, a checksum is a **calculated value** based on the **contents** of the **data packet**. When the packet is received at the destination node, the packet's checksum value is **recalculated** based on the data packet's **received contents**.

The new checksum is compared against the one sent.

If the checksums **match**, it is assumed that the data sent was **received successfully** (good data integrity).

If the checksums **don't match**, the destination node suspects that an **error** has occurred during transport. The destination node can then **request a retransmission** of the data from the source node.

Some checksums may simply be a **total of the bits** sent in the packet. In this case, the checksum is merely confirming **safe quantities** of data rather than the **quality** of the data.

Cyclic redundancy check (CRC)

A **CRC** is a **more thorough** form of checksum used for checking errors in data transmission (on the motherboard, in data files and in networking).

CRC error checking involves a **very complex algorithm** that generates a **numerical sequence** based on the **data** that was transmitted. CRCs are therefore able to guarantee (beyond a reasonable doubt) the **accuracy** and **quality** of the data transmitted; even a **transposed data sequence** (data in the wrong order) would be identified.

Sequence numbers

In systems where data is split up into a number of packets, it is important to know in which **order** a series of packets should be **read**.

This is vitally important as it is possible that they may arrive **out of sequence**; a consequence of packet-switched routes. For example:

◆ **Source node** sends packets: **1, 2, 3, 4 and 5**.
◆ **Destination node** receives packets: **2, 4, 1 and 5**.
◆ **Verdict**: the packets are in the wrong order and the message cannot be read until **3** (currently missing) is resent. **Please resend packet 3**.

Packets, datagrams and frames

Unfortunately these terms – all meaning something slightly different – are often used **interchangeably**. In reality, they are very often grouped together as **p**rotocol **d**ata **u**nits (**PDU**), collections of data which occur at different **layers** of the **ISO OSI model** (see 3.1).

Packet

A packet is a collection of data that has been created by **software**, not by a **hardware device**. For example, chunks of data created by **internet protocol** (IP) are called **IP packets**.

Crucially (and here's the important point), a packet contains **logical addressing** (e.g. IP addresses) for its data.

Frame

The term frame is normally used to describe a collection of data that has been created by **network hardware** (e.g. NICs or routers).

A frame contains **physical addresses** (e.g. MAC addresses).

Example frame types include **Ethernet frames** and **token ring frames**.

Datagram

A datagram is an independent, **self-contained collection of data** that is sent over the network. **Whether** it arrives, what **time** it arrives and what it will **contain** are not guaranteed.

User **d**atagram **p**rotocol (**UDP**) is a transport layer protocol used on IP networks. Unlike TCP (see 3.3), it is a simpler, **connectionless protocol**. As such, it cannot guarantee successful delivery nor does it have much functionality to **detect errors** or **data loss**.

The term packet and datagram are often used interchangeably.

1.4 Methods of electronic communication

In methods of communication, we examine **how** data gets from **point to point**.

Simplex

Simplex describes data transmission which is **one way** only.

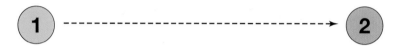

Half-duplex

Half-duplex describes data transmission that is **two-way**, just **not simultaneously** – each device **must wait** until the other has **finished** in order to transmit successfully.

Full-duplex

Full-duplex describes data transmission which can be **simultaneously two-way**.

Each device is capable of **transmitting** and **receiving** at the **same time**.

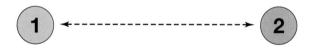

Sometimes this is referred to as just '**duplex**'.

Serial communication

Serial communication occurs when data is sent along a channel **bit-by-bit**, i.e. in a **sequence**.

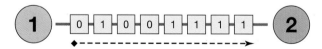

In reality, this can simply be the case of sending an electronic signal across a **single wire**.

Examples of forms of **serial communication** include the following.

Dating back to 1962, **RS-232** is an electrical signalling specification that was originally published by the Electronic Industries Association (**EIA**). It also has standards laid down by the International Telecommunication Union (**ITU**) known as **V.24** and **V.28**.

RS-232 is synonymous with **serial data transfer**; the earlier **25-pin** (DB25) and more recent **9-pin** serial connectors are still reasonably common on a motherboard's backplane. RS-232C offers a **full-duplex connection** and can be used to connect **DTE to DTE** and **DTE to DTC**.

The **communication protocol** between **two devices** using an RS-232 connection **has to agree**:

◆ **start bit**
◆ **data bits** (usually seven or eight)
◆ **parity bit** (odd, even or none)
◆ **stop bits** (usually one or two).

Figure 8.1 9-pin serial connector (male)

The **data packet** itself is typically stored in an **ASCII** (American Standard Code for Information Interchange) format.

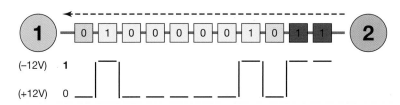

This transmission is sending the ASCII character 'A' (65 **10** or **1000001 2**) with **even parity** and **2 stop bits** from **device 2** to **device 1**.

Common RS-232 data transmission speeds are up to **1.5 Mbps** on the newest devices, with **20 Kbps** being the specified standard.

Parallel communication

In direct contrast to serial communication, parallel communication permits data transfer to occur in **groups**, across a **number of wires**.

Care has to be taken that data is **reassembled** in the **correct order** at the receiving end.

Example forms of parallel communication include **IEEE 1284**.

Figure 8.2 25-pin parallel connector (female)

Although now rapidly being overtaken in favour of **faster serial USB connection**, the older IEEE 1284 is a good example of parallel data transmission, used to connect printers and scanners.

The IEEE 1284 standard supports a number of different modes.

Mode	Description
Centronics (SPP)	Standard Parallel Port – unidirectional mode, providing backward compatibility
Nibble mode	Unidirectional mode, transmitting 4 bits per pulse
Byte mode	Transmits 8 bits per pulse
EPP	Enhanced Parallel Port – half-duplex transmission up to 2 Mbps
ECP	Extended Capability Port – supports compressed data and up to 1 Mbps

1.5 Transmission media

Modern communication systems use an array of different transmission media (the method used to get signals from point to point).

Here are the most common media used.

Coaxial

Although you are probably more familiar with these from **television aerials** and **cable equipment**, coaxial cable is used to connect telecommunication devices which use **high-frequency**, **broadband** connections.

A typical coaxial cable has a number of components.

A separate copper **braided shield** (also known as a **screen**) surrounds the insulator. This shield provides a **barrier** from **electromagnetic interference**.

Coaxial has a much higher **capacity** than a standard copper wire, which explains its use for carrying **radio frequency** (**RF**) **television signals**.

Various different types of coaxial cable exist and are used for:

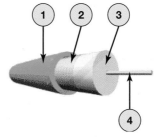

1	Outer plastic sheath
2	Braided copper shielding
3	White polyethylene inner insulator ('dielectric')
4	Copper core

Figure 8.3 Coaxial cable

◆ **thin Ethernet** (10 Base 2) – used for networking at 10 Mbps up to 200 metres.
◆ **thick Ethernet** (10 Base 5) – used for networking at 10 Mbps up to 500 metres.
◆ **amateur** ('Ham') **radio**.

Coaxial's use in building computer networks (**thin** or **thick Ethernet**) has mainly been superseded by **u**nshielded **t**wisted **p**air (**UTP**).

Optical fibre

Optical fibre uses light for data transmission; **LEDs** or a **laser** (**l**ight **a**mplification by **s**timulated **e**mission **r**adiation) generate light pulses which are sent down the **fibre** (actually a thin strand of **glass**). **Photodiodes** detect the light pulses at the far end.

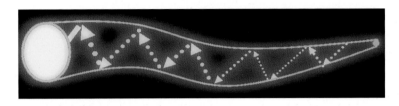

Each fibre is about **2 microns** in diameter – about **15 times thinner** than a **single human hair**.

Total internal reflection (about 41 or 42 degrees) prevents the majority of the beam's light from being **absorbed** by the outer cladding, leaving the remainder to safely reflect back along the fibre from one end to the other.

Optical fibres are **not affected** by stray electromagnetic interference (unlike copper cables). In addition, they are capable of sustaining **high transmission rates**, ideal for **broadband applications** such as **voice**, **music** and **video**.

Optical fibres can be manufactured into:

◆ **single mode** used for **longer distances** (3 km) carrying a **single beam** of light
◆ **multimode** used for **shorter distances** (2 km), carrying **multiple beams** of light (and therefore **more data simultaneously**).

UTP and STP

Unshielded and **s**hielded **t**wisted **p**air (STP) both use **copper wires** (the oldest type of transmission media).

STP has a **metallic-coated plastic foil** within the plastic sheath that is used to **screen out electromagnetic interference**. Because of this, STP is generally **more expensive** than its UTP counterpart.

Crosstalk can occur between two wires which run in **parallel**. In both UTP and STP cables, the individual wires are **twisted** in order to **cancel out** this form of interference.

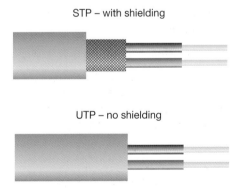

STP – with shielding

UTP – no shielding

The core of STP and UTP wires is **copper** as it is an **excellent conductor** (having low electrical resistance) and is an easy material to **work with**.

Wireless solutions

Wireless solutions use infrared (discussed at length in 3.2), radio, microwaves and satellite.

Radio

It is possible to convert the computer's digital signals into radio waves.

The transmitting device uses an antenna to **generate radio signals** which spread out in a **straight line**. Signals can be **reflected**, **absorbed** or **refracted** as they travel through **different materials** (e.g. wood, brick, moisture in the air etc.). As such, radio signals **weaken** over distance, necessitating the receiving device using an antenna to **amplify** the **weak** electrical signals.

Radio waves form the basis for **wireless LANs** (**WLANs**) and wireless technologies.

Microwave

Microwaves are electromagnetic waves in the range 1 to 30 GHz. Modern microwave-based networks are becoming more popular as the technology improves. They offer **high bandwidth** at a relatively **low cost**.

Satellite

Satellites are artificial orbiting devices which relay data between multiple **earth-based stations**. Satellites provide **high bandwidth** solutions.

Transmission media comparison grid

Transmission Media	Strengths	Weaknesses
Coaxial	Long runs (500 m) Relatively inexpensive Immunity to stray signals (noise ') Tried and trusted technology 10–100 Mbps	Rigid; difficult to install Expensive to install
Optical fibre	Very long runs (2000–3000 m) depending on the mode Not susceptible to electromagnetic interference Does not generate noise	Light signal strength diminishes over distance due to scattering and absorption Expensive to install
UTP	Reasonable runs (100 m) before repeating needed Inexpensive (cheapest per metre for LAN installation) Small – easy to install 10–1000 Mbps	Prone to interference from stray signals

STP	Reasonable runs (100 m) before repeating needed Shielded 10–100 Mbps	Moderately expensive (owing to extra weight and size)
Infrared	No wires Quick to install	Must have direct line of sight (LOS) Limited in range Easy to disrupt
Radio	No wires No LOS required Greater range possible	Signals become weaker over distance Wireless signals can be intercepted so security is an issue

2 Understand the communication principles of computer networks

2.1 Features of networks

Network size

Every network has a determined **size**. Common network sizes include the following (in **ascending order** of size).

Personal area network (PAN) or piconet

A piconet or **PAN** is a network of computing devices that use **Bluetooth technology** protocols to allow one master device to interconnect with up to **seven slave devices**. See IEEE 802.15.

Local area network (LAN)

A **LAN** is a computer network that covers a local area, typically like a home, connecting nearby offices or small clusters of buildings such as a college. These typically use **wired Ethernet (IEEE 802.3)** or **wireless RF** technology (**IEEE 802.11**).

Metropolitan area network (MAN)

A **MAN** is a computer network that covers a town or city. This type of solution often relies on **fibre-optic** solutions.

Wireless MANs (**WMANs**) using microwave technology are becoming increasingly popular, see **IEEE 802.16**.

Wide area network (WAN)

A **WAN** is a computer network (**public** or **privately owned**) that uses **high-speed, long-distance** communications technology (e.g. **telephone lines** and **satellite links**) to connect computers over long distances.

WANs can be used to connect LANs together, e.g. geographically distant branches of the same organisation.

Braincheck!

Decide whether the following are **PAN**, **LAN**, **MAN** or **WAN**:

◆ A public network paid for by a city council for all its residents.
◆ A network connecting the various national branches of Lee Office Supplies.
◆ Two friends exchanging .MP3 songs via their mobile telephones.
◆ A cluster of computer labs in a local school.
◆ A PDA transferring files to a notebook.

How well did you do? See page 421 for the answers!

Topology

Topology is the term used to describe the network's **shape** or **form**.

In simple terms, this is how the **nodes** (servers, workstations etc.) are **physically** or **logically** connected.

Common topologies include the following.

Star

One **central node** with **outlying** nodes.

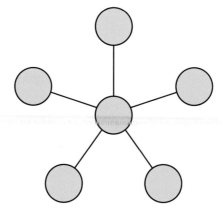

Ring

A series of nodes connected **daisy-chain** style.

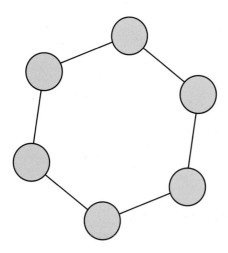

Mesh (fully connected)

Each node **interconnected** with others. The Internet could be viewed as the largest mesh topology network.

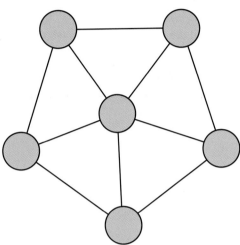

Tree

Nodes are linked in a **hierarchical structure**.

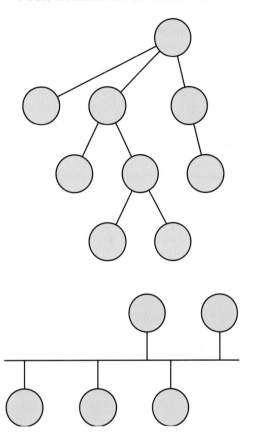

Bus

Different devices connected from a **common backbone** (a single run of cable). Any fault in the backbone will affect nodes beyond the break.

Network services

A number of different network services are available.

Packet-switched

This is the opposite of a **circuit-switched** network (where a **permanent circuit** is made between two nodes **before** communication can take place).

In a packet-switched network, data is **divided into packets** (see 1.2) and then moved from **source node** to **destination node** through a number of **different nodes**.

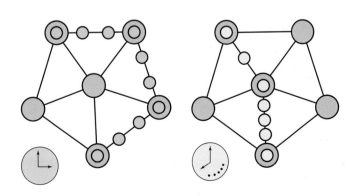

Depending on the **nodes available**, each packet may take **a different route** (see routers, 2.3)

Integrated services digital network (ISDN)

ISDN is a standard devised by the **C**omité **C**onsultatif **I**nternational **T**élégraphique et **T**éléphonique/International Telecommunication Union (**CCITT/ITU**) for digital data transmission. This type of network service occurs over ordinary telephone copper wire and thus is still popular where faster DSL and cable services are not available.

ISDN represented an upgrade from dial-up narrowband services (which relied on modems). Any home or business customers wanting to use this early broadband service would need to install an **ISDN adapter**.

Typical ISDN connections gave a bandwidth of about **128 Kbps**. At the time (mid to late 1990s) this was much faster than the **best modem speed** of **28.8 Kbps** so proved an attractive option.

ISDN has been mainly superseded in the UK through the mass availability of relatively inexpensive DSL and cable services.

Asynchronous transfer mode (ATM)

ATM is the **international standard** for dedicated connection-switching technology; a connection between source and destination nodes must be made **before** any data can be sent.

It organises **digital data** (voice, video and data) into **fixed-length** 53-byte cell units. This is different to packet-switched networks where the size of the data packets may **vary**.

Fixed-length cells allow processing to be easily implemented **by hardware**, resulting in **faster processing** and reductions in **transit delay**.

Broadband (Digital Subscriber Line etc.)

Broadband is a common term used to describe a transmission medium capable of supporting a wide range of frequencies – this **broad band** width is able to support large volumes of data, voice and video communication. The term is often used in comparison to older, analogue narrowband technology. Traditional telephone lines carrying voice conversations in an analogue signal form do not make full use of the transmission media's available bandwidth.

Digital signal-based DSL uses these unused frequencies available on the copper wire to transmit data traffic in addition to voice. This means that DSL allows voice and high-speed data to be sent simultaneously over the same connection.

A DSL **splitter** (also known as a **microfilter**), located at the customer's end, **separates** voice and data signals.

Wireless access point (WAP)

See 3.2

Network software e.g. network operating system (NOS)

A **NOS** is specifically written to support networking (especially LANs).

Its functions can include:

- ◆ **networking protocols** (e.g. TCP/IP)
- ◆ mechanisms for **sharing files** and **resources** such as **printers**
- ◆ facilities for managing **administrative functions** such as **security**.

Network basic input/output system (NetBIOS) is an application programming interface (API) that allows other applications to communicate with a LAN.

Originally created by International Business Machines (IBM), it was later adopted by Novell and Microsoft®. NetBIOS is used in modern Ethernet, token ring and Microsoft Windows® networks.

Access methods (e.g. CSMA/CD CSMA/CA token passing)

Access methods describe the ways in which a device knows when it can talk on a network.

Carrier sense multiple access collision detection (CSMA/CD)

This works like so:

1 Device '1' wants to transmit data so first checks the channel for a carrier…
2 If no carrier is sensed, device '1' can transmit, however…
3 If two devices transmit **simultaneously**, a **collision occurs** and each computer **stands back** and waits a **random interval** before attempting to **transmit again**.

Carrier sense multiple access with collision avoidance (**CSMA/CA**) is similar but sends a request-to-send (**RTS**) signal **which must be acknowledged** by other nodes **before** it transmits.

Token passing

Token passing is a network access method **particular** to **token ring** networks.

Token rings are a form of **LAN** developed and supported by **IBM**; they typically run at 4.16 or 16 Mbps over a **ring topology** (see 2.1).

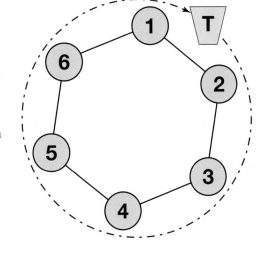

In a token-ring network, access is very orderly as it is based on the possession of a small frame called a token. Having a token gives a node the 'right' to talk…

In order to talk, a node does the following:

1 Captures a **token** as it moves around the ring.
2 **Inserts** its **data, target node address** and **control information into the token frame**.

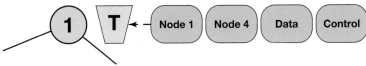

3 Changes the token frame to a **data frame**.
4 Node 1 then transmits the frame around the token ring towards the destination node.

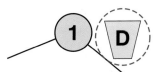

Nodes not targeted by the data frame just pass the token on.

The target node opens the data frame and reads the data stored inside.

After processing its data, the target node **releases** the data frame, and after a **complete circuit**, it finds itself back at its sending node. The sender node removes the frame and generates a **new token**.

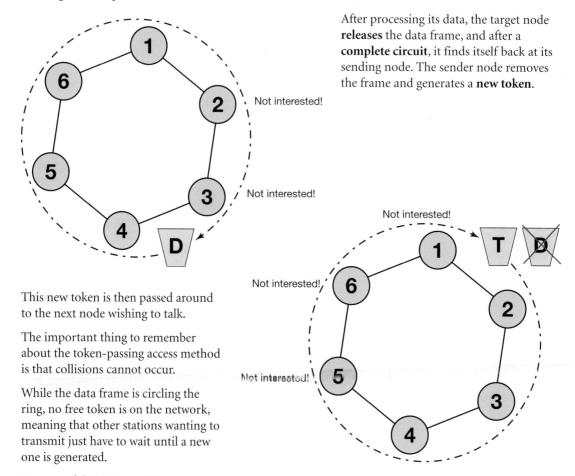

This new token is then passed around to the next node wishing to talk.

The important thing to remember about the token-passing access method is that collisions cannot occur.

While the data frame is circling the ring, no free token is on the network, meaning that other stations wanting to transmit just have to wait until a new one is generated.

Because of this, it is possible to calculate the **maximum amount** of time a node will have to **wait** to transmit; this is referred to as being **deterministic**.

Token rings and token passing are laid down in the **IEEE 802.5 standards**.

2.2 Network components

Aside from **cables** and **connectors** (see 1.5), a network consists of a number of typical components.

These include the following.

Server

A server is typically a power computer system that provides some form of **processing service** for **network clients** (or other servers).

Servers tend to be **well specified** (powerful CPU(s), large RAM and hard drive capacity) and have **u**ninterruptible **p**ower supplies (**UPS**s) to keep them going during an electrical power cut.

Typical services provided by a server include:

◆ **mail server** for processing **email** (electronic **mail**) **requests**
◆ **web server** for processing **h**yper **t**ext **t**ransfer **p**rotocol (**HTTP**) requests for **h**yper **t**ext **m**arkup language (**HTML**) **files** and associated **assets** (images, video, sound etc.)
◆ **file server** for managing **access** to **shared** network **drives** and **folders**
◆ **print server** for managing **print queues** to **network printing facilities**.

Workstation

A workstation is a common name for a computer system, particularly one operating within a **business environment** and **connected** to a **network**.

Network cards

A network card (more formally a **NIC**), sometimes called a network adaptor, is a **physical layer device** (see 3.1) which is used to **transmit data** from a computer system to a **target node** via some form of **transmission media**.

Depending on the type of transmission media, a number of different types of network card are available.

Ethernet

A **wired card**, offering an **RJ45 connection**. Ethernet cards may be plugged into **older i**ndustry **s**tandard **a**rchitecture (**ISA**) or **p**eripheral **c**omponent **i**nterconnect (**PCI**) slots on a motherboard. Like any other device, drivers for the operating system installed will be required before the card will work properly.

Figure 8.4 PCI network interface card

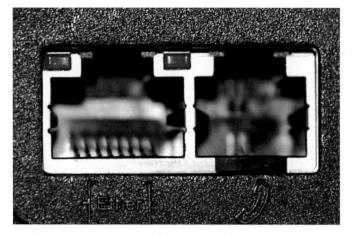

Modern motherboards have **onboard LAN** – Ethernet technology built into the motherboard as a single microprocessor.

Figure 8.5 Onboard Ethernet (RJ45) and modem (RJ11)

Personal **C**omputer **M**emory **C**ard **I**nternational **A**ssociation (**PCMCIA**) Ethernet adaptors are also available for notebooks although onboard LAN is now more commonplace.

Wireless

Wireless connectivity is very often built into modern portable devices such as PDAs and notebooks. Where wireless functionality is not available,

Figure 8.6 PCMCIA wireless NIC adaptor

PCI, USB and PCMCIA wireless adaptors are commercially available.

Token ring

Token ring networks (see 2.1) are **not compatible** with Ethernet networks. As a result, **specific network cards** must be used which process data in a way which is compatible with the **deterministic approach** used on a token ring. Physically, they are not dissimilar from their Ethernet counterparts.

Figure 8.7 PCMCIA token ring adaptor

2.3 Interconnection devices

A number of different devices are used to connect together different aspects of a network.

These include the following.

Repeater

A repeater is a device which can be used to extend cable runs and, as a result, the physical size of a network. One of the biggest problems with long cables is **signal attenuation** – the **decrease** in the **signal's strength** as it travels over a distance.

A repeater is simply an electronic device containing a **transceiver** (transmitter and receiver) that **receives**, **amplifies** ('**boosts'**), and then **retransmits** the signal.

At no point is it **aware** of what the signal actually represents (it does not know that it is network data).

Hub

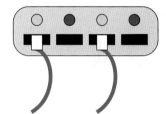

Also known as a **multiport repeater**, it performs the same basic function as the repeater. The number of ports (which typically can be up to **16**) allows a number of **different network devices** to be connected together.

Because hubs are **not** 'intelligent' (they are not interested in the data, only the electrical signals), any incoming signal is **retransmitted to all ports** of the hub, whether the transmission is targeted to its connected device or not.

Hubs are generally **cheaper than switches** and therefore, after a **crossover cable**, present the most inexpensive way of creating a simple **LAN**.

Hubs extend the **collision domain** – the network **segment** in which transmitted signals may **clash** (see 2.1 CSMA/CD).

Switch

These are **aesthetically** similar to a hub, however this is just **superficial**. Inside, a switch can **filter** and **forward packets** between **different LAN segments**. Because of this segmentation, a switch can improve network performance by **reducing competition** for **available bandwidth**.

When a packet of data is received, it is **only** forwarded onto the **appropriate port** for the **intended recipient** (by examining the **target node's MAC address**), thereby reducing **unnecessary** network traffic – compare this to the 'boost and repeat it all' tactic of the hub.

A switch therefore can be used to reduce the collision domain through segmentation.

Figure 8.8 USB-powered 5-port 10/100 Mbit switch (RJ45 sockets at the rear)

Router

A router is a complex device, making decisions about which of several possible paths should be used to relay network data (see mesh topology).

Figure 8.9 A router – 7 × RJ45 connectors for the LAN, 1 × RJ45 for a WAN

```
C:\WINDOWS\system32\cmd.exe                                    _ □ ×
C:\Documents and Settings\Mark>tracert www.google.com

Tracing route to www.l.google.com [64.233.183.99]
over a maximum of 30 hops:

  1    47 ms     9 ms     8 ms  192.168.123.254
  2    20 ms    18 ms    16 ms  ███ ███ ████ █
  3    21 ms    17 ms    17 ms  80-192-0-161.cable.ubr01.azte.blueyonder.co.uk [
80.192.0.161]
  4    28 ms    25 ms    27 ms  195.188.230.49
  5    21 ms    18 ms    19 ms  aztw-t3core-1a-ge-010-0.inet.ntl.com [80.1.240.6
9]
  6    21 ms    22 ms    20 ms  win-bb-a-so-200-0.inet.ntl.com [213.105.175.157]
  7    23 ms    21 ms    23 ms  gfd-bb-b-so-100-0.inet.ntl.com [213.105.172.130]
  8    25 ms    25 ms    24 ms  nth-bb-a-so-000-0.inet.ntl.com [62.253.185.97]
  9    33 ms    25 ms    47 ms  nth-bb-b-so-200-0.inet.ntl.com [213.105.172.194]
 10    25 ms    28 ms    26 ms  tele-ic-1-as0-0.inet.ntl.com [62.253.184.2]
 11    30 ms    27 ms    24 ms  212.250.14.66
 12    32 ms    25 ms    29 ms  72.14.238.244
 13    33 ms    31 ms    32 ms  209.85.248.80
 14    34 ms    33 ms    33 ms  209.85.248.87
 15    45 ms    42 ms    36 ms  64.233.175.246
 16    37 ms    35 ms    36 ms  72.14.233.81
 17    47 ms    51 ms    35 ms  216.239.43.30
 18    35 ms    35 ms    35 ms  nf-in-f99.google.com [64.233.183.99]

Trace complete.

C:\Documents and Settings\Mark>
```

Figure 8.10 A traceroute – following 18 hops from gateway to remote host

It does this by using a **routing protocol** to learn about the network, and has **algorithms** to help it select the best route based on several **criteria** (its **routing metrics**).

Sometimes the metric may be **time based** (which route is **quicker**); sometimes the metric may be **reliability** based. Uniquely, routes are **regularly updated** and, as part of a packet-switching solution, two consecutive packets could travel **completely different routes**.

Most NOSs have a **traceroute** command or utility which provides information about the route being taken by a sample test packet.

Each node along the route is called a **hop**.

Bridge

A bridge is a network device that is used to **connect two different network segments**, usually ones that use the **same communication protocol** (though not always).

Unlike a repeater, the bridge is usually intelligent (it learns) and can make **decisions** about which packets of data should move from one segment to another by examining the target **MAC address**. In this regard they are similar to a switch and, indeed, are often described as a switch on an **Ethernet network**. In addition, they can **remove targets** from their 'forward' list if they have not had contact with the destination for some time; this lets the segment on the other side of the bridge remain fluid (i.e. devices can be added and removed without incident). A **wireless bridge**, a more recent invention, allows **wired extension** of a **wireless** network.

Gateway

A gateway is a device that acts as a **direct interface** between two **different** networks.

It is the gateway's job to translate from one network's **set of protocols** to those of the other network so that its data can be relayed **out** of the network.

It also performs a **routing function** so acts like a router; on a TCP/IP network, any data that is destined for a host **not on the current network** is forwarded to the gateway for processing.

A gateway may be a **dedicated device** or a **computer** which has suitable **hardware** (two network interface cards, one for connecting to each network) and **appropriate routing software**.

Wireless access point (WAP)

A wireless access point may be used to connect **wireless nodes** to a **wired network**, forming what is described as an **infrastructure mode**.

Figure 8.11 A WAP showing external antenna and RJ45 socket

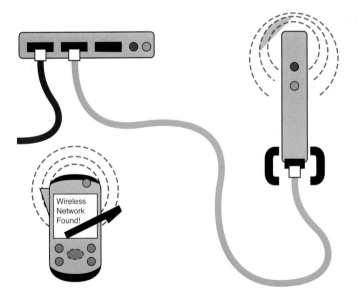

Figure 8.12 A PDA with wireless access connects to a WAP

A WAP is **wired traditionally** into a switch or router to gain access to the wider network.

From this point, the WAP usually broadcasts a **service set identifier** (**SSID**) – a **name** (up to **32 characters**) which is used to **identify it** to listening wireless devices. Broadcasting an SSID is a common practice, but **not ideal** from a security point of view.

In order to prevent unauthorised connection, WAPs typically feature **security** (**MAC filtering**) and **encryption facilities** (**WEP, WPA, WPA2 etc.**).

The MAC filtering prevents devices with **non-approved** **MAC addresses** from connecting wirelessly. This **access device list** is set up via the WAP's web-based user interface.

In addition, if encryption is enabled (and it really should be), a connecting device would need to have the correct **text** or **hexadecimal key** code in order to **decrypt** the transmitted data packets.

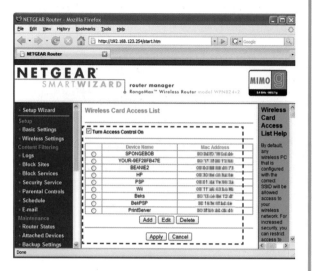

Figure 8.13 Filtering wireless devices by their MAC address

Planning a SoHO network

Your employer, **Lee Office Supplies**, is planning to network their current premises and has asked you to purchase equipment necessary to complete the task.

The building has a main office (ten PCs plus one printer), reception (one PC), the manager's office (one PC) and a storeroom (two PCs).

You have been asked to:

Supply all PCs with internet access

Share the office printer with all ten PCs

Draw up plans for this network, including costs for any network devices which must be purchased.

Building a simple LAN

Use the following **network diagram** as a **blueprint** to build a small **LAN** in a computer lab.

Shopping list:

◆ four PCs with NOSs (e.g. Microsoft Windows®)
◆ two wireless network cards (PCI)
◆ one WAP
◆ one switch (minimum four ports)
◆ two wired network cards (PCI)
◆ three × Cat 5 UTP cables.

The best way of checking your LAN is to assign each PC an IP address in the range **192.168.123.X** where X can be any value between 5 and 10. **No IP must be duplicated. Use a Ping command to check connectivity.**

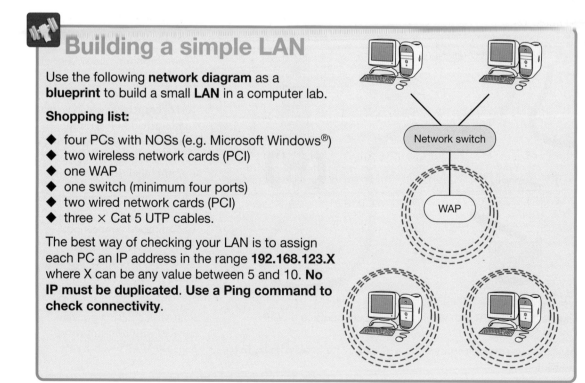

3 Understand transmission protocols and models

3.1 Model

Network technology comes in many different **shapes, sizes** and **configurations** and from many **different manufacturers worldwide**. Originally, manufacturers drew up their own **proprietary standards** which understandably generated **compatibility** issues.

In order to ensure i**nteroperability**, models were developed which provide **guidance standards** for creating **seamless network communication**, even though equipment and software will be created by different companies.

Perhaps the most **well-known standard** in communication technology is the **O**pen **S**ystems **I**nterconnection (**OSI**) model as pioneered by the **I**nternational **S**tandards **O**rganisation (**ISO**) back in 1984.

OSI

Commonly known as the **seven-layer model**, OSI looks like this.

7	Application layer
6	Presentation layer
5	Session layer
4	Transport layer
3	Network layer
2	Data link layer
1	Physical layer

What does OSI do?

As a conceptual framework, it defines all of the **basic services** a network should provide.

As noted, the model is divided into **seven layers**, each of which plays a key role in processing data and requests, enabling data to be transmitted between **any two points** in a network. Each layer **interacts directly** with the one **beneath** it and provides **functionality** for the layer **above** it.

How to remember the OSI model

Many **mnemonics** (memory aids) exist to help IT Practitioners remember the **seven layer names** and their **correct order**. Here are two common ones which may help:

(P)lease **(D)**o **(N)**ot **(T)**hrow **(S)**ausage **(P)**izza **(A)**way

(A)ll **(P)**eople **(S)**eem **(T)**o **(N)**eed **(D)**ata **(P)**rocessing

What does each stage do?

The following table describes the **purpose** of **each layer** and notes any **DCE** or **DTE** which are associated.

Layer number	Layer name	Purpose	Features
7	Application	A layer providing **network access** for **applications** (e.g. web browser etc.) A number of specific network protocols may occur here: ◆ **FTP** (file transfer protocol) ◆ **HTTP** (hypertext transfer protocol) ◆ **SMTP** (simple mail transfer protocol) ◆ **DNS** (domain name server) ◆ **TFTP** (trivial file transfer protocol) ◆ **NFS** (network file system) ◆ **Telnet** (terminal emulation) ◆ **Rlogin** (remote login)	Data
6	Presentation	This layer **translates data** into a **format usable** by the application layer above. In particular it is responsible for: ◆ **Translation** ◆ **Encryption** ◆ **Data compression**	Data (file formats include ASCII, .BMP, .JPG, .MPEG etc.)
5	Session	This layer allows applications on connecting systems to **establish** a **session**. It also provides **synchronisation** between **communicating computers**. In addition it **manages** and **terminates** these sessions as needed, determining how communications will occur.	Data
4	Transport	This layer is responsible for **end-to-end** communications; it **segments** and **reassembles** data into data streams. It **establishes**, **maintains**, and **ensures orderly termination** of virtual circuits. It can also **detect faults** in data transfer and can provide **recovery** and **information flow control**. The end result needs to be a **reliable service**.	Data is encapsulated into **segments**.
3	Network	The layer manages: ◆ **IP addressing** ◆ **Path selection** ◆ **Packet routing**	The **most important device** at this level is the **router**. Data is encapsulated into **packets**
2	Data link	Provides **point-to-point data transmission services** by **managing** the **physical layer** below. This layer has two sublayers: ◆ logical link control (**LLC**) ◆ media access control (**MAC**)	Devices such as **NICs, switches and bridges** Data is encapsulated into **frames**

1	Physical	The lowest level, it is concerned with the 'nuts and bolts' of the network; the electrical, the mechanical and timing issues etc.	Transmission media, e.g. cables and connectors, hubs, repeaters, DCE and DTE. Data is in bits

What are the advantages to breaking the model into separate layers?

There are many, but the main advantages are:

◆ easier to **develop network components**
◆ easier to **develop full networks**
◆ easier to **troubleshoot network problems**
◆ easier to **successfully manage a network** and **its resources**
◆ layers can be **improved in isolation** without **affecting others**.

Braincheck!

1 How many levels are there in the ISO OSI model?
2 Which level deals with end-to-end communication?
3 Name three data processes that the presentation is responsible for.
4 Which layer sees data in bits?
5 Which layer sees data encapsulated into segments?
6 Which layer sees data encapsulated into packets?
7 Which layer sees data encapsulated into frames?
8 Which layer would a router operate at?
9 Which layer would a NIC operate at?
10 When was the OSI created?

How well did you do? See page 421 for the answers!

3.2 Protocol

A number of different communication protocols may be found in a modern data communications network.

The following sections describes a number of **common technologies**, some **wired**, some **wireless**.

Bluetooth

Bluetooth is a wireless communication technology that was originally developed by Ericsson back in 1997.

Named after King Harald **Bluetooth** (Harold I of Denmark), Bluetooth is a popular IT industry specification for exchanging data between portable devices (**mobile telephones**, **PDAs**), **printers** and

notebook PCs. Although some computer systems have **onboard Bluetooth**, **inexpensive third-party USB Bluetooth adaptors** are **common** and relatively **inexpensive**, adding the facility to any PC.

It uses the **short-range**, **unlicensed** radio frequency of **2.45 GHz**.

As noted in **2.1**, Bluetooth can create secure **PANs**, connecting PCs together for the purpose of **exchanging data** and **sharing resources** and **services**.

Figure 8.14 A Belkin Bluetooth USB adaptor

Bluetooth scorecard

- Bluetooth supports data transfer rates of up to 2.1 Mbps.
- **Limited range** on low power (**<10 metres** is common).
+ Bluetooth **can penetrate** walls.
+ **Omnidirectional** – no direct **line of sight** (**LOS**) needed between devices.
+ Has **low power consumption**; ideal for mobile devices.
+ Use of **trusted pairs** to form secure connections.
+ **Configuration** is fairly simple.

Each Bluetooth device is identified by its own unique 48-bit number. Upon **discovery**, a Bluetooth device will reveal: its **name** (manufacturer and model), its **device class** (e.g. a PDA) and **a list of services it can provide** – the latter being supplied by the service discovery protocol (**SDP**).

In order to share these services, devices have to become **trusted**; this means sharing a **personal identification number** (**PIN**). The **PIN** is typically **alphanumeric** and up to **16 characters long**.

IrDA

IrDA®, which is a registered term for the Infrared Data Association, a non-profit organisation, specifies worldwide standards for infrared (IR) data transmission.

Members of the IrDA include a number of well-known 'household name' companies that specialise in **consumer electronics** and **telecommunications**.

Infrared (often abbreviated to **IR**) is a form of electromagnetic radiation that has a wavelength **longer** than visible light but **shorter** than that of microwaves and was discovered in the early nineteenth century.

Figure 8.15 A BAFO IrDA USB adaptor

Among its modern applications is **short-range data communication**, typically between portable devices such as **mobile telephones** and **PDA**s. You may be more familiar with IR as the method used to **change TV channels** via a **remote control handset**.

Infrared works by device 1 firing **LEDs** to create **data pulses** which are then received by **photodiodes** in a second device.

Excited by the light pulses received, the photodiodes **generate electrical current** which becomes an **electronic signal** for device 2 to process.

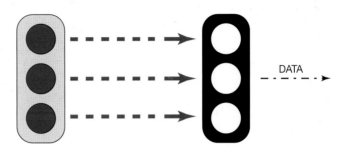

Infrared scorecard

- IrDA data standard has speeds up to 16 Mbps but is usually much slower.
- IR typically has a **short range** (limited to a few metres).
- IR **cannot penetrate** walls or solid objects.
- **Line of sight** (**LOS**) is required for IR to work effectively.
+ It is a tried and tested technology – it has been used for many years.

Wi-Fi (including 802.11x standards and security)

Wi-Fi (commonly and erroneously referred to as 'wireless fidelity') is the name given to the IEEE 802.11 **b** standards which cover **11 Mbps bandwidth** wireless networks operating in the **2.4 GHz** (unlicensed) frequency.

The Institute of **E**lectrical and **E**lectronic **E**ngineers (**IEEE**) is an international organisation that develops standards for many different types of modern technology.

The **802 committee** develops standards for **LANs** and **WANs**. A **subsection** of these standards, called **802.11**, concerns the use of **wireless networks**.

Here is a list of other notable 802.11 standards.

Standard	Year	Description
802.11	1997	Original 2 Mbps standard. **Now obsolete.**
802.11a	1999	Operates in 5 GHz frequency range, attracting less interference at a faster 54 Mbps. **Shorter range** than 802.11b and **not compatible.**
802.11d	2001	Standards for country-to-country roaming. Also known at the **global harmonisation** standard. It permits **location-sensitive** adjustments for **frequency, power levels** and **bandwidth.**
802.11e	2005 (delayed)	Incorporation of quality of service (**QoS**) to wireless network transmissions. QoS is vitally important for **time-critical** applications such as **voice over IP (VoIP)** and **streaming multimedia.**

Standard	Year	Description
802.11g	2003	Primarily for wireless LANs operating in **2.4 GHz** range but at a faster **54 Mbps**. Popular for small office, home office (**SoHO**) applications in the UK. Also **backwardly compatible** with **802.11b equipment**.
802.11i	2004	The introduction of enhanced security features (including **WPA2**).
802.11n	2004	A task force examining a theoretical speed increase to 540 Mbps.

Perhaps the biggest threat to wireless networking is **security**. In contrast to wired solutions, wireless networks are **particularly vulnerable** to **infiltration** and **data theft**.

It is possible to **unlawfully gain access** to a wireless connection using appropriate hardware and software. '**Wardriving**', the art of **driving around** looking for free, **unguarded** wireless signals, is well known, as is '**warchalking**' – **marking locations** of free wireless networks for **others** to exploit.

Security protocols used in 802.11

Security protocol	Year	Description	Strength
WEP Wired Equivalence Privacy	1999	Part of 802.11b standard. Optional security; not enabled on equipment by default. Weak encryption which can be cracked through network observation owing to recycled use of encryption keys.	●
WPA Wi-Fi Protection Access	2003	Released before 802.11i <u>finalised</u>. Replaces WEP, introduces temporal key integrity protocol TKIP which ensures that each data packet has a unique encryption key.	◐
WPA2 Wi-Fi Protection Access 2	2004	Part of 802.11i standard An enhanced form of WPA using advanced encryption standard (AES) rather than TKIP. AES is a US Federal standard for the encryption of commercial and government data.	○

Setting security on a wireless router

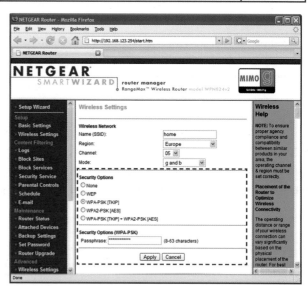

Figure 8.16 Enabling WPA passkey with TKIP

Wi-Fi Scorecard

+ Wi-Fi standards ensure global **interoperability** between different manufacturers' devices.
+ Wi-Fi signals **can** penetrate walls.
+ Enables easy, **inexpensive networking** in the home or small office where wired solutions are prohibitive.
+ **Ad hoc** or **infrastructure** modes available. Ad hoc mode allows wireless devices to connect to each other **without** a **WAP**. Infrastructure mode **requires** wireless devices to connect through a WAP.
− Normally uses unlicensed frequency of 2.4 GHz so **interference** can occur.
− **Slower** than a **physically wired** solution.
− **Security** can be **weak** if equipment is **obsolete** (WEP) or **badly configured**.
− **Three times more expensive** than Bluetooth.
− Uses **five times more power** then Bluetooth.

Cellular radio (e.g. GSM/UMTS, WAP, WML)

Mobile telephones act as **radio transceivers** meaning that they can both **transmit** and **receive** radio waves. These waves can be converted into **voice** or **data messages** depending on the type of call being made.

Messages are sent to other telephones via **base stations** (also know as **masts**). Large areas are covered by a **mosaic** of different cells. Each cell could cover up to **5 square miles** and sometimes their placement may cause them to **overlap**.

As a device **moves** from area to area, the device is **ordered** to move to a **new frequency** when a **new cell** is found with a **stronger signal**.

GSM

Global system for mobile communications (**GSM**) is a popular standard for mobile telephones in **Europe** and the rest of the world, providing a customer base of over **1.5 billion people**. GSM communication has a **narrow bandwidth** and, as a result, is primarily used for **voice communication**.

GSM standards are referred to as **second generation** (**2G**) because they use **digital signals** to communicate; earlier devices used **analogue signals** and are now retroactively referred to as 1G, although this term was never used then.

UMTS

The universal mobile telecommunications system (**UMTS**) is a **third generation** (**3G**) standard that supports **broadband**, data packet-based transmission of **text, music, video** and **digitised voice**.

An **extension** of GSM, it supports data rates up to a theoretical **2 Mbps**; fast enough to support **live video streaming** for films, television, sports events and video telephony.

WAP

Wireless Application Protocol is a **set of communication protocols** that allow **mobile telephones** to **access** online services and in particularly the **World Wide Web** (**WWW**).

WAP was originated by four companies: Phone.com, Ericsson, Motorola and Nokia.

WAP **content** is created in **wireless markup language** (**WML**), similar to **HTML** and **XML-compliant**, which is specifically designed for **portable devices** which have:

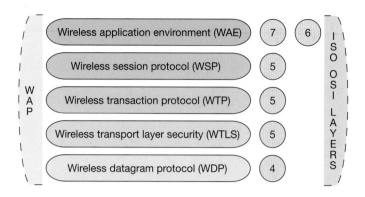

◆ limited bandwidth
◆ small screen size
◆ modest memory (RAM)
◆ short battery life
◆ low-powered CPU
◆ limited user-interface controls.

WML divides contents into **cards** (like a HTML page) and has various tags which permits fairly comprehensive user interfaces to be created.

```
<?xml version="1.0"?>

<wml>
<card id="Card1" title="WAP WML ">
<p>
This is basic WML.
</p>
</card>
</wml>
```

WAP has not been overly successful, particularly in its early days when mobile telephone WAP access (charged by the minute) proved **expensive** and delivered, compared to its PC + WWW 'big brother' a rather **lacklustre** experience.

Changes in **WAP billing** (measured by the downloaded data), **improved content** and cell provider **subsidised WAP minutes** have increased its popularity to a degree.

3.3 TCP/IP model

As its name suggests, the popular TCP/IP model consists of **two separate**, but **connected**, parts.

Both TCP and IP were developed by a United States Department of **De**fense's **A**dvanced **R**esearch **P**rojects **A**gency (**DARPA**) to connect a number of different networks together to form a much larger **inter-network** ('Arpanet', what became the 'internet').

In addition, the **inter-network** had to be reliable as even though it was envisaged that network links would be broken in times of armed conflict, communication and services would still be required.

As a result, DARPA designed TCP/IP to be **robust**, **automatically recovering** from any node failure; data would just get **routed** to the **destination** another way.

Let's examine each in a bit more detail.

Transmission control protocol (TCP)

TCP is a **connection-oriented** transport protocol.

TCP's primary job is to **verify that data** has been **correctly delivered** from **source node** to **destination node**.

In addition, TCP can:

◆ detect **errors**
◆ detect **duplicate messages**, **discarding** them as necessary
◆ detect **lost data**
◆ request **retransmission of data** until satisfied that it is both **correct** and **complete**
◆ use **flow control** to **slow data transfer** if the receiving node **cannot keep up**.

TCP works in conjunction with IBM's Network Basic Input/Output System (NetBIOS) to complete this task.

Internet protocol (IP)

As defined by IETF RFC791, IP's primary job is to **move data packets** from **one node** to the **next node**.

IP **forwards** each data packet based on a **4-octet** (8 bits) **destination address** (called the IP address). For example:

sender IP	192.168.123.**10**
destination IP	192.168.123.**20**
gateway IP	192.168.123.**254**

In this example, **host '10'** wants to send data to **host '20'**. All is fine as both machines are on the **same network** (192.168.123.0).

However, if a **different** destination IP (e.g. **4.233.183.99**) had been encountered, it would have been forwarded to the **gateway** IP (192.168.123.254) for routing out to another network.

Although the best-known version of IP is **IPv4**, it has its problems – **too few available IP addresses!** A newer version, IPv6 resolves this by having **128-bit addresses** (instead of 32 bits).

IP classes

Although IPv6 has been defined (increasing the addressing space to accommodate greater numbers of network-aware devices), it is version IPv4 that is in widespread use.

There are a number of IP classes currently in use.

Class A	Network addresses 1.0.0.0 through 127.0.0.0	N.H.H.H A 24-bit host part, allows 1.6 million hosts per network
Class B	Network addresses 128.0.0.0 through 191.255.0.0	N.N.H.H A 16-bit host part, allows for 16,320 nets with 65,024 hosts each
Class C	Networks addresses 192.0.0.0 through 223.255.255.0	N.N.N.H An 8-bit host part, allows for nearly 2 million networks with up to 254 hosts
Classes D, E and F	These network addresses, in the range 224.0.0.0 through 254.0.0.0, are either experimental or are reserved for special purpose (e.g. IP multicast)	

Some addresses are **reserved**: e.g. **127.0.0.1** is assigned as the 'loopback' interface.

This lets a networked computer system act like a closed circuit; any IP data packets sent to this address are returned to the client as if they had just arrived from some other network.

This lets the user develop and test networking software without ever using a 'live' network.

In addition, **hosts '0'** and **'255'** are **not permitted** as these represent the **number** and **broadcast address** respectively of the network.

```
C:\WINDOWS\system32\cmd.exe                                    _ □ ✕

C:\Documents and Settings\Mark>ping 127.0.0.1

Pinging 127.0.0.1 with 32 bytes of data:

Reply from 127.0.0.1: bytes=32 time<1ms TTL=128
Reply from 127.0.0.1: bytes=32 time<1ms TTL=128
Reply from 127.0.0.1: bytes=32 time<1ms TTL=128
Reply from 127.0.0.1: bytes=32 time<1ms TTL=128

Ping statistics for 127.0.0.1:
    Packets: Sent = 4, Received = 4, Lost = 0 (0% loss),
Approximate round trip times in milli-seconds:
    Minimum = 0ms, Maximum = 0ms, Average = 0ms

C:\Documents and Settings\Mark>
```

Figure 8.17 A ping is used to successfully test the loopback interface

An introduction to the subnet mask

The subnet mask is used to determine which parts of an IP address belong to the network (**N**) and which parts belong to the host (**H**).

In an example such as **192.168.123.45** (which is a **class C** address) the subnet mask (by default) will be:

255.255.255.0

This would indicate that the **first 3 octets** (**192.168.123**) are the **network address** and the connected device is **host number 45**.

The TCP/IP model

The TCP/IP model has **fewer levels** than the ISO OSI.

However, there is a clear **mapping** between TCP/IP **and** ISO OSI as shown by the following diagram.

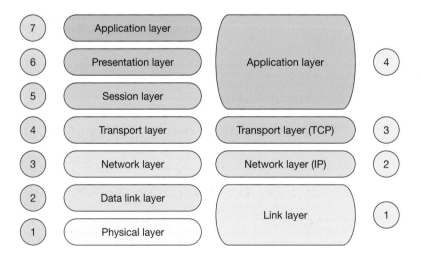

In more detail…

TCP layer number	Purpose
1	Defines the device driver and network hardware **NIC** – network interface card).
2	This layer handles basic communication, addressing and routing. Protocols seen here include **IP** (as discussed), **ARP** (address resolution protocol), **ICMP** (internet control message protocol) and **IGMP** (internet group management protocol).
3	This layer segments data into packets for transporting over the network. Both **TCP** and **UDP** (user datagram protocol) work at this layer. UDP is similar to TCP but **less reliable**; it does not **acknowledge** or **guarantee** safe delivery of data.
4	This layer deals with TCP/IP applications such as **Telnet, FTP, SMTP, Traceroute** etc.

4 Understand internet communications

4.1 Internet communication

Internet communication relies on a number of different technologies, each bringing its own terminology and jargon.

The more common ones are listed below.

Hypertext transfer protocol (HTTP)

Part of the internet suite of protocols, HTTP performs the **requests** and **retrieval** functions when a web browser tries to **load** a particular web page. This means that it is HTTP that is responsible for asking the **remote web server** for .html, images and sounds when they are specified by the **URL** input by the user in the address bar.

By default, HTTP operates through **port 80**. This is the same port that a remote web server would **listen to** (for requests). In addition, any **firewall** would need to **permit traffic** on this port.

The **HTTP protocol** is commonly seen as the **prefix** before the desired **website address**.

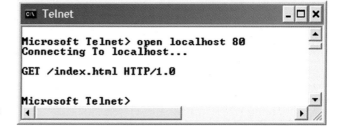

Figure 8.18 Telnet connects to the web server on port 80 and sends a HTTP request

In Figures 8.19 and 8.20, a **PC** is set up as a **web server** (using Apache) and is **simulating HTTP requests to itself.**

Figure 8.19 The web server responds to the HTTP request by returning the HTML file

This is essentially what is happening in the background when the same request is made from the web browser application.

It should be noted that '**localhost**' – the name being used for the web server – is actually the internal name for the **loopback address** (see 3.3)

Figure 8.20 The web browser client receives .HTML from the web server (localhost)

Do-it-yourself: installing a web server to test HTTP requests

What you will need:

◆ PC
◆ Windows® operating system (e.g. Windows 98, 2000, XP etc.)
◆ administrator rights to the operating system
◆ a copy of Apache HTTP web server (source: http://httpd.apache.org/).

Instructions:

1 Download and install the Apache HTTP web server.
2 Configure the web server correctly.
3 If firewalled, open port 80 for HTTP requests (likely to be open already).
4 Start the Apache web werver service.
5 Open a CMD prompt.
6 Start Telnet.
7 Connect to localhost.
8 Issue the HTTP request (ensure uppercase)

The web server should process the request and issue a 200 code ('OK – the requested resources have been sent').

Examine the HTTP header and HTML file returned.

Congratulations, you are now a **very basic** web browser!

Please remember to stop and uninstall the web server when you have finished!

URL

As we have seen, the **u**niform **r**esource **l**ocator (**URL**), is the **address of a resource** available on the internet.

Examples include:

◆ BBC News – World News main page   http://news.bbc.co.uk/1/hi/world/default.stm
◆ Doctor Who Web Page log   http://www.bbc.co.uk/doctorwho/images/furniture/tiny.gif

◆ Drunken Sailor midi sound file   http://www.contemplator.com/tunebook/midimusic/drnksailor.mid

HTTPS

HTTPS (**HTTP S**ecured) is similar to HTTP, however it uses **port 443** instead of the more familiar HTTP port 80.

This port change permits the use of an additional encryption/authentication layer **between** HTTP **and** TCP. It is often used for **security-sensitive communications** such as:

◆ online payment transactions
◆ online banking
◆ corporate log-ons.

Because the data being transmitted (e.g. credit cards, passwords etc.) is **encrypted** during **transport to** and **from** the server, any attempt to **intercept** the packets will be **pointless**; the data will be **meaningless** without the **decryption key**. The term **s**ecure **s**ockets **l**ayer (**SSL**) is often used in conjunction with this technology.

The HTTPS system was designed by **Netscape Communications Corporation** and is still in popular use today. However, it should be remembered that this technology only protects data **in transit, not at either end**: Both client and web server would still need to be protected from hackers.

Figure 8.21 Lloyds TSB Internet Banking – secured by HTTPS

File transfer protocol (FTP)

FTP is a common method for moving files over a network, from one computer system to another.

FTP predates the World Wide Web and has been popularised through the use of **anonymous FTP** – a file transfer between locations where the user does not need to specify a username or password.

FTP clients connect to an FTP server using **port 21**. The server responds on the same port, usually prompting for a username and password (unless it is anonymous FTP, of course).

Port 21 is only used for **server-side control**; the server and client would nominate **another port** for the actual data transfer itself.

FTP is generally seen as a **fast** and **reliable** file transfer protocol.

Simple mail transfer protocol (SMTP)

SMTP is a protocol used to **send** and **receive** email messages **between servers**. Another protocol (**p**ost **o**ffice **p**rotocol (**POP**) or the **newer**, more **flexible i**nternet **m**essage **a**ccess **p**rotocol (**IMAP**) is used by email client programs to **retrieve** the mail **from** a mail server.

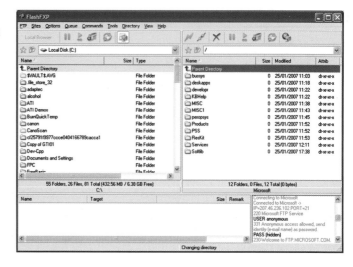

Figure 8.22 FlashFXP FTP client connects anonymously to the Microsoft® FTP site

SMTP is also used to send messages **from** a **mail client** to a **mail server**.

Mail client software needs to have server names specified for both incoming and outgoing mail. The incoming will be either POP or IMAP. The outgoing is likely to be SMTP.

Other forms of internet communication

Blogs

A **weblog** or just 'blog' is a **journal** (or **newsletter**), frequently updated and intended for public consumption on the World Wide Web.

Blogs generally mirror the **personality** of the author or the web site and may be **themed** or just present the **random musings** of the author as they reflect on the day's ups and downs, often revealing internal thought processes and ideas.

Readers are invited to **comment on** and **discuss** what they have read, sometimes helping the author to make sense of the events and life puzzles which have been perplexing them.

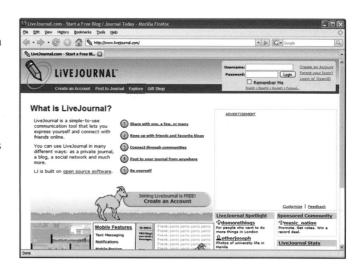

Figure 8.23 LiveJournal – a popular blogging community

Consequently, blogs can form an essential part of a **virtual community**.

A number of **blog communities** are active and popular:

◆ **LiveJournal** http://www.livejournal.com/
◆ **MySpace** http://blog.myspace.com/
◆ **Blogger** http://www.blogger.com/
◆ **TypePad** http://www.sixapart.com/typepad/

Wikis

A wiki is a **web-based application** that lets **normal users add new content** to existing online resources. In addition, it allows others to **edit the content** (though some user registration may be required).

Figure 8.24 A Wiki in progress

Complex **web-authoring functions** (such as **font, formatting, alignment, links** and **images**) are made simpler through a **basic user interface** that encourages **rapid creation** and **editing**. With the removal of **technical demands** from the process, the user can feel **creatively released** and **enjoy** the experience.

As such, it makes a wiki an effective tool for **performing mass collaborative authoring**. Wiki can also refer to the collaborative software used to create such web-based content.

Perhaps the most famous wiki is **Wikipedia** – an **online encyclopaedia**.

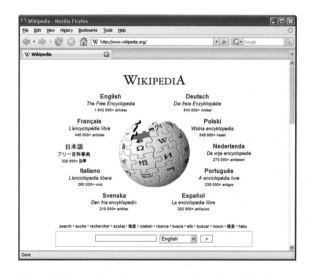

Figure 8.25 Wikipedia searchable front end

Video conferencing

Video conferencing is a system which uses a **computer**, **video camera** and a **broadband network** connection to conduct a **live conference** between two or more people, usually **geographically distant**.

It is a useful technique as it saves people the **expense** and **time-consuming travel** needed to accomplish face-to-face communication.

Instant messaging

Instant **messaging** (**IM**) is primarily **a text-based interface** that lets users **communicate in real time** over a network connection (including the internet).

When a message is received, the receiver is instantly notified and can choose to respond to the sender.

IM software and the IM network is generally free to use, often being supported through the use of **advertisements**. More advanced IM software permit group messaging and the use of **webcams** to provide **real-time video feeds**.

Functions such as **file transfer** are useful but can provide a way for **viruses** to enter a computer system, so **care** should be taken when accepting downloads.

Popular IM software applications include:

◆ **AIM®** (America On-line Instant Messenger) http://info.aol.co.uk/aim/

◆ **ICQ®** ('I seek you') http://www.icq.com/

◆ **Windows Live Messenger®** http://imagine-msn.com/ messenger/launch/en-GB/

◆ **Yahoo!® Messenger** http://messenger.yahoo.com/

Figure 8.26 AOL Instant Messenger

VoIP

VoIP is a technology which carries **voice communication** over an **existing IP network**; the specification includes the **digitisation** of the analogue voice signals and **conversion into packets** for transport.

VoIP is part of a larger scheme known as **IP Telephony**.

VoIP has become popular with larger **business corporations** and internet-enabled home users.

The major advantage to businesses is that VoIP helps **reduce running costs** because its telephone calls travel over its **own data network** rather than the **tele**phone **co**mpany's (Telco). In addition, it also means that a company using VoIP has better control over **security** and **voice quality**.

Figure 8.27 VoIP telephone

Skype, a free VoIP solution, was founded by Kazaa (peer-to-peer file sharing suite) creators Niklas Zennström and Janus Friis. With the free Skype application and a suitable headset/handset, users can call other Skype users for **free** and also call (SkypeOut) and receive calls (SkypeIn) from POTS numbers for a fee.

Skype: http://www.skype.com/

4.2 System requirements

Hardware and **software requirements** for **wired** and **wireless services** are discussed in 1.5, 2.2 and 2.3.

4.3 Direct communication

As discussed in **4.1**, direct communication can be achieved using video communication (webcams), instant messaging, email and VoIP.

Each of these electronic methods has a **social impact** – some **good** (distance is no longer a barrier to communication), some **bad** (not all forms of communication can be accurately duplicated using electronic means, e.g. body language etc.).

Links

Unit 8 is a **core unit** on the BTEC National Certificate and BTEC National Diploma for IT Practitioners (**Networking route**).

Unit 8 is also a **specialist unit** on the following BTEC National routes:

IT and Business

Software Development

Systems Support

There are particular links, however, to the following:

Unit 2 – Computer Systems

Unit 4 – IT Project

Unit 15 – Organisational Systems Security

Unit 16 – Maintaining Computer Systems

Unit 22 – Network Management

Unit 27 – Principles of Computer Networks

Unit 28 – IT Systems Troubleshooting and Repair

Unit 30 – Networked Systems Security

Unit 42 – Networking Basics (Cisco CCNA1)

Unit 43 – Routers and Routing Basics (Cisco CCNA2)

Unit 44 – Switching Basics and Intermediate Routing (Cisco CCNA3)

Unit 45 – WAN Technologies (Cisco CCNA4)

Unit 47 – Networking Essentials (Cisco IT Essentials 2)

Unit 50 – Networking Security (CompTIA Security+)

Unit 51 – Configuring and Troubleshooting Networks (CompTIA Network+)

Achieving success

This particular unit has 13 criteria to meet: 7 pass, 3 merit and 3 distinction.

For a **pass**:

You must achieve **all** 7 pass criteria.

For a **merit**:

You must achieve **all** 7 pass and **all** 3 merit criteria.

For a **distinction**:

You must achieve **all** 7 pass, **all** 3 merit **and all 3** distinction criteria.

So that you can monitor your own progress and achievement in each unit, a recording grid has been provided (see on next page). The full version of this grid is also included on the companion CD.

Assignment	Assignments in this unit			
	U8.01	U8.02	U8.03	U8.04
Referral				
Pass				
1				
2				
3				
4				
5				
6				
7				
Merit				
1				
2				
3				
Distinction				
1				
2				
3				

Help with assessment

This unit is fundamental to the Networking route. As such you are expected to **understand** and be able to **identify** and **explain** the underlying technologies and concepts related to the field of electronic communication.

The **merit** criteria see these concepts developed to ask you to understand the **need for error detection and correction** and the **circumstances** in which some **transmission media** are **preferred** over others. In addition, you will be required to **practically transfer data** between two devices.

For a **distinction** you must show **evaluation** and **justification** of particular **access methods**, be able to **compare wired** and wireless **networking** and be familiar with **network standardisation models** (ISO OSI and TCP/IP).

Online resources on the CD

Electronic glossary for this unit
Key fact sheets
Electronic slide show of key points
Flash animated tutorials

Further reading

Hallberg, B., 2005, *Networking: A Beginner's Guide*, 4th edn, Osborne/McGraw-Hill US, ISBN 0072262125.

Lowe, D., 2005, *Networking All-in-One Desk Reference for Dummies*, 2nd edn, Hungry Minds Inc US, ISBN 0764599399.

More, M., Southwick, P., Pritsky, T., and Riggs, C., 2001, *Telecommunications: A Beginner's Guide*, McGraw-Hill Education, ISBN 0072193565.

Schiller, J., 2003, Mobile communications, 2nd edn, Addison Wesley, ISBN 0321123816.

Unit 15

Organisational Systems Security

Capsule view

Organisational Systems Security is a full 60-hour unit that focuses on the **dangers** that **modern enterprises** face in the up-to-the-minute **digital** age.

Looking at both **internal** and **external threats**, this unit describes the **most common** forms of **attack**, the **best** forms of **defence** and the **resulting costs** of **being poorly protected**.

Additional themes will tackle **moral** and **ethical** use of ICT systems and the **professional bodies** that are there to help.

Learning aims

1 Know potential threats to ICT systems and organisations.
2 Understand how to keep systems and data secure.
3 Understand the organisational issues affecting the use of ICT systems.

> **Key Terms**
>
> **Unauthorised access** occurs when a person or group of individuals gain admission to a **location** or **use** a piece of **equipment**, **data** or **information** for which they have **no** permission.

1 Know potential threats to ICT systems and organisations

1.1 Unauthorised access

Unauthorised **internal** or **external** access can cause **damage** to data or the **blocking** of important **resources** (e.g. a virus scrambling vital data) or **services** (e.g. email being disabled).

It is also possible to access a system without authorisation and create **no** (or little) **damage**. When this happens, it may take **some time** before the infiltration is **noticed**.

Common examples of unauthorised access include:

◆ hacking
◆ phishing

- identity theft
- piggybacking.

While piggybacking is generally seen to be the act of using a legitimate user's credentials to follow them into a building or system, the other examples listed require a little more detailed explanation.

Figure 15.1 Phishing filter on Microsoft Internet Explorer® 7

Phishing filters tend to work by keeping **lists of reported phishing sites** on a **remote server** which the browser can **check against. Flagged sites** can then be **blocked** and the user **informed**.

Key Terms

Hacking was once a term used to describe programmers making harmless changes to existing programs. More commonly these days it is a term used to identify the **illegal practice** of an individual accessing **other people's computer systems** for the purpose of **destroying**, **copying** or **modifying** the data they find there, usually for **fun**, **spite** or **financial gain**.

Key Terms

A more modern and cynical tactic, **phishing** (pronounced 'fishing') is a type of **financial fraud** committed **over the Internet** that tries to **steal valuable personal information** (PIN, passwords, credit card numbers) by simply **asking** the **user** to **reveal them**!

The trick is that the **email** received (or **faked websites** visited) by the user are designed to look real, **imitating legitimate businesses** which the user **may** really have business with (e.g. a bank, insurance company or an online shop).

Phishing relies on the user **trusting** and **responding** to these requests. Modern **web-browsing software** such as Microsoft **Internet Explorer®** and Mozilla **Firefox®** have **phishing filters** which aim to **protect** their users against such threats.

Key Terms

Identity theft is **not** a new threat, but it does represent one of the **fastest growing crimes** in the United Kingdom.

A survey in 2005 by Which? Magazine discovered that **25 per cent** of **all UK adults** have either had **their identity stolen** or **know someone else** who **has**. This is a frightening statistic.

More traditional techniques typically involve **interception** or **theft** of **personal items**, for example:

- wallet, purse or handbag theft
- discarded bank statements, invoices, personal letters that may be found discarded in a rubbish bin
- mail deliveries.

Thieves committing 'ID theft' can **access** existing accounts, commit **fraud**, **start loans** or **buy expensive items** using credit agreements.

The increase in electronic data storage and transfer has meant that it is easier than ever to use another person's identity to perpetrate such illegal acts.

Chip and **PIN**

Figure 15.2 Chip and PIN logo

Activity

Find out what **forms of identity** are required to:

1 **open** a typical **current account** at a bank or building society in the United Kingdom
2 **purchase a car** from a showroom in the United Kingdom
3 **apply** for a United Kingdom **passport**
4 **open** an **email account** such as Gmail, AIM Mail or MSN Hotmail.

1.2 Damage to or destruction of systems or information

Damage to systems or information can be caused by **natural disasters (or 'Acts of God')**:

◆ fire
◆ flood
◆ earthquake

◆ hurricane
◆ tidal wave
◆ tornado.

Of course, as valuable as working systems or information are to an organisation, they **may not** be **mission critical**; **systems** can be **rebuilt**, **information** can be **reprocessed** from source data. Unique employees lost to such devastation **cannot** so easily be replaced.

Malicious damage may also occur through **internal** or **external** means.

Internal

◆ Disgruntled employee **breaks** or **sabotages equipment**.
◆ Disgruntled employee **deletes** or **tampers** with **sensitive data**.
◆ Disgruntled employee **makes sensitive data publicly known**.

External

◆ **Hacking**.
◆ **Theft**.

◆ **Criminal damage**.
◆ **Industrial espionage** from rivals and competitors.

Damage may also occur through less malicious means.

Technical failures

All devices have a **point of failure** – they will **inevitably** fail at some point in the future.

Generally, as devices **become more** complex, so does the act of predicting all of the **possible failures** that **might** occur.

Avoid technical failures through:

◆ **thorough user training** so equipment is used **properly** and **safely**
◆ **regular preventative maintenance** that **spots** faults **early**
◆ **investment** in **new, more reliable** (or **replacement**) technology
◆ having a **backup plan** – i.e. another way of doing things when technology fails.

Human errors

It is a basic fact: **people make mistakes**. Moreover, they can make **silly** mistakes (which may have little impact) and **colossal errors of judgement** which may be **life-threatening** to **themselves** or **others**.

In an organisation, it is **helpful** if employees **feel** that they can reveal any errors made without fear of **immediate** disciplinary action.

Organisations where employees **fear making errors** often lead to employees naturally **covering them up** and potentially **making matters worse** when the problem is **eventually discovered**.

1.3 Information security

It is an organisation's legal responsibility (see section 3.4) to ensure that information and data are:

◆ **kept confidentially** (access only given to those who have a **right** and **need** to know)
◆ **kept with integrity** (kept safely and in a state of completeness)
◆ **made available** (when asked for, with appropriate permission, as needed).

1.4 Threats related to e-commerce

Organisations that rely on e-commerce solutions are obviously open to threats through their ICT systems.

Although traditional organisations may be able to function while a loss of ICT service is encountered, the **impact** on e-commerce-reliant organisations is **much greater** and can completely **debilitate** their day-to-day **interactions** with their **customers**.

Common threats to ICT systems include:

◆ **website defacement**
◆ **DoS** (Denial of Service) **attacks**
◆ **customer phishing** (see section 1.1, phishing)
◆ **theft of customer information**.

Perhaps the most serious threat here is that of **website defacement**. Since an e-commerce organisation relies on its **website presence** to **attract** World Wide Web traffic and custom, its disruption can be fundamentally **crippling**.

During 2005, a survey produced by **Zone-H** revealed that the **majority** of **400,000 recorded web-server attacks** were due to **website defacement**. In simple terms that figure translates to over **2500 web servers** being the victims of **unauthorised access** and **malicious damage** each and **every single day**.

Most web-server attacks are **speculative**, taking **advantage** of **weak administration security** (guessable **passwords** or **unencrypted** files) or **security flaws** in the **software** itself.

Most website defacement is done for **fun**, acting as a twenty-first-century form of personal expression akin to street-level graffiti, with hackers leaving their distinctive 'tags' behind as a mark of achievement and expression. More damaging attacks are made for making **political** or **personal** views about the **organisation** or **its services**. Some case could be made that such attacks are highlighting the (sometimes) serious security flaws which exist in commercial websites that process sensitive customer information.

In either case, such defacements **undermine** both the organisation's **professional image** and their **current** clients' (and **potential** clients') **trust** and **faith** in them.

Organisations who have **suffered website defacements** are both **numerous** and **diverse**; they include:

- ◆ Panasonic
- ◆ Xerox Records.
- ◆ The Samaritans
- ◆ US Army
- ◆ Virgin

Unit Link

Unit 34 (e-Commerce) provides a more detailed insight into this relatively new and popular form of business and the organisations that use it.

1.5 Counterfeit goods

Counterfeit goods are those which are inferior, illegally copied and may be unsafe for use by the general public. They are placed on sale and advertised as the genuine article even though the seller will be aware that they are not real. This is a form of fraud, another illegal act.

Common **products** which are often counterfeited include:

- ◆ **commercial software applications** (including **games** for both PCs and consoles)
- ◆ **DVDs** (films, television, concerts)
- ◆ **games**
- ◆ **music**
- ◆ **clothes** (especially designer labels) and **shoes** (e.g. trainers).

Common **distribution mechanisms** for counterfeit goods include:

- ◆ **online auction sites** (e.g. eBay), although this is **against** online auction sites' code of practice and such lots are often pulled by the auction administrators.
- ◆ **car boot sales**

Figure 15.3 eBay policy on replica, counterfeit items and unauthorised copies

- **classified ads** in newspapers
- **personal contact**
- **peer-to-peer** (P2P) **networks** (e.g. BitTorrent, eDonkey, Gnutella etc.).

A peer-to-peer network operates by relying on the **distributed bandwidth** and **processing power** of a number of **different** computer systems. When a file (such as a .MP3 music track or game) is **announced**, a number of 'hosts' can be accessed which each have **small chunks** of the file. These chunks are then **glued together** to **reform** the complete **file**. While these chunks are being downloaded (in any order), the user's

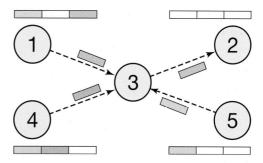

Figure 15.4 P2P network; computer 3 downloads from hosts 1, 4 and 5 and serves 2

computer system **becomes** a host **itself**, **serving** the file chunks it already has to **other** users. This process continues until **all users** have the files they want.

Although peer-to-peer networks have a **legitimate purpose** and **can** be used lawfully, a lot of **copied** (and therefore **counterfeit**) **electronic data** (images, video, music and software) is **illegally swapped** this way.

The difficultly in policing this type of network is that it is **decentralised** and therefore is **very robust** and **complicated** to **track**. It is precisely this threat that has mobilised the introduction of **d**igital **r**ights **m**anagement (**DRM**) in the **music industry**.

Trading Standards

In the UK, local **Trading Standards** are tasked with protecting customer interests when it comes to traditionally purchased counterfeit goods. They are guided by various pieces of legislation but primarily refer to:

- The Sale of Goods Act 1979 (as amended)
- The Supply of Goods and Services Act 1982

Jurisdiction over goods purchased online can sometimes be more difficult to decide.

1.6 Organisational impact

The impact of **weak systems security** on an organisation can be **severe.**

Common problems which occur as a result of security breaches include:

- **loss of service** – services such as email, customer order processing or finance not working
- **loss of business** or **income** e.g. through deletion or corruption of customer records, payments or orders
- **increased costs**, e.g. for repair of systems, recreation of lost data
- **poor image**, e.g. customers reacting to poor service or poor reputation.

It is not unknown for some organisations to become **bankrupt** (i.e. go out of business) through the **impact** of a security breach.

This is generally why organisations take security of ICT and non-ICT systems seriously and are willing to **invest money** into their **installation** and **maintenance.**

2 Understand how to keep systems and data secure

2.1 Physical security

These are **tangible** security measures – things that you can **see** and **touch**.

Physical security measures include:

◆ **locked doors** (manual or time based)
◆ use of **visitor identification passes** (ideally with a photograph)
◆ use of visitor or employee **sign in/out logs**
◆ use of **closed circuit television** (CC-TV)
◆ use of **security guards** and **regular patrols**
◆ use of **cable shielding** to prevent unwanted signal transmission.

> **Key Terms**
>
> **Biometrics** is a term used to describe systems which authenticate users by the use of **physical characteristics** such as **facial structure**, **hand geometry**, **fingerprints**, **retina patterns**, **DNA** (**d**eoxyribo**n**ucleic **a**cid), **signature** or **voice recognition**.

2.2 Biometrics

Additional security may be achieved through the use of biometric devices.

Biometric systems are generally **expensive** (as they require complex scanning equipment and processing software) but they do **provide highly distinctive** results.

Although simple fingerprint scanning is now available on upper-end notebooks, biometrics is usually reserved for **high-security applications** where the **costs of installing** such systems are far outweighed by the **fear** and **risk** of **compromised** system security.

Activity

Find out which **commercial biometric systems and devices** are currently available for:

◆ fingerprints
◆ voice pattern
◆ signature
◆ retina pattern.

Try to keep within a budget of £200 for each device.

Is this possible for each type of biometric device?

Figure 15.5 Fingerprint biometric device

2.3 Software and network security

In any organisation that uses ICT systems, a **mixture** of **different techniques** can (and should) be used to **improve security**. Some of these techniques are **software-based**, some are **procedural** (things to do) and some are **physical actions** (that must be performed).

The following sections examine each of these in more detail.

Software-based security

The most common types of software that can be used to improve security are:

◆ the **operating system** itself (and setting of appropriate **user rights** and **privileges**)
◆ **antivirus suites**
◆ **antispyware suites**
◆ **firewalls**.

In addition, the importance of keeping software **correctly updated** cannot be overstated. **Hackers** will often **exploit** known **security flaws** in an **application** or **operating system**. **Patches**, which address these **identified security loopholes**, are **released regularly** by software **developers** and **publishers**.

They should be **downloaded** and **installed** as a matter of organisational policy.

Unit links

Section 2.2, software utilities, in **Unit 2** (Computer Systems) provides a full overview of antivirus, antispyware and firewall software.

Unit links

Section 3.1, software maintenance, in **Unit 2** (Computer Systems) provides a full overview of installing patches.

Key Terms

Encryption is a **software-based technique** for improving an organisation's ICT security, used on both **local workstations** and **networks** (particularly those which are **wirelessly connected**). It is formally known as **cryptography**.

Encryption uses a **pairing** of a **private** and **public key** to create a **digital signature**.

Both must be known in order to **encode** and **decode** data **successfully** – the public key made freely available to 'lock' data, the private kept safely in order to decrypt.

Procedural

Procedural aspects of an organisation would include some elements that we will see in section 3.1 (security policies and guidelines).

Procedures may include the installation and routine running of certain software and network tools, these include:

◆ **scheduler** for **routine data backup** (e.g. each night)
◆ **creation** of **audit logs** to detail software and network usage
◆ **intruder-detection systems** to spot **attempts** at **accessing** particular **network addresses** or **ports**
◆ creation and use of **passwords**
◆ creation and use of **user accounts** which define **levels of access** to sensitive data.

Physical actions

Regular processes may include physical actions that must be undertaken in order to maintain the security of an organisation's ICT system.

An example of such an action is the installation of diskless workstations; these are simply desktop computer systems which have **no removable media drives** (e.g. **floppy diskette, magnetic tape, recordable** and/or **rewriteable CDs** and **DVDs**). In addition it is not unknown to find **external USB and fireware ports disabled** by the installation of **metal cover plates** or **hard resin plugs**.

This simple measure prevents organisational data from being **manually copied** from the network or local workstation. Conversely it **also prevents virus infection** of workstations which occurs when employees bring removable media from **outside**.

VPNs

The creation of **virtual private networks** (**VPNs**) is also a common technique that is used by organisations to secure their data.

The primary advantage is that the organisation can **safely** (and **securely**) **extend** its private network across a **much larger** geographic area. Using a **publicly available** infrastructure, it can also do this **exceptionally cheaply**.

It is a particularly popular method for connecting **distant branch offices** and **teleworkers** (employees working **flexibly from home**) who rely on **telephone** and **computer access** to perform their everyday job function).

> **Key Terms**
>
> A **VPN** works by transmitting **private** network data **over** a **public** telecommunication **infrastructure** (such as the **Internet**). It does this by using a **connection** formed by a **tunnelling protocol**.
>
> **Tunnelling** works by placing **packets of data** inside **other** data packets. The infrastructure network deals with (and routes) the 'outer' packet, leaving the 'inner' payload (the VPN data) alone.
>
> VPNs also make use of **encryption, firewalls** and **authentication services** to **secure both ends** of the VPN connection (i.e. the **remote end user** and the **organisation's network**).

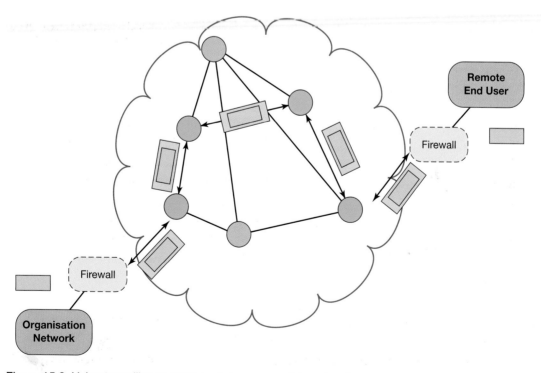

Figure 15.6 Using tunnelling to send packets over a public network

3 Understand the organisational issues affecting the use of ICT systems

3.1 Security policies and guidelines

Any organisation with **substantial** ICT system coverage will have a number of **policies** in place that **specify the actions required** to **deal** with **problems**, **routine** or **non-routine** circumstances that occur.

These can be categorised as follows.

Disaster recovery policy

This is a **statement** or **plan** of what to do when things go **horribly wrong**, through acts of theft, destruction (natural causes or through deliberate vandalism) or loss of data which **impact severely** on the business function (or security) of the organisation.

Updating of security procedures

As ICT technology is continually evolving, then so must the security procedures used within the organisation. This update should be done on a **regular basis**, usually **reviewed** by the organisation's head of ICT security or IT services. This may be achieved in conjunction with **outside agencies** (e.g. external security consultants or the police) and an **internal** IT strategy group.

Scheduling of security audits

Security audits on procedures, physical resources, equipment, software and logical protections need to be scheduled regularly. This will highlight any **irritations**, **opportunities** or **potential threats** that can be dealt with effectively by **strategic planning**.

Communications policy

In addition, many organisations ask employees to sign a **communications policy** as part of their **contract of employment**. It will detail their **permissions** and **rights** when interacting with an organisation's **ICT systems**.

This **code of conduct**, aimed at **improving** ICT systems security, may include guidance on:

◆ **email** usage
◆ **internet** usage
◆ **backing up data** files
◆ making **new** software and **hardware requests**
◆ software **installation**
◆ **reporting** of **system errors**
◆ **reporting** of **security breaches**.

Other

In addition, **surveillance** and **monitoring policies** will be introduced; the **exact details** of these **may** or **may not** be **made known** to general employees (see section 3.6).

Risk management (particularly **financial** and **health and safety** related) would also be examined documented.

Budget setting for purchasing of **new equipment** and **software** will also need to be considered as part of the organisation's **overall business plan**. Most organisations will use a **four-year cycle** for updating hardware with **major upgrades** to operating systems and application software being laid down in a **road map** or **implementation plan** that may be **drawn up** (and agreed) **many months** before it is **actually** begun.

Typically **ad hoc** (as and when needed) improvements to security through the use of **incremental software updates** will be considered **routine** and **not require** separate policies as this would prove **impractical** based on their high **frequency**.

3.2 Employment contracts and security

Hiring policies

Depending on the sensitive nature of the organisation's business, **hiring policies** will specify different levels of background check on a potential employee.

For example, a sensitive government organisation might interview family, friends and previous employers rather than just relying on information written on an application form.

Generally, the following information may be requested and checked to help screen out undesirable applicants:

◆ previous employment
◆ criminal record (convictions and cautions)
◆ health records.

Employees who are later found to have **lied** (or **deliberately misled** their employers through failing to mention pertinent facts about themselves) may find themselves **dismissed**.

Separation of duties

This is an **internal security tool** used by organisations to ensure that **no one employee** has **100 per cent control** of a process from **start** to **finish**.

Separation of duties typically works by giving **checking duties** to **another employee** who can catch **deliberate** (i.e. **fraudulent** or **malicious**) **actions** or **genuine mistakes** in a system. The availability of detailed **audit tools** and **activity logs** makes this process much easier.

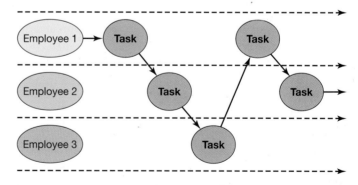

Figure 15.7 Task is split across three employees, with each tasked with checking

Training and communication

Regular training is part of an organisation's **commitment** to its staff's continuing and professional development (**CPD**). In addition, it **ensures** that the employee is both **capable** of **performing** the **tasks required** of them and **aware** of **recent changes** to **policy** that may **affect them** or **their role**.

Internal communication is also a **vital tool** to **improve security**, helping employees to understand their **personal and professional responsibilities within** the organisation and the **overall strategic aims** which are being pursued.

Ensuring compliance

Compliance is generally **assumed** in an organisation but employees are usually **made aware** of the **penalties** of **not working** to policies as agreed; this will obviously include security-related issues.

A code of conduct as laid down in their **contract of employment** (and usually an **organisational handbook**) will detail the **disciplinary steps** taken for unacceptable breaches.

These breaches may typically include (in ascending order of severity): **verbal warning**, **written warning**, **final interview** and **then dismissal** (the 'sack').

3.3 Code of conduct

As discussed in overview (section 3.1), many organisations use a **communications policy** to specify a **code of conduct** for employees when **interacting** with their ICT systems.

Typically this revolves around **key** ICT concerns that affect an organisation's security.

Non-compliance with such policies will undoubtedly lead to disciplinary action.

Email usage policy
◆ Acceptable language to use in an email.
◆ What personal views can be expressed in an email.
◆ What can be emailed externally (i.e. sent to clients and external entities).
◆ Printing restrictions.
◆ Inbox restrictions.
◆ Frequency of reading and replying to email communication.
◆ Attachments.
◆ Forwarding of spoofs, jokes or chain mail.

Internet usage policy
◆ **Which** web sites can be visited (appropriate content).
◆ **When** the Internet (World Wide Web) can be used for personal use (i.e. lunch time only).
◆ What can be **uploaded** or **downloaded** to/from a web site (e.g. inappropriate images).
◆ What can be **posted** on an online **message board, forum** or **newsgroup**.

Software acquisition

◆ What software **can** be used on an internal system.
◆ What software **must not** be used on an internal system (e.g. illegal or insecure).
◆ How to **officially request new** software or hardware.

User area usage policy

◆ How much **storage space** a user has in their own personal area.
◆ **What** can be **stored** in this storage space.
◆ **Who** is a**llowed access** to this storage space.

Account management policy

◆ Regular update of password (e.g. every 30 days).
◆ Robustness of password (e.g. alphanumeric, minimum six letters, upper and lower case).
◆ Letting other users know your password and use your account.
◆ Rights and privileges given to a user account based on organisational role.

3.4 Laws

Security-related legislation can vary from country to country and this can cause problems for organisations which operate globally. In the UK however, familiarisation with the following laws can be seen as a good starting point.

Protecting the organisation and the customer

UK Data Protection Act 1998

This legislation ensures that any **personal data** is:

1 processed **fairly** and **lawfully**
2 obtained for **specified** and **lawful** purposes
3 **adequate, relevant** and not **excessive**
4 **accurate** and **kept up to date**
5 **not** kept **any longer than necessary**
6 **processed** in accordance with the data subject's (the individual's) **rights**
7 kept reasonably **secure**
8 **not transferred** to any **other country without** adequate **protection**.

The original Data Protection Act was published in **1984** with **revisions** in **1998** designed to incorporate the European Union's (EU) 'Directive 95/46/EC on the protection of individuals with regard to the processing of personal data and on the free movement of such data'.

UK Copyright Designs and Patents Act 1988

In simple terms, a **copyright** is the **exclusive legal right** to **use** an **expression** or **idea** (known as intellectual property). It is indicated by use of the familiar © **symbol**.

In British law, the **initial** owner of a copyright is **assumed** to be the original **creator** of the intellectual property (IP).

However, any work that is created by an **employee** in the course of their **employment** gives the **employer** copyright ownership. This is usually part of the **employee's contract**.

In addition the **owner** of the work **may not** be the actual **copyright holder**; for example a letter sent from Person A to Person B is **owned** by Person B, but **cannot be published without the permission** of Person A (as the creator, **they** are the copyright **holder**).

The purpose of copyright is to **give** the **creator protection** against **unauthorised duplication** of their IP. **IP** covered by copyright can include such creative works as books, films, music, photographs, paintings and software (see **FAST**, section 3.6). When **copyright expires**, the IP is said to have **lapsed** into the **public domain**.

In 1996, the EU **extended** the period of copyright to **70 years after the year** in which the **creator died** (although there are some exceptions). This is often referred to as **post mortem auctoris (PMA)**.

In the UK, a concept called '**fair dealing**' grants some **exclusions** to copyright for the purposes of **academic** or **review purposes**, particularly where the IP is used in a **non-profit making** venture. As a matter of courtesy, an **acknowledgement** of the copyright holder's **permission** should be publicly made.

Computer Misuse Act 1990

This act **helps organisations** by providing **three basic protections** against:

1 **unauthorised access** to computer **material**
2 **unauthorised access** to a computer system with **intent to commit** or **facilitate the commission of a further offence**
3 **unauthorised modification** of computer **material**.

Of particular interest are parts 1 and 3; part 1 targets **hacking** (whether the **unauthorised access** is **internal** or **external**). Part 3 targets **deliberate damage** caused to **programs** or **data**; this would include deliberate **virus infection** or **deletion** and **alteration** of data.

Offenders caught breaking these laws would be subject to either a Magistrates or Crown court; depending on the **severity** of the offence and damage incurred, punishment could range from **substantial fines** and **community service** to **one or two years in prison**.

Activity

The following website lists **real-world cases** where individuals have been taken to court for charges associated with the **Computer Misuse Act 1990**.

http://www.computerevidence.co.uk/Cases/CMA.htm

Explore this resource (and its news site links) and determine which parts of the act are most commonly broken and the types of security breach which have been attempted.

Freedom of Information Act 2000 (Scotland 2002)

Introduced in **November 2000** and coming into full effect from **1 January 2005**, the Freedom of Information Act (**FOIA**) gives its citizens **right of access** to **any information that is held about them** by **public bodies**.

The range of public bodies is quite broad, but **notable** examples include:

◆ local authorities (e.g. council departments etc.)
◆ police authorities
◆ National Health Service (NHS) authorities
◆ schools and colleges.

There are some **exceptions** to these, of course, but generally a **written request** to any such body under this act should **force** the authority to confirm **whether** they have information, **what it is** and require them to **provide a copy** of it.

For further information see: www.opsi.gov.uk/acts/acts2000/20000036.htm

3.5 Copyrights

In addition to being aware of the various laws related to security, organisations which deal with operating systems and applications software must be clear on the **distinction between** their **different legal categorisations**.

Key Terms

Open source can be **freely distributed** and users can **make changes** to the program's **source code** and **modify it** as they see fit. Well-known examples include: **Linux** and the **Apache HTTP Web Server**.

Freeware is copyrighted software offered 'as is' with **no charge** to the user. Some commercial software is offered as **scaled-down**, fully functional freeware as an attempt to **encourage users** to buy the fuller versions. It may be **limited** to **non-commercial use**, however (i.e. for students or personal use only).

Shareware is typically a '**try before you buy**' **time-limited trial** or **function-limited version** of commercial software. Users happy with the software then purchase the full version when the **evaluation period** has expired.

Commercial software is software **purchased** (usually at **retail**) from a software publisher which has **extensive legal protection** in the form of an **end user licence agreement** (**EULA**) which prohibits **illegal duplication**, **reverse engineering** and **modification** of the program's code. Source code is **not** usually made available. Well-known examples include: **Microsoft Windows®**.

Braincheck!

Investigate the following software applications and operating systems and decide whether they are available as open source, freeware, shareware or commercial software:

◆ OpenOffice suite
◆ WinZip
◆ CutePDF Writer
◆ AVG Anti-virus
◆ Apple QuickTime
◆ FreeBSD

How well did you do? See page 421 for the answers!

3.6 Ethical decision making

Security concerns often **clash** with the concept of **personal privacy** and the **rights** of the **individual** in **society**.

For example, information about **where** an individual **lives** can be easily **pieced together** through examination of the local council's **electoral roll**, the **telephone book** and available **street maps**.

It is perhaps fair to say that **ethical decision making** takes over where the legislation **stops**, forcing the **organisation** or **individual** to examine **whether** what they are doing is **crossing** any **moral** or **ethical boundaries**. Examples of this may include:

◆ **use** of **photographs** in an **appropriate** way
◆ **placement** and **use** of **video** captured by **CCTV cameras**
◆ **logging** of employee **activities**.

In most cases it may be sufficient to simply **ask for permission** to commit such actions or at least make people **aware** that **it is happening** (and **why**).

3.7 Professional bodies

Many professional bodies exist which offer organisations advice and guidance on security issues. As an IT student you should be familiar with the following bodies:

◆ Business Software Alliance (**BSA**)
◆ Federation Against Software Theft (**FAST**)
◆ British Computing Society (**BCS**)
◆ Association for Computing Machinery (**ACM**).

Let's examine each one in a little more detail:

Professional body	Description
Business Software Alliance (BSA)	 Figure 15.8 BSA logo Established in 1988, the BSA is the leading voice of software industry before governments and businesses around the world. It serves to educate business owners and IT decision-makers about software management and intellectual property rights in order to encourage use of legitimate software and reduce software piracy. BSA programmes also advocate for technology innovation through education and public policy to promote copyright protection, cyber-security trade and e-commerce. **UK website presence:** http://www.bsa.org/uk/
Federation Against Software Theft (FAST)	 Figure 15.9 FAST logo Source: http://www.fast.org.uk/logo. jpg Established in 1984, it was the world's first antipiracy organisation that worked to protect a creator's IP (intellectual property). In 1988 it succeeded in lobbying the UK Parliament to include the phrase 'computer program' in the Copyright, Designs and Patents Act, thereby formally defining programs as literary works and as a result providing them the same rights and copyright protections as a book, magazine or journal. Since then it has focused on pursuing software copyright infringement through the UK's civil and criminal procedures. It has also attempted to educate consumers, students, organisations and the media about infringement of copyright for software-based IP. **UK website presence:** http://www.fast.org.uk/
British Computing Society (BCS)	 Figure 15.10 BCS logo Source: http://www.bcs.org/img/bcs/ bcslogo.gif

British Computing Society (BCS) cont.	The BCS was formed in 1957 and now has a worldwide membership of over 55,000 IT professionals. It is seen as the leading body for those working in the IT industry. A registered charity, the core objectives of the BCS are to encourage the study and practice of computing, advancing the public's knowledge and skills in IT. **UK website presence:** http://www.bcs.org/
Association for Computing Machinery (ACM)	 *Advancing Computing as a Science & Profession* **Figure 15.11** ACM logo ACM www.acm.org, established in 1947, is an educational and scientific society uniting the world's computing educators, researchers and professionals to inspire dialogue, share resources and address the field's most pressing challenges. ACM strengthens the profession's collective voice through strong leadership, promotion of the highest standards, and recognition of technical excellence. ACM supports the professional growth of its members – over 84,000 from more than 140 countries – by providing opportunities for life-long learning, career development, and professional networking.

Activity

Using an active internet connection and access to the World Wide Web, find out about the following professional bodies:

1 Investors in **S**oftware (**IIS**)
2 **S**oftware and **I**nformation **I**ndustry **A**ssociation (**SIIA**)
3 **I**nstitute of **I**nformation **S**ecurity **P**rofessionals (**IISP**).

What does each organisation do?
Who runs it?
Who is it for?
Is it profit making?

Braincheck!

1 Name two techniques for accessing systems without damage.
2 What is phishing?
3 What is identity theft?
4 Name three types of natural disaster.
5 How do you protect against human errors?
6 How do you provide information security?
7 What is website defacement?
8 What is a P2P network?
9 Give three organisational impacts from security breaches.
10 Give three forms of physical security.
11 What is biometrics?
12 Name three forms of biometric measurement.
13 What is a VPN?
15 Give two advantages for having diskless workstations.
16 What might be in a communications policy?
17 What is 'separation of duties'?
18 Which three security aspects does the Computer Misuse Act 1990 cover?
19 What are you most uniquely going to get in open source programs?
20 Ethical decision making is a balance between _____ and _____ .
21 What is FAST?

How well did you do? See page 421 for the answers!

Links

Unit 15 is a **core unit** on the BTEC National Diploma for IT Practitioners (**IT and Business** and **Networking routes**) and a **specialist unit** on the Certificate on the same routes.

Unit 15 is also a **specialist unit** on the following BTEC National routes:

Software Development

Systems Support

As such it has links to a number of other units, principally:

Unit 3 – Information Systems

Unit 16 – Maintaining Computer Systems

Unit 22 – Network Management

Unit 23 – Installing and Upgrading Software

Unit 27 – Principles of Computer Networks

Unit 28 – IT Technical Support

Unit 30 – Networking Systems Security

Unit 31 – Exploring Business Activity

Unit 35 – Impact of the Use of IT on Business Systems

In addition this unit has identified direct links with:

Unit 2 – Computer Systems

Unit 34 – e-Commerce

Achieving success

In order to achieve each unit you will complete a series of coursework activities. Each time you hand in work, your tutor will return this to you with a record of your achievement.

This particular unit has 12 criteria to meet: 7 Pass, 3 Merit and 2 Distinction.

For a **pass**:

You must achieve **all** 7 pass criteria.

For a **merit**:

You must achieve **all** 7 pass and **all** 3 merit criteria.

For a **Distinction**:

You must achieve **all** 7 pass, **all** 3 merit **and both** distinction criteria.

So that you can monitor your own progress and achievement in each unit, a recording grid has been provided (see below). The full version of this grid is also included on the companion CD.

	Assignments in this unit			
Assignment	U15.01	U15.02	U15.03	U15.04
Referral				
Pass				
1				
2				
3				
4				
5				
6				
7				
Merit				
1				
2				
3				
Distinction				
1				
2				

Help with assessment

Pass criteria for this unit focus on ensuring that you are aware of the various types of threats that exist, how they might impact and can be protected against. In addition, you need to be aware of organisational policies (both procedural and personal) that can be adopted to manage organisational security issues.

Merit grades will require you to explain security issues which exist in a given system (i.e. a real-world scenario), linked to two possible threats which may lead to information being accessed without damage to a system. Knowledge and understanding of a particular encryption technique will also be necessary.

Distinction grades require a deeper analysis of the likelihood of certain security issues occurring within an example system; you will be asked to match suitable countermeasures to these, justifying their selection (this will almost certainly include the use of written organisation policies).

Online resources on the CD

Electronic glossary for this unit
Key fact sheets
Electronic slide show of key points
Multiple-choice self-test quizzes

Further reading

Textbooks

Beekman, G., 2005, *Computer Confluence Complete: and Student CD*, Prentice Hall, ISBN 1405835796.

Heathcote, P., 2000, *A Level ICT*, Payne Gallway, ISBN 0953249085.

Websites

www.acm.org
Association of Computing Machinery

www.bcs.org
British Computing Society

www.bsa.org.uk
Business Software Alliance

www.fast.org.uk
Federation Against Software Theft

www.ico.gov.uk
Information Commissioners Office

www.patent.gov.uk
The UK Patent Office

Principles of Software Design and Development

Capsule view

Principles of Software Design and Development is a 60-hour unit which is designed to **introduce** the learner to the **processes** involved in creating a **bespoke** (or tailor-made) program for a **business client**.

It focuses on the steps required to get the job done **properly**, from understanding the client's **initial request**, to **selecting** an **appropriate programming language** and then proceeding to **create a workable solution** that **meets** the client's **needs**.

Although this unit **does not** specify a target programming language, we have decided to focus on those languages that are **most likely** to be used in both a **learning** and **commercial environment**. It is through examining such examples that the world of programming will open up to **you**!

1 Know the nature and features of programming languages

Before we can examine different types of programming languages it is worthwhile taking a pause to explain just **what** a programming language actually **is**!

Computers only understand **binary** instructions, sequences of patterned **1s** and **0s** which **open** and **close** electronic circuits **inside the CPU**.

Learning aims

1 Know the nature and features of programming languages.
2 Be able to use software design and development tools.
3 Be able to design and create a program.
4 Be able to document, test, debug and review a programmed solution.

Programming a computer in binary is often referred to as **machine-code programming** or **low-level programming**. In the earliest days of computing, this was the only option!

Modern programming languages are designed to be more **person-readable** than binary. As such, these **high-level languages** require **translation** into their **machine-code equivalents** so that the CPU can **execute** them.

The diagram in **Figure 18.1** illustrates this point:

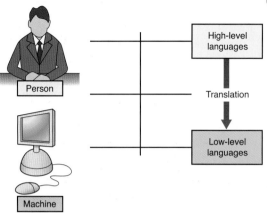

Figure 18.1 Low- and high-level languages

The following demonstrates a comparison between high- and low-level languages.

```
cout << "BTEC National Diploma";
```

```
10110100 00000101
10111010 00000101 00000001
11001101 00100001
11001101 00100000

01000010
01010100
01000101
01000011
00010000
01001110
01100001
01110100
01101001
01101111
01101110
01100001
01101100
00010000
01000100
01101001
01110000
01101100
01101111
01101101
01100001
00100100
```

Both programs output the phrase 'BTEC National Diploma' on a PC using an Intel x86-compatible processor (e.g. Pentium 4 or AMD Sempron).

The upper example is written in **C++**, a popular language developed in 1983 as an extension to an earlier language called C.

The lower example is **machine code** as shown in **binary**.

Although both samples of code do the same thing, the C++ code would need to be translated into the machine code in order for it to work.

Of course, if we had written the code in binary originally then no such translation needs to take place.

Which would *you* prefer to learn?

Which do you think is more *commercially productive?*

1.1 Types of language

Although there are hundreds of different programming languages, they can be categorised in a number of ways. The **style** or **approach** to problem solving (often called its '**paradigm**') can be used to group together similar languages.

The following section discusses this method of grouping.

Procedural languages

Procedural languages, developed from the 1960s onwards, are still popular today.

These types of languages rely on the programmer writing the solution to a problem as an **algorithm** or, put simply, **a logical series of steps** which provide an answer. It is seen as a very **traditional approach** to programming and, as such, it is highly likely that the majority of today's commercial programmers started their careers working this way.

Common procedural languages include the following.

BASIC (Beginners All-purpose Symbolic Instruction Code)

During the 1970s and 1980s, BASIC was the language of choice. Originally it relied on **line numbers** and was home to the infamous '**goto' statement** whose misuse resulted in **horribly complicated** 'spaghetti' code. Later versions remove the line numbers and use a more structured approach. BASIC often came in many different (and non-compatible) **dialects**, many of which were developed by Microsoft® in the 1980s.

Early BASIC (e.g. Microsoft's 'Gee-Whiz' GW-BASIC®)

```
10 let stars = 0
20 let count = 0
30 print "How many stars would you like?"
40 input stars
50 for count = 1 to stars
60 print "*"
70 next count
80 end
```

Modern BASIC

For example **Rockerfer BASIC**, online at: **http://www.pachesoft.com/rockerferbasic/index.html**.

```
declare variable integer count
declare variable integer stars
print "How many stars would you like?"
input stars
for count from 1 to stars do
  print "*"
end for
end
```

Though no longer popular as a commercial option, as we will see later in this book, **Microsoft®** used BASIC as the foundation for its popular **Visual Basic®** and **Visual Basic® .NET** products.

Pascal (named after seventeenth-century mathematician and philosopher Blaise Pascal)

Although over 30 years' old now, Pascal remains a popular language for **teaching programming** in schools and colleges as it encourages **good planning** and a **structured approach** to problem solving. It was created in 1970 by Niklaus Wirth.

Today, many different versions of Pascal exist for many different computer system platforms (e.g. Apple Mac, PC – Windows, Linux etc) although there is a **standard dialect** defined by the International Organisation for Standardisation (**ISO**).

```
Program mystars (input,output);

{A short program to demonstrate the
 use of a for loop in Pascal.

 Author: M Fishpool
 Date   : January 2007
 Ref    : BND                            }

Var
   stars: integer; {How many stars the user wants to see}
   count: integer; {The for loop counter}

Begin
   writeln('How many stars would you like?');
   readln(stars);
   for count := 1 to stars do
     writeln('*');
   {endfor}
   readln;
End.
```

Pascal

Borland's '**Turbo Pascal**' was a popular version, leading to its object-oriented extension, 'Delphi', challenging Microsoft's Visual Basic® in rapid Microsoft Windows® development.

A modern implementation of the language called '**Free Pascal**' is functionally similar to Turbo Pascal and can be freely downloaded from **http://www. freepascal.org/**.

C

C is considered to be a general-purpose, work-horse language, which is ideal for creating **applications**, **operating systems** and **interfacing** with **electronic control systems**. It was developed in 1972 by Dennis Ritchie at the Bell Telephone Laboratories.

Unlike languages such as BASIC and Pascal, C relies on **symbols** rather than **friendlier keywords**. As

```
/* mystars.c

   A short program to demonstrate the
   use of a for loop in C.

   Author: M Fishpool
   Date   : January 2007
   Ref    : BND                            */

// header files
#include <stdio.h>
#include <stdlib.h>

// main function
int main(int argc, char *argv[])
{
   int stars;   // How many stars the user wants to see
   int count;   // The for loop counter

   printf("How many stars would you like?");
   scanf("%d",&stars);
   for (count=0; count<stars; count++)
     printf("*\n");
   //endfor

   system("PAUSE");
   return 0;
}
```

such, it is often described as being 'terse'; **more difficult to learn** but typically offering **more powerful solutions** in **fewer** lines of code.

By 1989, the **A**merican **N**ational **S**tandards **I**nstitute (**ANSI**) had decided upon an agreed dialect of the language (now commonly known as ANSI 'C'), followed a year later by ISO.

Many versions of C exist, both commercially and as downloadable freeware.

The previous example was written and tested using Bloodshed's Dev-C++, a modern development suite which is freely available from **http://www. bloodshed.net/**.

Working with procedural languages

Following the provided links, **download** and **install** freeware procedural languages on machines for which you have administrator rights.

Try to get the sample programs running!

Finally, it is worth mentioning that procedural languages are also commonly referred to as **imperative programming**.

Object-oriented (OO)

Object-**o**riented **d**esign (**OOD**) and **o**bject-**o**riented **p**rogramming (**OOP**) are not new ideas. They have been around in one form or another since the late 1960s.

However, in the 1980s the OOP approach to programming became **popular** and has since been a common feature of most current commercial programming languages.

The following popular programming languages **all** use object-oriented techniques:

◆ **C++**
◆ **Microsoft C#®** (C 'Sharp')
◆ **Sun Java**
◆ **Microsoft Visual Basic .NET®**

> **Key Terms**
>
> **Classes and objects**
>
> In procedural programming, **data** and **functions** (which work on the data) are usually **kept separate**. The object-oriented approach does things a little differently; it packages the data and its functions **together**. This is called **encapsulation**.
>
> The collection of data and functions is called a **class**.
>
> These classes act like a template, mould, stencil for creating solid **objects**.

In object-oriented programming, the programmer has to examine the problem in a less traditional way; instead of **writing an algorithm**, they seek to **break down** elements of the problem into a number of **classes**.

Objects are created through a process called **instantiation**. This sounds awfully complex but in reality it simply means making **solid instances** (objects) **from** a class.

Let's do an example.

If I wanted to create **circle objects**, I first need to design a **circle class**.

This type of diagram is called a **schema**. The schema shows: the **name** of the class, the **data** (or **properties**) of a circle and a number of **functions** (or **methods**). A design tool present within Unified Modelling Language (**UML**) is very similar – it's simply called a **UML class diagram**.

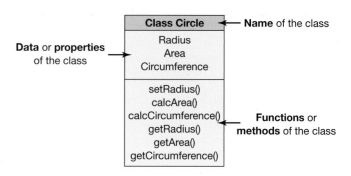

In this class we imagine that it will store **three items of data** (the radius, the calculated area and circumference).

Also, we think that we will need **six functions**:

◆ **setRadius**() – to give the circle its radius
◆ **calcArea**() – to calculate the area using the formula: **Area = Pi × Radius^2**
◆ **calcCircumference**() – to calculate the circumference using the formula: **Circumference = 2 × Pi × radius**
◆ **getRadius**() – to get the radius value
◆ **getArea**() – to get the calculated area value
◆ **getCircumference**() – to get the calculated circumference value

The order in which the functions (or methods) are coded in the class is **not really important**.

So, if we examine this as a Microsoft **C#®** solution the class code becomes (see right):

```
class Circle
{
    private float radius;
    private float area;
    private float circumference;

    public void setRadius(int r)
    {
        radius = r;
    }

    public void calcArea()
    {
        area = 3.14f * radius * radius;
    }

    public void calcCircumference()
    {
        circumference = 2 * 3.14f * radius;
    }

    public float getRadius()
    {
        return radius;
    }

    public float getArea()
    {
        return area;
    }

    public float getCircumference()
    {
        return circumference;
    }
}
```

However, in order to make it work, we must create some **objects** and **use** the methods in a **logical order**.

```
class CircleTest
{
  public static void Main()
  {
    Circle Circle1 = new Circle();         // create 1st object
    Circle1.setRadius(10);                 // give it a radius
    Circle1.calcCircumference();
    Circle1.calcArea();

    Console.WriteLine("1st Circle");
    Console.WriteLine("Radius of Circle is {0:F}", Circle1.getRadius());
    Console.WriteLine("Circumference is {0:F}", Circle1.getCircumference());
    Console.WriteLine("Area is {0:F}", Circle1.getArea());

    Circle Circle2 = new Circle();         // create 2nd object
    Circle2.setRadius(15);                 // give it a radius
    Circle2.calcCircumference();
    Circle2.calcArea();

    Console.WriteLine("\n2nd Circle");
    Console.WriteLine("Radius of Circle is {0:F}", Circle2.getRadius());
    Console.WriteLine("Circumference is {0:F}", Circle2.getCircumference());
    Console.WriteLine("Area is {0:F}", Circle2.getArea());

    Console.ReadLine();
  }
}
```

In this example, **two objects** are created (**Circle1** and **Circle2**). The program gives **each object** a radius (10 and 15 respectively) and then **uses** their functions (or methods) to **calculate** and **return** the resulting values.

This Microsoft C#® program would generate the output shown in Figure 18.2.

Object-oriented programming works in a similar fashion in other OOP languages.

One thing to remember though: classes may represent **anything** – an operating system 'window', a folder on a hard drive or even a type of opponent in an online game!

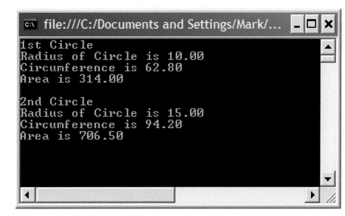

file:///C:/Documents and Settings/Mark/...

```
1st Circle
Radius of Circle is 10.00
Circumference is 62.80
Area is 314.00

2nd Circle
Radius of Circle is 15.00
Circumference is 94.20
Area is 706.50
```

Figure 18.2 Output from Microsoft C#® program

Building programs the object-oriented way

Using the schema and the Circle class examples as shown on the previous pages, design the following class:

Rectangle class

A rectangle has a **long side** and a **short side** measurement.

Its **perimeter** is measured by **adding up** the **two longest sides** and the **two shortest sides**.

It also has an **area** calculated by **multiplying** the length of the **longest side** by the length of the **shortest side**.

Visual languages

This category is **often misused**. Be careful!

Visual languages are best described as using **graphical development tools** to **create software**. The user can often create basic programs by the use of 'drag and drop' of icons, logic pathways and special symbols.

Every visual component (its appearance and function) may in fact represent many **thousands of lines** of traditional program code in a non-visual language.

A typical visual language is **VisSim©**.

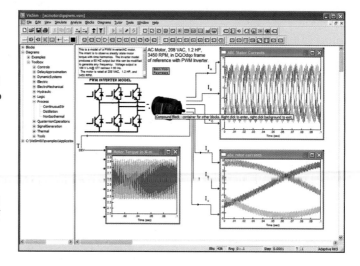

Figure 18.3 VisSim© Visual Solutions Incorporated 2007

Other languages such as Microsoft **Visual Basic® .NET** and **Visual C#®** have **visual development environments** but are **not** truly visual programming languages as they still rely on traditional **text-based** program code. Many books make this error however and, as a result, it has become commonly accepted as fact.

Other types of language

As well as procedural and object-oriented, a number of other types of programming language exist.

The following pages detail the types you are most likely to encounter on the BTEC National Diploma.

Scripting

'Scripting' (or 'script') languages are usually formed from **short**, **meaningful** instructions which are used to **automate processes** in a computer system. **Batch files** and **job control languages (JCL)** are typical examples of scripting.

PHP

PHP (**PHP H**ypertext **P**re-processor) is a **server-side scripting** language which works on a number of different hardware platforms and operating systems (this makes it '**cross-platform**').

PHP's job is to **create dynamic web page content**. What this means is that the actual HTML sent to the client PC requesting the page is **written by a PHP script** rather than being coded **manually** by a person. The generated HTML often comes from **live database queries** so the information sent to the client's web browser should be **up to date**.

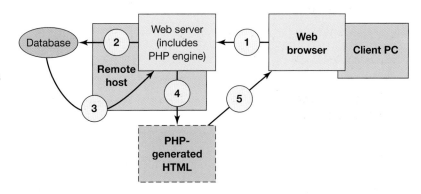

Figure 18.4 How server-side scripting works

The steps in a typical PHP scenario are:

```
<?php
  echo "<b>BTEC</b> National Diploma";
?>
```

1 The user's web browser makes a **request** for a particular piece of information; this request is sent **via the Internet** to a **remote host** running a w**eb server**.
2 The PHP script **queries** (usually with a **d**ata **m**anipulation language such as **SQL**), a linked **database** and a **results set** (of data) is created.
3 The **results set** is returned to the PHP engine.
4 The PHP engine **converts** the data in the results set into **valid HTML**, adding **formatting** as necessary.
5 The web server '**serves**' the **dynamically created HTML** page **back** to the client PC's web browser.

A common use of such scripting is in **search engines**, particularly those used to check **stock** in an **online shop**. **Message boards** and **forums** can also use PHP extensively.

Because the client PC only ever receives the generated HTML document, the end user **never gets to see** the PHP scripts involved.

ASP.NET

ASP.NET ('dot net') is the follow-up to Microsoft's earlier **A**ctive **S**erver **P**ages® (**ASP**).

As with PHP, it can be used to create **dynamic web page content**. **Unlike** PHP, which is available on a number of different computer platforms, ASP.NET is designed to run specifically on Microsoft Windows® operating systems.

ASP.NET is part of Microsoft's larger **.NET platform** – a **framework** of software components which are built **onto** the Windows operating system. The .NET framework provides a **large collection** of **reusable classe**s which are ideal for creating **new Windows applications**.

```
Response.Write("<b>BTEC</b> National Diploma");
```

JavaScript

Despite what some people may say, **JavaScript®** and **Java®** are **not** the same thing! Although the name is similar, JavaScript is only distantly related to Sun's full object-oriented programming language.

JavaScript is Netscape Communications' name for its own ECMAscript dialect.

Figure 18.5 JavaScript working in a web page

JavaScript's primary purpose is to provide **automation** and **interactivity** for existing **web pages**. Because of this, JavaScript is often included within the **HTML** page itself, although it is possible to store it **separately** in **.JS** files.

Figure 18.5 and the code below demonstrate a simple JavaScript automation of a web page.

```
<html>
<head>
<script = "JavaScript">

function check()
{
  var reply = confirm("Return to www.edexcel.org.uk?")
  if (reply)
  {
    window.location = "http://www.edexcel.org.uk";
  }
}
</script>
</head>
<body>
<form>
<input type="button" onclick="check()" value="Leave this page?">
</form>
</body>
</html>
```

Markup languages

Markup languages are used to **describe** the **way** in which **text is presented to a reader**. A number of markup languages are available and, while they are **not** programming languages in the truest sense, **do** provide solutions to set problems.

HTML

Hypertext Markup Language (**HTML**) is currently the most popular way of creating web pages for publishing on the World Wide Web (**WWW**). It was created by Tim Berners-Lee, who now leads the World Wide Web Consortium (**WC3**) which regularly publishes **standards** for web page creation to ensure that pages remain **interoperable** – that they 'work together' – on different computer systems.

HTML uses a series of **block tags** to indicate the **start** and **end** of **structured text** and web page **elements** (e.g. images, tables, bulleted lists etc.).

```
<html>
<head>
<title>BTEC National Diploma for IT Practitioners</title>
<META name="Author" content="M Fishpool">
</head>
<body>
<p>Welcome to the BTEC National Diploma for IT Practitioners!

<IMG src="computer.jpg" alt="Computer System">

</p>
</body>
</html>
```

The central idea of HTML is the **hyperlink**; a special link which, when clicked, takes the user to another **resource** (e.g. an image, piece of music, document or video) which may be on the same page or on another computer system located somewhere else.

CSS

CSS (**c**ascading **s**tyle **s**heets) is the preferred technique for **formatting the appearance** of modern web pages (e.g. **fonts**, **colours**, **alignment**, text effects such as **bold**, **underline**, **italics** etc.).

The following example shows **embedded CSS**, using the <style> tag to set formatting of the HTML elements.

This would produce the following formatted content.

```
<html>
<head>
<style type="text/css">
h1 {color: #ff0000}
h2 {color: rgb(0,0,255)}
</style>
</head>
<body>
<h1>Welcome to BTEC National Diploma</h1>
<h2>Welcome to BTEC National Diploma</h2>
</body>
</html>
```

Welcome to BTEC National Diploma

Welcome to BTEC National Diploma

The preferred option is to keep the **content** of a web page in one file (the .HTML) and the **formatting** in **another** (a .CSS file).

XML

XML is the abbreviation for **e**xtensible **m**arkup **l**anguage, a specification also developed by the **W3C**. XML allows programmers to **create their own** personalised tags. As such, .XML documents are exceptionally portable across different systems.

Formatting (or '**style information**') for .XML documents can be achieved by using **CSS**.

```
<!--
 Written by M Fishpool, 2007
-->
<announcement>
<to>BTEC Students</to>
<from>M Fishpool</from>
<heading>Welcome</heading>
<body>Enjoy your BTEC National Diploma!</body>
</note>
```

1.2 Reasons for choice of language

Why does a programmer choose a particular language?

If the programmer is able to choose which language to use, it may simply be a case of **familiarity** – they will tend to use the language that **they know best**.

However, there are **other** important factors to take into consideration.

These include the following.

> ### Choosing the right language can be a *rough* decision!
>
> Having trouble remembering these?
>
> Think: **C – O – A – R – S – E**

Cost

Languages have **development** costs (incurred **during** production) and **maintenance** costs (incurred **after** the solution has been delivered). Some languages prove more costly than others, for example a solution that is **not that reliable** will create a lot of **costly maintenance** over a period of time.

Organisational policy

Many organisations specify both the **language** and **development environment** to use. This is particularly true in **governmental** work where **security** is vital. A famous example of this is the programming language called **Ada** – it was **designed specifically** for use by the United States Department of Defense.

Availability

Programming languages are just like any other language; they have to be **learned** and **practised** for some time before a level of competency is reached. How many **trained** and **experienced** staff are **available**?

Reliability

Different languages may be seen to be **more reliable** than others. **Mission-critical systems** would not be created using a programming language whose **dependability** is **less than** 100 per cent.

Suitability

It is absolutely critical that programming languages are **suitable** for the task at hand, particularly when taking into consideration their **features** and **tools**. For example Java, while being very useful for **web-based applications**, is perhaps not so suitable for controlling **real-time systems** where **rapid response** to **real-world events** is crucial.

Expandability

A critical part of ongoing maintenance is the ability **to expand an existing solution**. Some programming languages, particularly **object-oriented** ones, are good at this.

Braincheck!

1 Name four different programming paradigms.
2 Name two organisations responsible for establishing standards for languages.
3 How do HTML and CSS differ?
4 What is a script language?
5 What is another name for a procedural language?

How well did you do? See page 421 for the answers!

1.3 Features

Although it is fair to say that all programming languages were created as **tools to solve problems**, they do not all approach this job in the same way!

While languages may vary in their **syntax** (the rules governing how statements are written), they are fortunately built from a collection of **similar features**.

In this section we will examine some of these common building blocks, using **C#** as our reference language.

Variables

A variable is a form of **identifier**; a 'name' which **represents** a **value**.

In programming, a variable is used to **store** and **retrieve data** from the computer's RAM. Every variable should have a **unique** (and **meaningful**) name.

In order to reserve **enough RAM** for the variable we must select an **appropriate data type** (see 1.4 for more on this).

For example, if we want to store our user's age in a variable:

```
int iAge;
```

This is called a **declaration**.

This line of code essentially **reserves enough RAM** to store an **integer** (a whole number) and allows us to **refer** to that reserved RAM by the **name** we have picked: **iAge**.

Professional programmers often **prefix** the name of their variables with an **initial letter** which **indicates** the variable's **data type**. This is called '**Hungarian notation**' and is considered to be good practice.

Even better practice would have been to add a **comment**, so:

```
int iAge;    // Will store the user's age
```

Variables can also be 'local' or 'global'.

In simple terms, what this means is: **how visible is the variable?** In a large program split into a number of different modules (**see 2.1**), a global variable would be visible to **all modules** whereas a local variable would **only** be visible **within** the module it was declared.

Professional programmers prefer to use local variables where possible because it tends to make programs **easier to debug**, as any faults with the variable have to be in a particular module.

Constants

In addition to variables, it is possible to create another type of identifier: a constant.

As the name suggests, it **does not change its value** once the program starts running.

```
const int MAXAGE = 125;   // oldest allowable age
```

In this example, 'MAXAGE' is declared as a **constant** and given the value of 125.

In the program we will now use the constant 'MAXAGE' whenever we want to refer to the value 125. The advantages of this are **two-fold**: it **improves** the **readability** of the program code and, secondarily, if we want to change the maximum age we **only** have to alter the constant's declaration – **not** find **every occurrence** of '125' in the code.

Assignment statements

An assignment statement is used to **give** a variable a value.

When an assignment is successfully performed, the **previous value** stored in the variable is **overwritten**.

```
iAge = 16;    // set user's age
```

In most languages an '=' (**equal sign**) is used for the **assignment operator**.

If the variable is being assigned for the **first time** we call this process '**initialisation**'. Some programming languages **do not** initialise new variables to **sensible** starting values (e.g. zero). Where this does not happen automatically, initialisation must occur to ensure that the variables are ready for use.

Output statements

All programming languages have a method for generating output, normally to screen.

In C# the '**Write**' or '**WriteLine**' method can be used:

```
Console.Write("Please enter your age: ");
```

```
Console.WriteLine("Please enter your age: ");
```

Both these methods will output text to the **console** (or command-line interface). The only difference is that the second method (WriteLine) will **move** the **cursor** to the **start of the next line** once the text has been displayed.

A more advanced version of Write allows us to output the contents of a variable.

```
Console.Write("Do you still feel young at {0}?", iAge);
```

If iAge currently had the integer value 16, the associated screen output would be:

`Do you still feel young at 16?`

The content (16) of the variable (iAge) is inserted into the correct part of the message.

Input statements

There are many different ways of obtaining input. For now we will just focus on basic **keyboard input**.

The following code **prompts** the user for a value (their name) and **stores it** in a variable ('username').

The stored **string** (their name) is then repeated to the user, complete with a greeting.

```
string username;

Console.WriteLine("What is your name?");
username = Console.ReadLine();

Console.WriteLine("Hello, {0}!", username);
```

Arithmetic operators

These are the basic building blocks for forming **arithmetic expression**–number calculations for want of a better phrase.

The number of arithmetic operators in programming languages varies greatly but there are some that are absolutely fundamental.

Here they are with their C# symbols.

Arithmetic operation	C# implementation
Add	+
Subtract	–
Multiply	* (asterisk)
Divide	/ (forward slash)
Modulus (obtains the remainder)	% (percentage)
Increment (increase by 1)	++
Decrement (decrease by 1)	--

In addition, **parentheses** (brackets) may be used to alter the natural order of operations (division, multiplication, addition and subtraction).

For example:

average = num1 + num2 + num3 / 3

isn't the same as:

average = (num1 + num2 + num3) / 3

The **second** version (forcing all the **addition** to be **performed first**) is the **correct one** and requires the use of parentheses.

Logical operators

Most programming languages have **keywords** or **operators** to process **logical operations**.

The following table lists these logical operations and their C# implementations.

Logical operation	C# implementation
AND	&&
OR	||
NOT	!

Logical operators can be used to create more complex compound conditions (**see conditional statements**).

Relational operators

In most languages these are a set of operators that make **direct comparisons between values**. The **result** of this type of comparison can **only** be **true** or **false**.

This table lists these relational operations and their C# implementations.

Relational operator	C# implementation
==	Equal to (test for equality)
!=	Not equal to (test for inequality)
>	Greater than
<	Less than
>=	Greater than or equal to
<=	Less than *or* equal to

Help on relational operators

Can't remember which symbol is '**Less than**'?

It's just a **squashed** 'L'.

< ess than

Braincheck

Work out whether these expressions **evaluate** to **TRUE** or **FALSE**.
10 > 5
6 < 6.1
'A' != 'B'
FALSE == FALSE
7 > 2 AND 5>=5
3 < 10 OR 99 < 67
'REBEKAH' == 'rebekah'
(10+2) >= (60/5)

How well did you do? See page 421 for the answers!

Conditional statements

Although programs can be built from a **simple sequence** (one event following another), these only provide limited solutions.

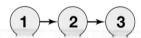

Here, as you can see, the solution follows steps **1**, **2** and **3**. **No step is missed, no step is repeated**.

More complex solutions require the ability to **make choices**.

For example:

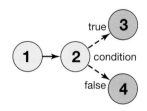

In this example, a condition is made **after** step 2.

If the condition is **true**, **step 3** is performed.

If the condition is **false**, **step 4** is performed **instead**.

It **is not** possible to perform **both** steps 3 and 4 – the program has a **choice** to make.

If…else statement

Most programming languages, including C#, perform these types of decision using an **if…else statement**.

```
                condition
if (iAge >= 18)
{
   Console.Write("In the UK, you are now a responsible adult.");      true
}
else
{
   Console.Write("In the UK, you are still a minor");      false
}
```

Any iAge value of 18 (or more) would cause the 'Responsible Adult' message to be output.

Any iAge value less than 18 would cause the 'Minor' message to be output.

The '**else**' part of the **if…else statement** is **optional** in most programming languages. If you do not have any action for the 'false' part, **don't have** an 'else'.

Case statements

Sometimes the programmer wishes to check for **multiple possibilities**.

Two primary techniques are available: first the '**nested**' **if…else**.

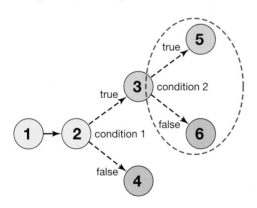

As you can see from this diagram, the **second if…else is nested** into the '**true**' **part** of the **first if…else**.

Use of nested if…else is common but can lead to unnecessary over-complication.

Case (or switch) statements simplify things somewhat by being able to pick a single matching value from a list of possibilities.

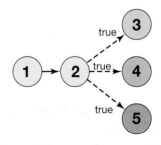

The **case** statement works **more effectively** because it can make **individual comparisons** against **each possible matching value**. If the comparison is **true** (they match), the resulting action (3, 4 or 5) is performed.

Let's put this into a practical C# example!

Imagine that we have stored the **day of the week** as an **integer variable** (e.g. 1 is Monday, 2 is Tuesday etc.). What we would like to do is examine the variable and be able to **output the correct day** of the week in text, i.e. 'It's Monday!'

Examine the following C# example which is coded using nested if…else statements.

```csharp
    if (iDayofWeek == 1)
A   {
        Console.WriteLine("It's Monday!");
A   }
    else
B   {
        if (iDayofWeek == 2)
    C   {
            Console.WriteLine("It's Tuesday!");
    C   }
        else
    D   {
            if (iDayofWeek == 3)
        E   {
                Console.WriteLine("It's Wednesday!");
        E   }
            else
        F   {
                if (iDayofWeek == 4)
            G   {
                    Console.WriteLine("It's Thursday!");
            G   }
                else
            H   {
                    if (iDayofWeek == 5)
                I   {
                        Console.WriteLine("It's Friday!");
                I   }
                    else
                J   {
                        if (iDayofWeek == 6)
                    K   {
                            Console.WriteLine("It's Saturday!");
                    K   }
                        else
                    L   {
                            if (iDayofWeek == 7)
                        M   {
                                Console.WriteLine("It's Sunday!");
                        M   }

                    L   }

                J   }

            H   }

        F   }

    D   }

B   }
```

As you can see, even though the **matching pairs of open and close braces** have been **visibly linked**, this still looks rather **untidy** and **inefficient**.

The **case/switch statement** version of this in C# is fortunately a bit more straightforward.

```
switch (iDayofWeek)
{
    case 1: Console.WriteLine("It's Monday!");
            break;

    case 2: Console.WriteLine("It's Tuesday!");
            break;

    case 3: Console.WriteLine("It's Wednesday!");
            break;

    case 4: Console.WriteLine("It's Thursday!");
            break;

    case 5: Console.WriteLine("It's Friday!");
            break;

    case 6: Console.WriteLine("It's Saturday!");
            break;

    case 7: Console.WriteLine("It's Sunday!");
            break;
}
```

Case/switch statements can also handle **multiple matches**; for example if we want to **cheer** on the **weekend** a **minor modification** is needed.

```
    case 6:
    case 7: Console.WriteLine("Yay! It's the weekend!!!");
            break;
    }
```

A **default option** is available to **catch** any **unexpected values**.

```
    case 6: Console.WriteLine("It's Saturday!");
            break;

    case 7: Console.WriteLine("It's Sunday!");
            break;

    default:Console.WriteLine("That isn't a valid day");
            break;
}
```

Loops

Loops or **iterations** allow the programmer to make something happen **repeatedly**.

Normally loops will repeat **until** they are **told to stop**. This is achieved by using a **conditional statement**, e.g. **reply == 'Y'** will repeat the loop while a reply is 'Y' (for 'Yes').

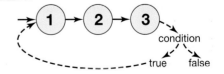

Post-check conditioning occurs when the conditional statement is placed **after the actions**.

Because of this, the actions in a post-check conditioned loop will **always work at least** once.

```
int counter;

counter = 1;

do
{
  Console.WriteLine("Counter is currently {0}", counter);
  counter++;
} while (counter <= 10);
```

In C# a post-check loop can be created by using a '**do…while**' like this:

In this example, a post-check condition is used to repeat the loop **while** the **counter** is **less than or equal to 10**. Each **cycle** of the loop **outputs** the counter's

current value (starting from 1) and **increments** the counter. The loop **stops** when the condition is **no longer true**: when the counter gets to **11**.

The resulting screen output is shown in Figure 18.6.

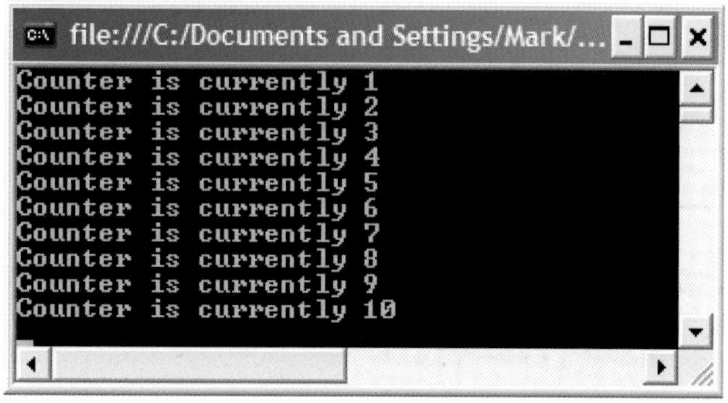

Pre-check conditioning occurs when the conditional statement is placed **before** the actions.

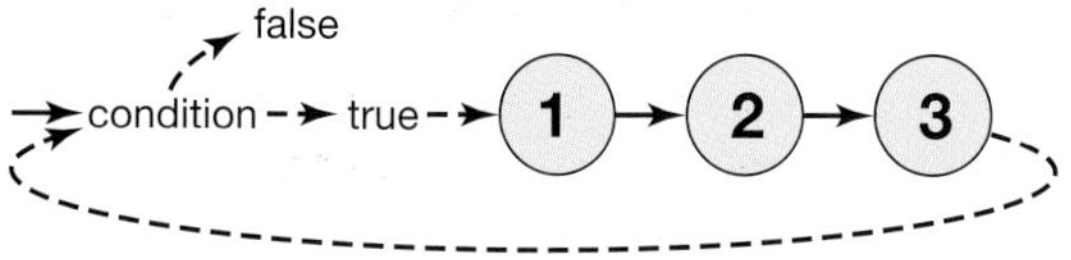

Figure 18.6 Output from post-check do…while loop

Placing the condition at the start of the loop has an interesting effect; if the loop condition is found to be false to begin with, its actions will **never** be processed.

```
int counter;

counter = 1;

while (counter <=10)
{
  Console.WriteLine("Counter is currently {0}", counter);
  counter++;
}
```

In C# a pre-check loop can be created by using a '**while**' loop like this:

The resulting screen output is shown in Figure 18.7.

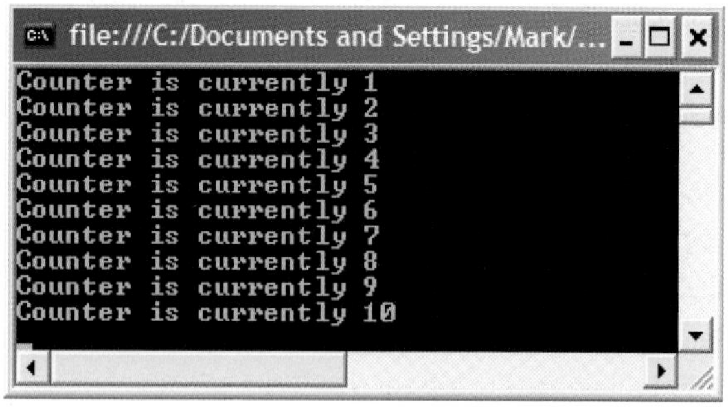

Figure 18.7 Output from pre-check do…while loop

Arrays

In programming, an array is a form of **data structure** – a way of **collecting together data items** of the **same type**.

Arrays can be **one-dimensional** (**1D**):

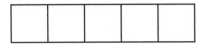

Two-dimensional (**2D**):

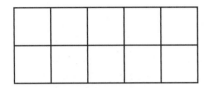

Three-dimensional (**3D**):

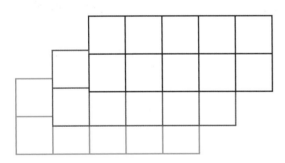

In C# this can be created by a simple line of code.

Higher-dimensional arrays are possible but these are more difficult to **represent** on paper.

Programmers use arrays to help solve **complex problems** as they provide an easy way to **access** similar data values in a **specific** order.

Let's start by examining a **1D array of integers**.

```
int[] iaMyNumbers = new int[5];
```

This will create an **array** of **five integers**. Notice that we have not said **which** integer values we wish to use!

C# will handle this **automatically**, giving each box (or **element**) its **default** value. For an **integer**, this is the value **0**. Not all programming languages are this helpful.

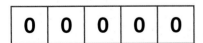

If we had wanted to give each element an initial value, the code would have been slightly different.

```
int[] iaMyNumbers = new int[5] { 9, -2, 8, 4, 3};
```

Notice that the elements values are added to the **end** of the declaration.

This will create a slightly different array.

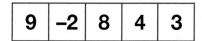

Once the array has been **created**, it typically stays this size (five elements) in the **majority** of programming languages; it is called a **static data structure** – it does not **shrink** or **grow**.

Another point to remember is that **elements** are **numbered** with the **first element** (**left-most**) being **element 0**.

0	1	2	3	4
9	–2	8	4	3

Because of their **fixed size**, programmers often use a special form of **pre-check loop** called a '**for**' loop.

Here is an example '**for**' loop in C# being used to '**walk along**' the array and output **each element's value**.

```
int counter;
int[] iaMyNumbers = new int[5] { 9, -2, 8, 4, 3 };

for (counter=0;counter<5;counter++)
{
    Console.Write("The value in element ");
    Console.WriteLine("{0} is {1}.",counter,iaMyNumbers[counter]);
}
```

Figure 18.8 shows the resulting output.

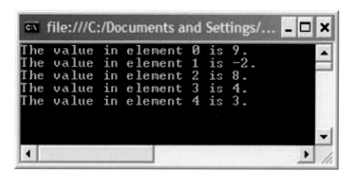

Figure 18.8 The results of using a 'for' loop to walk an array.

1.4 Data types

Specific data types **vary** from language to language but **common categories** are found.

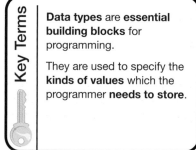

Key Terms

Data types are **essential building blocks** for programming.

They are used to specify the **kinds of values** which the programmer **needs to store**.

Let's take a look at these in a little more detail:

Categories

Character

This can store **one character**, any symbol in the computer system's character set e.g. alphabetic, digit, punctuation, currency symbols etc.

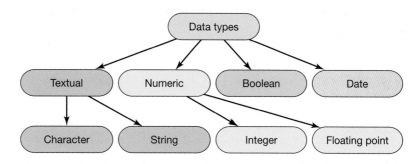

Figure 18.9 Data types family

For example:

A & " @ 9 #

A character normally needs 1 byte of RAM.

String

A string is a **number of characters joined together**. Again the string can be composed of any number of **valid symbols**. Some languages may define a **limit** for the **length** of the string (e.g. **255 characters**).

For example:

'BTEC National Diploma' '01412 989922' 'Jane Smith' '#123'

Some languages use what are called **ASCIIZ** strings – they use a **Zero (0)** value to **mark the end of a string**.

Other languages place the **length** of the string in the **first byte**.

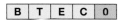

Integer

An integer is a **whole** number, i.e. it has **no decimal part**. Integers can also be **positive** or **negative** or **neither** ('unsigned').

For example:

2814   +52   −7

Languages place a **limit** on the **size** of integers. However, this usually depends on **how much RAM** an integer is allocated and whether the integer is **signed** (positive or negative) or **unsigned**.

Unit Link

See also: **Unit 7** (IT Systems Analysis and Design) 3.1.

For example, for an **8 bit integer:**

Signed range (max & min)   **Unsigned range (max & min)**

		128	64	32	16	8	4	2	1
⊞127		0	1	1	1	1	1	1	1

		128	64	32	16	8	4	2	1
■128		1	0	0	0	0	0	0	0

		128	64	32	16	8	4	2	1
255		1	1	1	1	1	1	1	1

		128	64	32	16	8	4	2	1
0		0	0	0	0	0	0	0	0

Integer sizes in most modern programming languages are **minimally** 16 bits in size.

Floating point

These are '**real**' numbers, ones which have a **decimal point and fractional part.**

For example:

+1025.34   −117.1234   +0.4

Floating-point numbers have **two** main components: the **mantissa** and the **exponent.**

For example:

$+1.34\,E + 2$ or 1.34×10^2

In this example, both values equal **134.**

1.34 E + 2 means move **the decimal point** two places to the **right.**
1.34×10^2 means **multiply** 1.34 by 100 (**10 squared**).

The **mantissa** represents the **accuracy** of the number whereas the **exponent** represents the magnitude.

In programming languages, floating-point numbers come in various sizes. **Larger** floating-point numbers offer **greater magnitude** and **accuracy** of numerical data.

Boolean

The name reflects the field of **mathematical logic** developed by nineteenth-century English mathematician **George Boole**; Boolean values are **true** or **false, yes** or **no.**

This reflects the 0 and 1 binary values used by computer systems.

Date

Computer systems typically have a **real-time clock** (**RTC**). Date and time processing is fairly easy. Date data types may be stored in different ways.

For example:

As **YYYY-MM-DD** – 10 July 2008 would be **2008-07-10.**
As **DD-MM-YYYY** – 10 July 2008 would be **10-07-2008.**

Data types in an example language

The following table reflects actual primitive data types available in Sun's **Java.**

Java data type	Range	RAM requirement
byte	+127 to -128	8 bits (1 byte)
short	+32,767 to -32,768	16 bits (2 bytes)
int	+2,147,483,647 to -2,147,483,648	32 bits (4 bytes)
long	+9,223,372,036,854,775,807 to -9,223,372,036,854,775,808	64 bits (8 bytes)
float	1.40129846432481707 E-45 to 3.40282346638528860 E+38 (positive or negative)	32 bits (4 bytes)
double	4.94065645841246544 E-324 to 1.79769313486231570 E+308 (positive or negative)	64 bits (8 bytes)
Boolean	True/False	1 bit
char	Any **Unicode** character, the theoretical range being any one of 65,536 different global symbols	16 bits (2 bytes)

Investigating data types

Select **one** of the following popular programming languages:

◆ C++
◆ C#
◆ Pascal
◆ Microsoft Visual Basic® .NET

Investigate **which data types** the language **would use** to store the **following data values**:

400 'C' 6.7 false 'Saturn'

Unit Link

See also: **Unit 7** (IT Systems Analysis and Design) 3.1 for data types in the C# programming language.

Other programming languages have data types with **different names**. When you start to program in a specific language, an **important first step** should be to **familiarise yourself** with the **data types available**.

Benefits of appropriate choice of data

As a programmer, selecting the correct data type for a value is **vitally important** as choosing badly can generate serious **run-time** problems.

A number of **benefits** are associated with picking the correct data type.

Accurate storage

This is vitally important for numeric values. If the data type is too small to store a value, it becomes truncated (chopped) and accuracy is lost. Using a data type of the right size prevents this happening.

Efficiency of storage

Although greater quantities of cheaper RAM have reduced the need for programmers to be as efficient as they once were, there are still occasions when using data types efficiently is recommended. This can be particularly important in **embedded computer systems** where **free RAM** or **processing power** may be **limited**.

Additional validation

Entering **non-numeric data** into a **numeric data** type **can cause a program to crash at run time**. One simple technique is to enter all data into a text data type, **validate** the characters and then only convert to a true numeric data type if the contents are correct.

Braincheck!

1 What are the **four basic categories** of data types?
2 Numeric data types can be _____ or _____.
3 How **many** characters can be stored in a **char** data type?
4 What **kind** of numbers does a floating-point data type store?
5 Which **part** of a floating-point number does the mantissa **represent**?
6 What is a **typical maximum length** of a string data type?
7 What is the **difference** between signed and unsigned numbers?
8 **Which** data type can only store True and False values?
9 What is the **real value** of 0.1963 E + 3?
10 Select appropriate data types for the following values:
   −5.8
   A
   +7800
   (0120) 101000
   04/09/2012
   Miss Helena Wayne

How well did you do? See page 421 for the answers!

Activity

Frankoni T-Shirts Ltd requires a program that will calculate the **production cost** and **projected sales price** of a designer T-shirt.

Frankoni buy blank shirts at the following rates: small (£3 each), medium (£4 each), large (£6 each) and extra large (£7 each).

It costs Frankoni £2.50 to print the customer's design on the T-shirt.

Frankoni aims to make a 30 per cent profit on each T-shirt sold.

Write a program that will calculate and output production costs, projected sales and the profit of selling a user-specified quantity of each type of T-shirt.

2 Be able to use software design and development tools

2.1 Software development life cycle

Program development forms part of a natural life cycle.

New solutions are designed and implemented because:

◆ **an older system is failing**
◆ **user needs have changed**.

In order to design and implement a new solution it is important to put this activity into a wider context, to see what part of the overall process it represents.

Let's examine each **stage** of this cycle in more detail.

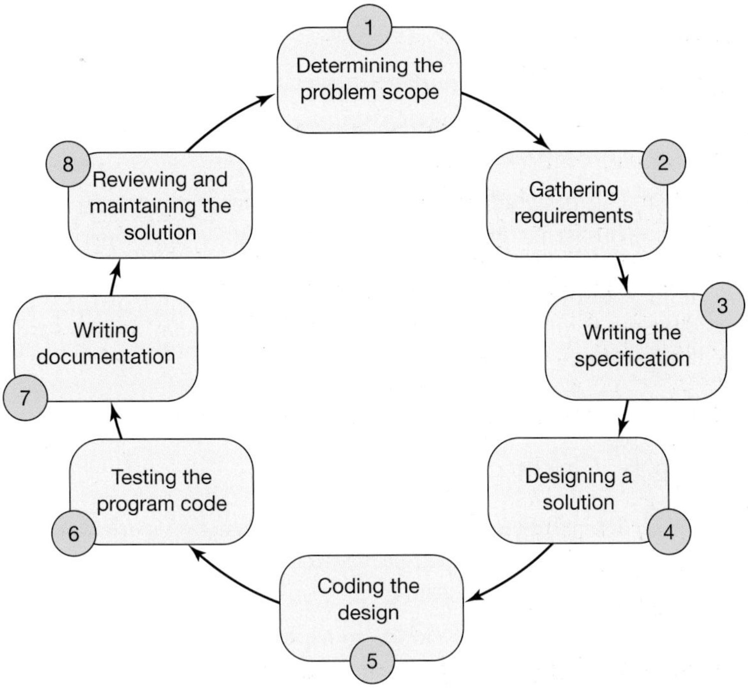

Stage 1: Determining the problem scope

Figure 18.10 Software development life cycle

Scope is a term used to describe the **boundaries** of the problem (often called the '**problem domain**'). In particular, it is a **definition** of **what is** and **what is not** covered by the identified problem. It also includes those who are affected by the problem (e.g. people, organisations etc.) and **how** they are affected.

Understanding the scope is vital in order to understand the nature of the problem.

Stage 2: Gathering requirements

Before the problem is tackled, it is vital that the **functional requirements** – what is **wanted** from the solution **by those who are affected** – are clearly known. Those affected by the problem are commonly referred to as **stakeholders**.

This will absolutely specify what the solution **does** and **does not** cover. A staggeringly high number of commercial solutions fail because these requirements are poorly researched; it is a common failure of IT projects worldwide.

Functional requirements may be collected in the form of **use cases**; a use case is simply a way of **describing how** a single task is achieved.

Unit Link

See also: **Unit 7** (IT Systems Analysis and Design) 2.1 for more on information gathering techniques.

Stage 3: Writing the specification

This is a categorised list of the elements required in order to start designing a solution:

- ◆ inputs
- ◆ outputs
- ◆ processing
- ◆ storage
- ◆ user interface
- ◆ constraints.

Section 3.1 examines the **requirements specification** in greater detail.

Stage 4: Designing a solution

Using a suitable **design tool** or **methodology** (a set of procedures or methods) a solution is built. This may be **paper based** or **electronic** depending on the design tools being used.

Modern IT solutions can be partly solved by software tools; programs effectively writing new solutions.

Avoid the temptation to rush ahead into the coding; many mistakes are made this way and a lot of time is needlessly wasted!

A number of different design tools are examined in **Section 2.2**.

Stage 5: Coding the design

From here, designs are converted into program code by experienced software developers. The programming language will have been selected before they start as some design features will lend themselves to particular languages.

It is common for software developers to work in a team. If this is the case, it is important that they are all clear about their **individual responsibilities** and adopt similar **working practices** and the **'in-house' style in an effort to standardise.**

Programs written in a **modular** way (broken into **smaller modules** such as **procedures** and **functions**) ensure **reusability** through **shared libraries**. Use of **classes** will also permit easy code reuse and speed up the development process.

Ideally, all developers need to have an understanding of how their modules **fit** into the larger solution, even if they **do not know** how modules which they have not written **actually** work.

Stage 6: Testing the program code

This is vital.

Two common testing methods are used: **black box** and **white box**.

Black box testing does not **care** about **how** the program was written (i.e. peeking inside). It only wants to see how closely a program meets its list of **functional requirements: Does it do what it is supposed to do?**

White box testing examines the **performance** of the program code, ensuring that what has been programmed is generating the **right** results. White box testing takes **much more time** and usually starts **after** black box testing has been completed.

Section 4.1 examines testing in greater detail.

Stage 7: Writing documentation

Documentation is **also** vital!

Generally there will be three types of documentation:

◆ **internal documentation**
◆ **technical documentation**
◆ **user documentation**.

Internal documentation is documentation that is actually **inside** the program's code.

All good programs should be self-documenting; there are some easy ways to achieve this:

◆ **meaningful** and **sensible** variable names
◆ good use of **comments**, written to describe the **code's purpose in the solution**, **not** the **syntax** of the actual code itself
◆ good **indentation** and tidy **layout** (most modern **IDE**s do this automatically for the programmer).

Section 3.3 looks at **technical documentation** in greater detail.

Section 4.2 focuses on **user documentation**.

Stage 8: Reviewing and maintaining the solution

This stage's components can be examined separately.

Review is a reflective process, **looking** at the solution and **comparing** it to the **stakeholders' original requirements. Have** they been met? And if so, **how well** is the solution working?

Maintenance is an ongoing process. Programs are written to solve a problem which exists at a particular point in time; as business or personal needs change, the solution will seem less ideal.

Maintenance is the process of **keeping** the solution **working**, **fixing** minor errors that occur, making **small adjustments** which **expand** the **scope** of the program.

If the maintenance requirements become too severe, it may be necessary to redevelop – to start the cycle again.

2.2 Design tools

There are a number of design tools available. In order to use the tool effectively, it has to be **appropriate** to the type of solution in hand. For example, coding a **scientific solution** often requires **different** design tools than a solution which involves a **database**.

The most common techniques are listed below. Familiarise yourself with them.

Flowchart

Flowcharts are a familiar **visual tool** for describing the **logical steps** needed to solve a problem. Many user manuals use them to explain complex sequences of instructions.

Flowcharts use a standard set of drawn symbols.

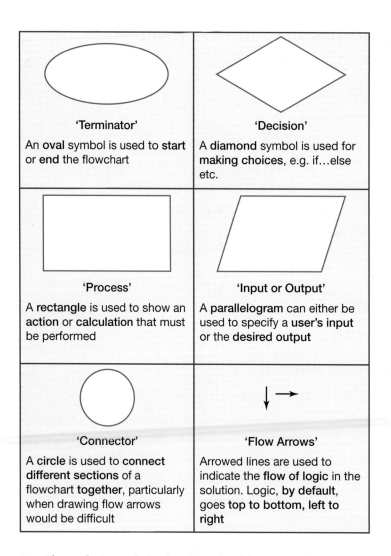

'Terminator' An **oval** symbol is used to **start** or **end** the flowchart	**'Decision'** A **diamond** symbol is used for **making choices**, e.g. if…else etc.
'Process' A **rectangle** is used to show an **action** or **calculation** that must be performed	**'Input or Output'** A **parallelogram** can either be used to specify a **user's input** or the **desired output**
'Connector' A **circle** is used to **connect different sections** of a flowchart **together**, particularly when drawing flow arrows would be difficult	**'Flow Arrows'** Arrowed lines are used to indicate the **flow of logic** in the solution. Logic, **by default**, goes **top to bottom, left to right**

As with any design tool, the flowchart **should not contain any programming language**, only **natural language**, e.g. English should be used. A limited use of general symbols is acceptable.

An example flowchart follows which checks an inputted password. The user has three opportunities to get it correct before the program identifies them as an 'Unauthorised User'.

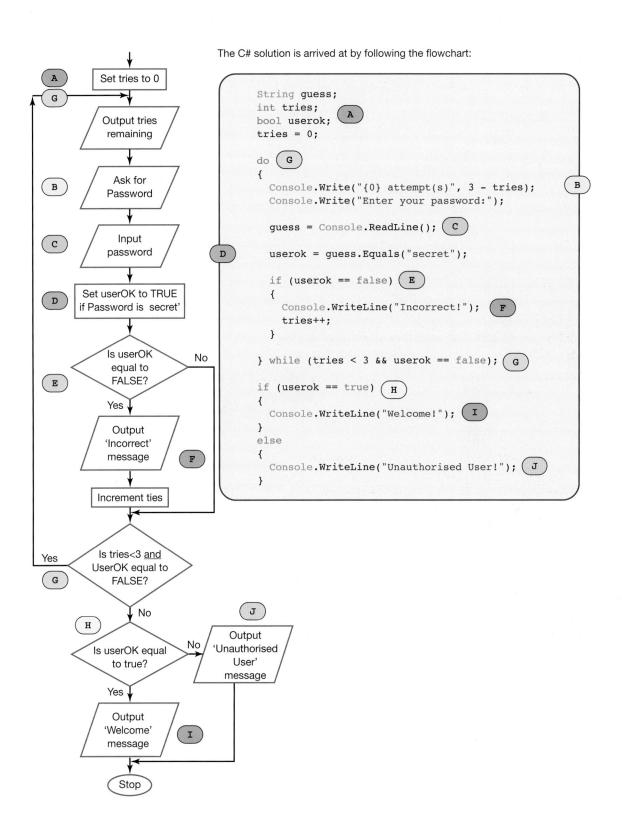

The C# solution is arrived at by following the flowchart:

```csharp
String guess;
int tries;          A
bool userok;
tries = 0;

do  G
{
  Console.Write("{0} attempt(s)", 3 - tries);        B
  Console.Write("Enter your password:");

  guess = Console.ReadLine();      C

  userok = guess.Equals("secret");

  if (userok == false)    E
  {
     Console.WriteLine("Incorrect!");      F
     tries++;
  }

} while (tries < 3 && userok == false);      G

if (userok == true)    H
{
   Console.WriteLine("Welcome!");    I
}
else
{
   Console.WriteLine("Unauthorised User!");    J
}
```

Jackson structured programming (JSP)

As you have seen, a flowchart is good at demonstrating the **logical flow** of a solution.

Unfortunately, even short solutions quickly become **large** and **confusing**, preventing the reader from grasping the **underlying structure** of the code, e.g. where the conditional statements or loops actually are.

JSP uses a simple system which breaks solutions down into three **basic building blocks** – **sequence**, **selection** and **iteration**.

Sequence

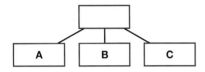

This is a sequence; first action A, then action B, followed by action C.

Selection

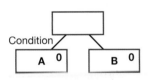

O = option!

Notice the small 'O' in the **top-right** corners of each option box to show they are **selections** rather than a **sequence**.

Unlike the sequence, the selection uses a condition to perform either A or B, not both.

If the condition is true, A is performed else B is performed.

Iteration

* = loop!

Notice the small '*' symbol (asterisk) in the **top-right** corner of lower box. This indicates that the box will occur a number of times.

Iterations are shown by a **pair of boxes**. The parent box indicates a **plural**, built from the **lower** box **repeating** zero or more times (as specified by the condition).

JSP design tool

Let's examine that 'Password' solution **again**, but this time using the **JSP** design tool.

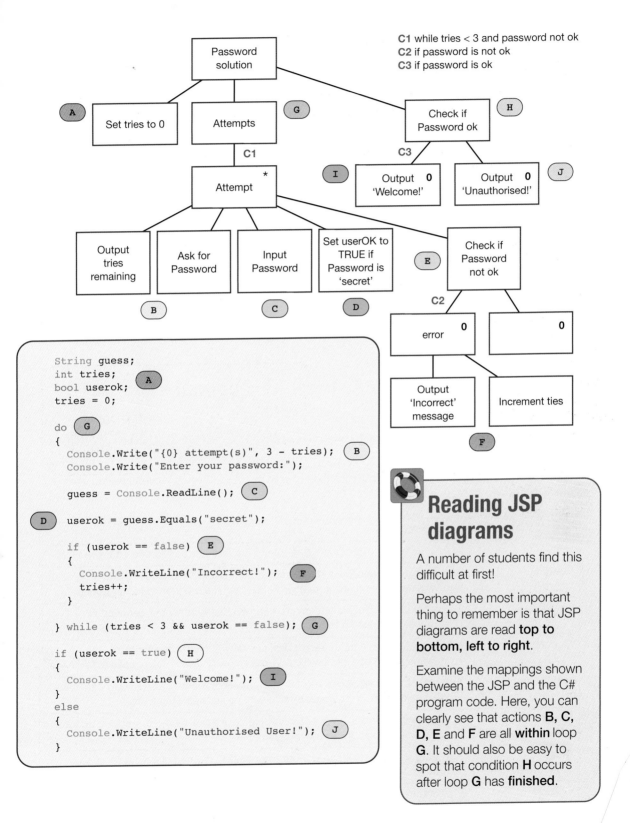

C1 while tries < 3 and password not ok
C2 if password is not ok
C3 if password is ok

Password solution

(A) Set tries to 0

(G) Attempts

(H) Check if Password ok

C1

C3

(I) Output 0 'Welcome!'

(J) Output 0 'Unauthorised!'

* Attempt

Output tries remaining (B)

Ask for Password

Input Password (C)

Set userOK to TRUE if Password is 'secret' (D)

(E) Check if Password not ok

C2

error 0

0

Output 'Incorrect' message

Increment ties

(F)

```
String guess;
int tries;           (A)
bool userok;
tries = 0;

do  (G)
{
  Console.Write("{0} attempt(s)", 3 - tries);  (B)
  Console.Write("Enter your password:");

  guess = Console.ReadLine();  (C)

(D) userok = guess.Equals("secret");

  if (userok == false)  (E)
  {
    Console.WriteLine("Incorrect!");  (F)
    tries++;
  }

} while (tries < 3 && userok == false);  (G)

if (userok == true)  (H)
{
  Console.WriteLine("Welcome!");  (I)
}
else
{
  Console.WriteLine("Unauthorised User!");  (J)
}
```

Reading JSP diagrams

A number of students find this difficult at first!

Perhaps the most important thing to remember is that JSP diagrams are read **top to bottom, left to right**.

Examine the mappings shown between the JSP and the C# program code. Here, you can clearly see that actions B, C, D, E and F are all **within** loop G. It should also be easy to spot that condition H occurs after loop G has **finished**.

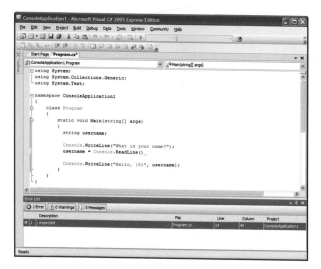

Figure 18.11 Sample output from the Password program

🔗 **Unit Link**

Unit 7 (IT Systems Analysis and Design) 1.2 and 3.1 has extended coverage on **DFD** and **ERM**.

- ◆ **UML** – discussed as part of object-oriented programming back in 1.1 Types of Languages
- ◆ **DFD** – **d**ata **f**low **d**iagram
- ◆ **ERM** – **e**ntity **r**elationship **m**odel

2.3 Software structures

Software is built from a number of different **constructs** (including the variables and data types we have already seen).

These constructs cover a number of different language elements. The following section gives an overview of these elements.

Software structure	Overview
Sequence	Any collection of program statements that are performed one after the other.
Selection	A decision or conditional statement whose result lets the program execute one set of program statements or another. These form the program's logical pathways.
Iteration	A block of statements which are repeated based on some conditional statement evaluating to true.
Modules	In programming, a term used to describe different parts of a program. The implementation of a module (size, layout etc.) will vary from language to language.
Functions	A practical example of a module. Functions, generally, are used to calculate a value, although some may perform actions instead. Reusable.
Procedures	Another practical example of a module. Procedures tend to perform actions. As with functions, these are reusable.
Classes	Part of the object-oriented programming paradigm, a class contains both data and functions which describe a real-world 'thing'.
Objects	A concrete instance of a class, complete with its personal data.

Most programs are built from **combining** these **different constructs** in various **patterns** and **quantities**.

3 Be able to design and create a program

3.1 Requirements specification

As previously discussed, the requirements specification starts to identify the following before a full design is produced.

Inputs

Nice and simple; essentially any **data** that is **entered into** the **system** by its **target user**. **Every input** will need to be **separately identified** and listed. This can take some time to investigate fully.

Outputs

More complex; this is the output required from the system, as requested by the user. In order to program the solution correctly the designer will need to know:

◆ **what the outputs are**
◆ **how the outputs should be displayed**
◆ **when the outputs should be generated**.

Processing

These should be basic descriptions of the processing that is required, for example:

◆ **calculate tax**
◆ **verify user account**
◆ **print customer report**.

These process descriptions can then be **decomposed** (broken down) into more **detailed algorithms** as part of the design phase.

Storage

Storage typically means two things:

◆ **temporary** data stored in **RAM (variables)**
◆ **permanent** data stored on **backing storage** (e.g. hard disk).

Any identified data should include:

◆ any piece of data **mentioned** in the problem
◆ any **calculated value** needed to solve the problem
◆ any value which will be **output**.

At this point it is worthwhile identifying whether these storage items are numeric, text, date or Boolean. More complex types such as arrays could also be considered.

User interface

A separate study in itself (**HCI** – **h**uman–**c**omputer **i**nterface), there should be a detailed look at how the end-user will **interact** with the program. Mouse or keyboard only? Which colours to use? Size of font? How is the screen laid out? **Forms design** is an important part of this aspect.

Constraints

A constraint is some kind of **limiting factor**; something which could **prevent** you completing the task satisfactorily.

Common constraints to plan for are:

◆ **operating-system software** availability and compatibility
◆ **hardware availability** and compatibility
◆ **timescale for development** (i.e. is there enough time)
◆ **funding** (i.e. money)
◆ **workforce** (availability of trained developers, quality assurance testers etc.).

3.2 Design

Once the **requirements specification** has been **created** (and **agreed** by all **stakeholders**), it will be time to **design** a **solution** which takes into account all of the **factors** discussed so far.

A particular design tool will be selected that is appropriate to the type of problem at hand, for example:

◆ **flowchart** – general use
◆ **JSP** – procedural and modular problems
◆ **UML** – problems which lend themselves to an object-oriented approach
◆ **DFD, ERM** – database-related problems.

Some designs may use a number of different design tools and diagrams.

3.3 Technical documentation

Technical documentation is written by **developers** for **other developers** to read.

This means that programming **terminology** (jargon) may be freely used, as long as it is sufficiently explained.

Technical documentation may often include, depending on how the design was developed:

◆ requirements specification
◆ forms design (**manual** or **electronic**, particularly for data entry)
◆ flowcharts
◆ JSP diagrams
◆ UML diagrams
◆ DFDs, ERMs
◆ data dictionary (a table listing data items and data types used in the solution)
◆ class schemas.

It should also contain:

◆ test strategy
◆ test results (predicted and actual)
◆ error messages (and corrective actions)
◆ fully commented program code
◆ recommendations for future enhancements.

Perhaps the most important factor to consider is that software **needs to be maintained**; even with the best programming it is unlikely to have covered all potential outcomes.

As such the technical documentation is the ultimate handbook which tells another programmer **how** the program was created and **why** it was done **that way**. This is particularly important when maintenance has to be performed by **another programmer**; the original programmers of a solution often become **unavailable** after a period of time (i.e. they may have changed job or be busy on other projects).

In addition it is also **live documentation**; as changes are made to the program code so should the technical documentation be updated to reflect those changes.

4 Be able to document, test, debug and review a programmed solution

4.1 Testing and debugging

Testing is the part of the **quality assurance** process in the software development life cycle (**See 2.1**).

Thorough testing **guarantees** that the solution should **work properly** and **meet** the **identified needs** of the **stakeholders** (as detailed in the **requirements specification**).

As a general rule, **good** programs are **RARE**!

Having a thorough **testing strategy** is the key to creating RARE programs. This starts with the concept of a **test plan**.

Test plan

A test plan should attempt to:

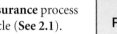

Help with assessment

RARE programs are:

Robust – they do not crash when given bad or silly input.

Accurate – they produce results with an acceptable level of accuracy.

Reliable – they work the same way every time they are used; no unexpected surprises.

Efficient – they calculate results and perform operations as quickly as possibly.

◆ Check different **logical pathways**, e.g. does the test check **both halves** (true and false) of a **conditional statement** (e.g. an if…else) or **all possible outcomes** of a **case** statement? Have all the **loops** been successfully tested? **Flowcharts** are particularly good for this as the **logical pathways** are easy to see. The tests should touch upon all **flow arrows** on the diagram.
◆ Check **normal data**. The program needs to be tested with data that is **within a sensible range**; data **likely** to be input.

- Check **extreme data**. It should also be tested with values, which while still within a sensible range, are **less likely** to be input; these are the values on the **extremes** (both **high** and **low**). For example, an age over 115 years is not impossible, but it is **extreme** (1 in 2.1 billion approximately!)
- Check **erroneous data**. Not all data entered into a program **will** be sensible. In order to ensure it is robust, **spurious** data should be tested. This typically included **values outside valid ranges** and **wrong types of value** (e.g. alphabetic when a number is expected).

Collecting suitable test data is important, both in **quantity** and **quality** of **spread**.

The test plan structure should include:

- **Test** – **what** is being tested; which **part** of the program is being tested.
- **Date** – **when** the test is taking place; this is important as it may link to a particular version of the program.
- **Expected result** – what results **we** expected to get out of the program by **tracing through first** on paper.
- **Actual result** – the results generated by the computer using our supplied test data.
- **Corrective action** – if a problem was discovered, what was done to the program to fix it.

Many formats exist for this type of content. A **trace table** is often seen as a simple way of **tabulating** and **comparing** such results.

Trace table for program 'Water Mover'								
Date: 12 September 2007								
Test: Calculation of water weight based on volume								
Number	Box H	Box W	Box L	Vol cm cubed expected	Vol cm cubed actual	Calculated weight expected kg	Calculated weight actual kg	Corrective Action
1	10	20	30	6000	6000.0	0.001 × 6000 = 6kg	6.0	None!
2	20	40	60	48,000	48,000.0	0.001 × 48,000 = 48kg	12.0	Fix data type problem

The trace table allows us to record the **values entered** and **logical pathways used** when a program runs both on paper (the 'dry run') or live.

The **comparison** between the **actual** and **expected results** will quickly show how **accurate** the programmed solution is and also, given the variables involved in any particularly test, where any possible problem will be found.

Screen captures are a good addition to any trace table as they **reinforce** the **actual results** of the program running.

Error messages

The process of **finding** and **removing** errors from program code is known as '**debugging**'.

Some errors occur at **compile time**, found as the high-level language is translated into low-level language. Statements which break the language's syntax generate **compilation errors**.

When errors occur while the programming is running, they are referred to as **run-time errors**.

Warnings are **minor issues** discovered during translation; they are **not fatal** (like an error) but may indicate possible run-time errors. A common example is using a **data type** which is **too small** to **hold** a **calculated result**. The run-time effect would be **truncation** and, therefore, **inaccurate results**.

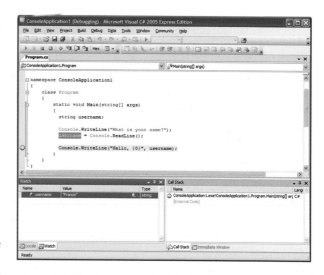

Figure 18.12 The C# IDE highlights a certain error (a missing semi-colon)

Specialist software tools

Modern programming software has feature-rich tools to assist the specialist while debugging a solution.

In a typical IDE, the three most commonly used **debug tools** are the following.

Trace

A trace allows the programmer to **follow** a program **line by line** as it executes, walking through the different **logical pathways** as the program progresses.

Tracing is very useful when **conditional statements** (if…else, case etc) are present. If the **trace** shows **unexpected behaviour** (going down the wrong logical pathway, for example) the programmer will need to **check their logic** to see where things have gone wrong.

Watches

A watch lets the programmer **spy** on the **contents** of a variable while the program is running, usually during a **trace**.

One of the most common programming problems is a variable storing **unexpected values**. The watch feature lets the programmer **see the changes in a variable's contents** as different lines of the program code are executed.

The appearance of an unexpected value in a watched variable will allow the programmer to **narrow their search** to just a few lines of program code.

Breakpoint

A breakpoint is a debugging feature which lets the programmer **mark a line of code** with a **physical breakpoint**. When the program runs it will **halt temporarily** at this point.

From here the programmer can decide to **trace the remaining code** and/or **inspect variable watches** they have set.

The clear advantage here is that parts of the program that are functioning correctly **need not be traced**; the breakpoint can be placed after these sections have finished.

4.2 User documentation

Unlike **technical documentation** (**see 3.3**), this type of documentation is meant to be read by a **typical** end-user – **not** a developer.

As a result, the user instructions should **avoid the use of technical terms or jargon** where possible.

Typical content may include:

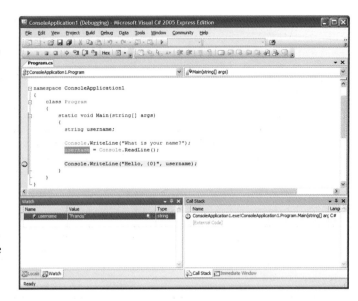

Figure 18.13 The C# IDE demonstrates tracing, watches and breakpoints

◆ how to **install** the program (including 'loading' instructions and hardware/operating-system requirements)
◆ how to **safely uninstall** the program
◆ how to **start** and **end** the program
◆ how to **use** the program **properly**
◆ **how to resolve** problems that might occur (also known as a '**troubleshooting**' guide)
◆ how to get **further help** (online forums, files on disk, telephone support etc.).

A common tactic is for the user guide to hold the user's hand by taking them through a typical example of the program working.

In addition, keeping the instructions brief (**step-by-step** are ideal), with accurate **screen**, **mouse** or **keyboard** diagrams or **screen captures** to show the program running.

The move from paperware

Over the last 15 years or so there has been a determined shift from producing printed program documentation to electronic distribution.

Text files (e.g. Readme.txt)
An **ASCII** (American Standard Code for Information Interchange) **text file** containing basic information about the program. This is usually stored as a file on a disk or in a downloaded archive (e.g. .ZIP or .RAR). Text files can be opened and created by using a **text editor** such as Microsoft Windows **Notepad**.

.PDF document
Adobe's portable document format file – a **popular**, **secure** and **reliable** way of **sharing electronic documents**. A copy of the freely downloadable Adobe **Acrobat Reader**® application is required in order to read a .PDF file.   Acro Software's **CutePDF** – a freely downloadable PDF creation tool

Screencast videos and animations
Why **describe** how something works when you can **show it**? Applications such as **Wink**® and **Adobe Captivate**® can be used to **create recordings** of programs **being used**. These **recorded tutorials** ('**screencasts**') often have additional **highlighting** and **narration** to help explain what is being seen on screen.

4.3 Review

A formal, reflective procedure that should clearly identify:

◆ the program's **strengths**
◆ the program's **weaknesses**
◆ **how well** the program **meets the stakeholders' needs**.

This is essentially a comparison of the **final product** and the **requirements specification**.

It will require the **cooperation** of all the stakeholders in order to secure the necessary findings and could take some time.

End-users of the software can be **interviewed**, **observed** or be given a **questionnaire** to complete.

The use of **focus groups** to **dig down** into **user viewpoint** is also valuable.

In addition it is likely that a section on further developments will be required, listing:

◆ an overview of **corrections** made (to errors)
◆ **improvements** (to existing performance) that could be made
◆ **expansions** (to existing functionality) that could be invested in.

Review should be an **ongoing process**, exploring program **performance** and **end-user satisfaction** at **regular intervals**. If faults are found which cannot be remedied using minor maintenance, the software development life cycle (as seen in **2.1**) will start once more.

Braincheck

1 Name four qualities a good program should possess.
2 Name four properties that a test strategy should cover.
3 Explain the difference between an error and a warning.
4 Name three specialist tools which assist the debugging process.
5 Name four different aspects a user guide should cover.
6 Name three different forms of documentation media.
7 Which three points should a formal program review identify?
8 What further developments can be identified during review?
9 What should user documentation avoid?

How well did you do? See page 421 for the answers!

Links

Unit 18 is a **core unit** on the BTEC National Certificate and BTEC National Diploma for IT Practitioners (**Software Development route**).

Unit 18 is also a **specialist unit** on the following BTEC National routes:

IT and Business

Networking

Systems Support

As such it has links to a number of other units, principally:

Unit 4 – IT project

Unit 10 – Client Side Customisation of Web Pages

Unit 11 – Data Analysis and Design

Unit 12 – Developing Computer Games

Unit 13 – Human Computer Interaction

Unit 19 – Web Server Scripting

Unit 20 – Event Driven Programming

Unit 25 – Object Oriented Programming

In addition this unit has identified direct links with:

Unit 7 – IT Systems Analysis and Design

Achieving success

In order to achieve each unit you will complete a series of coursework activities. Each time you hand in work, your tutor will return this to you with a record of your achievement.

This particular unit has 11 criteria to meet: 6 Pass, 3 Merit and 2 Distinction.

For a **pass**:

You must achieve **all** 6 pass criteria.

For a **merit**:

You must achieve **all** 6 pass and **all** 3 merit criteria.

For a **distinction**:

You must achieve **all** 6 Pass, **all** 3 merit **and both** distinction criteria.

So that you can monitor your own progress and achievement in each unit, a recording grid has been provided (see below). The full version of this grid is also included on the companion CD.

	Assignments in this unit			
Assignment	U18.01	U18.02	U18.03	U18.04
Referral				
Pass				
1				
2				
3				
4				
5				
6				
Merit				
1				
2				
3				
Distinction				
1				
2				

Help with assessment

The key issues with this unit are to ensure that you can select an appropriate programming language for a set problem, design a solution, implement it and document it for the target users.

An awareness of different programming languages is vital, as is the need to test the solution fully.

The **merit criteria** focus on **your ability to compare different programming languages** (to appreciate their suitability to any given problem), your **understanding of different data types** and how to **justify their selection**. Furthermore, there is an expectation that **testing** and **review** should be thorough enough to point towards **corrections** and **improvements** of an **existing solution**.

For a **distinction** you need to be able to **identify which language to use** in different scenarios and be able to **fully justify your selection**. In addition, you will be expected to **design**, **implement** and **test** full programs, demonstrating the ability to **review them** and suggest **possible improvements**.

Online resources on the CD

Electronic glossary for this unit

Key fact sheets

Electronic slide show of key points

Sample program code in a number of programming languages

Multiple choice self-test quizzes

Flash animated tutorials for C#

Further reading

Knuth, D., 1998, *The Art of Computer Programming*, 3 vol., 2nd edn, Addison Wesley, ISBN 0201485419.

Wender, K., 1995, *Cognition and Computer Programming*, Intellect Books, ISBN 1567500951.

Event-driven Programming

Capsule view

Event-driven Programming (EDP) is a full 60-hour unit that is intended to build on programming skills developed in Unit 18 Principles of Software Development and Design.

Programs developed using an **event-driven approach** differ from traditional algorithm-oriented solutions. In EDP, the key is to understand **what kinds of events** can be **triggered** and how the program can best **respond** to them. For some learners, event-driven programming can be much more **rewarding** and **fun**!

The unit itself will use **Microsoft Visual Basic® .NET** as its language of choice but the accompanying CD will have comparable Microsoft **Visual Basic 6®** and Microsoft **Visual C++®** samples for all code given in the main body of the text.

Learning aims

1 Understand the characteristics and used of event-driven programming.
2 Be able to use the tools and techniques of an event-driven language.
3 Be able to design and create an event-driven application.
4 Be able to test and review an event-driven application.

1 Understand the characteristics and used of EDP

1.1 Key characteristics

Perhaps the obvious starting point is to define the key characteristics of EDP languages.

To start with it will help if we can define a few new terms.

Key Terms

A **form** is a **visual container** used to **group together** user interface **components** such as text boxes, buttons, labels, checkboxes etc. It is used to provide an **input mechanism** for a user that is both **approachable** and **functional**.

Event loops are **processing cycles** which **continually look for events to happen** (e.g. a button click, file deletion or arrival of a data packet over a network).

Trigger functions are used by event loops to identify and **launch** a **response** to an **event** which has happened in an event loop.

Event handlers are the actual **program code modules** which are **executed** when a particular **trigger** has **occurred**. For example, if a user clicked a button, this would **trigger** an **event handler** for the **code actions associated** with the **button**.

EDP uses all four of these elements to form an effective **software development solution**.

Here is a **visual representation** of the key EDP **characteristics**.

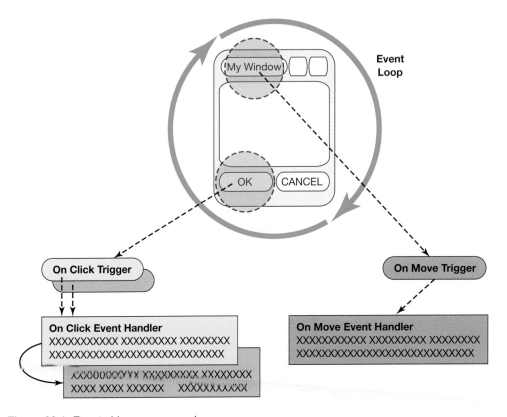

Figure 20.1 Event-driven programming

In the example shown in **Figure 20.1**, a **form** is enclosed in an **event loop**.

Two trigger functions are specifically available:

◆ **Form Move**
◆ **Button Click**

When the '**Form Move' trigger** is **detected** (by the user **manually repositioning** the form on screen), the '**On Move**' event handler is called and executed.

When the '**Button Click' trigger** is **detected** in response to the 'OK' button being **clicked**, an '**On Click**' event handler is called and executed.

Please note that the On Click event handler could perform an action that would trigger **another** event to occur. This is called an **event cascade**; in theory a number of events could be cascaded in an event-driven solution.

1.2 Advantages of EDP

There are clear advantages to using EDP:

◆ **flexibility**
◆ **suitability** for **graphical user interfaces** (**GUIs**)
◆ **simplicity of programming** (visual components autogenerate code for the programmer)
◆ **ease of development,** particularly for **r**apid **a**pplication **d**evelopment (**RAD**).

1.3 Disadvantages

There are also some clear disadvantages that come with an EDP approach:

◆ Can be **slow** – especially if software needs to work in **real time,** with **time-critical** responses.
◆ Can be **inefficient** – EDP does not always make efficient use of operating system resources.
◆ **Large footprint** – solutions can use a **disproportionate** amount of RAM.
◆ **Does not teach developer** algorithmic skills.
◆ **Difficult to translate** into **other languages.**
◆ **Solution** can be **platform dependent** (e.g. only work on Microsoft Windows®) and **cannot** be recompiled for other operating system platforms.

1.4 Examples

An operating system is a **good example** of an **event-driven system**. For example, a modern **GUI** is a **collection** of a number of **visual components** that **each** have to respond to user input, e.g. the Microsoft Windows® **calculator applet** has a surprising number of potential **triggers**.

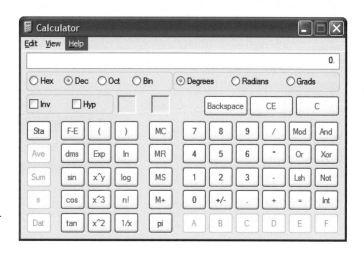

This applet has to deal with triggers for button clicks, key presses, menu selection, radio buttons, checkboxes, minimising and window movement – and that is before the functional part (i.e. doing the actual calculations) is considered.

Figure 20.2 Microsoft Windows® calculator applet

As you can see, any simple program that awaits unpredictable user input has to be ready to handle any event, depending on the trigger.

1.5 Programming languages

There are a number of programming languages which adopt the **event-driven paradigm**.

The following pages discuss the most common ones.

Microsoft Visual Basic®

Visual Basic®, often abbreviated by developers to just 'VB', is an EDP language that was created by **Microsoft**.

The language itself is heavily derived from **BASIC** (**B**eginner's **A**ll-purpose **S**ymbolic **I**nstruction **C**ode) and shares many of its **keywords** and **constructs**. In addition, Microsoft Visual Basic® provides opportunities for RAD applications which often rely on a GUI.

It also has simple integration with **Microsoft Access®** and **Excel®** and provides relatively straightforward use of **Windows® libraries** (in the form of .DLL files and **ActiveX controls**) to tap into **prewritten routines** such as the Common Dialogue Box for Open/Save/Font/Colour components.

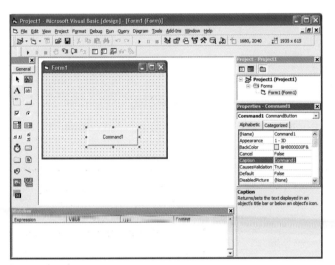

Visual Basic® programs are **only intended** to run on a **Microsoft Windows® operating system**. The Visual Basic® language and **integrated development environment** (**IDE**) have the **same limitation**.

Visual Basic® is **slowly being replaced** by its **successor** (**Visual Basic® .NET**) although, as there is a wealth of **legacy Visual Basic® code** still in use today, it is **unlikely** to disappear that soon.

The last version of traditional Visual Basic® is VB6.

Its successor is **Microsoft Visual Basic® .NET.**

Figure 20.3 Visual Basic 6® IDE

Microsoft Visual Basic® .NET

Visual Basic® .NET is effectively version 7 of Visual Basic®.

However, VB® .NET is a true **object-oriented version** of the language, built on Microsoft®'s .NET framework. As a consequence, some **language syntax** and **features** available in Visual Basic® no longer worked as they once did, causing developers much pain during transition.

The newest version is part of **Microsoft Visual Studio 2005®**.

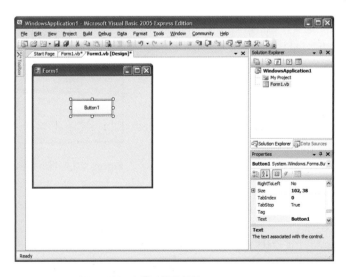

Figure 20.4 Visual Basic® .NET IDE

VBA

VBA or **V**isual **B**asic for **A**pplications is a dialect of Microsoft's Visual Basic that is **built into Microsoft Office applications** such as **Microsoft Word®** and **Microsoft Excel®**.

VBA gives developers a way to **add functionality** to Microsoft applications and to **customise** them to form **tailored solutions**. In addition, VBA also allows developers to **automate** these packages using **macros**, which represent a **quick, low-cost, low-risk approach** to designing **bespoke solutions**.

This example, accessed from a **toolbar button click event**, highlights the **selected text** in **yellow**.

VBA also has a **poor reputation** for **security**; many **macro viruses** have been successfully written which **infect** Microsoft Office® **documents**, often causing **annoying side effects** and **disabling** an **application's key features**. As such, **security features** have been added to these applications to **screen malicious** ('unsafe') VBA code.

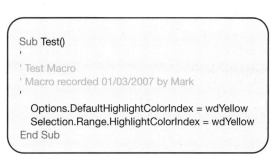

```
Sub Test()
'
' Test Macro
' Macro recorded 01/03/2007 by Mark
'

    Options.DefaultHighlightColorIndex = wdYellow
    Selection.Range.HighlightColorIndex = wdYellow
End Sub
```

VBA has been superseded by Microsoft Visual Studio 2005® **Tools for Applications**, a .NET implementation.

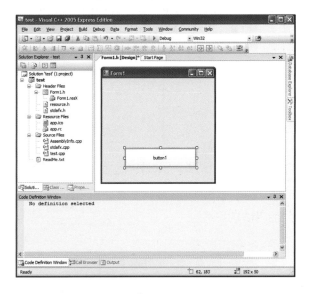

Figure 20.5 Visual C++® IDE

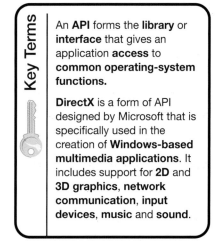

Key Terms

An **API** forms the **library** or **interface** that gives an application **access** to **common operating-system functions**.

DirectX is a form of API designed by Microsoft that is specifically used in the creation of **Windows-based multimedia applications**. It includes support for **2D** and **3D graphics, network communication, input devices, music** and **sound**.

Visual C++

Visual C++ is Microsoft's own C++ dialect which has added functionality that allows software developers to build event-driven GUIs.

Microsoft Visual C++® (often abbreviated to MSVC) contains support for the **Windows API** (**a**pplication **p**rogramming **i**nterface), **DirectX** and the **.NET framework**. As such it represents a comprehensive language for developing Windows-oriented event-driven programs.

Downloading Visual Basic 2005® Express Edition

Following the provided link, **download**, **install** and **register** the **free version** of Microsoft's Visual Basic 2005® **Express Edition**.

http://msdn.microsoft.com/vstudio/express/vb/

Try to get the sample programs on the **companion CD** running!

2 Be able to use the tools and techniques of an event-driven language

2.1 Triggers

Common triggers are typically either:

◆ **user events**
◆ **system events**

It is important that **you** can use EDP language to **respond** to such event triggers. The following Visual Basic .NET example demonstrates handling both **user events** (key presses, mouse click etc.) and **system-generated events**.

This simple example is created by selecting a **Button Control** (actually a .NET component) from the VB® .NET **Toolbox**. This is then **drawn** on the form.

The Button Control's **Text property** is changed to 'What time is it?'

The Button is then **double-clicked** to display the **VB® .NET code window**.

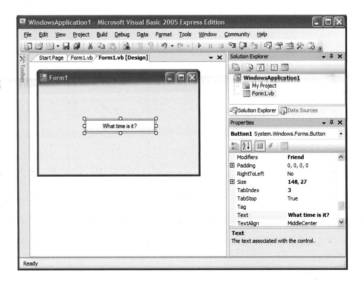

Figure 20.6 Creating a simple user event in VB® .NET

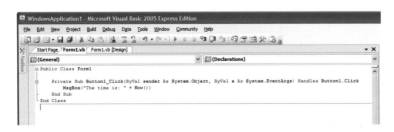

Figure 20.7 Coding the event handler in VB® .NET

It is here that an **empty** 'stub' **event handler** is shown. As a software developer, we need to **add** the **appropriate actions** to this **event handler**.

In this case we will use a VB® .NET **function** called '**MsgBox**' which displays **customised Message Boxes** on the Windows screen. In addition, we will use the 'Now' function which returns the current date and time (as stored in the PC's RTC).

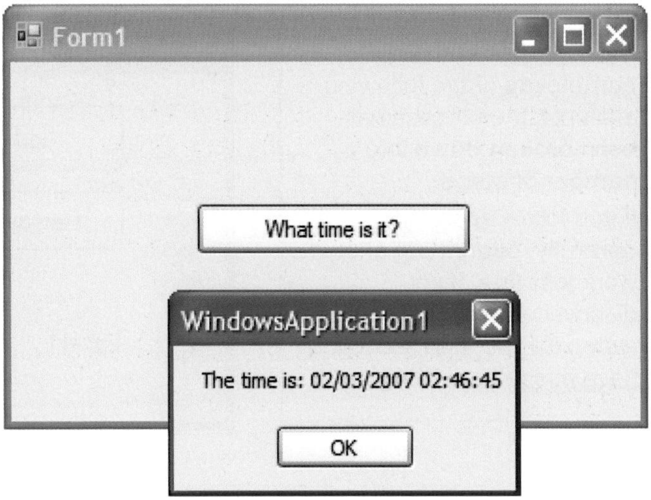

In this nice, simple example, the VB® .NET application simply executes the 'Button_Click' event handler when the user triggers the event by clicking on the 'What time is it?' button.

The 'Button_Click' event handler responds to the trigger by displaying a Message Box which shows the current date and time; displaying the 'OK' button is the default behaviour for a Message Box.

As you can see, coding a basic event handler is a fairly straightforward practice in VB® .NET. Don't worry, though, the examples will get more challenging as we work through.

Figure 20.8 Running the VB® .NET application and triggering the user event

Modifying the code

VB® .NET programs are modified by altering the form contents and its associated event handlers.

Try to **modify** the Button so that the **Text property** says 'Play Windows Alert!'

Delete the Msgbox line of code and **replace** with the following:

```
My.Computer.Audio.PlaySystemSound(System.Media.SystemSounds.Asterisk)
```

Now **rerun the VB® .NET** program and **test** the **new user event**.

Hopefully, if you have modified the code **correctly**, your PC should make your **Windows Alert** sound when the 'Button_Click' event is **triggered**.

System events are a bit trickier!

First we need to select a suitable system event.

System events are directly connected to the operating system on a computer system. As such, any demonstration created using VB® .NET will be using Microsoft Windows.

Common **Windows system events** include **triggers** for:

◆ **low RAM**
◆ change of **display settings** (the video mode)
◆ change of **power mode** (e.g. moving to and from suspend mode)
◆ change of **RTC settings** (date and time).

> ⚠ Because of the **complexity** of the following example, the process has been **broken down** into a **number** of **steps**.
>
> If you follow each step **carefully, everything** should work **just fine**. If you discover a **problem**, go back a step (or two) and see if you have **missed anything**.

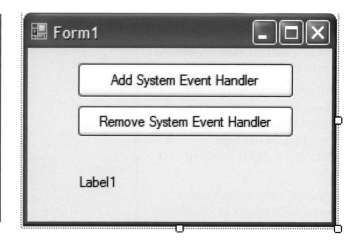

Figure 20.9 Creating the form for system events

Step 1

Create a new project, adding these two labelled buttons (Button1 and Button2) and a label (Label1).

Step 2

Double-click on **Button1** and add the **following** VB® .NET code.

```
AddHandler SystemEvents.TimeChanged, AddressOf MyEventHandler
```

Step 3

Double-click on **Button2** and add the **following** VB® .NET code.

```
RemoveHandler SystemEvents.TimeChanged, AddressOf MyEventHandler
Label1.Text = ""
```

This will have added **code** to **both buttons' event handlers** to add a **system event handler** (when Button1 is **triggered**) and **remove** the **system event handler** (when Button2 is **triggered**).

The handler is for the **TimeChanged system event**. VB® .NET will need to know **what we want to do when** the **system event is triggered** (i.e. **when** the **user changes** the **RTC**). To do this we simply give the **RAM address** of a **new event handler** we are going to write (we have called this '**MyEventHandler**').

Creating the new event handler comes **next**.

Step 4

Right-click on 'WindowsApplication1' in VB® .NET's **Solution Explorer** pane.

VB® .NET uses modules as separate .vb files which can store our functions. This new module is where we will put our new program code for the TimeChanged system event handler (i.e. saying what will happen).

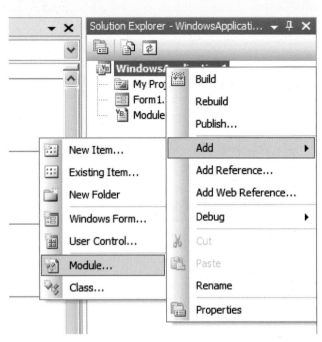

Figure 20.10 Adding a new module to the current application

Step 5

Select module which opens up the 'Add New Item' window.

Choose 'Module' and ensure that that the module is called 'Module1.vb' (it should be).

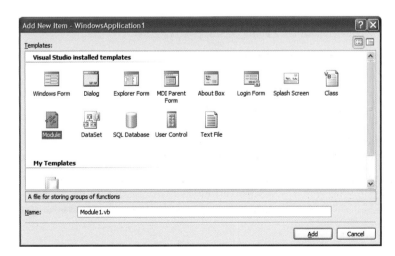

Figure 20.11 Adding a new module to the current application

Step 6

Double-click the new 'Module1.vb' entry in the **Solution Explorer**.

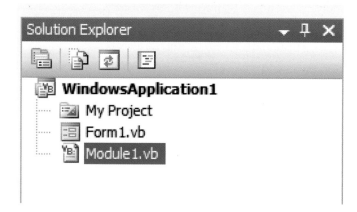

Figure 20.12 Opening the new module

Then add the following VB® .NET code into the empty module.

```
Public Sub MyEventHandler(ByVal sender As Object, ByVal e As EventArgs)
    Form1.Label1.Text = "User has changed the system time"
End Sub
```

Step 7

Double-click 'Form1.vb' in the **Solution Explorer**.

Then, **double click the form itself** to create the **empty 'Form1_Load'** event handler.

Add this code to it:

```
Label1.Text = " "
```

Step 8

Move the cursor into the 'General' section of the VB® .NET code window.

Add the following line.

```
Imports Microsoft.Win32
```

Step 9

That should be it!

Let's recap those steps by first looking at the **form's** ('Form1.vb') code.

Figure 20.13 VB® .NET code related to the form

Step 10

And then do the same but for the module ('Module1.vb').

Figure 20.14 VB® .NET code related to the module

Step 11

Save all the files (CTRL+SHIFT+S)!

Step 12

It should now be possible to **run the application** to test our **handling** of the Windows 'TimeChanged' **trigger**.

Step 13

Enable our **system event handler** by **clicking** the '**Add System Event Handler**' button **once**.

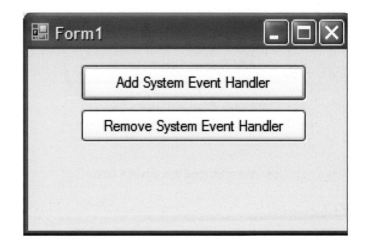

Figure 20.15 The form as it first appears

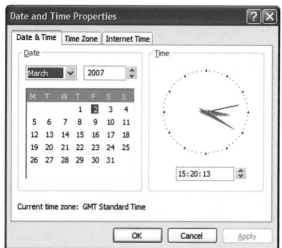

Figure 20.16 Changing the time in the Windows 'Date and Time' applet

Step 14

Change your PC's **system time.**

Step 15

Re-examine our form.

As you can hopefully see, our homemade system event handler has been triggered by the operating system. This is shown by the change of the label's text (beneath the buttons). Compare this to Figure 20.15.

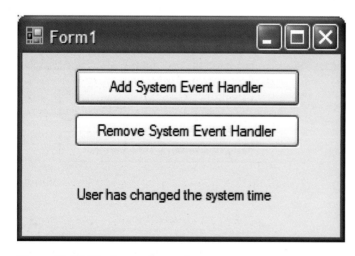

Figure 20.17 The forms changed appearance

Step 16

Click the 'Remove System Event Handler' and **change** the **time back.**

Although the 'TimeChanged' **trigger** will still occur, our system event handler has been removed. As a result, there will be nothing to deal with it.

Modifying the code

Attempt to modify the example application by writing a simple event handler for the 'change of display settings' trigger.

This is known as **'DisplaySettingsChanged'**.

As you may have guessed, the "`Imports Microsoft.Win32`" is used to give the developer access to the **system events** listed in the **Win32 API**.

Your homemade event handler can simply display a message that says 'Display settings have been changed'.

If you feel really confident, add a Windows alert sound.

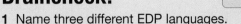
Braincheck!

1 Name three different EDP languages.
2 Common triggers can be caused by the _____ or the _____.
3 Name three possible system events.
4 Give three advantages of EDP languages.
5 Give three disadvantages of EDP languages.

How well did you do? See page 421 for the answers!

2.2 Tools and techniques

An EDP language such as VB® .NET has a number of different elements. In this section we will take a closer look at these elements and look at putting them together to form more complex solutions.

Use of controls

Controls are the **basic elements** of a VB® .NET application.

Most of the common controls can be found in the **Toolbox**, a **categorised collection** of **visual elements** that can be added to a standard form. It is accessed by pressing the **button** to the **left** of the **form design view**.

The Common Controls represent the category which most developers will initially rely on to build their solutions as they form the core of most GUIs.

It is also the category that we will focus on in this book.

When a control is added to a form, it allows the developer to **add event-handler code** to specific **triggers** and change the control's **properties**.

Clicking the *Auto Hide icon* will toggle (swap) the Tool Box between *automatically hiding* when not in use and being *permanently pinned* to the *left-hand side* of the screen.

Figure 20.18 VB® .NET Toolbox with Common Controls expanded

In this regard it is similar to an **object**, having both **properties** and **methods**.

Unit Link

Unit 18 (Principles of Software Design and Development) section 1.1 introduces object-oriented programming concepts. In addition, **Unit 25** (Object Oriented Programming) which is located in the companion book, deals with the topic in far greater detail than is possible here.

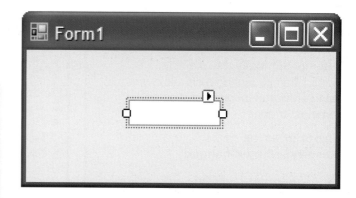

Figure 20.19 VB® .NET TextBox control

The control's properties can be seen in VB® .NET's **Properties Window**.

VB® .NET controls can therefore be seen as **classes**, with the **actual instances** of the **controls** (sat on the form) as the **true objects**.

This is a logical view as **changing the properties** of **one** TextBox 'object' **does not change** the **properties** of **another** (much as in OOP).

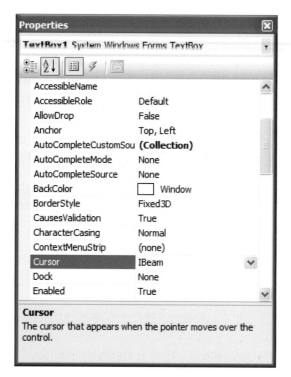

Figure 20.20 VB® .NET TextBox control's properties (alphabetical)

As you have seen already, most (but not all) **properties** can either be **changed** at **design-time** or at **run-time** (through the VB® .NET program code itself).

For example, we can use the **Properties Window** and alter the correct property **manually**.

But we can also achieve the **same affect** via **VB® .NET code**, executed at run-time.

```
TextBox1.BackColor = Color.Cyan
```

VB® has a number of predefined colours in its **Colour structure;** 'Cyan' is just one of them.

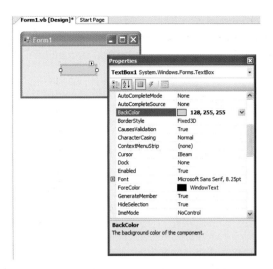

Figure 20.21 Changing the TextBox object's BackColour property to cyan at design-time

A more complex method would be as follows.

```
TextBox1.BackColor = System.Drawing.Color.FromArgb(128, 255, 255)
```

The latter example uses the **FromArgb function** (or method) to **generate** a colour based on its **red, green** and **blue values**. If you look back at Figure 20.21, you will see that these are the **same RGB values** as selected in the Properties Window.

Event handlers

VB® .NET has a **number** of **event handlers;** some are **generic** ('**Click**' being fairly common) but **others** are **specific** to **certain controls**.

Here is a list of some event handlers for the **Button** control:

◆ **Click**   occurs when user triggers by **clicking** the button.
◆ **DoubleClick**   occurs when user triggers by **double-clicking** the button.
◆ **KeyDown**   occurs when button has **focus** (it is **selected**) and a **key** is **pressed**.
◆ **MouseHover**   occurs when user **hovers mouse over** the button

And some **different** event handlers for a **TextBox** control:

◆ **Enter**   occurs when user triggers by moving **into** the TextBox.
◆ **TextChanged**   occurs when user triggers by **altering the text inside** the TextBox.
◆ **Leave**   occurs when user triggers by **moving away** from the TextBox (i.e. **clicks** or **tabs** to **another** control).

The **full list** of event handlers available for a control can be found in the VB® .NET **help system**.

Selection

A selection is a type of **conditional statement**, allowing the developer to **make a choice** about **which lines** of code to execute.

VB® .NET has a number of selection mechanisms but perhaps the most frequently used are **If…then…else** and **Select…Case statements**.

Let's take a look at the If…then…else statement first.

If…then…else

Here is a practical example of using an If…then…else statement.

```
Private Sub TextBox1_Leave(ByVal sender As Object, ByVal e As
System.EventArgs) Handles TextBox1.Leave

  If Not IsDate(TextBox1.Text) Then
    MsgBox("Please enter date (dd/mm/yy)", MsgBoxStyle.Information)
    TextBox1.Focus()
  Else
    MsgBox("Date acceptable", MsgBoxStyle.Information)
  End If
End Sub
```

In this example a sample form (as shown in Figure 20.22) has two TextBoxes.

The **first** TextBox control (**TextBox1**) will allow the user to store a **date** in the format **dd/mm/yy**, e.g. **04/09/07** would be entered for **September 4 2007**.

The **second** TextBox control (**TextBox2**) will allow the user to store a **time**.

If an **invalid date is** entered (tested using the **IsDate function** in VB® .NET), the **first part** of the **If…then….else statement** displays a **message box** and the user is **returned** to the **Date TextBox** (**TextBox1**) for **another** try.

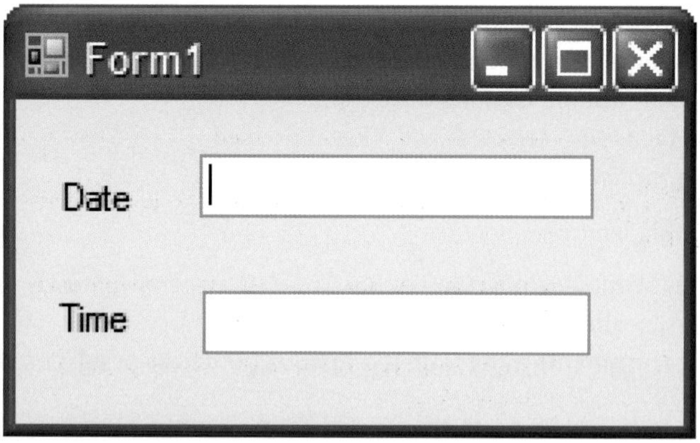

Figure 20.22 The sample form

The **test** for a **valid date** is performed **when** the user **moves away from** the Date TextBox, i.e. when they **click** on the Time TextBox. This is performed by the '**Leave**' **event handler**.

Figure 20.23 Getting the input wrong

However, if a **valid date** is entered, the '**else**' part of the **If…then…else** is **executed**. All this does is to simply pop up **another** message box, but this time it displays a **confirmation** that the date was **acceptable**.

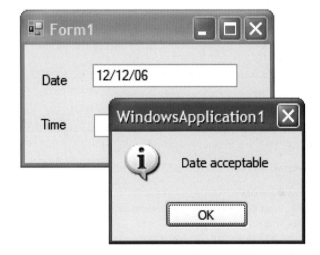

Figure 20.24 Getting the input right

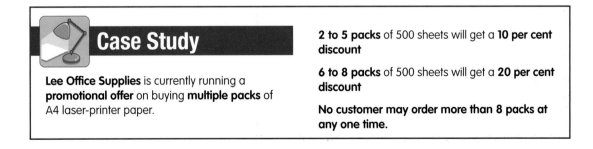

Case Study

Lee Office Supplies is currently running a **promotional offer** on buying **multiple packs** of A4 laser-printer paper.

2 to 5 packs of 500 sheets will get a **10 per cent discount**

6 to 8 packs of 500 sheets will get a **20 per cent discount**

No customer may order more than 8 packs at any one time.

Select...Case statement

Case statements are often used to simplify program code when it is necessary to match a single value (or range of values) from a list of given possibilities.

Here is a practical example of the Select...Case statement at work.

First we create a simple form with **Label**, **TextBox** and **Button** controls.

Figure 20.25 Lee Office Supplies' quantity check

And add the following code to the **Click event** of the **'What's my discount?' button** control.

```
Select Case (Val(TextBox1.Text))
   Case 1
     MsgBox("Sorry, no discount!", MsgBoxStyle.Information)

   Case 2 To 5
     MsgBox("10% discount.", MsgBoxStyle.Information)

   Case 6, 7, 8
     MsgBox("20% discount.", MsgBoxStyle.Exclamation)

   Case Else
     MsgBox("Sorry, you can't order more than 8.", MsgBoxStyle.Critical)
     TextBox1.Focus()

End Select
```

If you examine this closely, you will see that the text value entered into the 'Quantity Required' TextBox is converted to a number (with the VB® .NET Val function). This is then checked by the Select...Case statement against a list of possible values (and ranges).

Note that the case statements may check a **single value**, a **range** (e.g. '**2 To 5**') or a **comma-separated list**. The **Else part** of the Select...Case statement is used to process **any other value** which **is not matched** by any **previous** case statement.

Let's test this code with some sample input values that a customer might enter.

Entering a quantity of **1**:

Figure 20.26 No discount awarded

Entering a quantity of **3**:

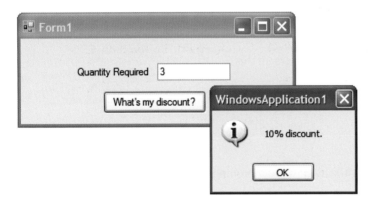

Figure 20.27 10 per cent discount awarded

Entering a quantity of **7**:

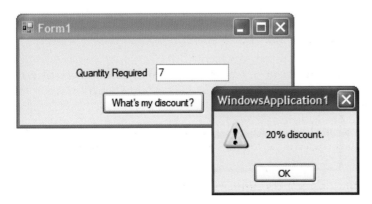

Figure 20.28 20 per cent discount awarded

And, finally, entering a quantity of **10**:

Figure 20.29 Invalid quantity requested

In most EDP languages, **similar types of selections** exist; they are **fundamental building blocks** which let the developer **make choices** in their programs.

Loops

Unit Link

Unit 18 (Principles of Software Design and Development) section 1.3 also examines selections (or conditional statements) but does so from a Microsoft C#® perspective. You will notice that although the C# syntax is different, If and Case statements are similarly constructed in different languages.

Loops or **iterations** allow the developer to perform a group of actions **repeatedly**. Unless the loop is infinite (goes on endlessly), it will have some kind of conditional statement that will force it to stop.

VB® .NET has a number of different loops. Perhaps the most commonly used are the following.

For…Next statement

The **For…Next** statement is a common tool in most programming languages; VB® .NET is no exception to this rule.

It is used to run a loop a **preset number** of times, usually controlled by a **counter**.

The following example application demonstrates the use of a **For…Next** loop to **generate** a child's **times tables** based on **two inputs** (the **table number** itself and the **number of rows** required).

TextBox3 will be treated **slightly differently**; please **modify** the following **properties:**
◆ **Multiline** set to **True**
◆ **ScrollBars** set to **Both**

Next, add the **following code** to the **click event** of the 'Make Table!' **button** control.

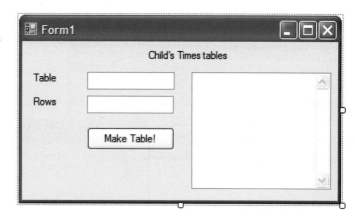

Figure 20.30 Form design for child's times tables

```
Dim counter As Byte
Dim newline As String

TextBox3.Text = TextBox1.Text & " times table" & vbCrLf
```
Pre-check condition
```
For counter = 0 To Val(TextBox2.Text)

    newline = counter & " X " & TextBox1.Text & " = " & _
    Val(TextBox1.Text) * counter & vbCrLf

    TextBox3.AppendText(newline)
Next counter
```

Next, run the application and some sample values.

In this example I have asked for **10 rows** of the **4 times table**.

If you take a look back at the code, you will see that the **For...Next loop** is **instructed** to run **from 0 up to the value entered into TextBox2** (the **number of rows**). If we entered **10** into that TextBox, the For loop will indeed run from **0 to 10** (rows 8, 9 and 10 need to be scrolled down to in Figure 20.31).

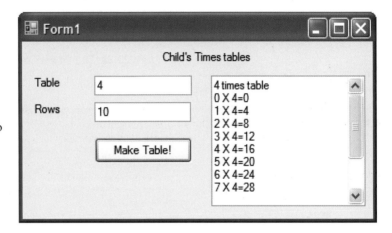

Figure 20.31 The 4 times table

Inside the For...Next loop **a new string** (**see 2.3**) is created which is used to **assemble** a line of output that includes the counter, 'X' and '=' symbols, the table number and the calculated result (which is also stored in a new variable (again, **see 2.3** for details). This is then **appended** into the multiline TextBox3.

It is because of the fixed-length nature of the For...Next loop that it is invariably used to repeat code where the developer knows how many times it is to be repeated before it starts.

Do...Loop

The **second** type of **loop** we will look at is the **Do...Loop**.

In VB® .NET the **Do...Loop** can either be **pre-** or **post-check conditioned**. What this means is that the **controlling condition** is put either **before** (pre-check) or **after** (post-check) the **lines of code** being **repeated**. The following example (a **vowel counter**) is written twice, using **two forms** of the Do...Loop.

First, **create the form** as indicated.

Again, in preparation the following **properties** must be set on the **TextBox1** control:

◆ **Multiline** set to **True**
◆ **ScrollBars** set to **Both**

Unit Link

Unit 18 (Principles of Software Design and Development) section 1.3 also examines loops but does so from a C# perspective. You will notice that although the C# syntax is different, loops tend to be similarly constructed in different languages.

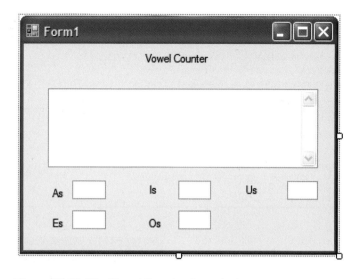

Figure 20.32 The Vowel Counter form design

The following code is added to the **TextChanged event handler** of **TextBox1**:

```
Dim counter As Byte
Dim nextchar As Char
Dim acount As Byte
Dim ecount As Byte
Dim icount As Byte
Dim ocount As Byte
Dim ucount As Byte

counter = 1
Do
  nextchar = Mid(TextBox1.Text, counter, 1)
  Select Case (nextchar)
    Case "a", "A"
      acount = acount + 1
      TextBox2.Text = acount
    Case "e", "E"
      ecount = ecount + 1
      TextBox3.Text = ecount
    Case "i", "I"
      icount = icount + 1
      TextBox4.Text = icount
    Case "o", "O"
      ocount = ocount + 1
      TextBox5.Text = ocount
    Case "u", "U"
      ucount = ucount + 1
      TextBox6.Text = ucount
  End Select
  counter = counter + 1
Loop Until counter > TextBox1.TextLength
```

Post-check condition

When this application runs, the **event handler** is **triggered** when a **new keystroke** is made. The application then runs a **post-check conditioned Do…Loop** which **repeats until** the **counter** is **greater** than the **length** of the current text **stored** in **TextBox1**. **Inside** the loop, a **Select…Case** is used to **examine each character** (by using the **MID function**) and **increment the appropriate counter** when a **vowel** is **matched**.

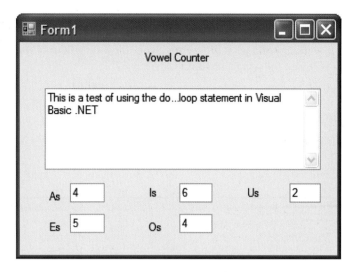

Figure 20.33 The Vowel Counter application running

The same code can be re-written as:

```
Dim counter As Byte
Dim nextchar As Char
Dim acount As Byte
Dim ecount As Byte
Dim icount As Byte
Dim ocount As Byte
Dim ucount As Byte

counter = 1                                        Pre-check condition
Do While counter <= TextBox1.TextLength
   nextchar = Mid(TextBox1.Text, counter, 1)
   Select Case (nextchar)
     Case "a", "A"
        acount = acount + 1
        TextBox2.Text = acount
     Case "e", "E"
        ecount = ecount + 1
        TextBox3.Text = ecount
     Case "i", "I"
        icount = icount + 1
        TextBox4.Text = icount
     Case "o", "O"
        ocount = ocount + 1
        TextBox5.Text = ocount
     Case "u", "U"
        ucount = ucount + 1
        TextBox6.Text = ucount
   End Select
   counter = counter + 1
Loop
```

In this example, a **pre-check condition Do…Loop** is used, **moving** the condition to the **beginning of the loop**. Also notice that the **condition statement** has **changed** to 'while counter <=' to reflect the fact that it is working **somewhat differently**. Now, the loop **will only work** while counter is still **less than or equal to** length of the text in TextBox1.

In VB® .NET it is possible to use the **Until** and **While** forms in **both pre- and post-check forms**.

The **final** VB® .NET loop type is the **While…End While**.

It works in a **similar fashion** to the **pre-check Do…Loop** as shown above, so we will not dwell too much on it here!

Its VB® .NET **syntax** is:

```
Dim counter As Byte
counter = 0
While counter < 10
    counter = counter + 1
    MsgBox("Loop has run " & counter & " time(s)!")
End While
```

Menu

Perhaps one of the most important aspects of any EDP application is its ability to respond to **triggers** generated by **menu systems. Drop-down** menus are a popular component of modern software applications, so you have to be able to **create** them and program their **event handlers**.

Creating a menu

Step 1

Have a good idea of the menu functions you require and how you want the menu organised. This can be achieved by drawing up a quick plan of the options and how they are grouped.

For example:

File	Edit	View	Help
Open File	Copy	Orders	Help about this program
Save File	Paste	Sales	About this program
Exit			

Where possible, and to improve human-computer interaction (HCI), it is advisable to try and keep menu options **similar** to those seen in **other commercial programs** (or even the **operating system's GUI**). This gives **the user** an **instant familiarity** with your software and makes it **more approachable** and **user-friendly**.

Step 2

VB® .NET approach to creating menus is different to its predecessor (VB6).

In VB® .NET a **new category** of controls is present in the **ToolBox: Menus & Toolbars**.

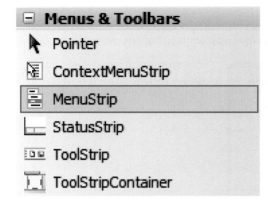

Figure 20.34 VB® .NET ToolBox category Menus & Toolbars

The control we want to use is the **MenuStrip**. **Select** this and **draw** on your empty form.

Note. Do not worry about **where** you draw it; it will automatically **default** to the **top** of the form. This is shown in Figure 20.35.

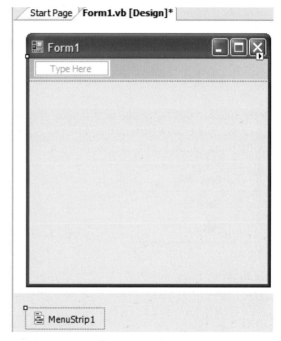

Figure 20.35 VB® .NET Form with empty MenuStrip

Step 3

You can now start to add in the text labels (as planned in Step 1) that represent your menu options. Click **each** 'Type Here' box and **enter the appropriate label** (moving down **or** across).

Figure 20.36 Adding the MenuStrip labels

Step 4

When you have finished, you should have a MenuStrip that looks like the plan from Step 1.

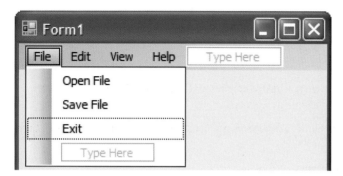

Any **unwanted** menu items can be **selected** and **removed** with the **Delete key**.

Figure 20.37 Completed MenuStrip

Step 5

Running the EDP application will result in a partially working menu system; it will appear and you will be able to navigate through the options but it will not respond to any triggers as we have not yet coded any event handlers.

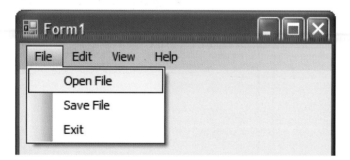

The next step is therefore to add an event handler.

Figure 20.38 Menu in action

Step 6

In design mode, **double-click** the '**Open File**' menu option and **add the following code** to the '**OpenFileToolStripMenuItem**' **click event handler**.

```
MsgBox("This would open a new file", MsgBoxStyle.Information)
```

This will simply pop-up a message box until we are ready to code the full actions of this menu option. It will, however, let us check to see our menu is working when the program is run.

From here, you can simply repeat Step 6 for each menu option and add program code appropriate to each event handler.

VB® .NET allows us to make functional improvements to our menu system.

What follows is a basic overview of three possible improvements to the existing menu that you could consider.

Use of shortcut keys

Shortcut keys can be used to access menu systems **without** relying on the mouse. For users who remember **keyboard shortcuts**, this can be a useful **time saver**.

It is recommended that you select shortcuts which are **commonly used** on **commercial software** so that you keep your application **consistent**.

For example, File Open is usually given the keyboard shortcut **CTRL + O**.

This would mean the user **holding down CTRL** (Control key) and pressing the 'O' **key**.

To add this, **select the required menu label** in the design view and **modify** the appropriate **properties** of this **menu option** in the **Properties** window.

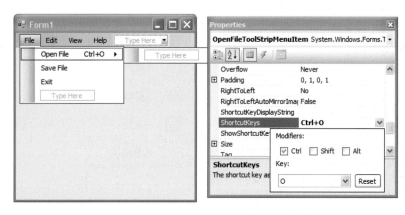

When the application is run again, the menu option can now be accessed using the CTRL+O shortcut.

Figure 20.39 Adding a shortcut

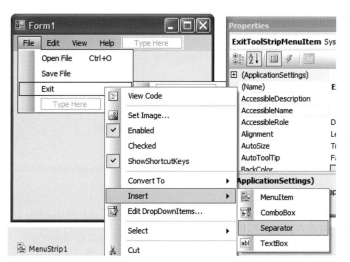

Figure 20.40 Adding a separator

Using a separator

As the name suggests, a **separator** is a **horizontal line** that is used to **distinguish different parts** of a menu system.

A common usage is to separate **loading, saving, printing** and **exit** options **underneath** the **File menu option**.

We can add a separator to our File menu option by selecting the Exit option and choosing the 'Insert a separator' option from the **right-click context menu**.

When the application is run again, the separator is clearly visible.

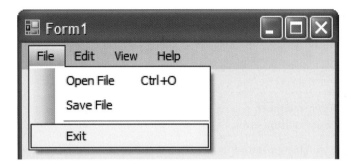

Figure 20.41 Separator between 'Save File' and 'Exit' options

Adding a single letter key press for each menu item

You may have seen a Windows application where **menu items** have **certain letters underlined**, e.g. in **Microsoft Word®**.

This is achieved by use of the **ampersand symbol** (**&**) in the menu item's **Text property**. Simply place the ampersand **before the letter** you wish to use as a key press alternative for the menu item.

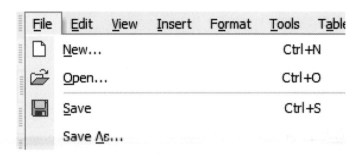

Figure 20.42 Single-letter keyboard shortcuts

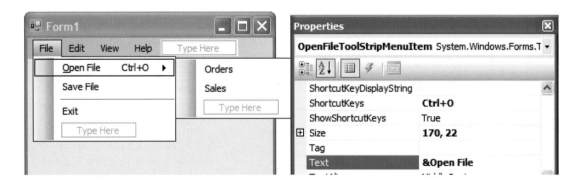

Figure 20.43 Adding single-letter keyboard shortcuts

Many other options for enhancing (including **ToolTips** – see 3.2) exist in VB® .NET.

It is recommended that you **experiment** with the **settings** and **facilities** available in order to create **intuitive** and **functional** menu systems for your own EDP applications.

Creating a menu system

Use VB® .NET's **MenuStrip control** to create the **following menu system**.

File		Reports	Help
O̲pen	CTRL+O	Customers	About this Program
S̲ave	CTRL+S	Orders	
_____		Sales	
E̲xit			

Remember to create shortcuts, separators and key-press options as indicated!

Debugging tools

Like most programming languages with an IDE, VB® .NET has extensive debugging tools.

Perhaps the most common debugging tools are:

◆ **Breakpoint**
◆ **Step Into (similar to a Trace)**
◆ **Watch**
◆ **Immediate Window**

Let's examine each of these in turn.

Unit Link

Unit 18 (Principles of Software Design and Development) section 4.1 also examines debugging tools but does so from a Microsoft C#® perspective. You will notice that debugging tools tend to function similarly from language to language. Therefore to avoid unnecessary duplication, the **tool definitions** are **not** repeated here and instead the focus is on **how** these tools are used in **VB® .NET**.

Breakpoint

Breakpoints can be placed in to a VB® .NET program by either **clicking** in the **left-hand margin** (alongside the code window), by using the **Debug menu** or by pressing the **F9 key** which **toggles** the breakpoint **on** and **off**.

A breakpoint is signified by a **red ball** and **inverse colouring** of the line of code.

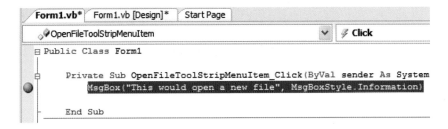

Figure 20.44 A breakpoint is marked on a specific line of code

When the EDP application is run, it will temporarily halt at the breakpoint as shown in Figure 20.45.

The developer can then decide how to proceed; this might mean **examining variables** (see 2.3) or **tracing the remainder of the code** line by line.

Figure 20.45 An active breakpoint on a line of code

Step Into

Step Into is activated by either using the **Debug menu** or by pressing the **F8 key**, which **will let the** developer trace the **execution** of **each line of code separately**.

Another feature called **Step Over** (Shift+F8 key or the Debug menu) can be used in a similar fashion but it executes **all the statements** in a block of code **at once**; this is useful if you are **moving between** sections of the program that need to be traced line by line (**Step Into**) and sections which you are confident are OK (**Step Over**).

Step Out can be used to **move** from Step Into **to** Step Over functionality.

Watch

A watch may be added to a **variable** (see 2.3) in a number of ways.

The most straightforward way to **add a watch** is to **Debug** the program (**F5**), **pause** the execution (**Break All** toolbar button) and **right click** on the variable you wish to watch. This will display a shortcut menu which has an option '**Add Watch**'.

Adding a watch will result in the **chosen variable appearing** in a separate **Watch window**.

Once the program is **paused** it can be **traced** using F8 (**Step Into**). This allows the developer to see the values in the **Watch window changing** as the variables are **processed** by each **active line** of program code.

Figure 20.46 Debug window showing contents of variables being processed

Right-clicking on the variable's name in the Watch window will display a further shortcut menu. One of the options is to **delete the watch**, allowing the developer to manage active watches effectively.

Immediate Window

This is a **separate window** which can be used to **output debugging information** while the VB® .NET application is running. If it disappears it can be made visible again with **CTRL+G**.

Usually located at the **bottom-left of the design screen**, it can be made to **float** as required or added as a tab (alongside the Form Design and Code windows).

A **simple use** of the Immediate Window is to **output calculated values** as the application runs, without **affecting** the **appearance** of the **form**.

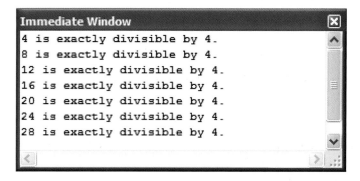

Immediate Window

```
4 is exactly divisible by 4.
8 is exactly divisible by 4.
12 is exactly divisible by 4.
16 is exactly divisible by 4.
20 is exactly divisible by 4.
24 is exactly divisible by 4.
28 is exactly divisible by 4.
```

Figure 20.47 Floating Immediate Window displays debug information

This can be achieved using **Debug.Print**.

```
Dim counter As Byte
counter = 1
Do While counter < 30
  Dim remainder As Byte
  remainder = counter Mod 4
  If remainder = 0 Then
    Debug.Print(counter & " is exactly divisible by 4.")
  End If
  counter = counter + 1
Loop
```

In this example, the Mod (modulus) operator is used to discover **whether or not** a number is **exactly divisible by four** (it will have **a zero remainder** if this **is** the case).

The output is **sent directly** to the **Immediate Window** by use of the **Debug.Print** statement.

2.3 Data

Identifiers – variables and constants

An identifier is simply a **name** which **represents** a **value**. The name is used as an **alternative** to **referring** to a value's **memory address** in **RAM** (names are **friendlier** and **easier to remember**). Identifier names **should not be the same** as any existing **control's property**.

Key Terms

A **variable** is an identifier whose **value can change while** the program **runs**. Variables can **only** store **one value at a time**; if a second value is assigned, the **older value** is **overwritten**.

A **constant** is an identifier whose value **cannot change while the program is running**. Constants represent **fixed values** which may be used in program code **instead** of using text or numeric **values**, e.g. '**PI**' instead of **3.14**, to **improve** both its **readability** and **maintainability**.

VB® .NET uses **two kinds** of identifier; **variables** and **constants**.

Variables and constants are **absolutely critical** to writing program code; **without these** there could be no true **processing** (see 3.1).

Data types and declaration

In order to **create** a variable or constant, it is necessary to **write a declaration**. In VB® .NET a variable is created through the use of the '**Dim**' keyword (standing for **dimension**). In addition, the programmer must **select** the **correct data type** for the variable or constant.

The following example demonstrates **declarations** of **variables** and **constants** in VB® .NET.

```
Dim bAge As Byte
Dim iMatchAttendance As Integer
Dim sUsername As String
Dim dItemPrice As Decimal

Const PI As Double = 3.141592
Const PASSWORD As String = "LETMEIN"
```

In VB® .NET, **constants** are created by using the '**Const**' keyword.

The following **table** lists **popular VB® .NET data types**.

Data type	RAM requirement	
Boolean	4 bytes	True or False
Byte	1 byte	0 to 255 (unsigned)
Char	2 bytes	0 to 65535 (unsigned)
Date	8 bytes	January 1, 1 Common Era to December 31, 9999 CE
Decimal	12 bytes	+/–79,228,162,514,264,337,593,543,950,335 with no decimal point +/–7.9228162514264337593543950335 with 28 places to the right of the decimal The smallest non-zero number is +/–0.0000000000000000000000000001
Double	8 bytes	–1.79769313486231E308 to –4.94065645841247E–324 +4.94065645841247E–324 to +1.79769313486232E308
Integer	4 bytes	–2,147,483,648 to 2,147,483,647

Long	8 bytes	–9,223,372,036,854,775,808 to 9,223,372,036,854,775,807
Object	4 bytes	Any type can be stored in a variable of type Object; it is often referred to as a universal data type. Similar to a 'variant' in Visual Basic 6®
Short	2 bytes	–32,768 to 32,767
Single	4 bytes	–3.402823E38 to –1.401298E–45; +1.401298E–45 to +3.402823E38
String	10 bytes + (2 * string length)	0 to 2 billion **Unicode characters** (approximately)
User-defined type (structure)	Sum of the sizes of its members	Each member of the structure has a range determined by its data type and independent of the ranges of the other members

When creating variables and constants it is usually considered **good practice** to select a data type which can store **expected values** in the **most efficient manner**. For example, selecting a 'Long' data type to store a **user's age in years** would **not** be appropriate; it is wasteful of RAM.

Scope of variables

Scope refers to the **visibility** of a variable; whereabouts in the program it **can be seen** (and therefore **used**).

For example, a variable **declared inside** an **event handler** (e.g. 'Click') can **only** be **used inside that** event handler; it does not **exist outside** it. This is called a **local variable**.

A variable declared inside the Form **Class** can be used in any of the event handlers; it has **wider scope**.

In addition, the keywords **public** and **private** are also used to mark variables (and event handlers) as accessible from **only within** (private) their class or **from outside** (public). These are called **access modifiers**. Unless **made** public, variables are private **by default**.

In VB® .NET, variables can belong to one of four basic **scopes**.

Block

New in VB® .NET, these are variables declared **within a construct**, e.g. a loop or selection, and cannot be used outside it.

```
Dim counter As Byte
counter = 1
Do While counter < 30
  Dim remainder As Byte
  remainder = counter Mod 4
  If remainder = 0 Then
    Debug.Print(counter & " is exactly divisible by 4.")
  End If
  counter = counter + 1
Loop
```

In this example the variable called '**remainder**' can **only** be used **within** the Do…Loop block.

Procedure

Variables declared **within an event handler** are available **throughout** that event handler, e.g:

```
Private Sub Button2_Click(ByVal sender As System.Object, _
ByVal e As System.EventArgs) Handles Button2.Click

  Dim counter As Byte
    counter = 1
  Do While counter < 30
    Dim remainder As Byte
    remainder = counter Mod 4
    If remainder = 0 Then
      Debug.Print(counter & " is exactly divisible by 4.")
    End If
    counter = counter + 1
  Loop
End Sub
```

Module

Variables declared within a **separate** module are limited to use **within that** module.

The term can also apply when a variable is declared **within a class** (e.g. a Form class), effectively limiting the use of the variable **to** that class, but **any event handler** inside it.

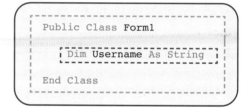

```
Public Class Form1

    Dim Username As String

End Class
```

Namespace

This is a more modern programming idea where **defined namespaces** are used to **collect together identifiers** (variables and constants). When a namespace is used, its set of variables and constants is active.

Where possible, scope should be kept as **local as possible** – it **reduces memory consumption** and reduces the opportunity for variables to be **incorrectly used**; this also helps **debugging** by limited the opportunities where variables can be given 'bad' values.

3 Be able to design and create an event-driven application

3.1 Specification

The specification of an event-driven application relies on the developer assembling the following:

◆ **Purpose** – What is the program **for**? What is it supposed to **achieve**?
◆ **User needs** – What **are** the user's needs? What **do** they want the program to achieve? **How** do they want it to work? **Who** is going to use it? How **accurate** does it **need** to be? How **reliable** and **robust** does it need to be?

- **Inputs** – What are the **inputs**? What **type** and **quantity** are they? How **frequently** are they required?
- **Processes** – What processes are **required** to **calculate** the outputs required by the user? **How** do we get from the input to the output?
- **Outputs** – What outputs are required? How are they to be **presented**? How should the information be **formatted**? **How often** is the output to be generated?
- **Backing storage** – What **kind** of data needs to be stored? How is the data to be **organised**? **How long** does the data need to be kept? How will this data be **accessed**?

Unit Link

Unit 7 (IT Systems Analysis and Design) deals with this topic in far greater detail than is possible here.

3.2 Design

Owing to its event-driven approach, VB® .NET does not really lend itself to **traditional design techniques** such as **pseudocode**, **flowcharts** and **structure diagrams**.

Other techniques such as **form design, storyboards** and **action/event charts** are preferable.

Form design

Good form design is **critical** to the success of a **GUI**-based event-driven program. As such there are a number of **simple rules** we can apply to **ensure** the best **user interaction experience** possible.

Forms should:

- be **sensibly laid out** – with related information grouped together
- not have any **spelling** or **grammatical errors** (users will lose faith in the software)
- use a **logical tab order** (Tab key) to move **between** form elements
- use **consistent formatting** (colours, font etc.)
- use helpful **labelling**
- have **error detection** built in
- ideally support users with **disabilities**: have font-size changes, audible prompts to **improve accessibility**
- have **online help** available.

Unit Link

Unit 13 (Human Computer Interaction), which is to be found in the companion book, deals with this topic in far greater detail.

Form design concepts also affect web pages as discussed in **Unit 10** (Client Side Customisation of Web Pages) and **Unit 21** (Website Production and Management). These are also to be found in the companion book.

Case Study

The management at **Frankoni T-Shirts** have asked you to design a new application, which they can install on PCs in their retail outlets, that allows users to **select the design** and **features** of their personalised T-shirt.

The program will then produce a **rough image** showing the **final product** and generate **its cost** based on **size**, **quantity** etc.

Form designs may be drawn manually (i.e. by hand) or developed using a graphical package on a computer system.

The following image is a **hand-drawn form design** for the **case study** described earlier.

As you can see, the designer has taken the **initial needs** as identified by the user (Frankoni T-Shirts) and has sketched a **suggested** user interface. **No functionality** has been specified yet. The sketch should be **presented** to the user for **feedback** and (if necessary) **revision**.

The final form design will be **implemented** using a suitable EDP language such as VB® .NET (see 3.3).

Storyboard

Storyboards can be created as a way of seeing an event-driven solution in an **outline fashion**.

There is **no need** to **specify functionality** (**how** the event handlers work); all that is necessary is to

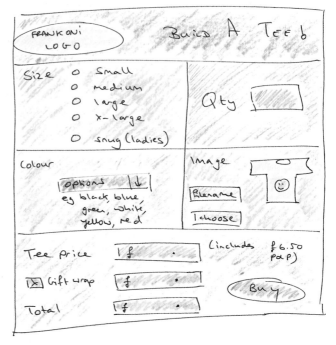

Figure 20.48 Frankoni T-Shirts form design sketch

identify what needs to be done and **how multiple forms** and **components link together** and are **triggered**.

Creating a **simple storyboard** for this is the logical solution.

Storyboard scorecard

+ Easy to show to others and discuss as it is a visual tool.
+ Can get quick feedback.
+ Not linked to any programming language.
+ Can be quickly redrawn; more efficient than prototypes (see RAD).
− Cannot be tested interactively.
− Can become outdated quickly as designs can change rapidly.

Figure 20.49 shows a typical storyboard for a **password-controlled stock control system**.

The designer has drawn a few forms and given basic linkage through the use of arrows. Additional notes are included to help explain the linkage of the forms.

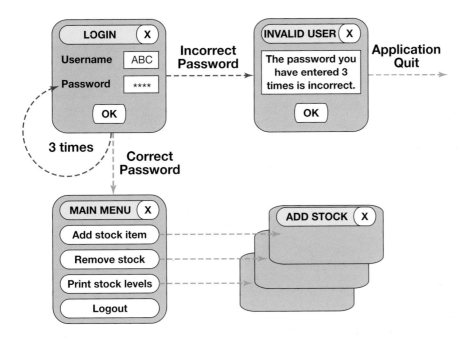

Figure 20.49 Storyboard for a password-controlled stock control system

Action/ event table

This is a useful reference table that lists each form, trigger and event handler for an application.

For example, here is a suggested **action/event table** for the **storyboard** shown in **Figure 20.49**.

Form name	Trigger	Event handler	Event handler description
Login	OK button clicked	OKbutton_Click()	**Checks** to see if password is correct for the given user name. Also **keeps a track** of the **number of attempts** the user has made.
			An **incorrect** attempt adds one to the **number of attempts** and **clears** the TextBoxes.
			If three attempts are made **unsuccessfully** the **Invalid User form** is opened.
			A **correct** attempt opens the **Main Menu form**.

Form name	Trigger	Event handler	Event handler description
Login	Close window button clicked	'Windows Close' System event handler	A **System Event** which closes the application.
Invalid User	OK button clicked	OKbutton_Click()	**Closes** the **application** after the warning has been displayed.
Invalid User	Close window button clicked	'Windows Close' System event handler	A **System Event** which closes the application
Main Menu	Add stock item button clicked	Addstock_Click()	Opens the **Add Stock item form** when clicked
Main Menu	Remove stock item button clicked	Removestock_Click()	Opens the **Remove Stock form** when clicked
Main Menu	Print stock levels button clicked	Printstocklevel_Click()	Opens the **Print stock levels form** when clicked
Main Menu	Logout button clicked	Logout_Click()	Closes the **current form** and **reopens** the **Login form**.
Main Menu	Close window button clicked	'Windows Close' System event handler	A **System Event** which closes the application

As you can see, between them the form design, storyboard and action/event table start to build the **mechanics** and **appearance** of the **required EDP solution**. From here, these designs are **implemented** using a suitable EDP language such as VB® .NET.

3.3 Creation of application

This section will walk you through the creation of a new EDP application. We will use the **Frankoni T-Shirt** company **case study** and **form design** as introduced in **section 3.2** as our active problem.

> ⚠ Once again the following example has been **broken down** into a **number** of **steps** owing to its **complexity**.
>
> If you follow each step **carefully**, **everything** should work **just fine**. If you discover a **problem**, go back a step (or two) and see if you have **missed anything**.

Step 1

Create a **new VB® .NET project**, adding these **controls** based on the original form design's **elements** and **layout**.

Step 2

All of these **controls** can be found in the various **subcategories** in the VB® .NET **ToolBox** (see 2.2).

Figure 20.51 represents an attempt at recreating the form in VB® .NET.

Although functional and as close to the suggested form design as possible, it looks a bit unbalanced; particularly with the 'Qty' TextBox seemingly floating alone in the middle of the form. In reality this would be an **iterative process** with the design being shown to the end-users to make suggestions until they are happy with the final product.

Some minor changes have been made; two Panel controls have been added to the 'Colour' and 'Image' parts of the form. In addition, there are now two PictureBoxes in the Image panel – one inside the other. The inner one will show our image, the outer

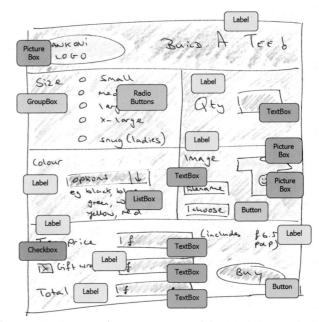

Figure 20.50 Identifying the VB® .NET controls

one will display the correct colour T-shirt (as selected from the Colour ListBox to the left). The colours in the ListBox (stored in the Items property) have also been put into ascending alphabetical order, i.e. A to Z.

All of the text is formatted to Tahoma, 12pt regular.

Figure 20.51 VB® .NET recreation

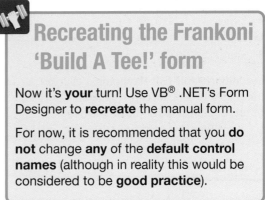

Recreating the Frankoni 'Build A Tee!' form

Now it's **your** turn! Use VB® .NET's Form Designer to **recreate** the manual form.

For now, it is recommended that you **do not** change **any** of the **default control names** (although in reality this would be considered to be **good practice**).

Step 3

The next step is to code the functionality of the form, identifying the triggers and necessary event handlers which are needed.

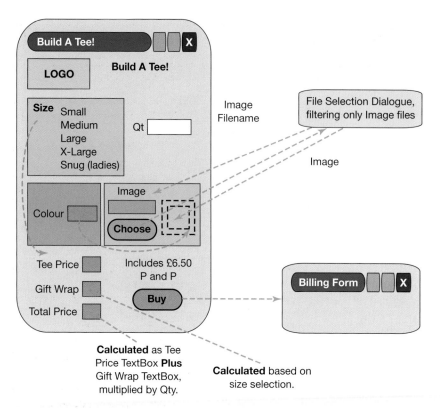

Perhaps the best way to do this is to produce the **Storyboard**.

Figure 20.52 Storyboard

As you can see there are a number of calculations to perform.

Upon investigation we find that the current T-shirt prices are:

- **Small –**   £7.50
- **Medium –**   £9.50
- **Large –**   £10.50
- **X-Large –**   £12.50
- **Snug (Ladies)** £11.00

In addition, while **Gift Wrapping** is charged per Tee (£2.00), the £6.50 **Postage and Package** is considered to be a **flat rate** (Frankoni absorbs the postal charges on larger shipments as a goodwill gesture and the hope of future business).

The 'File Selection' dialogue will be a **Control** which exists as part of the Windows API.

Step 4

The next step is to build a basic **action/event table**.

Form name	Trigger	Event handler	Event handler description
BuildATee	Buy button clicked	BuyButton_Click()	**Opens** the **Billing Form**.
BuildATee	Choose button clicked	ChooseButton_Click()	Opens a File Open Dialogue. The selected image's filename is stored in the Filename TextBox. The selected image itself is loaded into the inner PictureBox.
BuildATee	Colour is selected from Listbox	ColourList_SelectedIndexChanged()	The colour is used to select the correct image for the T-shirt background which forms the outer PictureBox
BuildATee	Close window button clicked	'Windows Close' System event handler	A **System Event** which closes the application.
BuildATee	Gift Wrap checkbox is checked or unchecked	GiftWrap_CheckedChanged()	If the GiftWrap option is selected, the associated TextBox is set to £2.00. If the option is unchecked the TextBox is cleared. TotalPrice TextBox is also updated to show TeePrice + GiftWrap values.
BuildATee	Small Size is selected from radio buttons	SmallSize_CheckedChanged()	Tee Price TextBox is given the value of: £7.50 × Qty TextBox + £6.50
BuildATee	Medium Size is selected from radio buttons	MediumSize_CheckedChanged()	Tee Price TextBox is given the value of: £9.50 × Qty TextBox + £6.50
BuildATee	Large Size is selected from radio buttons	LargeSize_CheckedChanged()	Tee Price TextBox is given the value of: £10.50 × Qty TextBox + £6.50
BuildATee	X-Large Size is selected from radio buttons	XLargeSize_CheckedChanged()	Tee Price TextBox is given the value of: £12.50 × Qty TextBox + £6.50
BuildATee	Snug Size is selected from radio buttons	SnugSize_CheckedChanged()	Tee Price TextBox is given the value of: £11.00 × Qty TextBox + £6.50
BuildATee	Value in Qty TextBox is changed	Qtychosen_TextChanged()	Cascade to appropriate radio button event handler to recalculate the total price.

Step 5

You will notice that the design work has necessitated us changing the **object names** into something **more meaningful**.

This is achieved by **selecting** the **form object** and **changing** its (**Name**) **property** in the **Property Window**.

As noted, changing the names of form objects is **good practice** as it makes it easy for the developer to **remember** what an object **actually is** when reading through a section of code. It also helps to **self-document** the **program code**.

Various techniques are used to name objects in professional development environments. For now, we will keep things straightforward and use simple, understandable names.

The **recommended changes** to this EDP application are shown in **Figure 20.54**.

Figure 20.53 Changing the object names

Note. It is, of course, possible that you may have added objects to the form in a **different** order. If this has happened, **ignore** the 'old name' column and just **focus** on the **key letter** and the **new name**.

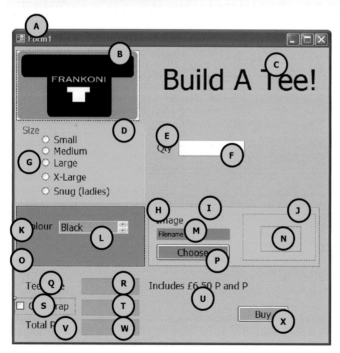

Figure 20.54 Application with renamed objects

Key	Control	Old name	New name	Additional new properties
A	Form	Form1	BuyATee	**Text** = Buy A Tee!
B	PictureBox	PictureBox1	Logo	**SizeMode** = StretchImage (will help to autoscale the image selected)
C	Label	Label1	Title	
D	GroupBox	GroupBox1	SizeSelector	
E	Label	Label2	Qty	
F	TextBox	TextBox1	Qtychosen	
G	RadioButton	RadioButton1 RadioButton2 RadioButton3 RadioButton4 RadioButton5	SmallSize MediumSize LargeSize XLargeSize SnugSize	Checked = True (SmallSize)
H	Label	Label4	Image	
I	Panel	Panel2	ImagePanel	
J	PictureBox	PictureBox2	TeeImage	
K	Label	Label3	Colour	
L	ListBox	ListBox1	ColourList	Has to have entries in the **Items property**: Black, Blue, Green, Yellow, Red and White
M	TextBox	TextBox2	Imagename	
N	PictureBox	PictureBox3	Teedesign	**SizeMode** = StretchImage (will help to autoscale the image selected)
O	Panel	Panel1	ColourPanel	
P	Button	Button1	ChooseButton	
Q	Label	Label5	TeePrice	
R	TextBox	TextBox3	TeePriceBox	**TextAlign** = Right
S	CheckBox	CheckBox1	GiftWrap	
T	TextBox	TextBox4	GiftWrapBox	**TextAlign** = Right
U	Label	Label7	PandP	
V	Label	Label6	TotalPrice	
W	TextBox	TextBox5	TotalPriceBox	**TextAlign** = Right
X	Button	Button2	BuyButton	

Step 6

Creating **variables** and **constants** for the application is also necessary. These can be recorded in a simplified form of **data dictionary** which describes **each** identifier.

Identifier name	Var or Const	Scope	Value	Date type	Description
dpostpack	Const	Module	6.5	Decimal	Current price of postage and packing
dindgiftwrap	Const	Module	2.0	Decimal	Current price of gift wrapping each Tee
dsmallprice	Const	Module	7.5	Decimal	Current price for a small Tee
dmediumprice	Const	Module	9.5	Decimal	Current price for a medium Tee
dlargeprice	Const	Module	10.5	Decimal	Current price for a large Tee
dxlargeprice	Const	Module	12.5	Decimal	Current price for an extra large Tee
dsnugprice	Const	Module	11.5	Decimal	Current price for a snug (ladies) Tee
dqty	Var	Module	–	Byte	Quantity of Tees wanted by user
dgiftprice	Var	Module	–	Decimal	Cost of gift wrapping based on quantity of Tees wanted
dteeprice	Var	Module	–	Decimal	Price of Tees – includes P&P for quantity wanted
dtotalprice	Var	Module	–	Decimal	Total Price – includes gift wrapping (if required)

These variables are then added to the program code **under** the **Public Class line**.

```
Public Class BuyATee

    Const dpostpack As Decimal = 6.5
    Const dindgiftwrap As Decimal = 2.0
    Const dsmallprice As Decimal = 7.5
    Const dmediumprice As Decimal = 9.5
    Const dlargeprice As Decimal = 10.5
    Const dxlargeprice As Decimal = 12.5
    Const dsnugprice As Decimal = 11.5


    Dim dqty As Byte = 0
    Dim dgiftprice As Decimal = 0.0
    Dim dteeprice As Decimal = 0.0
    Dim dtotalprice As Decimal = 0.0
```

Step 7

Now starts the fun part; we have to **code** some of the **event handlers** that match to the **identified triggers** in the **action/event table**.

We will start by coding the **size radio buttons** (SmallSize, MediumSize, LargeSize, XLargeSize and SnugSize).

Let's code the **SmallSize_CheckedChanged**() **event handler** by **double clicking** on this radio button.

Add the following code:

```
dqty = Val(Qtychosen.Text)

dteeprice = dsmallprice * dqty + dpostpack

TeePriceBox.Text = Str(dteeprice)
TeePriceBox.Text = Format(TeePriceBox.Text, "Currency")
dtotalprice = dteeprice + dgiftprice
TotalPriceBox.Text = Str(dtotalprice)
TotalPriceBox.Text = Format(TotalPriceBox.Text, "Currency")
```

Similar code will then be added to **each** radio button's event handler, making **modifications** to the **Tee price** being charged in the calculation, e.g. for **MediumSize_ CheckedChanged() event handler.**

Step 8

The next step is to code the Qtychosen TextBox.

This is a little more complex as **changing the quantity** will **result** in **changes to the Tee Price** and the **Total Price.** In other words, we will have to recalculate these costs as the quantity changes.

```
If SmallSize.Checked Then
   SmallSize_CheckedChanged(sender, e)
End If

If MediumSize.Checked Then
   MediumSize_CheckedChanged(sender, e)
End If

If LargeSize.Checked Then
   LargeSize_CheckedChanged(sender, e)
End If

If XLargeSize.Checked Then
   XLargeSize_CheckedChanged(sender, e)
End If

If SnugSize.Checked Then
   SnugSize_CheckedChanged(sender, e)
End If
```

These calculations **already exist** in each size radio button's CheckChanged() event handler (as seen in Step 7). Because of this, it seems a little **silly** to simply **repeat the code.** There **must** be another way!

One technique involves using the **GroupBox** (SizeSelector) to determine which radio button has been selected, but this is a little too **complex** to be described here.

Instead, we will **manually** check (with **If…Then…Else** statements) **which** size radio button has been **selected** and **trigger** its **event handler** accordingly. This is effectively **cascading an event** (**from** the TextChanged() event handler in the Qty TextBox **to** the CheckChanged() event handler of the **currently selected** radio button.

Here is the code for the TextChanged() event handler for the Qtychosen TextBox.

Step 9

This step involves **adding** the **GiftWrap price** of £2 per Tee **to the bill** if the **associated checkbox** is selected. Of course, if the checkbox is unselected, the Giftwrap costs must be set to £0.00.

Here is the appropriate code.

```
If GiftWrap.Checked Then
  dgiftprice = dindgiftwrap * dqty
  GiftWrapBox.Text = Str(dgiftprice)
  GiftWrapBox.Text = Format(GiftWrapBox.Text, "Currency")
Else
  dgiftprice = 0.0
  GiftWrapBox.Text = Format("0.0", "Currency")
End If
dtotalprice = dteeprice + dgiftprice
TotalPriceBox.Text = Str(dtotalprice)
TotalPriceBox.Text = Format(TotalPriceBox.Text, "Currency")
```

This code is added to **GiftWrap_CheckedChanged**() event handler.

Step 10

Next let's try coding the **change of T-shirt colour** – the **ListBox** we have called **ColourList**.

This is reasonably straightforward but relies on good preparation. The easiest way to do this (without accessing Windows graphics API) is to use simple bitmaps to represent each plain T-shirt. These will be created using a graphic package such as Microsoft Paint®, Adobe Photoshop® or Corel Paintshop Pro®.

We will need to create six T-shirt bitmap images, one for each option with uniform size, format and filename.

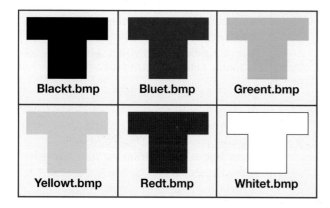

| Blackt.bmp | Bluet.bmp | Greent.bmp |
| Yellowt.bmp | Redt.bmp | Whitet.bmp |

Double-click the **ColourList** to access the **code window** and add the following VB® .NET code to the **ChooseButton_SelectedIndexChanged handler**.

```
TeeImage.Image = System.Drawing.Image.FromFile("C:\MyFolder\" +
ColourList.SelectedItem + "t.bmp")
```

This code will **load** a **T-shirt bitmap image** into the **outer PictureBox object** (**TeeImage**).

The bitmap loaded will be the **value picked** from the **ListBox** (e.g. **Red**) **plus** the **string 't.bmp'** giving the **full filename** of 'Redt.bmp'. Here is an example of this code in action.

Step 11

Let's move our attention to ChooseButton's Click() event.

In order to code this we have to **add another object** to the form. In this case, it is a **special type** of dialogue called the **OpenFileDialog**. It is located in the **Dialogues category** in the **ToolBox**.

Figure 20.55 Selecting a plain red T-shirt

Figure 20.56 Adding an OpenFileDialog

Once selected, it is added to the **bottom** of your form in a **separate area**.

Double-click the **ChooseButton** to access the **code window** and add the following VB® .NET code to the **ChooseButton_ Click handler**.

```
OpenFileDialog1.Filter = "Image Files(*.BMP;*.JPG)|*.BMP;*.JPG"
OpenFileDialog1.ShowDialog()
Imagename.Text = OpenFileDialog1.FileName
Teedesign.Image = System.Drawing.Image.FromFile(Imagename.Text)
```

This section of code:

1   sets a filter for only .JPG and .BMP files
2   shows the OpenFileDialog
3   stores the selected filename in the text property of our **Imagename TextBox**
4   loads the image selected into the Image property of the **inner PictureBox object** (Teedesign).

Figure 20.57 is an **example OpenFileDialog** – I'm sure you will have **seen** this **before** while using **Windows**.

Putting this together now means we can select the size, T-shirt colour and image.

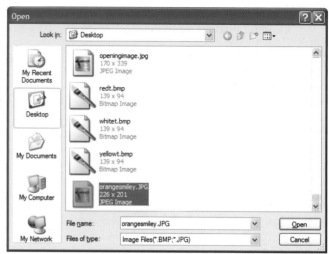

Figure 20.57 Our OpenFileDialog browsing for Image files only

Figure 20.58 One white small Tee with an orange smiley and no giftwrap

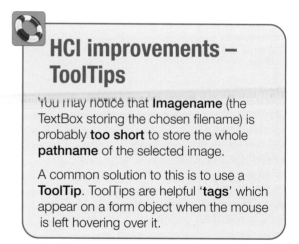

HCI improvements – ToolTips

You may notice that **Imagename** (the TextBox storing the chosen filename) is probably **too short** to store the whole **pathname** of the selected image.

A common solution to this is to use a **ToolTip**. ToolTips are helpful '**tags**' which appear on a form object when the mouse is left hovering over it.

We can add a ToolTip to our EDP solution to improve the **HCI** as shown in Figure 20.60.

The ToolTip control can be found in the Common Controls category in the ToolBox.

Figure 20.59 An example ToolTip in Microsoft Word®

The ToolTip control will be added to the separate area alongside the OpenFileDialog.

The next step is to **add** a line of code (**ringed below**) into the existing **ChooseButton_Click handler.**

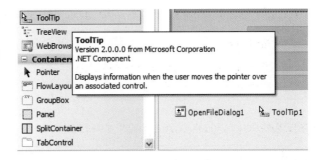

Figure 20.60 Adding a ToolTip to the EDP application

```
  OpenFileDialog1.Filter = "Image Files(*.BMP;*.JPG)|*.BMP;*.JPG"
OpenFileDialog1.ShowDialog()
Imagename.Text = OpenFileDialog1.FileName
Teedesign.Image = System.Drawing.Image.FromFile(Imagename.Text)

  ToolTip1.SetToolTip(Imagename, Imagename.Text)
```

Run the application again, **select** an **image file** and then **hover** over the **Imagename TextBox.**

Putting it all together

A **Frankoni** customer tries the program, selecting **five large white Tees** with an **orange smiley logo**; they would also like them **giftwrapped**.

Figure 20.61 An example ToolTip, improving the HCI

Let's see if these calculations are correct.

Figure 20.62 Testing the full application

Tee price: 5 x £9.50 =	£47.50
Add P&P (£6.50) =	£ 6.50
Plus gift wrap (5 @ £2.00) =	£10.00
Total Price =	**£69.00**

From this calculation, it would appear that the program is **functioning correctly**. In addition, all **triggers** and **event handlers** seem to be working properly.

Finally, you may wish to check the **Tab order** of each form control to ensure that the form can be easily (and logically) navigated, i.e. top to bottom, left to right.

The full Frankoni EDP solution (with comments)

```
' Frankoni BuildaTee
'
' Written by M Fishpool
' January 2007
' Version 1


Public Class BuyATee

    Const dpostpack As Decimal = 6.5        ' price of packing and postage
    Const dindgiftwrap As Decimal = 2.0     ' price of individually gift wrapping 1 Tee
    Const dsmallprice As Decimal = 7.5      ' price of 1 small Tee
    Const dmediumprice As Decimal = 9.5     ' price of 1 medium Tee
    Const dlargeprice As Decimal = 10.5     ' price of 1 large Tee
    Const dxlargeprice As Decimal = 12.5    ' price of 1 extra large Tee
    Const dsnugprice As Decimal = 11.5      ' price of 1 snug Tee

    Dim dqty As Byte = 0                    ' quantity required as a whole number
    Dim dgiftprice As Decimal = 0.0         ' gift wrapping price as a decimal number
    Dim dteeprice As Decimal = 0.0          ' tee shirt price as a decimal number
    Dim dtotalprice As Decimal = 0.0        ' total price of order as a decimal number

    Private Sub ChooseButton_Click(ByVal sender As System.Object, ByVal e As _
    System.EventArgs) Handles ChooseButton.Click
        '   Code to select an image file and load it onto the form
        OpenFileDialog1.Filter = "Image Files(*.BMP;*.JPG)|*.BMP;*.JPG"
        OpenFileDialog1.ShowDialog()
        Imagename.Text = OpenFileDialog1.FileName
        Teedesign.Image = System.Drawing.Image.FromFile(Imagename.Text)
        ToolTip1.SetToolTip(Imagename, Imagename.Text)
    End Sub


    Private Sub ColourList_SelectedIndexChanged(ByValsender As System.Object,ByVal e As _
    System.EventArgs) Handles ColourList.SelectedIndexChanged
        '   Code to load the appropriate plain Tee image onto the form
        TeeImage.Image = System.Drawing.Image.FromFile("C:\"+ColourList.SelectedItem+ _
        "t.bmp")
    End Sub


    Private Sub SmallSize_CheckedChanged(ByVal sender As System.Object, ByVal e As _
    System.EventArgs) Handles SmallSize.CheckedChanged
        '   Code to recalculate costs if a small Tee is selected
        dqty = Val(Qtychosen.Text)
        dteeprice = dsmallprice * dqty + dpostpack
        TeePriceBox.Text = Str(dteeprice)
        TeePriceBox.Text = Format(TeePriceBox.Text, "Currency")
        dtotalprice = dteeprice + dgiftprice
        TotalPriceBox.Text = Str(dtotalprice)
        TotalPriceBox.Text = Format(TotalPriceBox.Text, "Currency")
    End Sub
```

```
    Private Sub MediumSize_CheckedChanged(ByVal sender As System.Object, ByVal e As _
    System.EventArgs) Handles MediumSize.CheckedChanged
        ' Code to recalculate costs if a medium Tee is selected
        dqty = Val(Qtychosen.Text)
        dteeprice = dmediumprice * dqty + dpostpack
        TeePriceBox.Text = Str(dteeprice)
        TeePriceBox.Text = Format(TeePriceBox.Text, "Currency")
        dtotalprice = dteeprice + dgiftprice
        TotalPriceBox.Text = Str(dtotalprice)
        TotalPriceBox.Text = Format(TotalPriceBox.Text, "Currency")
    End Sub

    Private Sub LargeSize_CheckedChanged(ByVal sender As System.Object, ByVal e As _
    System.EventArgs) Handles LargeSize.CheckedChanged
        ' Code to recalculate costs if a large Tee is selected
        dqty = Val(Qtychosen.Text)
        dteeprice = dlargeprice * dqty + dpostpack
        TeePriceBox.Text = Str(dteeprice)
        TeePriceBox.Text = Format(TeePriceBox.Text, "Currency")
        dtotalprice = dteeprice + dgiftprice
        TotalPriceBox.Text = Str(dtotalprice)
        TotalPriceBox.Text = Format(TotalPriceBox.Text, "Currency")
    End Sub
```

```
    Private Sub XLargeSize_CheckedChanged(ByVal sender As System.Object,ByVal e _
    As System.EventArgs) Handles XLargeSize.CheckedChanged
        ' Code to recalculate costs if a large Tee is selected
        dqty = Val(Qtychosen.Text)
        dteeprice = dxlargeprice * dqty + dpostpack
        TeePriceBox.Text = Str(dteeprice)
        TeePriceBox.Text = Format(TeePriceBox.Text, "Currency")
        dtotalprice = dteeprice + dgiftprice
        TotalPriceBox.Text = Str(dtotalprice)
        TotalPriceBox.Text = Format(TotalPriceBox.Text, "Currency")
    End Sub

    Private Sub SnugSize_CheckedChanged(ByVal sender As System.Object, ByVal e As _
    System.EventArgs) Handles SnugSize.CheckedChanged
        ' Code to recalculate costs if a snug Tee is selected
        dqty = Val(Qtychosen.Text)
        dteeprice = dsnugprice * dqty + dpostpack
        TeePriceBox.Text = Str(dteeprice)
        TeePriceBox.Text = Format(TeePriceBox.Text, "Currency")
        dtotalprice = dteeprice + dgiftprice
        TotalPriceBox.Text = Str(dtotalprice)
        TotalPriceBox.Text = Format(TotalPriceBox.Text, "Currency")
    End Sub

    Private Sub Qtychosen_TextChanged(ByVal sender As System.Object, ByVal e As _
    System.EventArgs) Handles Qtychosen.TextChanged
        ' Code to recalculate costs by cascading the correct event handler when
        ' quantity changes
        If SmallSize.Checked Then
            SmallSize_CheckedChanged(sender, e)
        End If

        If MediumSize.Checked Then
            MediumSize_CheckedChanged(sender, e)
        End If
```

```
            If LargeSize.Checked Then
                LargeSize_CheckedChanged(sender, e)
            End If

            If XLargeSize.Checked Then
               XLargeSize_CheckedChanged(sender, e)
            End If

            If SnugSize.Checked Then
                SnugSize_CheckedChanged(sender, e)
            End If
        End Sub

    Private Sub BuyButton_Click(ByVal sender As System.Object, ByVal e As _
    System.EventArgs) Handles BuyButton.Click
        MsgBox("Would display the customer information form")
    End Sub

    Private Sub GiftWrap_CheckedChanged(ByVal sender As System.Object,ByVal e As _
    System.EventArgs) Handles GiftWrap.CheckedChanged
        ' to recalculate costs based on whether or not the customer has asked for
        ' Tees to be gift wrapped
        If GiftWrap.Checked Then
            dgiftprice = dindgiftwrap * dqty
            GiftWrapBox.Text = Str(dgiftprice)
            GiftWrapBox.Text = Format(GiftWrapBox.Text, "Currency")
        Else
            dgiftprice = 0.0
            GiftWrapBox.Text = Format("0.0", "Currency")
        End If
        dtotalprice = dteeprice + dgiftprice
        TotalPriceBox.Text = Str(dtotalprice)
        TotalPriceBox.Text = Format(TotalPriceBox.Text, "Currency")
    End Sub

End Class
```

4 Be able to test and review an event-driven application

4.1 Testing and debugging

Although **testing** and **debugging** can be seen as two separate stages of the EDP development path, they are linked to a degree.

Vigorous testing should discover the following types of error in a typical EDP:

◆ Triggers not working or incorrectly identified.
◆ Event handlers not working properly.
◆ Calculations incorrect or with insufficient accuracy.
◆ Calculations not correctly formatted.
◆ Some functionality missing or incorrectly implemented.

Testing an EDP **relies** on the following:

1 Creating a test strategy (how you are going to test the application).

2 Creating a test plan structure – specifically:
- ◆ **What** is being tested?
- ◆ **When** is it being tested?
- ◆ What are the **expected results**?
- ◆ What are the **actual results**?

3 Comparing the expected and actual results:
- ◆ Did it work as expected?
- ◆ If not, what **corrective action** needs to be performed?
- ◆ Which **error messages** occurred?

As we have already seen, **specialist debug tools** available in VB® .NET (**Breakpoint**, **Step Into**, **Watch** and the **Immediate Window**) are invaluable in the quest to **identify** and **correct errors** in the program code.

Unit Link

Unit 18 (Principles of Software Design and Development) section 4.1 also examines testing and debugging and while it does so from a C# perspective, concepts such as **white-box testing**, **black-box testing** and **trace tables** are still relevant.

Refer to these for additional guidance.

4.2 Review

Review is a **critical process** which occurs after testing and debugging.

Initially the major concern should be: **How does the EDP compare to the user's original specifications**?

If the correct level of **fact-finding** was **conducted** as part of the **design** (see 3.1), the program should meet the user's needs **accurately**.

At the risk of finding out at the **end of the process** that considerable **time** and **money** has been wasted in creating something which **does not** meet the user's needs, the use of interim reviews which are regularly spaced along the development period are a good idea. These will prevent a program getting **too far** from its original design (something which is called 'feature drift').

Review **feeds** back into the **design** and **implementation** stages of EDP, helping the programmer to understand what is **really** wanted rather than what they **think** is wanted.

Unit Link

Unit 18 (Principles of Software Design and Development) section 4.3 also examines the review process.

Refer to this for additional guidance.

EDP stages of development

1 Understand the user's needs.
2 Design screen layouts, work out data storage etc.
3 Implement forms and controls to reflect approved screen layouts.
4 Identify triggers needed.
5 Code associated event handlers (including documentation).
6 Debug the program.
7 Test the program.
8 Review (may occur during stages if required).

In addition, documentation (for the user and future developers) should be produced.

More EDP problems

Problem 1

Kris Arts and Media Ltd requires EDP which will calculate a quote for specific **marketing** and **advertising** jobs.

Generally they use the following formula when creating a sales brochure.

One-off costs for the one-off sample brochure:

◆ Black and white printing   £300
◆ Greyscale printing   £500
◆ Full colour printing   £900
◆ Costs are £3 per page (matt stock paper)
◆ Costs are £5 per page (gloss stock paper)
◆ Costs are £25 per illustration/graphic
◆ Costs are £35 per photograph (black and white)
◆ Costs are £45 per photograph (colour)
◆ Duplication of the brochure to PDF format for electronic distribution: £100

Costs per printed brochure:

◆ Duplication of each brochure is £1.25

Problem 2

Kris Arts and Media Ltd would like a simple **colour 'picker'** which allows them to use three scrollbars (Red, Green, Blue) to **generate** a true-colour shade. **Each scrollbar** should permit movement between 0 and 255.

The program should display the RGB colour code and generated colour.

Links

Unit 20 is a **core unit** on the BTEC National Diploma for IT Practitioners (**Software Development route**) and a **specialist unit** on the Certificate of the same route.

Unit 20 is also a **specialist unit** on the following BTEC National routes:

IT and Business

Networking

Systems Support

As such it has links to a number of other units, principally:

Unit 4 – IT project

Unit 5 – Advanced Database Skills

Unit 6 – Advanced Spreadsheet Skills

Unit 7 – IT Systems Analysis and Design

Unit 25 – Object Oriented Programming

In addition this unit has identified direct links with:

Unit 10 – Client-side Customisation of Web Pages

Unit 13 – Human Computer Interaction

Unit 18 – Principles of Software Design and Development

Achieving success

In order to achieve each unit you will complete a series of coursework activities. Each time you hand in work, your tutor will return this to you with a record of your achievement.

This particular unit has 11 criteria to meet: 5 pass, 3 merit and 3 distinction.

For a **pass**:

You must achieve **all** 5 pass criteria.

For a **merit**:

You must achieve **all** 5 pass and **all** 3 merit criteria.

For a **distinction**:

You must achieve **all** 5 pass, **all** 3 merit **and all** 3 distinction criteria.

So that you can monitor your own progress and achievement in each unit, a recording grid has been provided (see below). The full version of this grid is also included on the companion CD.

	Assignments in this unit			
Assignment	**U20.01**	**U20.02**	**U20.03**	**U20.04**
Referral				
Pass				
1				
2				
3				
4				
5				
Merit				
1				
2				
3				
Distinction				
1				
2				
3				

Help with assessment

The key issue with this unit is to ensure that you can identify and work with EDP languages. You are likely to examine several but focus on one for implementation.

To **pass**, it is important that you can accurately describe different EDP languages and be able to give their typical uses and advantages. In addition you will be expected to be able to demonstrate the use of a chosen EDP, using different tools and techniques to build two different applications that meet a user's needs. These applications will also need to be documented and tested.

Merit grades ask you to investigate the EDP a little further, explaining how EDP may occur in an operating system, and how you can improve a user interface and functionality after review. You will also need to know the difference (and explain it) between different variable scopes.

Distinction grades focus on evaluation and justification; they ask you to examine EDP techniques with non-GUIs, the tools and techniques you have used to build an EDP application and how well it meets the user needs in review.

Online resources on the CD

Electronic glossary for this unit

Key fact sheets

Electronic slide show of key points

Sample program code in a number of programming languages

Multiple choice self-test quizzes

Flash animated tutorials for Microsoft Visual Basic®, Visual C++® and Visual Basic® .NET

Further reading

Balena, F., 2005, *Programming Microsoft Visual Basic 2005: The Language*, Microsoft Press US, ISBN 0735621837.

Bond, M., Law D, Longshaw, A., Haywood, D., and Roxburgh, P., 2003, *Sams Teach Yourself J2EE in 21 Days*, 2nd edn, Sams, ISBN 0672325586.

Palmer, G., 2001, *Java Event Handling*, Prentice Hall, ISBN 0130418021.

Sharp, J., 2002, *Visual J#.NET Core Reference*, Microsoft Press US, ISBN 0735615500.

Suddeth, J., 2006, *Programming with Visual Studio .NET 2005*, Lulu.com, ISBN 1411664477.

Troelsen, A., 2004, *Pro C# 2005 and the .NET 2.0 Platform*, 3rd edn, Apress US, ISBN 1590594193.

e-Commerce

Capsule view

With the **development** of the **Internet** and **World Wide Web**, the face of business changed forever. Suddenly **products** and **services** were **easier to come by**, the **range** and **choice expanded** beyond anything experienced previously, and **businesses** suddenly had **more opportunities**. In fact, some would say that organisations that fail to explore and use e-commerce could be in danger of losing business, being passed over for organisations that are willing to invest in the relevant technologies.

This unit considers the **effects** that e-commerce has on **society** and on the world at large, and **focuses** on the **technologies** that **support** it and the **legislation** that **attempts** to **control** it.

1 Know the effects on society of e-commerce

1.1 Social implications

Changing customer perspectives (e.g. providing added value, providing service, ease and security)

Learning aims

1 Know the effects on society of e-commerce.
2 Understand the technologies involved in e-commerce.
3 Understand the security issues in e-commerce and the laws and guidelines that regulate it.

The growth of internet trading has been of particular benefit to customers **throughout** the world. Quite apart from the obvious advantage of being able to buy a **wider** range of products at increasingly competitive prices, improved business efficiency and distribution logistics have ensured that online purchases **do not** take weeks to arrive. There certainly was a time when if you bought anything over the phone, or by completing order forms or coupons from magazines or newspapers, you would be advised that you should 'allow 28 days for delivery'. In those days, a 28-day wait was standard practice.

Today, however, it is not unusual for you to receive goods you have purchased within 24 to 72 hours after payment to the seller has been confirmed.

What has the Internet really done for us as consumers?

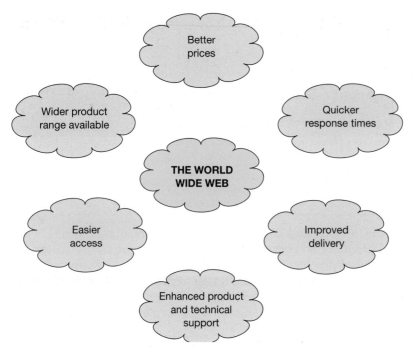

Figure 34.1 Added value for consumers

The **internet** has **widened consumer participation** by **enabling** those who might not be able to easily **access goods** and **services** to have the opportunity to do so, particularly those who are **ill**, **housebound** or who are **caring for others**. Equally it has offered businesses new customers to whom they would have had little or no access, so potentially increasing sales revenue.

Customers can now explore **wider product ranges** because they are not limited to the items on display in high-street outlets, but can effectively choose from a **whole range** of **companies**. The days where you would have to walk from shop to shop with a notebook, comparing products and prices, are long gone. This can all now be done from the comfort of your own home, using a keyboard, mouse and screen. Some websites even do it for you! PriceRunner®, for example, compares the costs of a DVD box set and as you

can see, prices range from £17.99 to £39.99 – quite a difference.

This in turn has meant that the **consumer** has become **more informed**, and it has encouraged consumers to take that little bit of extra time to shop for **better prices**.

Customers are not satisfied unless they receive **quick response times** from the organisations with whom they trade. As such, the businesses have had to find ways to become more efficient. **Email**, certainly, has ensured that **dialogue** between the consumer and the trader has **improved**.

Equally, better technology has also ensured that customers can **receive** their **goods more quickly**, and has offered them the ability to **track** their **orders** through business systems and with the delivery company through online **track and trace** facilities like the one provided by **Royal Mail** shown in Figure 34.3.

Figure 34.2 Price comparison website

Organisations can now provide enhanced product and technical support by, for example, simply having product manuals available online.

Keying the words **nokia 6610 manual** into a search engine provided the guide as shown in Figure 34.4.

Initial customer **fears** that trading with organisations online would tend to make them **more remote** and **less likely** to provide a **good service** have not been realised although, as with anything, there are exceptions to this and there clearly has been significant internet-facilitated fraud over the last few years.

In general, businesses have seen the rise of the Internet as an opportunity, and they have embraced this fully. As a footnote, there are organisations who have failed to take advantage of the Internet and who have, as a result, seen a large part of their customer base disappear.

Figure 34.3 Royal Mail website

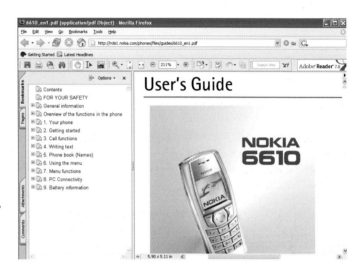

Figure 34.4 Nokia 6610 online user's guide

Impact on business and society as a whole

Most people would agree that the impact on business and society as a whole has generally been a positive one. There are, however, those who would **not** agree. Some critics who believe that advances in technology are essentially negative would bring some convincing counterclaims into the debate:

◆ Older people who might **not have** the **relevant IT skills** would be disadvantaged.
◆ It will increase **desire** for products people **cannot afford** and so increase **frustration** and possibly **debt** levels.
◆ It **increases expectations** and **impatience** because the wait should be short.

In an effort to **upskill** our older citizens, many colleges of further education, along with schools and local communities, have started laying on a range of courses targeted at older learners. With titles like *Computers for the over 50s, Working with email* or *Surfing the Internet* many of these courses are either free or have minimal enrolment costs.

Economic and social impact owing to speed of changes

What the whole concept of the Internet **has** done, however, is to create an **economic impact** on organisations, who initially found they had to **invest heavily** in new technology, as well as paying website designers and other specialists for website services, particularly while these technologies were new. Those who did invest, largely felt they had seen a **good return on** their **investment**. For some small and medium enterprises (**SMEs**) however, the situation was **less favourable** and many were **unable** to **invest**, **particularly** in the **hardware** that would be required to have a website managed in-house. The result of this was that small website companies were founded and these grew, offering **outsourced services** to those organisations that did not have the technical skills or the money to acquire them.

The **speed of change** also caused problems for many because of the **constant requirement** to upgrade, particularly hardware, to improve download speeds and remain competitive.

In terms of society at large, it would be fair to say that most of us choose **not** to stay 100 per cent up to date with **every** technological advance that comes along, although there are those people who do. Some individuals feel that not keeping up with such change would be equivalent to failing, and they do not see that as an option.

No-one would argue that technology **will** continue to change and, as with most technology, the cyclical nature of change (it speeds up, it slows down) will see times of **heavy transformation**, and other times of **relative calm**.

From a business perspective, companies must try as hard as possible to stay ahead of their competitors, and investing in new technology is one way to do this. Individuals are less likely to see the need for constantly staying up to date as important.

Bricks and clicks (integrating high-street and online presence)

One of the biggest dilemmas for companies that have a high-street presence is whether to set up online trading facilities. Initially, companies set up websites which were effectively nothing more than **online brochures**, providing images and descriptions of products and services, but which were not interactive and where the user was unable to purchase any of the goods or services **directly**. This quickly became unsatisfactory for consumers, and most of the major high-street companies, who were already in the **brick** world, joined the **click** world. Figure 34.5 shows just a few examples.

Conversely, there are those companies who began with an online presence, then later made the decision to open a high-street shop. The Spice of Life® is just such a company.

Having originally started the business trading solely via the Internet, the company recently opened its first high-street shop.

```
Tesco
HMV
Sainsbury's
Marks and Spencer
Tesco
Asda
```

Figure 34.5 High-street outlets with an online presence

1.2 Benefits

The main reason for the success of internet trading has been the many benefits of which companies can take advantage. Let's not forget at this stage that non-profit-making organisations such as charities also have websites as a means of collecting donations and subscription fees.

Let's investigate some of the numerous benefits.

Figure 34.6 The Spice of Life® website

Global marketplace and alternative income sources

For some time now we have all accepted that the world is getting smaller! With advances in transportation, we now go further on holiday than most of our grandparents would have done. This is because faster planes, cars and trains have enabled us to go further, more quickly, which has truly opened up new horizons for all of us.

Similarly, we might now consider buying a CD, DVD or computer game from Japan or the USA, particularly if it was not available in the UK (as long as we have region-free machines to play DVDs and computer games from other regions on – it does not apply with CDs).

We can buy textiles from Asia and South America, we can buy sculptures from Italy and Africa…the list goes on.

As businesses, we can similarly find our own products and services being purchased by individuals living or working outside our usual **trading regions**, adding to our **sources of income**.

Today we really can say that the world is our **global marketplace**; our **customers** can be situated anywhere in the world and **so can** our **suppliers**.

24/7 trading

Another advantage of trading online is that we do not have to have any particular **opening** or **closing times**. If customers order online, orders are stored in a database until they are processed. At the point of ordering, **no human intervention** is required. If customers have queries, they will send an email which can then be answered when the staff are at work. For this reason it does not actually matter whether the customer is buying at 9.00 am, 3.00 pm, 8.00 am or at midnight.

This means that, effectively, the **online shop** is **open** 24 hours a day, 7 days a week (**24/7**), and **restrictive time-zones** no longer have an impact on an organisation's **ability to trade**.

Relatively low start-up and running costs

The emergence of companies offering web-hosting services to small businesses has ensured that the **start-up** and **running costs** of having a website can be very low indeed. This is an option that many organisations pursue, specifically because it means that they do not have to find the money for hardware and software, but more importantly, they do not have to employ skilled staff to maintain the website and hardware if they are using the services of a web-hosting company.

Competitive edge and pricing opportunities (e.g. differences, fluid pricing)

Any organisation that has an online presence is going to have a **competitive advantage** over any company that does not. In the simplest terms, this will be because e-commerce offers increased trading opportunities and those companies that do not have this facility will clearly have the potential for less business.

The other aspect to the concept of securing a competitive edge is that if your competitors are advertising their goods and services online, including prices, delivery services etc., your organisation will be able to see the type and level of service **your competitors** are offering **their customers**. This will enable **you** to find ways of making your own offers **more attractive** to customers (lowering prices, or offering cheaper or no delivery costs). Because it is easy to change the prices you display on your website, you can respond easily to the activities of your competitors and apply **fluid pricing** principles, which is to adjust your prices quickly in response to competitor activity.

Always remember that if you can do this to your competitors, they can do it to you!

Search facilities

Most websites have **search facilities** built into them. This is to help users **to find information**, **products** or **website services quickly** and **efficiently**.

Figure 34.7 HMV online search facility

Using a search facility requires the user to input **key words**, which the system will then use to look for matches in its product database. The matches are then listed for the user, but if the user then decides that this was not what they were looking for, the search can be done again.

Gathering customer information

Software now exists that can report on the **visitor traffic** experienced by a website, detailing which products or web pages they viewed, and how many times they returned to the website etc. This information, stored in log form, is then analysed to build up a picture of the site usage.

The simplest log is a hit counter, which can be made visible, or kept invisible, on the site.

This allows companies to compare the number of hits they receive with the number of orders generated. If the hit count is **high**, but the number of orders is **low**, the company should be trying to establish why this has occurred.

Figure 34.8 A hit counter

Is there something **unsatisfactory** about the website?

◆ Are the prices too high?
◆ Are delivery times too long?
◆ Too difficult to find the right product?
◆ Not enough product information given?
◆ Checkout procedures too time-consuming?

Another positive aspect of gathering customer information is that if your organisation knows that particular products are **selling better** than others, they can **change** their **stock levels** of less popular items, ensure they have increased numbers of the more popular items, and even look for other similar items that could be equally popular. This is **online supply and demand**.

Alternative income sources

The main additional income source that can be accessed as a direct result of e-Commerce activities comes from potential advertising revenue. For example, company A could adds links or popups to its own website that advertises company B's products or services, for which company A then gets paid a fee. Equally, some complementary organisations advertise each other's products – for example, a sports equipment manufacturer advertises a sports clothing retailer and vice versa. Neither is in direct competition to the other, so this can be a mutually beneficial relationship bringing additional income to both.

The growth in charity search engines is an example of using e-Commerce as an alternative income source. Charities that traditionally relay on public donations, can be more proactive in generating income by offering advertising space or displaying web links to businesses. Example include:

GoodSearch.com
Everyclick.com
SearchKindly.org
CharityCafe.com

Clearly, the advantages of trading online are extensive. There are also, however, **drawbacks**.

1.3 Drawbacks

Consumer trust

Gaining the **trust** of your customers is **paramount** if you trade in remote locations and do not have the potential for **face-to-face contact** with your customers. Companies must therefore place great importance on the customer service function.

The two main concerns for customers who buy goods online are:

◆ How will the company respond to complaints if goods are faulty when purchased, become faulty within their guarantee period or if they were damaged in transit?
◆ Will my goods actually ever arrive?
◆ Will my payment details (e.g. credit card information) be secure?

Certainly there will be **unscrupulous companies** that will attempt to avoid **their legal obligations** in such situations, and if this is experienced by customers they would a) have the **right** to take action against the organisation and b) they would be **unlikely to recommend** the organisation to others, or more importantly, would be **unlikely to use them again**.

If an organisation is determined to **behave badly** towards its customers then it will do so, regardless of whether it is trading online or on the high street. The only difference is that on the high street the company is more visible than it is online.

In the long run, the best way an organisation can ensure that it earns the trust of its customers is by keeping its promises:

◆ Delivering **on time**.
◆ Keeping prices **low**.
◆ Dealing with queries **quickly** and **effectively**.

- Handling complaints **without a fuss**.
- Using appropriate security to protect customer data.

Lack of human contact

One of the main problems of trading through an online medium is the **lack of human contact** you will experience, because your **suppliers** and **customers** will feel extremely remote. If you are a very small business, maybe even a **sole trader**, you might, therefore, not have any contact with the outside world at all, other than by post or email. What are the **implications** of this?

Consider the image in Figure 34.9.

This image might look **peaceful** and **inviting** – but consider the one person in the image. What happens if anything **goes wrong**? What can that one person **do**? Who can they **turn to** for support? As with the person in this image, an online trader could only be reliant on themselves. This can be a **stressful** situation.

According to published theory, human beings are fundamentally **social animals** – we generally live in **groups** and we **form relationships**. Failure to have this kind of interaction can make individuals **socially** isolated. This is a serious issue and anyone who works alone, or works from home, should be aware of the problems that this could cause.

Delivery issues

Before the growth of e-commerce, when companies traditionally traded with individuals and organisations in more or less the same location, the delivery costs were relatively straightforward, and largely inexpensive.

Figure 34.9 Isolation

Now, with the global market, it is not unusual for organisations to trade with businesses and individuals in other countries. This has presented a number of issues:

1 The first is that there will be **greater costs** in getting goods to their **destination** – companies have two choices:
   - **Absorb** the cost and **reduce** their own **profit**.
   - **Add** the costs of delivery and **risk losing** the sale if these costs make the purchase **unattractive**.
2 Secondly, in some countries there are **regulations about packaging** – not only product packaging, but delivery packaging – sometimes this must be of a specific type. In the first instance, the company should be **fully aware** of the **legislation** in the destination country. Then the company has three choices:
   - Use **specialist packaging** and **absorb** the **cost** (so as not to pass it on to the customer), thereby **reducing profit**.
   - **Add** the costs of specialist packaging and **risk losing** the sale if these costs make the purchase **unattractive**.
   - Send the goods in **standard packaging** and risk being caught breaking the law – which clearly is not a serious option.

Clearly, increased costs to customers might make sales **unattractive**. Organisations with **specialist** or **rare** products may have no difficulty adding delivery costs, because in this instance it would be a **seller's** market (this means that the buyer has limited choice about where they can obtain the product – so the seller is really in control of the transaction). In the event that the product is **more easily** accessible, it would be considered a **buyer's market** (where the buyer has a large choice about where they can obtain the product, and so can be choosy about trying to find the best deal).

This will have implications for the overall success of the business.

International legislation

As organisations and businesses are now able to increasingly access global markets, they will have a growing number of laws to contend with. In recognition of these issues, the International Organization for Standardization (**ISO**) was formed, and working as a combined body with a large number of member states, it has attempted to ensure that issues such as legally defined **safety standards** and **product standards** are set, **adhered to** and **policed**.

Unit Link

For more on the **ISO** see **Unit 33** – Impact of the Use of IT on Business Systems, section 2.1.

Product description problems

Once you begin to cross country boundaries, the issues of language and understanding have an impact on the success of communication! This is because sometimes when sentences are transferred from one language to another, something can be **lost in translation** – maybe the **spirit** in which something was said, maybe the **actual meaning**. Even when countries share a common language, there can still be misunderstandings.

Term	Meaning in English	Meaning in the USA
AC	Alternating current – an electrical term to do with domestic and industrial power supply	Air conditioning
Chips	Sliced and fried potatoes	Crisps
ER	The Queen, e.g. Elizabeth II	Emergency room, which is usually known as A & E – accident and emergency – in the UK!
Holiday	Time taken away from normal routine – a day off school, college or work, often associated with spending time away from home, in a resort for example	A public festival like Christmas or Thanksgiving
NHS	The National Health Service	National Historic Site
Pants	Underwear	Trousers
Subway	A pedestrian underpass under a road for example	The underground rail network
The tube	UK terminology for the underground rail network – primarily in London	The television
Vest	An undergarment like a sleeveless T-shirt worn under main clothes	A waistcoat – part of a 3-piece suit!
Vet	Abbreviation of veterinarian (a doctor for animals)	Abbreviation of veteran (someone who has served in the armed forces during a conflict or war is said to be a veteran of that conflict)

Similarly, in different countries the same words can be spelled in different ways, although in that instance, the words still (usually) mean the same thing

UK	USA
Organisation	Organization
Colour	Color
Centre	Center
Analogue	Analog
Theatre	Theater

Interestingly, the word organisation, spelled with a z, is now in the UK dictionary as an acceptable alternative spelling.

Similarly, there can be issues even within the same country!

Unit Link

For more on **cultural differences with words** see **Unit 1** – Communication and Employability Skills for IT, section 2.1.

Security issues

One of the fundamental problems with distributing goods over large areas is the amount of time that passes between the goods **leaving** the supplier and being **received** by the purchaser. During this period any number of things could happen, including the goods could be:

◆ **damaged** (the item could be damaged in transit)
◆ **stolen** (although with modern tracking systems this is less likely as losses are identified more quickly)
◆ **lost** (there have been many instances of letters arriving a considerable time after they were posted).

Activity

Using the Internet, see how many instances you can find of letters, postcards and parcels arriving years after they were posted.

http://news.bbc.co.uk/1/hi/england/1934116.stm
http://news.bbc.co.uk/1/hi/world/europe/2221882.stm

The above news items are an interesting place to start!

Overland transit is likely to be the **least secure** as goods will tend to change transportation vehicles a number of times between origin and destination.

Air freight will probably be the **quickest** and least likely to be open to experiencing difficulties. It is usually, however, the most expensive method of delivery.

Essentially, companies need to be aware that as much as there is a major benefit from e-commerce, there can also be significant disadvantages which can, usually, be overcome once organisations have become aware of them and have put some sort of remedial action in place!

1.4 e-Commerce entities

In section 1.1 we considered some of the organisations that have an online presence, and some of the services we can now find online. In section 1.2 we investigated the ways that organisations can use the Internet as part of their activities and the impact this has had on the way businesses function.

Now we will look at the range of entities that have online activity.

Category and definition	Name of entity	What they do!
e-tailers – these are companies that trade solely online. The term probably comes from the abbreviation of e-commerce and retailers.	**amazon.com**	Amazon began by selling books, CDs and DVDs to the general public, largely for less than customers would expect to pay on the high street, largely because of the lower overheads with not having to have a high-street presence. Initially trading only in the USA, an English .co.uk site soon followed. The company now deals in a large range of products including electronics.
	ebuyer.co.uk	Ebuyer sells a wide range of white goods – that is computer products and accessories, and audio-visual products such as TVs and cameras.
Manufacturers – companies that produce goods for sale, either direct to the general public or through other outlets.	**dell.com**	Unlike most other brands of computer, Dell computers can only be purchased through online retailers. As such, Dell is a rare example of a manufacturer that trades solely online.
Existing retailers – this is where companies originated in other formats, either on the high street or as mail-order companies that have now opted to have an online presence.	**tesco.com**	A clever concept as an extension to a supermarket, customers can now do their weekly shopping online, from the comfort of their own computers. One of the advantages of this particular service is that you can configure your account to order specific items that you purchase regularly as part of your order, with you only then having to add the items that would not form part of your usual shopping list. One huge benefit for the customer of shopping this way is that you tend to spend less money overall, and you are less likely to succumb to impulse purchases. In addition you can check whether you have pasta in the cupboard before you buy another bag to add to the four you forgot you had! Subsequently, Tesco has also diversified their business by providing other services such as insurance, entertainment products such as CD, book and DVD sales, loans and personal finance products and mobile communications.
	argos.co.uk	As a high-street catalogue shop, customers were generally unable to browse the actual products prior to buying them. They were only able to look at pictures in a catalogue. However, as a lower-price store, the shops themselves were often full of customers, particularly around Christmas. When Argos opened its online shop, its range expanded dramatically because now products that would ordinarily be too costly to store or too heavy for staff to move, could be held by the store, and delivered directly to the customer's front door.

▶

Category and definition	Name of entity	What they do!
	trutex.com	Originally a mail-order-only distributor for school uniforms, this organisation has now invested in a website, although it still publishes its printed catalogue for those customers who have no internet access.
Consumer led – an online site that is controlled largely by the activities of consumers.	eBay.co.uk	At its outset, eBay was simply an online auction site, where individuals could sell products they no longer wanted. Rather than throwing them away, they were now able to offer them for sale. Examples might include baby products that were still in good condition but which children had outgrown, unwanted gifts, old records and books. More recently, however, many small-business owners have used eBay as an outlet for their own goods and services via online shops.
Informative – generally these are websites that are intended to provide information, although as in the case of National Rail, this can also include providing services such as ticket sales.	bbc.co.uk	As an online news service, the BBC is still one of the most successful services which is accessed around the world. The advantage of a news website is that information can be accurately and quickly updated, prior to any general TV news update. Other services include: http://www.bbc.co.uk/learning/ where students can access learning and revision materials for a variety of subjects. http://www.bbc.co.uk/health/ contains health-related information including physical and mental health. http://www.bbc.co.uk/relationships/ has pages containing general relationship advice. All in all, the assortment of information available on the BBC website is expanding all the time.
	nationalrail.co.uk	This website is useful for the traveller as it contains all the information you might need for planning a rail journey. Train times, ticket prices (including offers as a result of different pricing bands), journey stops etc. can all be viewed online, then printed for reference purposes. If there is sufficient time when you plan your journey, you can ask for the tickets to be sent to you. If there is insufficient time, you can print out the information and book the tickets at a station ticket office.
Service providers – companies that provide low-cost services or act as agents for third parties.	easyjet.co.uk	A low-cost airline, easyjet.co.uk was one of the first companies that traded solely online to offer cheap flights to the general public. It also allows you to book hotels independently of the flights, thereby allowing you to customise your own trip.
	lastminute.com	Lastminute.com is also a travel organisation, although it offers more to its service as it also allows customers to book car hire, restaurants and theatre tickets in their destination location.

	seetickets.com	An event tickets service – once you have purchased gig or concert tickets from this website, you can register to receive regular updates. Then as new gigs, concerts and tours are added, you can be automatically notified.
		The company acts as an agent for ticket sales for venues across the UK. The events are listed; the tickets are then ordered and paid for online, before being delivered to your front door.
Financial – this category would include internet banks, loan providers and online insurers.	esure.com	Essentially an insurance company, esure.com now provides a range of insurances and subsidiary services.
		Now on offer, customers can purchase car, home, pet and travel insurance from one website, along with securing a personal loan.
	egg.com	Egg.com was one of the first banks to be created that traded solely online. While most high-street branch services can be obtained from an online bank, clearly one major problem remains. The technology does not yet exist that will allow you to use your computer base unit as a cash dispenser!

Activity

You have been consulted by **Frankoni T-Shirts Limited** regarding the value of trading through e-commerce.

Create an A5 booklet that will be distributed to Frankoni employees about the notion of trading online.

NB: You should ensure that you discuss the benefits (see section 1.2) and the drawbacks (see section 1.3) that the organisation would experience, and make sure that you link your discussion directly to Frankoni and its activities.

Show the leaflet to your tutor.

Braincheck

Test your understanding of your learning so far by answering the following questions:

1 How has the Internet **widened consumer participation**?
2 What is **track and trace**?
3 Why might some **older users** be **disadvantaged** in using e-commerce sites?
4 What are **bricks and clicks** companies?
5 Name three **benefits** of e-commerce.
6 Name four **drawbacks** of e-commerce.
7 What is a **hit counter**?
8 What is **ISO** and what does it do?
9 What are the two interpretations of the term '**The Tube**'?
10 What is an **e-tailer**?

How well did you do? See answers on page 421!

2 Understand the technologies involved in e-commerce

2.1 Hardware and software

Firstly it should be noted that this section is intended to help you understand what e-commerce is, what the security and legal implications of trading via e-commerce are, and give you an overview of the technologies involved. Other units that concentrate on server scripting, website production and management and customisation of web pages are included in the companion options book.

Links

The companion book contains the following units:

Unit 10 – Client Side Customisation of Web Pages

Unit 19 – Web Server Scripting

Unit 21 – Website Production and Management

Web servers

The web server, which is made up of the usual computer components such as a motherboard, memory and one or more hard drives, depending on the capacity required, will be controlled by designated software such as Microsoft OEM Windows Server 2003 Web Edition®, which has versions for both Mac and Windows-based hardware.

The software, supplemented and supported by security utilities such as firewalls, virus protection, spyware and adware products, controls user access to the content stored on the server.

Key Terms

A **web server** is essentially a computer that stores and organises website content written in **H**yper**T**ext **M**arkup **L**anguage (**HTML**). Users will access this material via a **web browser**.

Essentially, the server manages the process as users access the information via the Internet, and with a large and busy website, this functionality might not be provided by a single server but by a number of web servers working together.

Browsers

In order to access the content of internet sites, users need to have a **web browser** client. A browser is a specialist software application which locates and then facilitates the display of the hypertext (stored on the server) on your computer's monitor. Through the browser the user is then able to interact with the web content.

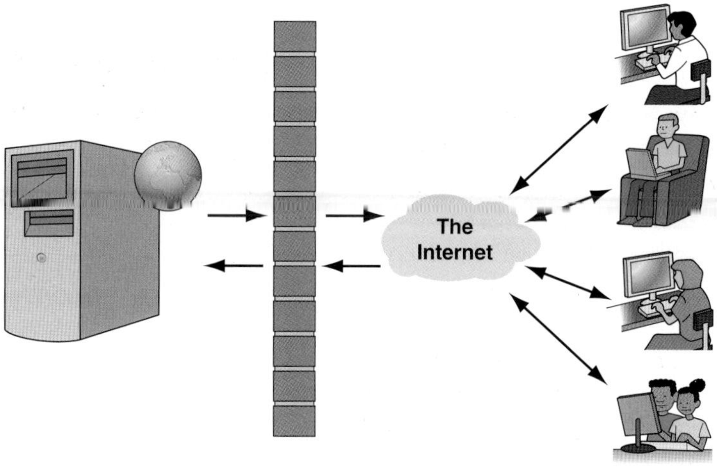

Current software includes:

◆ Microsoft IE® (Internet Explorer) 7
◆ Mozilla Firefox®
◆ Avant Browser® 11
◆ Smart Bro® 2.6
◆ Netscape® 8.1.2
◆ Safari RRS®

Figure 34.10 How a web server communicates with the outside world

Unlike many other types of software, downloading a web browser client is usually free. The example shown in Figure 34.12 is Mozilla Firefox® version 1.5.0.10.

The primary common components of all web browsers are as follows:

1 The **address bar** – this is where the user can type in the **u**niform **r**esource **l**ocator(**URL**) of the page they would like to view. The address is translated to a server's network address by a **d**omain **n**ame **s**erver (**DNS**). Alternatively the user can key some search terms into the search bar and choose from a list of addresses which, when clicked, will automatically move into the address bar.

2 The **search engine** – this is the tool that users use in order to find specific web content. These search engines are created by organisations and, in some cases, they offer a free service, where in others there can be a small indirect charge. Most search engines **receive income** through **advertising** and **sponsored links**.

There are a large number of charity-based web browsers currently active on the Internet such as the one shown in Figure 34.13.

Through advertising revenue received from companies who use this service as one of the media for users to access their web pages, the organisation donates money to the charity of the user's choice. This is one way to passively donate to charity.

3 The **search bar** – this is where the user keys in one or more **search terms** that will be used to explore the content of websites, looking for particular subject matter. Where the subject matter is found, the system will filter out the relevant **hits** and list them. The user can then look through the list to find the exact content required.

Figure 34.11 A typical web browser

Figure 34.12 Everyclick web browser

Key Terms

A **meta tag** is data that is included in code at the beginning of a web page that contains information on which a user might search. For example, the name of the author, a company name, a list of key words. The more matches there are between the detail in the meta tag and the search criteria input by the user, the higher up the results list the page is likely to be. Not all web pages, however, contain meta tags.

The principle is relatively straightforward: authors of web pages can create a **meta tag**. This is not visible to the user; it bears a description of the **page's contents** and a number of **key words**. When the user enters the relevant search terms into the browser, the software will search these mega tags and list those pages that are relevant because they contain those key terms. The HTML script for a meta tag would look something like this:

<META name='Web Browsers' content='Everyclick'>

Not all internet documents contain meta tags and not all search engines are set up to use this information. However, as the quantity of information on the World Wide Web continues to increase, it is more likely that the use of meta tags will become more and more important to reduce the search time (rather than search each page manually).

4 **Bookmarks** are a useful tool if you find that you have found a website you might wish to return to at a later date.

Figure 34.13 Bookmarking a page

Once you have found a page, you simply click on the bookmark menu on the toolbar, and then click on **Bookmark This Page**. As part of the process, the browser will offer you a suggested title for the bookmark. You may, however, choose your own.

5 **Done** – while it might seem odd to draw your attention to this data item on the bottom toolbar, it is actually an important one. There will be times, for example, where a website loads and is appears blank. If the word **Done** appears in the toolbar, then it means that as far as the computer is concerned, it has downloaded the requested web-page content. If it is **not** yet done, there will be other messages in the toolbar, like the one shown in Figure 3.15.

As long as the word **Done** is not visible, the page loading is still active.

Waiting for www.google.co.uk

Figure 34.14 Internet activity guidance

Around the **search bar** you will see a number of options.

Figure 34.15 Google™'s search bar

We will take them in order (top row first).

Web

This option or category is the most general term. In fact, if this option is selected, the search engine will explore the content of most of the other categories as well!

The **hits** are displayed in order of **relevance** – an item is deemed more or less relevant depending on the number of matching words there are between the search terms and the article.

If the search terms were 'New York Hotel Offers' then the pages that would be listed first would contain all the search terms. Following these would be pages where two of the search terms occur, followed by pages where only one of the search terms occur.

There are other ways of refining a search by using symbols to influence how the search is executed, for example the inclusion of a '+' symbol between two words will ensure that the only hits returned will include both search terms.

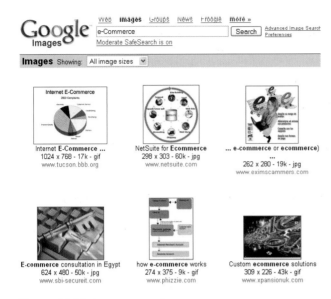

Images

Clicking on the images tab before entering the relevant key word will ensure that the search only returns image files that contain the keyword(s) in the file name.

The hits returned when **e-commerce** was keyed into the search bar with the image tab selected are a range of photographic images and diagrams, although these searches can often also return clipart illustrations.

Groups

Selecting the groups option will search for message boards for groups interested in a particular subject. Inserting BTEC into the search bar found the pages shown in Figure 34.18.

Figure 34.16 Images search

Figure 34.17 Groups search

News

A news search will filter for articles associated with a given topic. As can be seen in Figure 34.19, since articles will be published at a specific time point, users can filter in different time periods. As you can see, Google News UK® has now also added an **Archive** feature.

Figure 34.18 News search interface menu options

Google Product Search

The Google Product Search tab is a portal that gives you access to pages about products you can buy.

You will also notice that the website even provides you with a definition of what it is!

Figure 34.19 Google Product Search interface

Google™ Search button

Clicking on this button will search the net and return a list of matches that the user can then browse.

I'm Feeling Lucky button

Clicking this button, however, will simply take the user to what would have been the **first hit** in their list had they chosen the Google™ Search option, and will open up the page. There are times when this is a very useful feature, but then you must be very careful to choose your keywords accurately!

Search the web radio button

If selected, this option will search the web for information based on the key words or search terms input by the user, and may include pages from anywhere in the world.

Search pages from the UK button

This option will **only** return pages from the UK.

More>>

This contains a number of other features available through the browser, which includes those shown in Figure 34.21.

Below the search bar are four additional options. These are straightforward.

Google™ Search button

Figure 34.20 Other Google™ utilities and services

To use browsers and search engines effectively is a skill, and the more you use and experiment with them, the better you will become.

Server software

The two main server software solutions are **Microsoft IIS®** (internet information server) and **Apache HTTP Server®**, which is usually simply referred to as just **Apache®**. Recently surveys by **Netcraft** (**http://news.netcraft.com/**) show that Apache® has approximately **60 per cent** of the web-server market, with **Microsoft IIS®** taking a further 30 per cent and the remaining server software coming from companies such as **Sun** and **Zeus**.

Both products contain a series of **utilities** and **services** specifically directed at **managing** the **serving** of **web-page content** to **remote clients**.

These may include:

◆ **organising** multiple web sites
◆ **logging requests** and resources successfully served to clients

- **logging faults** and **errors**
- **filtering requests** based on client IP addresses
- **interfacing** with **server-side scripting** languages to provide **automation** and **user interaction**
- interfacing with **server-side database systems** to provide **dynamic content.**

Web-authoring tools

A web-authoring tool is basically a software application that is used to generate web pages. This software includes HTML/text editors such as:

- Adobe Page Mill®
- Adobe homesite®
- AOL Press®
- Coffee Cup® HTML editor

and **combined** site management and editing products such as:

- Adobe Dreamweaver®
- Microsoft FrontPage®
- HoTMetal Pro®

The most common web-authoring techniques are text and html editors.

Even simple text editors such as Microsoft Notepad® can be used in the creation of web pages. Here the user will key in HTML code. Sample code would look something like this:

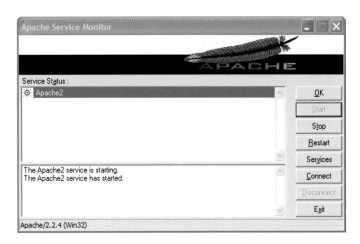

Figure 34.21 Apache Service Monitor – a simple front end to start and stop Apache®

```
<html>
<head>
<title>Frankoni Hompage<\title>
</head>
<body>
<b>Welcome to the Frankoni Website!<b>
</body>
</html>
```

Discreet HTML editing suites that include combined functionality such as management and editing facilities can be purchased, although the price, functions and complexity of the software varies greatly. Many of these suites also have W3C validation for HTML standardization, support for JavaScript, Java and CSS (cascading style sheets) for formatting. They help with the organisation and interconnectivity of pages on the site.

Many of these products are defined as being either **WYSIWYG** or **non-WYSIWYG**, although some of the authoring tools have combined functionality and allow the developer to work in either way.

Some more traditional text editors have developers working with descriptive codes known as **markup** (e.g. HTML) which **describe** the text (for example 'text colour blue' or 'text bold' immediately prior to the text that will ultimately be output will ensure that the relevant text when viewed will be blue and emboldened).

As with most software types today, some products can be downloaded freely from the Internet, although it is unlikely that they will have all the features and functionality of their commercially available alternatives!

Portability

Published guidelines and standards for web page creation help to ensure that there is greater portability for pages across a range of different computer systems. This is achieved, for example, through the use of HTML (HyperText Markup Languages) as a universally recognized and valid web page syntax.

There can be noticeable difference between the rending of html and CSS on different browsers. Before an e-Commerce website is published it should be tested on a number of browsers and platforms (i.e. hardware and operating systems) to reflect the potential audience.

The adoption of globally developed WAI (Web Accessibility Initiative) standards has also helped to remove barriers to those with disabilities who otherwise would not be able to contribute to or access the Web.

Database systems

Developers of websites, where database functionality is essential, have a number of options in terms of how this functionality can be achieved.

Although not ideal, the simplest and probably most easily understandable solution would be to create a database using proprietary enterprise-level software like **Microsoft SQL Server**®, then manipulate the database using, for example, **Adobe Dreamweaver**®. Basically, Dreamweaver will be using the database purely as the **data source** it uses to generate its **dynamic content**.

Alternatively, the database can be developed using combinations of **open source** tools like **PHP**® and **MYSQL**®, where **PHP** (PHP hypertext preprocessor), which is a server-side scripting language that can be used across different platforms (e.g. Microsoft Windows or Linux), is typically used alongside MYSQL (**SQL** stands for **s**tructured **q**uery **l**anguage), which is a database system based on relational principles. Requiring heavy coding, these products are generally classified as non-WYSIWYG.

Links

For more on PHP, see **Unit 19** – Web Server Scripting, in the companion book.

So, the range of alternatives for creating **dynamic** web-based database solutions includes:

Tool	Description
ASP® **ASP .NET**	Active Server Page® From the Microsoft stable, ASP creates web pages dynamically using **scripts**, **HTML** and **ActiveX** components.
JSP®	Java Server Page® Developed by the Sun Corporation, uses **servlets** to modify the HTML content of a web page once it has been requested and before it is sent to the user.
CGI®	Common Gateway Interface® This is relatively standard technology that extends web-server utilisation capabilities.

Clearly, which options are chosen will be dependent on the skills and abilities of the developer or the development team.

Storage size

Just as with all other data, web pages need to be stored, and developers must ensure that the hardware that will be **running** and **managing** the website has the capacity not only to **store** the relevant **pages**, **documents**, **images** and any relevant databases, but that it also has **sufficient spare capacity** to store any **data** that might be **input** into the system by the user.

This is particularly relevant where **databases** are used that support ordering systems. **Insufficient storage capacity** will slow down the system's ability to **search**, **sort** and **filter** the website's content.

Download speeds

When websites are being built, developers should ensure that the system that is produced can be used on a variety of hardware specifications – for example, the download speed of **narrowband** solutions like dial-up will be **much slower** than for **broadband** access through **cable** or **ADSL**. Some websites achieve this by providing **graphic** and **text-only versions** of their content, **enabling customers** to choose which is **most appropriate** to their download capabilities.

Essentially, developers must ensure that all of the technical aspects of the system have been fully considered in terms of the **volumes of data** that the system will need to **handle**, but more importantly, in terms of the potential number of **simultaneous users** that may want to **access** the website, **download specific resources** or **query** underlying 'back-end' **databases**.

Browser and platform compatibility

Care should be taken when building web sites as, despite firm standards being laid down by the World Wide Web Consortium (W3C), many browsers interpret and render HTML and cascading style sheets (CSS) differently.

Although Microsoft's Internet Explorer® for Windows is by far the most popular browser used, potential web-page content should be tested with other browsers (such as those listed earlier) and on different computer platforms (i.e. hardware and operating system combinations).

2.2 Networking

TCP/IP addresses, ports and protocols

Links

For this topic, see **Unit 8** – Communication Technologies, sections 3.3 and 4.1.

In URLs there are a range of protocols that allow users to access different aspects of the Internet. Here are some examples:

Protocol	Accesses
http://	Web servers
https://	Secure web servers (often used when you are trying to gain remote access to secure web content) for example when someone accesses their organisation's email systems remotely, transmitting credit-card information or logon details
news://	Newsgroups (as long as the user has subscribed)
ftp://	File transfer protocol servers and related files
file://	HTML documents stored on your local hard drive (although the full path does need to be defined)

Domain names

Like any computer system connected to the Internet, a **web server** is **identified** by a **unique IP address**. However, asking **customers** to **remember** an address such as **123.12.7.8** is obviously **unrealistic!** This is the reason why **user-friendly** domain names are used instead.

A domain name acts as a type of **alias** to the actual IP address. The domain has to be **unique**, should be **memorable** and be **registered** with a **domain authority**. These domain and IP address **pairs** can then be **linked** so that when a customer **looks** for a particular domain, it is **converted** to a **target IP** address by a **domain name server** (**DNS**), typically at the customer's **internet services provider** (**ISP**). This process is **completely invisible** to the user.

For example:

www.google.com is **really** IP address 64.233.183.103
www.apple.com is **really** IP address 17.112.152.32
www.microsoft.com is **really** IP address 207.46.199.30

Domain registration companies (e.g. www.UKreg.com) can **reserve domains** for customers and will usually **charge** on an **annual basis** for the **right** of an organisation to use that name. Different **types** of domain exist, usually indicating the **country of origin** (e.g. uk = United Kingdom, fr = France) and the **type of organisation** (e.g. .co is a company, .org is an organisation, .gov is a government department etc.). The .com (commercial domain) is typically used by **multinational** organisations. Apart from **cost**, there is **nothing** stopping a company from registering **multiple** domains.

For example:

www.google.co.uk (Google, company, UK)
www.ford.com (Ford, commercial – multinational)
www.ford.co.uk (Ford, same company but UK only)

There are some important things to remember when considering site and domain names, including choosing names that are:

◆ Easily remembered.
◆ Reflective of the business they represent.
◆ Unlikely to cause offence in other countries.

2.3 Payment systems

Services available

Clearly with so many commercial enterprises selling their goods and services through online sites, finding ways for customers to **pay quickly** is essential in maintaining the **throughput** of orders through any system. If companies had to wait for **traditional cheques** to arrive then allow time for them to be cashed through **banking systems**, it would create a **backlog of orders** awaiting distribution. Not a satisfactory situation! For this reason a number of **electronic payments systems** have been created over the last few years. The most commonly used services, however are:

◆ PayPal®
◆ NoChex®

PayPal® and NoChex®

Both of these organisations are **intermediaries**. They provide a **secure service** between **sellers** and **buyers** that allows **money** to be **transferred**. This process is described fully in unit 35, section 3.1, and can be seen as a visual representation in the same unit, Figure 35.15.

The main selling point of such a service is that the **intermediary promises** a **secure service** where the buyer can register their card details. When the buyer then needs to make an online payment, the buyer authorises the transaction with the intermediary and using buyer and seller identification numbers, and information about the amount of the money to be transferred, the transaction takes place with no other information being exchanged. Therefore, the seller **does not** receive the buyer's **personal** financial information.

The account holder can manage their account through the **account interface** seen in Figure 34.22.

1 The user's name is displayed, along with their email address. You will notice that the user can add email addresses meaning that they can use a single PayPal® account to pay for items that might have been purchased through different email accounts.
2 Each transaction will be listed and will include the name of the recipient or the contributor, depending on whether a payment was made or a transfer was received.
3 An additional column will list the amount of the transaction.

Both PayPal® and NoChex® are advertised as being fully secure methods of transferring funds online.

Debit and credit cards

Using a credit or debit card is a relatively straightforward process. The buyer keys in their account number, card start and expiry dates, and a security number taken from the reverse of the card.

The transaction is then **electronically authorised** by either the **bank** (or **credit-card** company **before** the seller will despatch the goods.

Remember, however, that you should **never** input **personal information** into a website **unless absolutely certain** that the website is

---

Premier Account Overview

Name:
Email: [Add email]
Status: UK - Unverified (0)

PayPal Account Balance❓ [View Limits | Manage Currency]

	Currency	Available Balance ❓
	US Dollars (Primary):	$0.00 USD
	Pound Sterling:	£0.00 GBP
	Current Total in US Dollars:	$0.00 USD
❓	Current Total in Pounds Sterling:	£0.00 GBP

Recent Activity | All Activity | Items Won 🅮

File	Type	To/From	Name/Email/Phone	Date
☐	Payment	To		15 Mar. 2007
☐	Transfer	From		15 Mar. 2007

Figure 34.22 PayPal® Account Overview interface

In this example the CCV is 999

Figure 34.23 Reverse of credit or debit card

genuine and is **secure**. The small **closed** padlock symbol on the **status bar** at the bottom of a web page gives an indication that the site is probably safe.

Customers will want **reassurance** that their personal information is **safe** and that it can **not** be accessed by **unscrupulous individuals** who might want to use it for **fraudulent purposes**. This is known as **identity theft**. Not only will the criminal be able to access bank, building-society or credit-card accounts, but with this type of personal information they will be able to **purchase goods** or **services** in someone else's name – so ultimately the payment will come from them!

2.4 Promotion

Effective use of search engines

In order to promote their own websites, organisations can use a series of techniques to ensure that their sites are among the first in the list when a search is run. The options are:

♦ using **meta tags**
♦ **spiders**
♦ **paying for prominence** in a search-result listing (a sponsored link).

> ## Key Terms
>
> A **spider** is a program within a search engine that accesses and reads web-page content to extract information that will be used in search-engine indexes. It will also 'crawl' through web links in a web page to find other pages, hence the name!

In addition to these options, some organisations are prepared to pay organisations for the privilege of being one of the first **hits** in a search list.

Figure 34.24 Search engine ranking providers

It is clear from the ranking service's claim that companies can buy **guaranteed first-page ranking** relatively cheaply. With a current exchange rate of $1.95 to each £ sterling, the $2.75 per day converts to about £1.40.

Newsgroups and forums

Newsgroup and forums are **discussion groups** that concentrate on **specific subjects.**

As you can see in Figure 34.25, there are 65 News newsgroups that, when clicked, reveal organisations such as human rights groups and cultural groups. Not surprisingly perhaps, the largest topic grouping is computers!

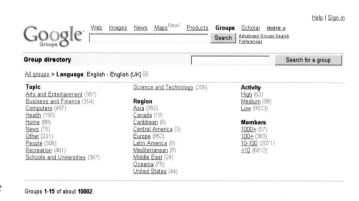

Figure 34.25 Current Google™ Group categories

What you will notice is that Google™ has created some main categories for the groups:

◆ groups by topic or interest
◆ groups by geographical region
◆ groups by the level of activity
◆ groups by the number of members they contain.

Banners and pop-ups

Banners and **pop-ups** are used very effectively to **promote** organisations, **goods** or **services** to users. Sometimes these can be really useful – for example, a company could add a pop-up or banner to their website containing **special offers**. At times these are likely to generate impulse purchases.

Sometimes, however, they can be extremely **irritating**. For this reason, most web browsers contain options to suppress pop-ups ('**pop-up blockers**'), as can be seen in Figure 34.27.

In this case the user would simply click on the relevant checkbox to block pop-up windows; the user does then have the option to **allow** particular sites if they choose.

Figure 34.26 Mozilla Firefox® Options window

PCWorld's izone puts a world of knowledge at your fingertips
Offering sound advice, buyer's guides and technical explanations

i ZONE
Learn More ▶

Banners are useful for **free advertising**, although they do not always publicise chargeable products!

Figure 34.27 Advertising banner from PC World's website

Spam

This is another term for **junk-email**. It is basically **unsolicited email** (mail that you did **not** request **or** want), that can be sent to you from a variety of sources.

In order to partially **protect** yourself against spam, you should always ensure that if you are keying your email address into a web page, you look for the checkbox that so often exists that usually looks something like this:

☐ Click here if you do not wish to receive notification of other goods and services

Quite often this is written in a very small font, and if you fail to click where required, your email address will undoubtedly be added to a **mailing list**!

There are times, however, where if you want to access particular information you have to submit an email address. As such, another strategy that might help you to avoid excessive spam is to have **two email accounts**. Your main account and a second **junk** account which bears a different email address. If you then have to submit an email address you can input your junk account address and any spam will be sent to your alternative mailbox.

Clearly there are also software utilities that help you manage your account against spam:

◆ One solution is to add each spam address to a **banned list** – but as spam regularly comes from addresses you will not yet have added, you may reduce the amount of spam you get, but you will not eradicate it.

◆ The second solution is to activate a **spam filter**. This filter will instantly divert any emails it **believes** to be spam to a particular directory and folder. However, this is not **foolproof** as it relies on being able to scan the **subject line** on the email, comparing the **content** to a list of particular words. If the subject contains any of these words, the email will be **filtered**. There will be times that a particular word will be included in the subject line **legitimately** and in this instance the email might be **incorrectly** identified as spam.

Spam is clearly a growing problem and organisations are constantly looking for new ways to block and eradicate it!

Direct marketing

Most commercial enterprises that have an online presence will have a **direct marketing** strategy, but depending on the organisation, the strategy will be implemented differently. Some companies may send **regular emails** to **existing** customers (those who have purchased goods previously) or **potential** customers, which could be those who have previously requested information from a website and, in some cases, those who have visited a website.

This could result in **monthly**, **weekly** or **ad hoc** emails, or could even result in traditional snail mail! It is certainly true that many mail-order companies, who now have websites, frequently follow up online orders by sending printed catalogues to customers.

Ensuring an effective user interface

One of the key principles of web page design has to be understanding the importance of the interface design. Websites that are **too crowded** (have too much information in a confined space), are too sparse (have too little information) or require **too much navigation** (movement between pages and around the screen) will be unattractive to the user, and the user will be less likely to visit the website again.

In addition, there are aspects such as **colour combination**, **font choices** etc. which have an impact on the effectiveness of any website.

You should also be aware that the Disability Discrimination Act (DDA) has been modified to cover accessibility issues, to specifically ensure that physically less able users will not be disadvantaged

Links

For more on website design and the user interface, see **Unit 21** – Website Production and Management and **Unit 13** – Human Computer Interaction, in the companion options book.

because of the way that websites are constructed.

The **RNIB** (Royal National Institute of the Blind) website provides a good overview of how the October 2004 changes to the DDA directly relate to websites (among other things).

In addition to laws such as the DDA, the **WAI** (**w**eb **a**ccessibility **i**nitiative) developed by the **W3C** provides advice, guidance,

When must a site be accessible by?

The Disability Discrimination Act 1995 - Word (the DDA), was introduced with the intention of comprehensively tackling the discrimination which many disabled people face. The part of the DDA that states websites must be made accessible came into force on 1 October 1999 and the Code of Practice for this section of the Act was published on 27 May 2002.

What are the October 2004 changes to the DDA?

The DDA changes that came into effect on October 1 2004 are as follows:

- small employer exemption removed. All employers are now legally obliged to make all their services accessible including websites, intranets and extranets accessible
- police and fire services are now also legally obliged to make their websites, intranets and extranets accessible. Previously they were exempt. The only area of employment still specifically excluded is the armed forces.
- service providers will have to make physical adjustments to their premises where these features make it impossible or unreasonably difficult for disabled people to use the service they provide.

- Note that since 1999 websites have had a legal obligation to be accessible.

Web access centre
Design and management resources

Figure 34.28 DDA modifications from the RNIB website

strategies and resources to help organisations who might be new to the concepts of accessibility, which will help these organisations make sites more accessible to those with disabilities.

For further information see:

http://www.w3.org/WAI/gettingstarted/Overview.html

Activity

This legislation is clearly very important. To ensure that you understand and appreciate its intricacies, log on to the URL shown above and write a short set of revision notes for the questions listed. The information is readily available and is easy to understand.

1 Explain the obligations of organisations as defined by the DDA.
2 Explain how it applies specifically to websites.
3 The term **reasonable adjustments** has been used to guide organisations – what does this mean?
4 Explain what can happen if companies do not adhere to the legislation and its requirements.

Once you have completed your revision notes, discuss them with your tutor.

Establishing customer loyalty in a virtual environment

While **customer loyalty** is what most companies strive for, many find it very **difficult to achieve** as most customers will ultimately shop around to find the best deals.

As such, enterprises have had to find new ways of encouraging customers to stay with them. The two main ways that they have done this include examples of both commercial and social strategies:

◆ One current **commercial** strategy has come directly from high-street retail, which is the concept of **loyalty points**. The customer will be given a proportional number of points against the money that they spend through the website. The points can then either be **exchanged for gifts** or can be **converted into money** which will be **deducted** from a subsequent order. Amazon® has incorporated this concept into its own credit card, where users will earn double points if they use the card to purchase goods from the Amazon® website, but single points if they use the card in other outlets.

◆ On a slightly different track, one of the major **social** strategies is where organisations give to charity when their search engines are used. This is known as a **passive** donation. Two examples are **Charitycafe** and **GoodSearch**, as can be seen in Figures 34.30 and 34.31.

Figure 34.29 GoodSearch

Unlike some charity search engines, GoodSearch allows the user to choose the charity to which they would like to contribute. Prior to using the search facilities, the charity is entered and verified. Users are able to enter a category like **Aids** for example, and they will then be presented with a list from which to choose. You should be aware, however, that the beneficiaries will largely be US charities

Figure 34.30 Charitycafe.com

This website donates 100 per cent of its profits to major charities which have worldwide activities.

2.5 Customer interface

Usability issues

As suggested in the earlier section, the **customer interface** is paramount if the organisation wishes to **widen participation** (that is to encourage the widest range of users to use the website). As part of their efforts to do this, they should ensure that they **ask regularly** for **user feedback** and should be prepared to **act** on this feedback when it is received.

Adapting and **modifying** the customer interface to improve its usability should be a standard maintenance activity for any good website. Online customer feedback forms are the obvious way to achieve this.

Feedback form: TrafficMap

Please tell us about how you use our service. Your information will help us improve. We appreciate your time.

1. How would describe your main use of the web site? (select one)

   ○ As a daily commuter
   ○ As a private traveller (e.g. leisure or personal travel)
   ○ As a long distance business traveller
   ○ As a media organisation
   ○ As a freight operator
   ○ As a public transport operator
   ○ Other

2. "How often" or "When" do you use the web site? (tick all that apply)

   ☐ Every day
   ☐ At least once a week
   ☐ Before a routine journey
   ☐ Before a new journey
   ☐ In response to a specific event (e.g. incident report by the media or bad weather)
   ☐ First time user

3. Has this web site influenced a recent journey? (tick all that apply)

   ☐ Yes, delayed or postponed a journey.
   ☐ Yes, diverted via another route.
   ☐ Yes, I have taken public transport as an alternative.
   ☐ No, I made the journey regardless.

4. a) How useful do you find this site and its content? (select one)

   1. ○ Extremely useful and informative
   2. ○ Useful
   3. ○ Sometimes disappointed by the extent or level of detail
   4. ○ Not at all useful

   b) Please outline reasons for your choice above.

Figure 34.31 Customer feedback form taken from the Highways Agency website

What is appropriate for any particular organisation will depend on its activities.

Providing customer account/profile

If you have an account with any online organisation, you will have

Contact information (e.g. email, phone contact, FAQ, live chat)

Almost all websites contain a **Contact Us** tab or window that contains a range of contact opportunities. Depending on the website (and **size** of the organisation) this might just include **email information**, but could also include categorised telephone numbers, for example **sales team** or **accounts enquiries** numbers.

Charitycafe.com, for example, limits contact opportunities to email, although it does also contain an **FAQ** (**f**requently **a**sked **q**uestions) window.

Other organisations, however, will additionally offer a range of **telephone numbers** and in some cases a **message board** or **live-chat** window.

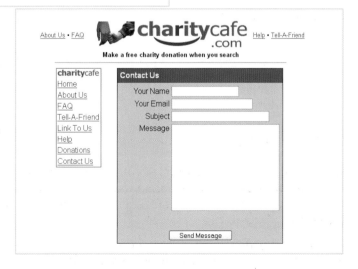

Figure 34.32 Charitycafe.com contact method

options about how you **set up** your own **account**. Under normal circumstances you will input all the relevant information at the start. You may, however, need to **change** some of your settings from time to time – for example, you may need to change your password. You would usually do this through some sort of **self-care**, **profile** or **account** settings interface, much like the one shown in Figure 34.34.

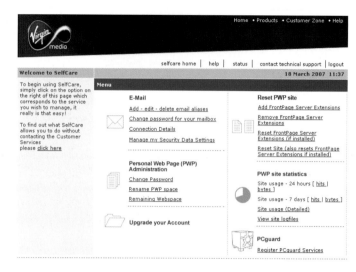

Figure 34.33 Virgin Media SelfCare interface

Order tracking

Similarly, part of the customer interface will include functionality to **track orders**. Figure 34.35 shows such an interface.

You should always remember, however, that some of the functionality is not always available depending on where the item is in the despatch system (for example you can not change a delivery address after the item(s) have been despatched).

Figure 34.34 Amazon® order tracking interface

Dealing with enquiries and complaints

Most organisations will actively promote an **enquiries** service, but often will not have an **obvious route** for directing **complaints**, perhaps because they do not really want to encourage complaints by highlighting this as a possible activity! Most **enquiries** and **complaints** are usually made **via email** and initially they result in an **automated email response**.

While the **automated response** in Figure 34.36 was to an **enquiry**, and **not** to a **complaint**, the principle should be the same. Organisations

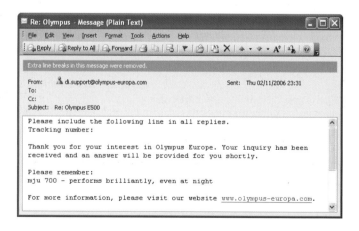

Figure 34.35 Olympus automated response to an enquiry

should **acknowledge** the **receipt** of emails; most do this by returning a simple email that acknowledges receipt of the email and allocates a **tracking number** which recipients are asked to **quote** in future communications.

In some situations, the company may respond with a telephone call – it will usually depend on the nature of the enquiry or complaint.

Either way, responding quickly and consistently is essential if the organisation wants to maintain good customer service.

Braincheck

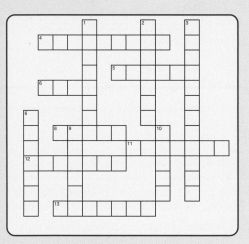

ACROSS
4 An email that is immediatlley gnerated in response to an enquiry or complaint
5 One of the two comon web server software solutions
6 Unscolicted email
8 The A in FAQ
11 Infomation about user that can be changed
12 What you see is what you get?
13 A Google facility for accessing shopping websites

DOWN
1 A link to page saved byt the user to enable quicker page access
2 Information at th begining of a website that contains key words
3 An organisation that acts as an agent between two companies to facilitiate transactions
7 The interface for accessing web pages
9 A program within a search engine that accesses, reads and extracts key information to add to an index
10 A window that appears when accessing and which often includes advertising material

See answers on page 421

3 Understand the security issues in e-commerce and the laws and guidelines that regulate it

3.1 Security

As **Unit 15** – Organisational Systems Security covers many of these subcategories in some depth, the topics will only be briefly covered here.

Prevention of hacking

Hacking is the unauthorised access of a computer system via a network. It is the intentional accessing of computer systems to **illegally gain access to data** for the purposes of theft, or with other **malicious** (and sometimes quite serious) **intent**.

Some hackers are merely pranksters who will attempt to access systems they know to be secure just to see if they can.

The intention of the activity is irrelevant when it comes to the consequences in law. It is an **illegal** and **criminal activity** and can result in **imprisonment**.

Viruses

Categories of virus include the following:

◆ **Email** viruses enter your system as attachments to emails you receive, and may well be passed on by you inadvertently because part of the virus **payload** (the action the virus is intended to perform) is to pass itself on to every contact in your address book.

◆ **Worm** viruses are designed to **reproduce** and they are capable of transmitting themselves across networks so that they can infect other systems. They do not need any help to reproduce; they can do this without any user intervention. Worm viruses are designed to harm networks, sometimes contributing to DOS attacks by reducing bandwidth, and some viruses will corrupt and destroy files.

◆ **Macro** viruses usually cause the least damage. They are only activated when the host program is activated and largely their payload will include **irritants** like **inserting unwanted phrases** or words in **documents** and **changing** font types, styles and colours.

◆ **Trojans** are hidden inside other programs and are designed to cause as much destruction as possible, including hiding files and directories, or encrypting system files with the intention of rendering systems unusable. The main problem with Trojans is that they can be difficult to find and difficult to destroy.

If detected, most viruses can either be **healed** or **deleted**. However, this is only possible if you have installed a good-quality antivirus product and you keep the software up to date.

Links

For more on **hacking** see **Unit 15** – Organisational Systems Security, section 1.1.

Key Terms

A **virus** is mini program that is attached to a genuine executable file and which is intended to damage the carrier file or other files on the system. The intended damage may be very severe, such as destroying directories or particular file types, or it can be more of an irritant, like generating pop-up messages that have to be closed down.

Some viruses have **time delays**; in other words some time may elapse between your machine becoming infected and the virus activating.

Links

For more on **viruses** see **Unit 15** – Organisational Systems Security, section 1.1.

Identity theft

Identity theft is a serious issue worldwide. It occurs where individuals or groups intentionally gain unauthorised access to information, particularly financial information, and use this to support criminal activity. This can include directly accessing someone's bank account to divert funds, and using someone's account numbers and codes to purchase goods (often online).

To make sure that your details are safe you should avoid giving any information unless you are absolutely sure who it is you are giving it to.

Firewall impact on site performance

Links

For more on **identity theft** see **Unit 15** – Organisational Systems Security, section 1.1.

Firewalls are programs that monitor a computer's **traffic** (which is the **incoming** and **outgoing** data communication that takes place when the user is online). The software needs to be **configured** to **permit** or **deny** communication with websites, as chosen by the user.

In general, once configured, there is **no real impact** on the performance of websites, but it can take time to set up the relevant **permissions** between the site and the user's computer.

Firewall software includes products such as:

◆ McAfee® Firewall Plus
◆ Zone Labs® ZoneAlarm 6.1.737
◆ Norton Personal Firewall as part of the Norton AntiVirus™ 2007 bundle
◆ Sygate Personal Firewall Pro User Version 5.6.

SSL (Secure Socket Layer)

Originally developed by the Netscape Corporation, this technology is a protocol that manages the **confidentiality** and security of transmissions. Data that is being transmitted is effectively **encrypted**, and then **decrypted** at its **destination**.

Links

For more on **firewalls** see **Unit 15** – Organisational Systems Security, section 1.1 and **Unit 2** – Computer Systems, section 2.2.

HTTPS

HTTPS uses SSL technologies to make web servers more secure. This is frequently used when accessing private data (organisational email or personal bank account information which is accessed remotely is usually accessed through an HTTPS secure web server).

Links

For more on **SSL** see **Unit 19** – Web Server Scripting, **Unit 21** – Website Production and Management in the companion book.

RSA certificates

This is a security method that is used for encryption, decryption and authentication, and which is based on mathematical principles – specifically the pairing of prime numbers.

Links

For more on **RSA certificates** see **Unit 30** – Networked Systems Security in the companion book.

Strong passwords

To demonstrate password strength we will set up a **Hotmail account** for Frankoni T-Shirts Limited.

Activity

Activate Hotmail and select the option that allows you to create a free email account.

You will be asked to select your country from a drop-down list, then create an email address.

In this instance, frankoni@hotmail.co.uk **is** available – it is likely that when you undertake this activity it will **not** be, so you might need to add some numbers on the end to create a potential account.

Figure 34.36 Creating the email address

Figure 34.37 A weak password

You will then need to choose a **password** – this is where the guide to password strength is visible. To see how it works, we will now enter three different passwords and look at the response we receive from the interface:

The first password is **pickles**.

Having input the word pickles as a password, the system estimates that this is probably not a very secure choice. This is because simple dictionary words that have a recognisable structure are probably easy to guess. Some individuals, for example, use the names of boyfriends, girlfriends, wives, husbands or children, which will clearly not be difficult to find out.

Let's try again!

The second password is **pickles1992.**

Now we have added some numbers to the password (this can be done before or after any text), which means that this password would be considered more secure.

How can we make this even more secure?

The third password is **P1ckles 1992** (where the **P** is a Capital and the **1** is numeric).

Create your password

Please type a password, and then retype it to confirm.

Password: ***********

The password must contain at least six characters and is case sensitive.

Password strength: **Medium**   Strong

Retype password:

Figure 34.38 A medium password

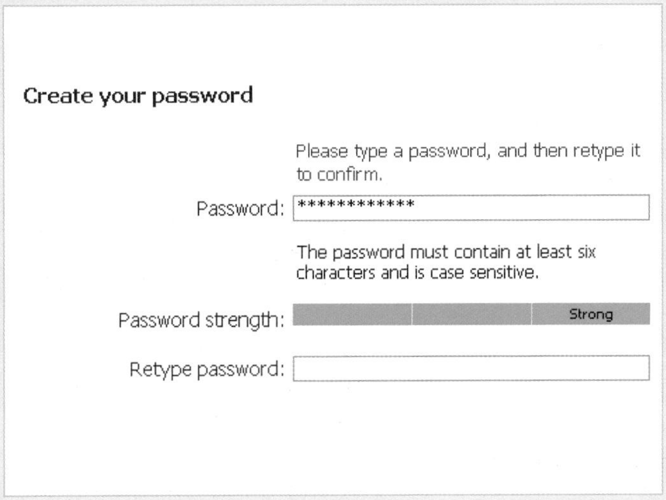

Create your password

Please type a password, and then retype it to confirm.

Password: ***********

The password must contain at least six characters and is case sensitive.

Password strength: **Strong**

Retype password:

The more secure a password is, the less likely it is that someone else will be able to **guess it** or **crack it** using **hacking** tools.

Now that you have seen this in action, close down the setup process without creating the account!

Figure 34.39 A very strong password

Alternative authentication methods

Links

For more on **biometrics** see **Unit 15** – Organisational Systems Security, section 2.2.

There are clearly alternative authentication methods for systems including **biometrics** (such as fingerprints, retinal scans or voice patterns) that can be used in preference (or addition to) traditional username and password combinations.

The hardware required to facilitate this type of authentication, however, is not yet in the general public domain – as such, organisations would be unable to use this to authenticate access to their websites.

3.2 Legislation

Legislation in general is so important that it is mentioned many times in different units. Why is it mentioned quite so often? Simply to ensure that one way or another it will be studied, regardless of which qualification pathway you follow and units you choose.

As such, the basic principles of the legislation will be mentioned here, and you will be referred to other units in this text for the main content.

Relevant legislation

Data Protection Act 1998

The Data Protection Act sets out enforceable guidelines on how data about us is stored and used. It also makes organisations responsible for ensuring that the data being stored is accurate. Organisations that fail to implement the regulations as laid out in this Act can be prosecuted by both individuals and organisations.

Computer Misuse Act 1990

Essentially, this legislation is designed to prevent users from using computer systems intentionally for criminal activities such as theft, pornography and terrorism.

Consumer Credit Act 1974

This act was designed to protect individuals against being drawn into credit agreements, in many cases, without the full facts.

Under the terms of the law, companies must (in addition to other aspects of the law):

Links

For more on the **Data Protection Act 1998** see **Unit 3** – Information Systems, section 3.1 and **Unit 15** – Organisational Systems Security, section 3.4.

Links

For more on the **Computer Misuse Act 1990** see **Unit 3** – Information Systems, section 3.1 and **Unit 15** – Organisational Systems Security, section 3.4.

◆ set out the repayment expectations (both the repayment amounts and dates when payments should be received)
◆ explain what will happen if payments are missed
◆ explain how the contract can be terminated
◆ explain the charges that will be applicable (including the interest rate and any penalties).

Also, to protect individuals who feel coerced into signing credit agreements in their own homes, the amendments to this legislation offer additional protection known as a **cooling-off period** (usually seven days) during which you can withdraw from the agreement if you change your mind.

For more information about this important law see the following website:

http://www.compactlaw.co.uk/free_legal_information/consumer_law/consumf 4.html

Trading Standards

Trading Standards legislation is made up of content from the Sale of Goods Act 1979 (as amended) and The Supply of Goods and Services Act 1982.

It is designed to regulate the quality of the goods and services we buy and fundamentally decrees that these should be **fit for purpose** and **safe to use**.

Freedom of Information Act 2000

Clearly a new law, having only been passed in 2000, this act enables individuals to see the information that is being stored about them.

This is an important step forward, particularly if you find you are one of those unfortunate individuals who is being disadvantaged by data that may not be **correct**.

Links

For more on the **Freedom of Information Act 2000** see **Unit 3** – Information Systems, section 3.1 and **Unit 15** – Organisational Systems Security, section 3.4.

Copyright legislation

Interestingly, when it comes to website content, there is no need for specific legislation, as current legislation will still apply. Simply, this legislation deals with the ownership of visual **content**, whether that be through books, magazines, journals, music, images or, indeed, websites.

Links

For more on the **copyright and patent legislation** see **Unit 15** – Organisational Systems Security, section 3.4.

For further information you can also see:
http://www.copyrightservice.co.uk/ copyright/p01_uk_copyright_law

Activity

Create a series of passwords for the following:

◆ Lee Office Supplies
◆ Frankoni T-shirts
◆ Kris Arts and Media.

In each case, create a weak, medium and strong password, using words that you would associate with the activities of each organisation.

Once you have done this, reconsider your own system passwords and create a new **strong** password for your own account. Implement the new password.

Links

Unit 34 – e-Commerce is a **Core Unit** on the BTEC National Diploma for IT Practitioners (**IT and Business** route) and a **Specialist Unit** on the Certificate on the same route.

Unit 34 is also a **Specialist Unit** on the following BTEC National routes:

Software Development

Systems Support

Networking

As such it has links to a number of other units, principally:

Unit 1 – Communication and Employability Skills

Unit 3 – Information Systems

Unit 8 – Communication Technologies

Unit 10 – Client Side Customisation of Web Pages

Unit 13 – Human Computer Interaction

Unit 15 – Organisational Systems Security

Unit 19 – Web Server Scripting

Unit 21 – Website Production and Management

Unit 30 – Networked Systems Security

Achieving success

In order to achieve each unit you will complete a series of coursework activities. Each time you hand in work, your tutor will return this to you with a record of your achievement.

This particular unit has 12 criteria to meet: 6 pass, 3 merit and 3 distinction.

For a **pass**:

You must achieve **all** 6 pass criteria.

For a **merit**:

You must achieve **all** 6 pass and **all** 3 merit criteria.

For a **distinction**:

You must achieve **all** 6 pass, **all** 3 merit and **all** 3 distinction criteria.

Help with assessment

In order to **pass** this unit you will need to show an understanding of the basic principles by being able to describe them. You will need to be able to highlight similarities, identify and comment on differences and be able to provide positive and negative views on various aspects of the topic. You will need to be able to demonstrate a sound understanding of systems security and legislation.

For a **merit** you will also need to explain potential threats and risks to organisations that choose to commit to e-commerce systems, be able to explain security issues in context and be able to demonstrate a knowledge of countermeasures to any issues identified. You should also be able to compare different types of payment systems used in e-commerce systems.

For a **distinction** you will need to expand your coursework to include evidence of justification and evaluation. You will need to be able to justify your choices, and evaluate the impact that e-commerce has had on the high street.

So that you can monitor your own progress and achievement in each unit, a recording grid has been provided (see opposite). The full version of this grid is also included on the companion CD.

Assignment	Assignments in this unit			
	U34.01	U34.02	U34.03	U34.04
Referral				
Pass				
1				
2				
3				
4				
5				
6				
Merit				
1				
2				
3				
Distinction				
1				
2				
3				

 ## Online resources on the CD

Electronic glossary for this Unit
Key fact sheets
Electronic slide show of key points
Multiple choice self-test quizzes

 ## Further reading

Textbooks

Chaffey, D., 2003, *E-business and E-Commerce Management*, 2nd edn, FT Prentice Hall, ISBN 0273683780.

Malmsten, E., Leander, K., Portanger, E., and Drazin, C., 2002, *Boo Hoo: A Dot.com Story from Concept to Catastrophe*, Arrow Books Ltd, ISBN 0099418371.

Vise, D., 2005, *The Google Story*, Macmillan, ISBN 1405053712.

Websites

www.ico.gov.uk
www.w3.org

Impact of the Use of IT on Business Systems

Capsule view

With IT-related products and services under constant development, **technological change** is a constant **feature** of the **face of business** today.

Whether or not organisations choose to **explore** and **embrace** new technologies will be **their choice**. If, however, they **do** decide to exploit such opportunities, they will need to be **clear** about the **impact** that the use of such systems will have on the **business**. They will also need to understand the **potential costs** of **not** investing.

1 Know the information technology developments that have had an impact on organisations

Extensive technological developments that have been made over the last three decades have seen:

◆ a **wider range** of **software**
◆ **more** business **functionality supported**
◆ the **resolution** of **compatibility issues** between different packages
◆ **better integration** of products.

How do organisations **use** this improved technology? Through:

◆ better information management
◆ improved presentation
◆ increased ability to manipulate data in different ways
◆ better communication.

Learning aims

1 Know the information technology developments that have had an impact on organisations.
2 Understand why organisations need to change in response to information technology developments.
3 Understand how organisations adapt activities in response to information technology developments.

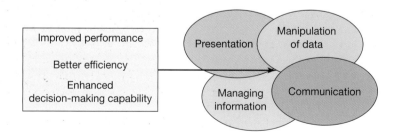

Figure 35.1 Business uses of ICT

This means that organisations can **perform more effectively** and it will be seen as **more professional**, and by embracing these technologies significantly **enhance** managers **decision-making** capabilities.

1.1 Hardware, systems and increasing power

Anyone who has been **technologically aware** since the late 1980s or early 1990s can give you lots of anecdotes about how **slow** computers used to be and how you had time to go and make a cup of coffee and a sandwich while the machine went through its boot sequence or attempted to open an application!

Computers at this stage would have run on Intel 80286 or 80386 processors which, when compared with modern processors, would have been like comparing the tortoise and the hare.

Having said that, users would not really have considered the speed of a 386 16 MHz processor as particularly slow, as at the time when these

Figure 35.2 Old technology

processors were commercially available, there was nothing faster to compare them with. It was only as new technology (in this case the 80486 processor) came into the public arena that the 80386 technology began to look jaded. So it is with any technological advances.

The upsurge in computer-aided design/computer-aided manufacturing (**CAD/CAM**) technologies **triggered** huge **changes** in the way that **goods** are **produced**.

Automated car production is now commonplace, with the knock-on effect that jobs traditionally done by people are now being done by machines. The advantage of using machines over human workers is obvious: machines do not take holidays and can work long hours without breaks. While you might initially want to say that machines do not get sick, you would have to bear in mind that machines, like humans, can go wrong. However, if machines are regularly maintained and serviced, rather than being allowed to run until they break, then even downtime can be largely avoided.

Figure 35.3 Automated car plant

Some years ago, the United Colors of Benetton (the clothing manufacturing group) invested heavily in new **computerised CAD/CAM** and **logistics** systems which allowed them to **increase** their **competitive advantage** over their rivals by allowing them to get products into the marketplace **three weeks earlier** than they had previously experienced, while enabling them to reduce the amount of **manpower** required to achieve this. Effectively they **vastly increased efficiency** and **throughput**, while **decreasing** the need for **human workers**. The impact of new CAD/CAM technologies on the clothing industry has greatly improved its ability to respond to new markets.

The automotive and clothing industries are not the only ones that have been affected by advances in technology. Plastics production, bottling plants, food production, distribution and logistics and many more have seen a rise in technology investment, with a corresponding fall in the use of human workers.

Education, too, has been changed beyond all recognition through **i**nformation **l**earning **t**echnology (**ILT**); computers in the classroom have improved learners' **access** to **knowledge** and **information**, with the advantage that, unlike books, this resource can always be up to date.

There are some obvious **exceptions** to this trend – many of the **service industries** (e.g. nursing, hairdressing and the trades, such as plumbing, building, car maintenance), which rely on human interactions, have remained largely unaffected, although they increasingly use computerised equipment as part of the process.

Some people believe that advances in technology will slow down in the next few years as companies run out of invention ideas. Others, however, believe the opposite – that continued investment in development will see **even more** progress made.

Today, areas of major investment include **robotics** (specifically artificial intelligence), **medicine** (such as smart limbs which are capable of interfacing with the body's own nervous system) and **communications** (mobile telephones with even more functionality than at present).

Increasing capacity and sophistication of platforms

There are three main advances here:

1 Increased **hard-drive capacity** allows organisations to store more of their historic data than previously possible, giving them access to larger **datasets** for analysis.
2 Faster **processors** allow much more complex tasks to be undertaken more quickly.
3 **Operating systems** have improved **functionality**, enabling systems and networks to work together more **efficiently**, including allowing users to share resources and offering a wider range of utilities for system management.

Availability of new communication technologies (e.g. mobile communication, networks, email, electronic data interchange)

The developments in communications technology have probably had the most impact on the way in which organisations operate.

Mobile phones ensure that working teams, customers, suppliers and distributors **maintain contact** much more easily than ever really thought possible. **Electronic systems** that **track goods** in **transit** have enabled businesses to demand a **better service** from their delivery agents, and ensure that customers' needs are met more effectively.

Networks have ensured that individuals inside companies can have **access to** and can **share information** more easily: information can be quickly **updated**, improving **response times** and **timeliness** of **information**, and generally making up-to-date facts and figures available at the touch of a button. In addition, many organisations have their own **intranet**, through which they share news and event information.

Prior to email, almost all companies had busy **internal mail** systems, where memos and other documents were **physically moved** between departments, even across sites. While this certainly does still exist (as there will be instances where documents cannot be sent electronically), more and more internal communication is now supported through the use of **email** and, in some cases, organisational **online messaging systems**.

Electronic data interchange (EDI)

This is a system that allows **inter-organisational communication** of **business documents** such as orders and invoices, and which through its use has reduced the amount of paperwork needed to support most business activities. Boeing, for example, schedule their manufacture of aircraft well in advance, and as they are unable to stock many of the components that go into aircraft building, specifically because of the size of an engine, set of wings, fuselage pieces, they need these components to be delivered to them immediately prior to them being installed into an aeroplane. They use EDI-style systems to **communicate** with their suppliers, who then produce the components and get them to the Boeing factory immediately before they are needed (**JIT** – Just In Time).

> ## Key Terms
>
> What is **EDI**?
>
> Essentially EDI is a method of exchanging controlled information between companies using information technology.

The advantage of all of the above communications technologies is that many of them are **effectively time-independent**. If tracking a parcel through an electronic system, using a computer, this can be done at any time of the day or night. Email from customers in **different time zones** can be sent to you while your company is closed, and will be held on file until your workers return. EDI systems can be operating day and night, again because any documents sent through such a system will be stored until the employees are there to respond to them.

1.2 Software

Software is becoming **increasingly complex**, but is also offering more and more **advanced functionality** over its predecessors.

Increased sophistication and integration of application software

The main difficulty for software manufacturers when developing new applications software has always been the issue of **backward compatibility** (that is being able to open and upgrade files created in previous versions of a product). Files created in the original Microsoft Access® database software, for example, were not useable when Microsoft upgraded to Microsoft Access® 2.0. Many companies had to find ways of **exporting** huge **quantities** of **data**, **changing** its **format** and then **importing** it back into Microsoft Access®. At the time, Microsoft was aware of the problems that this would cause for companies, and it has endeavoured not to make the same mistakes with subsequent releases of software. The problem centred on the original data format and how it was stored, and the way that this functionality was differently handled by the newer product.

It has also long been recognised that being able to import tables of information from a database package, and maybe graphs or charts from a spreadsheet, will create **better presented**, more **interesting** and

professional word-processed reports. However, until more recently, simple copying and pasting was not an option, as there was a level of **incompatibility** between the products. Microsoft Office® is a truly integrated package, where copy and paste functionality is readily available. This has been followed by a number of similar integrated software packages.

Name of product	Manufacturer	Functionality
StarOffice 8	Sun Microsystems	Word processing, spreadsheet, presentation, drawing and database
WordPerfect® Suite	Corel® Corporation	Word processing, spreadsheet, database, presentation
Open Office Suite	Openoffice.com	Word processing, presentation, drawing, spreadsheet, database, advanced calculator, PDF creator

Many of these products have also been created for multiple platforms (e.g. MS Windows®, Mac OS, Linux).

Integrated software has also enabled organisations to produce **consistent documentation** across multiple applications, further enhancing their professional image.

Specialised support software (e.g. management information systems, decision support software, expert systems)

It should also come as no surprise that there are more and more specialist products on the market that have specific uses.

Middleware, for example, is **specialist communications** software that **enables applications** to **integrate** across networked systems and environments.

Management information systems (MIS)

An **MIS** is a system that is designed to help executives to **manage** an **organisation** by giving them sufficient **information** to help them **control** the **overall direction** and the day-to-day activities. The information the system produces must be in the right format, and must be available at the right time to provide the required support.

Decision support software

Decision support software is used to help managers **predict** the **future**, using 'what if.....?' scenarios, so that managers can, as far as possible, see the **consequences of decisions** that they make. The software is able to use **what is known** about a previous decision of the same type, plus a range of **other known** or **estimated factors**, to **simulate** the likely outcome.

Expert systems

Using a pre-programmed **knowledge base** and a set of **rules**, an expert system is designed to **act** as an **expert** in a given situation. One of the best-known expert systems is used by NHS Direct to help medical staff **diagnose** medical conditions

Unit Link

For more on management information systems and expert systems see **Unit 3** – Information Systems.

and **offer recommendations** on **treatment**. It should be noted, however, that this particular system is monitored by qualified staff, particularly as the decisions it makes could literally mean life or death for the caller.

Other (e.g. security software)

However, on the **negative** side, the increased ability to communicate electronically has equally increased an organisation's **need** for **better security** of **systems**, both in terms of **physical** and **logical** security, from physical security including locking rooms and employing security staff, to using logical security tools which are largely software based. In fact this has become such an important issue that this course has dedicated an entire unit to it.

Unit Link

For more on security see **Unit 15** – Organisational Systems Security, and **Unit 3** – Information Systems, section 3.3.

Braincheck

IT development crossword
Try the following crossword based on what we have covered **so far**. The **grid** and **clues** are provided, along with the **answers** (if you get stuck).

ACROSS

1 Something that has been manufactured?
5 A organisation's private internal network
11 A private network shared with selected external users
13 The World Wide Web!
14 Helped?
15 A knowledgeable person

DOWN

2 Machines that are able to perform tasks usually done by humans
3 The ability to understand and make sense of experiences
4 When two systems are unable to work together they are said to be this
6 Making a system safe from threat
7 The I in EDI?
8 Not forwards!
9 A process that doesn't require human intervention
10 To alter
12 A group of computers that are linked together (can be a LAN or a WAN)

See answers on page 421.

2 Understanding why organisations need to change in response to information technology developments

Why do organisations need to **change**? Why can't they just go on in the same way that they have been for years?

1 **Customers** make **demands** for new products and services.
   ◆ Companies that fail to respond to these demands will:
      a) **not** receive any **new business** and, more importantly,
      b) could **lose** their **existing business** as customers go elsewhere to buy the new products and find the other products also available!
2 **Companies** need to **grow**.
   ◆ While even a small profit is a good profit, because money put into companies is basically an **investment**, **investors** will want to see an improved **return** over a period of time. If this does not occur, then they will simply **withdraw** their money and invest it **somewhere else** where they **anticipate** that the **returns** will be **greater**.
   ◆ Eventually, as more and more demands are made on systems, they become increasingly inefficient – for example, the **volumes** of **data** they handle get **larger**, the **tasks** the computers are expected to perform become **more complex**.
3 **Competitors'** activities see them becoming **proportionally more successful.**
   ◆ Anything that **weakens** an organisation's **position** in the market will be **detrimental** to the **ultimate survival** of the organisation.

Managers, particularly, should fully appreciate where the organisation is **positioned** in relation to its **customers**, **investors** and **competitors** and should be prepared to respond to the challenges posed.

2.1 Organisational challenges

Constant changes needed for constant re-engineering of systems

In order to **respond** to **change**, organisations will need to **re-engineer** their **systems**. This means that the systems will need to be **modified** to ensure that they still meet the organisation's needs.

Some organisations involve IT staff in strategic planning – primarily in **strategic information planning**, so that those employees with the relevant knowledge and technical expertise can inform and support the process of change, ensuring that any changes that are implemented are appropriate and correct and will ultimately meet organisational needs.

The important aspect of this is understanding how the organisation currently works (**point A**), anticipating where the organisation wants to be (**point B**), and finding the relevant method of getting the organisation from point A to point B.

When the required change is major, then the existing system will be investigated, and a new system will be designed and then implemented, tested and reviewed. This is known as the **systems life cycle**.

Unit Link

The systems life cycle topic is covered in depth in **Unit 7** – IT Systems Analysis and Design, section 1.

Ensuring management is IT-aware

Many people assume that all managers have a good **understanding** and **awareness** of IT, its technologies and its uses. Sadly, this is **not** always the case – in fact, some managers are **barely** able to use email **effectively**! A significant number of senior staff rely on their IT managers and departmental employees to advise them as and when issues arise. For this reason it is common for the head of an IT department to be involved in **decision making**, and generally, it is this person who would be able to match up the **information needs** of managers with what the system can produce.

Need for reduction in complexity and for integrated systems

While systems need to be able to carry out **more complex tasks**, the actual system should, as far as possible, be **made easier to use**. This will mean that staff with fewer IT skills will find it easier to use the system and its features.

It is quite normal, as companies develop, for each functional area to create its **own system**, and do so in its own way! However, this means that sharing information effectively **might not** be possible because systems are **incompatible**, or information is not created in a format that is useable by other functional areas.

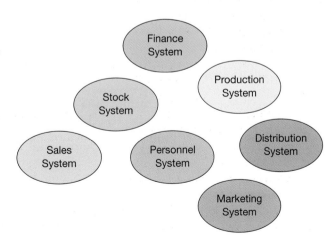

Figure 35.4 Sharing information?

Ideally the organisation should find a way of **integrating** the **individual systems**.

This will reduce the duplicated effort in making individual systems reproduce the same information, and will ensure that **management information** is available as and when needed in order to **support** the organisation's **activities**.

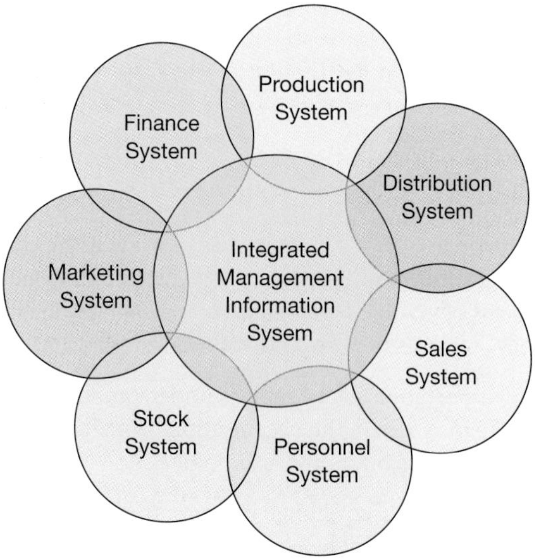

Ensuring payback on IT systems

No organisation should make an investment unless it is **confident** that it will receive full **payback** on any investment made. At the very least the company should **break even**. Here are some examples:

Figure 35.5 Integrated management information system

◆ Company A has a production line that designs and manufactures plastic products. It has an antiquated CAD/CAM system and a large number of operatives who use the system. The company decides to spend **£30,000**, **upgrading** the system and **retraining four** of the **six** employees who use the current system. Once implemented, the organisation **reduces** the workforce by **two people**, at **£15,000** each per year. This means that at the end of the first year the organisation has been able to break even. In the second year, the implemented system will be helping the organisation to make a profit.

◆ A company spends **£50,000** developing and implementing a new online presence (website and sales system). It anticipates that if it can increase sales by £10,000 per year over the next five years, the investment will have been worthwhile. In actual fact, because the organisation is now entering markets that were previously inaccessible, it **improves** sales by £30,000 in the first year, and a further £36,000 in the second year.

This means that the **improvements** made should help the organisation to **save money**, or be **more productive** (make and sell more), thereby **reducing costs while** potentially **increasing sales**.

Developing technical infrastructures

Having the right **technical infrastructure** is **not** something that can just happen overnight. It needs careful **planning** and **financing** over a period of time, particularly as technology can generally be expensive and the costs to an organisation of not investing wisely can be the difference between success and failure.

In general terms, how should technology be supporting an organisation?

The systems implemented should support an organisation in the ways shown in Figure 35.6.

REACTIVE	PROACTIVE
FOCUSED	PREDICTIVE

Figure 35.6 The support grid

Reactive

An organisation needs to be able to **respond to events** that occur, whether these events are triggered **internally** or **externally**. These events may be **opportunities** for the organisation, or **threats** to it.

The organisation needs to be able to **respond quickly** to take **advantage** of opportunities that present themselves, or to reduce the impact of perceived threats.

Proactive

It should have the infrastructure in place that will allow it to be proactive – this means that the organisation will have the **capacity to anticipate** and, in some situations, **lead the way** with **innovation** and **originality**.

Focused

One of the major advances of having a sound technical infrastructure is that employees and managers do not get bogged down with small details, as many of the standard, repetitive and routine tasks will be executed automatically, allowing staff to focus on **new horizons** and **improvements**.

Predictive

Simulation is one of the most important aspects of good business. If software can be used to **predict the future**, based on known factors and some careful estimations, it will be in a **better** position to be proactive in the first place, with some **confidence** in the projected outcomes of its activities.

Developing the technical infrastructure will require a significant investment in:

◆ **hardware**
◆ **software**
◆ **relevant IT skills**.

Some organisations do not pursue **improvements** in **technology** because they say that they cannot afford them. In today's markets, companies should realise that in most cases they **cannot afford not to invest**, as **failure** to do so may see their profits and business **eroded** by the activities of **competitors**.

As suggested earlier, there are a number of factors to which an organisation must be in a position to respond. These will be classified as either external or internal factors.

2.2 External environment

The external environment (the world outside the organisation) is changing all the time, and the organisation needs to:

1 be aware of the outside world
2 be prepared to modify its own activities accordingly.

The problem with the **outside world** is that the organisation has **no power** to **change** it – it can only **respond** to it!

Increasing globalisation

Key Terms

The concept of **globalisation** can be more or less defined from a number of different viewpoints. The following **perspectives** are all part of the globalisation framework:

◆ internationalism
◆ liberalism
◆ universalism

Internationalism – this is the concept that **international barriers are being overcome** and this is accepted as being the norm. Part of this is because of improved communications between most nations in the world, and we also need to remember how much easier world travel has become, making more of the world easily accessible. Taking Europe as an example, the countries within it were originally extremely well-defined and separated. Each had its own boundaries, language(s) and currency. In the last three or four decades, however, the **E**uropean **U**nion (**EU**) has been formed and the divisions between the countries of Europe have begun to diminish. While each country still has clear physical borders, English is becoming the main language of Europe, and the euro has replaced the traditional currency of many of the member countries. Britain has, so far, chosen to retain its own currency for the present, although this decision is under constant review.

Liberalism – in order to benefit from an improved world economy, many countries are becoming **more lenient** about their **borders**, encouraging **trade** and the **migration** of individuals (though this is not true in all countries), and in general there is more acceptance of other traditions and cultures. The world is, in many respects, becoming a much more integrated society. Similarly, in the UK we are required to comply with legislation created by the European Parliament (significant work-related legislation has come to the UK this way).

Universalism – items that have been hard to come by in some countries are now easier to get than before. This has resulted in some **technologies** becoming more **generic**, so that they fit with other technologies in different parts of the world. Consider the concept of the home-entertainment system. In principle, this technology could be easily effected – but in order for this to take place, all manufacturers would have to make agreements on standards, formats, and connections of certain types of device. Clearly, many companies will be reluctant to do this as they fear losing sales. Let's take a particular games console as an example. The console has a controller that is used to play games. Each make of console has a controller with the same functionality, largely with buttons and pads in the same place. What makes each controller different is the connection it has that goes into the main console. Wouldn't it be easier if there was only one type of controller, with a single type of connection? For consumers this would be easier, but companies would be reluctant to accept this standard because it would reduce the number of controllers sold for a particular console.

No-one would disagree that perspectives are increasingly important and companies that wish to succeed in the global market must accept these concepts, and be willing to work with them, rather than trying to avoid or work against them!

Potential for outsourcing and geosourcing

Companies that are willing to take advantage (and a little risk) by outsourcing or geosourcing will probably find that they can purchase good-quality solutions much more cheaply.

Key Terms

Outsourcing – is the practice of **buying in skills**, particularly **IT skills**, from **outside the organisation** when they are needed, on a fixed-term basis. This can be **cheaper** than **employing** and **training staff** who may not have sufficient work to do to make their employment viable.

Geosourcing – is similar, but the implication is that organisations can seek these skills **outside** the **UK** or the usual partner countries. For example, at the moment there is a surplus of available games-programming skills in **Eastern Europe** (in places like Poland, the Czech Republic and Serbia and Montenegro), with a similar surplus of skills in general applications programming in parts of **Asia**. The advantage here is that employees in these regions have the skills, but are willing to work for **significantly less money** than their European counterparts would demand.

Changing regulatory and legal frameworks

Unit 3 – Information Systems, section 3.1 discusses in depth the legal implications of using information, and considers the responsibilities of employers and employees in relation to Health and Safety in the workplace when using IT. Also mentioned are other **laws** and **acts** that have a **direct impact** on organisations and employees, particular in terms of IT-related issues.

You must understand that if markets have become more global, then organisations will have more laws and acts to contend with, as they will also need to observe and comply with any regulations in countries with which they trade. The **I**nternational **O**rganisation for **S**tandards (**ISO**) has a large number of member states with different levels of membership. Their level of membership has a bearing on the voting rights of each state or country.

A full list of the member states can be found at the following address:

http://www.iso.org/iso/en/aboutiso/isomembers/MemberCountryList.
MemberCountryList

These countries work together to ensure that issues such as safety standards and product standards are set, adhered to and policed in those countries. Clearly, membership of any multinational organisation is going to be optional! The ISO's own website describes its activities as follows:

> ◆ *ISO is the world's leading developer on International Standards.*
> ◆ *ISO standards specify the requirements for the state-of-the-art products, services, processes, materials and systems, and for good comformity assessment maagerial and organisational practice*
> ◆ *ISO standards are designed to be implemented worldwide*

Figure 35.7 The ISO's mission

In addition, the ISO claims that:

> ***ISO standards level playing field.***
> *They make transparent the requirements that products must meet on world markets, as well as the conformity assessment mechanisms for checking that those products measure up to standards. As a result, suppliers from developed and developing countries alike can compete on an equal basis on markets everywhere.*

Figure 35.8 The ISO's promise

And that:

> **ISO standards making the cake bigger.** *When new technologies or business sectors emerge, internationally agreed ISO standards on basic features, such as terminology, compatibility and interoperability, help to disseminate them and increase the size of the market for the derived products and services.*

Figure 35.9 The ISO's aims and objectives

Source: Taken from http://www.iso.org/iso/en/prods-services/otherpubs/pdf/isoinbrief_2006-en.pdf

The ISO is effectively trying to make the economic environment much fairer for all. With participation from a number of countries, in general, organisations can feel some sense of reassurance that the rules and regulations will be the same if they are trading with one of the member states. However, the list of countries has some interesting omissions!

Unit Link

For more on UK regulations see **Unit 3** – Information Systems, section 3.

For this reason, organisations must protect themselves by ensuring that they are not breaking any regional laws when trading in external environments.

Reduced costs of business start-ups

These days, businesses are relatively cheap to start up. In most cases, a few resources are required initially which, when sold, will provide the finance for a larger quantity of resources, and so on.

Technology, also, can be purchased relatively cheaply, including buying manufacturing equipment in trade journals and online. Similarly, computer equipment can be secured at relatively little cost.

There is also a wide range of financial support available, such as grants and loans from the government or its agencies, groups of businesses or organisations like the European Social Fund (**ESF**), which provide finance for projects. In order to secure this type of funding, particularly from the ESF, organisations must put together **sound business plans**, and explain **how** the money they request will be spent. Not surprisingly, **failure** to **meet agreements** made with ESF agencies will require any monies provided to be returned!

Increased potential for competition by global companies at local level using e-commerce

Clearly, improved technology and better logistics have made it possible for organisations to sell goods and services to more remote locations, thereby

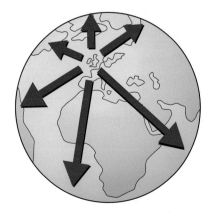

Figure 35.10 World trade

accessing new markets and opportunities. However, organisations must remember that just as trading has been made easier for them, so trading has been made easier for the competitors.

2.3 Internal environment

Need for constant upskilling of workforce

One of the most important **consequences** of the increased use of IT in the workplace has been the constant need for organisations to upskill their workforce through appropriate training. From an organisational perspective, this dramatically increases the cost of implementing new systems.

Figure 35.11 IT Training

How can relevant training be facilitated?

Nearly all Further Education (**FE**) colleges provide a wide range of IT courses, many of which may suit the needs of employees. In addition, college-supported venues and commercial training providers will also offer a similar if possibly more limited range. For those employees working with computer technology such as hardware and systems, any of the following might be appropriate:

◆ Computer hardware qualifications (maybe from the CompTIA® suite, such as A+, Security+ or Network+)
◆ Higher National Certificates, Diplomas and Foundation Degrees in Software Development (computer programming), Networking or IT Systems
◆ Specialist courses such as Microsoft Certified Systems Engineer® (**MCSE**) courses for managing servers and networks
◆ Cisco Certified Network Associate® (**CCNA**) courses for organisations that operate using Cisco systems.

Alternatively, if organisations need to provide user-level qualifications, the range offered might include:

◆ word processing
◆ spreadsheets
◆ database
◆ internet and email
◆ Outlook Express
◆ web page design
◆ desktop publishing
◆ presentation graphics
◆ Sage® accounting.

If, however, the systems implemented use **bespoke** (**purpose-built**) **software**, then it would be unlikely that any training would be available from the usual sources. At these times it is customary for the developers to provide some level of training as part of the development package.

Organisations must always weigh up the costs of training, which can be greater than simply the costs of courses:

Scorecard

+ Training on generic software such as word processing, internet or desk-top publishing (DTP), is likely to be relatively inexpensive, particularly if the courses are done in a college or community venue.
+ Using **cascade training** (such as training one or two individuals from an organisation, who in turn train others) can be an inexpensive way of ensuring that staff remain upskilled.
+ Staff feel valued if organisations invest in their skills.
+ If appropriate, training can be made specific to the needs of organisations (effectively tailored), and it can then be delivered **on site** (at the organisation's premises), to ensure that it exactly meets the needs of the organisation.
– Generic training might not always fully address the needs of users.
– When employees are being trained, they will not be doing their usual jobs and organisations either need to put cover arrangements in place, or accept that work will fall a little behind.
– **Tailored** training can be expensive, although most organisations would say that they feel the investment in such training would be worthwhile in the long run.

How are training needs identified?

Sometimes a need is easy to identify because **new systems** are being implemented and, as such, it is obvious that users will need to be trained to use these systems.

It is more likely, however, that training needs will be identified through the **annual appraisals** that most employees undergo. This is when the employee's **performance** over a period of time (usually one year) is discussed and evaluated. Employees are encouraged to **identify their own** training needs, but managers also may make suggestions.

Unit Link

For more on appraisals see **Unit 1** – Communication and Employability Skills for IT, section 4.2.

What is most important about this concept is that an organisation's failure to train employees to use systems correctly will merely result in staff not **working efficiently**, which ultimately will be to its detriment and to the benefit of its competitors.

Dealing with redundant skills and employees

The other consequence of improvements in technology has been that some employee skills have become **unnecessary** or **redundant**. For example, engineering parts once manufactured by highly skilled lathe workers are now produced by pre-programmed machines. One of the main advantages of this is that there are fewer reject parts, because machines can work **more closely** and **consistently** with very **accurate** machining tolerances.

So, what does an organisation do with employees like lathe workers, whose skills are no longer needed?

The company has a number of choices:

◆ **Use employees elsewhere** – it is possible that some employees will have other skills that could be further developed to make them useable elsewhere in the organisation.

◆ **Retrain** employees – bearing in mind that most organisations will have implemented new systems as the result of a strategic plan that was developed some time earlier, most organisations will have made decisions about what to do with redundant skills before the systems were installed. Some employees will be completely retrained to do something fundamentally different from the job they were doing previously.

◆ Make employees **redundant** – this means to actually ask the employees to leave the organisation (see the following case study). Organisations are generally reluctant to do this, because along with skills that the organisation will be losing, it will see a significant amount of knowledge about the organisation leave:

   a) that the organisation might not be able to replace very easily

   b) which could ultimately fall into the hands of competitors.

Even so, there are times when the organisation actually has no choice other than to make employees redundant. This was certainly the case in the 1980s when unemployment in the United Kingdom rose higher than it had in previous decades.

Case Study

In the early part of the 1980s when the manufacturing industry in the United Kingdom was greatly affected by the recession, one of the world's most well-known and largest photocopier and sundries manufacturers was forced to make most of the employees at a manufacturing plant redundant.

As a responsible employer, however, the senior management decided to do all that they could to help employees find alternative employment and, to this end, they set up their own employment agency where a group of personnel consultants were employed with the remit of contacting other local companies to try and relocate any staff who wanted that level of support. Although not all employees found new employment quickly, in general this strategy was successful because in addition to finding new opportunities for the majority, it ensured that the reputation of the manufacturer as a professional and caring company was maintained.

Home and remote working

A major advance in employment was made when it became technologically possible for employees to work from home, or from other remote locations. This had two distinct advantages:

◆ Organisations had a larger **skills** pool to choose from (because they could employ individuals outside their usual recruitment area).

◆ It now became possible for individuals who had not traditionally been able to enter mainstream employment to take up opportunities that would allow them to work from home.

The types of work that could now be done remotely included:

◆ freelance activities such as consultants
◆ writing
◆ teaching (for example the Open University uses tutors who work from home)

- graphic design
- specialist mail order
- product design
- web design and programming
- telesales
- web publishing.

To set themselves up to work from home, most workers simply needed a computer, network connection or modem, appropriate software and the time and skills to be able to do the job. In some instances, employers would actually provide the technology, from a desk and chair, to a broadband connection, computer and printer.

What you should remember, however, is that there are advantages and disadvantages to the concept of home working for both the employer and the employee.

Home working – the employer scorecard

+ Better **access** to a **wider** and more **diverse skills** set.
+ Employees are **less stressed**, particularly if travelling to and from work is effectively avoided.
+ **Less** need to **rent** large amounts of office space.
+ It is usually **easier** to **contact** your employees because they are likely to be in one fixed location.
+ Some employers believe that those who work from home are more **productive** because they often will be willing to work slightly longer hours (to get a job finished) and because they experience **fewer distractions** or **interruptions** in the working day as they do not have colleagues to chat to.
– Employees who become **unhappy** with their working situation can be **difficult** to **motivate** – this might be because initially the employer is unaware that there is a problem, so one or two minor problems that might have been resolvable have now developed into much bigger issues.
– Getting employees together for **meetings** is more **difficult** because they are not all working in the same location.
– The potential for **ad hoc interaction** is completely **diminished** (no bumping into each other in the corridor, no opportunity to have a quick meeting because the organisation is facing a sudden crisis).
– In order to **monitor** an **employee's activities** (and productivity), an employer might have to resort to using activity monitoring software, which in itself will have a detrimental effect on staff morale; they will feel that they are not trusted.

Home working – the employee scorecard

+ Employees can work at a time that suits them, which accommodates the basic needs of those who are better at working at a specific time of the day.
+ There is a sense of freedom and the feeling of trust that employers are not watching every move.
+ The job becomes more flexible as employees are able to work around dependants (commitments to children or other family responsibilities).
+ Home workers can work as many, or as few, hours as they choose.
– They might be tempted to work at times that are inappropriate, and where they might not be giving their employer a level of productivity that has any real quality.
– Many home workers become isolated because they have little or no direct contact with others apart from via email or the occasional phone call.
– Employees need to have a good level of self-discipline to work effectively from home as they might succumb to distractions and the work might not get done.

Working from home can, however, be exceptionally rewarding, particularly if all the systems have been put in place to enable you to do this.

Impact of regular restructuring and managing change

Implementing technology can quite often result in the need for organisations to be **restructured**. There are some organisations that are able to do this with a **minimum of fuss**, and where there is no real evidence of **resistance** from employees. Other organisations, however, often because of their **size** and **structure**, will find restructuring **very difficult** and consequently **demoralising** and **destabilising** for staff.

In many respects, the way that an organisation responds to the concept of change in general will be representative of the culture of the organisation.

Organisations that are **unwilling** to **respond to change** are generally **autocratic** and rooted in tradition and thereby the past, so will find the restructuring that is often required as part of the implementation of technology a difficult and costly experience:

◆ Employees may well be resistant to restructuring or change, particularly if they feel that their own jobs and livelihoods are under threat.
◆ Key employees may leave the organisation because they fear that technology or a new organisational structure might ultimately push them out.
◆ A lack of skills may make managers reluctant to implement change, and without planning may endanger the organisation's activities.
◆ Unless all parts and levels of the organisation buy into the change process, change may be successfully implemented in parts of the organisation, with other parts lagging behind, making it more difficult for the organisation to work effectively.
◆ Staff may well feel demotivated and demoralised because they do not feel valued.

This kind of response is often referred to as a **closed culture**.

Conversely, organisations that are **open** to the prospect of change are more likely to see change as a natural and important part of organisational development because change:

◆ means new opportunities (for promotion, or learning new skills)
◆ may see new employees joining the organisation (often referred to as bringing in new blood)
◆ is a healthy consequence of an organisation that is growing and that is becoming more prosperous
◆ makes individuals, generally, see themselves as part of the greater whole (as an important part of the organisation)
◆ makes people feel valued and thus motivated.

This is often referred to as an **open culture**.

Successful implementation of technology will be dependent on the **culture** of the organisation being an **enabling** one – this is a culture that effectively **makes things possible**.

Balance of core employees with contractors and outsourced staff

Increasingly, if an organisation is unable to afford to employ staff with particular skills or abilities, it may well have to resort to buying in these skills and experiences from contractors or other outsourced staff. However, it is likely that the organisation itself will maintain a number of key (or core) staff, primarily because of the disadvantages of using staff or services secured from outside the organisation.

The main advantage to using external staff is always going to be cost:

◆ You only pay for them when you need them.
◆ You do not have to train them.
◆ You will always have a service, because if a contracted member of staff is off sick, another one will normally be provided by the external agency. Why? Because there would be no reason for you to continue to pay for the service if staff were not available – if you are buying in these services, then it is not your problem.

The disadvantages, however, are also relatively severe:

◆ These staff may have little or no knowledge of the organisation, its products or services.
◆ External staff have no stake in the organisation and therefore might be less motivated.
◆ They can also walk away from the situation at any time.
◆ Turnover of staff can be high as the parent organisation pulls experienced staff off one job and puts them on another.
◆ The organisation effectively has little control over the individuals; it must trust the agency (at the end of the day, it can always fire a contractor if the job is not being done satisfactorily).

It would be extremely unwise for any organisation to outsource or contract staff into key positions within the organisation for the reasons listed above.

Companies are more likely to retain their own core staff who they will continue to develop, to ensure that the activities of contractors and agency staff are monitored.

Others (e.g. delayering as organisational structure flattens)

A traditional organisation is commonly quite tiered. This means that there are many levels of management, with formal lines of communication established and a clear chain of command. Figure 35.12 shows a typical example.

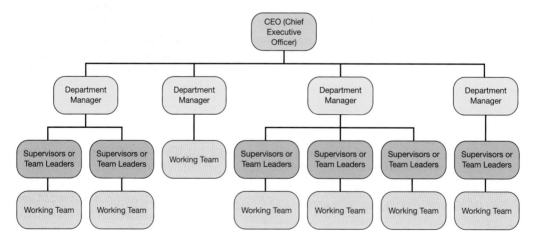

Figure 35.12 Tiered organisational hierarchy

In this type of hierarchical structure, members of the working teams at the bottom of the diagram would rarely communicate directly with department managers, they would ordinarily go through their own line managers (in this case supervisors or team leaders). Organisations built on this type of structure tend to be quite **dictatorial** with instructions, policy and working methods dictated **from above**.

The alternative to this type of structure is a flatter hierarchy, as shown in the typical example in Figure 35.13.

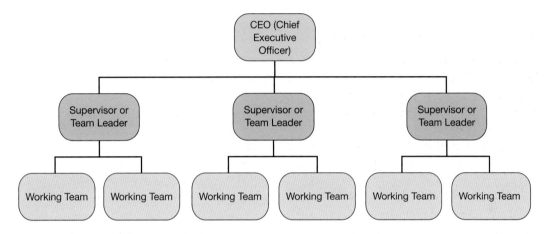

Figure 35.13 Flatter organisational hierarchy

In this example, the organisational structure has been **delayered** (management layers have been removed), making the chain of command much shorter. With this kind of scenario, communication would be more likely across layers of the organisation, with policies and methods of working negotiated and discussed.

When thinking back to the previous section where we considered change management and restructuring, you can probably see why it would be more difficult to implement change where communication is tighter and more controlled (so it would be more difficult in an organisation that is more tiered than in a flatter organisation). However, you should not assume that this is always going to be the case because there are a large number of organisations with highly tiered structures that are responsive and proactive, and that adapt easily. This is because even though they are tiered, communication across levels is actively encouraged and accepted.

General

Ultimately, organisations have to **balance internal** and **external factors**, the **benefits** and **disadvantages** of **technological change** and the **needs** of **employees,** to have an effective and successful establishment. Managers are usually trained to have the relevant management skills to identify, create and maintain this balance, although there are some extremely gifted and entrepreneurial managers who have never had any formal training!

Braincheck

Find the words in the grid below.

```
S F O D E T A R G E T N I E O
Y H C R A R E I H Z V X R E U
T T R P G G E R U T L U C H T
D G L O B A L I S A T I O N S
E H R S E K N L I C W M V Y O
M V W E V V A I U V E K G S U
S Q I O D N I R S W X O J I R
I L Z T R U T T O A L N P N C
L K L E C S N R C O T A D T I
A W T I A I K D N A Y I K E N
R X H R K I D H A B E J O R G
E C F G N S C E A N N R W N F
B N H G I E I C R F T H U A Y
I R E G T F K E H P N C R L J
L C H A L L E N G E R O N H S
```

CHALLENGE
GLOBALISATION
INFRASTRUCTURE
LIBERALISM
PAYBACK
REDUNDANT
CULTURE
HIERARCHY
INTEGRATED
ORGANISATION
PREDICTIVE
SKILLS
EXTERNAL
HOMEWORKING
INTERNAL
OUTSOURCING
REACTIVE
TECHNOLOGY

See answers on page 421.

Activity

Create an A4 leaflet that explains your school, college or institution to someone else. As part of the explanation, draw a diagram that represents the organisation's structure and explain, briefly, some of the technologies that are used to support your organisation's activities.

Once completed, discuss the leaflet with your tutor.

3 Understand how organisations adapt activities in response to information technology developments

The final section of this unit suggests some ways in which organisations have adapted their functional activities and their performance in line with advances in technology. Also covered is a short section on risk management, although security of IT systems is covered in depth in **Unit 15 –** Organisational Systems Security.

Unit Link

For more on systems security see **Unit 15 –** Organisational Systems Security.

3.1 Activities

Adapting sales and marketing strategies (global opportunities, sales management)

Sales and marketing have always been **data hungry** parts of any organisation. In order to understand markets, buying patterns, service users, peaks and troughs in demand, and activities of competitors, **large quantities of data** must first be **gathered**, then **analysed** and **interpreted** as useable information so that predictions about the future can be made, to which the organisation can then respond.

Gathering data has never been easier, with the wealth of information that is collected about us on a regular basis (some of which we might not even be aware of):

◆ Data is **gathered** about us through media such as **loyalty cards**, **credit** and **debit cards.**
◆ Organisations gather information through electronic point of sale (**EPOS**) systems such as supermarket checkouts.
◆ **Websites** record data about our **purchases** and, through the additional use of **hit counters**, can calculate the sorts of websites that have the most activity.
◆ **Demographic statistics** (such as age groups populating particular towns or villages, information about employment status) are **freely available** through government websites.
◆ **Data** is **not restricted** to particular locations.

Manipulating data is more straightforward:

◆ There is better **functionality** in traditional database and spreadsheet software.
◆ New products are **specifically designed to** work with and **interpret data**.
◆ **Identifying trends** is easier, particularly with the development of graphical tools.
◆ **Drill-down** functionality allows users to **interrogate data** at lower levels.
◆ The use of computer systems to undertake this task has seen **information** being **available** more **quickly**.

Interpreting data is easier:

◆ **Information** is **presented** in a more **user-friendly** way.
◆ **Exceptional events** are easier to **identify**.
◆ **Managers** will have more **confidence** in the outcomes of **analysis**.

Because of the way that information can now be managed, organisations can adapt their sales and marketing strategies. They can:

◆ gather and analyse data more promptly
◆ respond more quickly to opportunities
◆ manage sales teams more effectively
◆ provide information more successfully.

Adapting new purchasing opportunities (e.g. EDI and automated ordering)

Some organisations now refuse to do business with other organisations if they do not have access to **EDI** or other automated ordering systems. Certainly some of the larger supermarkets **will not** trade with smaller companies who **have not** invested in this technology because they do not feel that these companies will be able to respond quickly enough to **meet their needs**.

A number of different types of EDI currently exist:

An Applicability Statement 2 (**AS2**) **EDI** allows organisations to transmit electronic documents via the Internet. The AS2 standard dictates the way that the connection is created and the way that the data is actually transferred.

A **web-based EDI** on the other hand, uses a web browser to handle the data exchange process.

And finally, a **v**alue-**a**dded **n**etworks (**VANs**) **EDI** is usually set up using private networks to allow the secure exchange of information between business associates. An investment in this type of EDI, particularly with all the security requirements to ensure systems are fully protected, would be more likely with a large company involved in regular transactions with one of its trading partners.

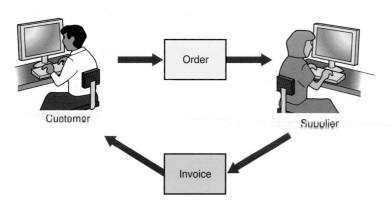

Figure 35.14 Typical EDI

As with other technical aspects of systems, an organisation's EDI requirements can also be outsourced.

Once the invoice has been received, a statement of account may well follow, prior to the payment being sent to the supplier.

Most of the larger supermarkets use EDI systems (possibly using VANs concepts) to pass orders to suppliers. This allows the supplier to respond almost instantly to the request, which has dramatically speeded up the supply chain and made transactions more accurate (there is less opportunity for error if information is digitally transmitted in this way).

Using new technology in customer support

Some would say that using technology in customer support is a **negative step**. Technology has, for example, enabled companies to outsource their customer support functionality (usually known as call centres) to other countries around the world. This is currently a controversial debate, as some customers are irritated by the fact that they find themselves **speaking** to someone a **long way away** when the business has premises **geographically close by**.

One of the main advantages, however, is that using internet technologies, for instance, allows organisations to give the appearance of providing customer support 24 hours per day, 7 days per week.

Often, if you email a company using their '**contact us**' link, an automated response email will be **automatically generated** and returned to you, usually suggesting some sort of **time frame** in which **you can expect a reply**. Generally in such an email, companies will state a longer time frame for a response than they actually intend to implement, simply so that when they reply sooner than you anticipate, it will give you a good impression of the organisation!

How is technology used in the customer support process? It can provide any or all of the following:

◆ **online** user **manuals**
◆ **health and safety** information
◆ **product specifications**
◆ frequently asked questions (**FAQs**), where queries by other users are logged, and the answers given recorded, for all to see
◆ **complaint** handling systems
◆ customer **feedback collection**.

With the exception of the last item in the above list, most of us are always ready to accept this type of online support – in actual fact, many of us would prefer to use websites to access this kind of information, as it allows us to view the content at our own pace and in our own time.

However, many of us will become frustrated if we have to make complaints in the same way, as we often want a quick response.

If organisations are offering excellent customer support, they may very well make almost immediate contact with a customer if an email suggests that a customer is potentially not happy. Other organisations, however, choose not to do this and continue to handle the complaint via email. There are times when this strategy is successful, but equally there are times when it is not. Good customer service is when a company knows the difference!

Secure funds transfer

On a personal level

Most people will, quite rightly, warn you about making payments for goods and services online using bank cards, particularly if you are not completely sure that the website is genuine.

For such eventualities, intermediary organisations like PayPal® and NoChex® exist.

It works as shown in Figure 35.15.

This system protects both the buyer and the seller:

◆ The buyer's information is not passed on.
◆ The seller has confirmation that the buyer is genuine because they know the funds are available.

Ultimately, the intermediary takes a small payment from the buyer for its services.

More and more companies like Paypal® and Nochex® are springing up all the time – very little time will elapse before yet more online payment companies will begin to offer their services. Before you use any such intermediary, you should always ensure that you have checked it out.

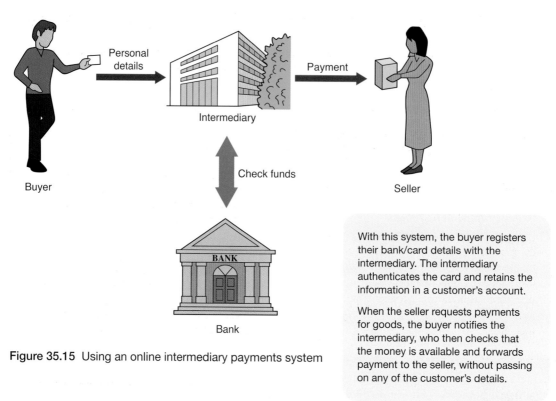

Buyer

Personal details

Intermediary

Payment

Check funds

Seller

BANK

Bank

With this system, the buyer registers their bank/card details with the intermediary. The intermediary authenticates the card and retains the information in a customer's account.

When the seller requests payments for goods, the buyer notifies the intermediary, who then checks that the money is available and forwards payment to the seller, without passing on any of the customer's details.

Figure 35.15 Using an online intermediary payments system

On an organisational level

Bankers **A**utomated **C**learing **S**ervice (**BACS**) is the most common business-to-business transfer method. For example, it is often used by companies to pay salaries into employee bank accounts. Similarly, it is often the preferred method of handling credit and debit card payments, and regular payments such as direct debits and standing orders.

Direct debit – an amount that you pay out of your bank account to an organisation on a regular basis (e.g. a monthly charge for your home utilities). In this instance you complete documentation and present it to your utilities company, who then present it each month to your bank, with notification of the amount of money it needs to pay on your behalf.

A **standing order**, on the other hand, is generally set up by the bank account holder, direct with their bank. An example would be making a monthly donation to charity. You would set up a standing order that would pay a fixed amount into the charity's bank account on a regular basis.

The key issue with any secure funds transfer system is that it is indeed **secure**! This is why it is extremely important that you check how any system you use is protected. Unless you are fully satisfied that your personal information is safe, find another service!

Supply chain management and integration with partner businesses

Information technologies have revolutionised supply chain management, and using EDI (as described earlier in this section) or other related systems has reduced the time it takes for suppliers to respond to customer demands.

Case Study

Boeing® uses a carefully orchestrated supply system to provide the parts and materials for its aircraft manufacture.

Using a system based on **JIT** principles, the company publishes its production schedules up to a year in advance on a secure system that links Boeing® with its suppliers.

The suppliers can then see when particular parts will be needed, and it becomes the suppliers' responsibility to ensure that the relevant parts are delivered to the factory floor just before they are needed.

From a supplier's perspective, this system is useful as, in addition to effectively being an ordering system, it can be used to help them plan their own production schedules.

Why does Boeing® use JIT? Because when you consider how big many of the parts are (aircraft engines, bodies, wings, etc.) the company would need to spend a large amount of money on storing these items prior to using them in production. Using JIT technology means that Boeing® only has to store these items for a very short time (sometimes only a matter of a day or two).

Logistics

Increasingly, organisations involved in the movement of goods are investing in IT systems to manage this process.

Let's consider this in terms of organisations such as **DHL**, **UPS** and **ParcelForce**. When a customer presents any one of these organisations with a parcel, the item is automatically given a tracking number. A copy of this number is then given to the customer for **tracking** purposes. Using the number that the item has been given, the customer can then log on to the relevant website and track where the parcel is, from the point it enters the DHL system, to the point where it reaches its destination.

Key Terms

Logistics

While there are many different, yet similar, definitions of the term logistics, in this instance we will consider it from a delivery perspective. This means the process of getting customer goods from the supplier to the customer's premises.

Figure 35.16 UPS shipment tracking interface

UPS offers additional functionality – which is that once the item has been delivered, the customer can view the signature of the person who signed for the item!

The ParcelForce shipment tracking service also has slightly different functionality to the other two providers.

To ensure that the shipments or parcels move quickly through the system, a barcode reader is generally used to scan the barcode on the item. The code itself is dictated by the thickness and quantity of lines contained in the image. The scanning device (that may be hand-held or in a fixed position, like the one at a supermarket checkout) contains a laser beam that provides a light source and which then passes over the code, reflecting the light back into the device as it hits the white space in the code. The device then receives the reflected light and translates this back into a sequence of numbers which can be stored, compared etc.

Figure 35.17 Sample barcode

Along with this data, the location of the item will be input (e.g. on final delivery van, with the van's identification number so that the actual van carrying the item can be identified). Some of these organisations also use **satellite-tracking equipment** to **track** their **delivery vehicles**, even to the extent that, if required, they can tell a customer how many **minutes away** the parcel actually is because they can track the vehicle down to road level!

Establishing an internet presence

As many high-street shops find sales dropping as customers increasingly favour the use of catalogues and online services, many companies feel that they are being forced to establish an internet **presence**. At a minimum, organisations could merely set up an **online brochure** which would show prospective customers what goods or services they provided, but without any possibility for the user to interact with the website (so no orders could be placed). In this instance the company would be hopeful that that customer will see a good deal, and will then be prepared to come in to the shop to make the actual purchase.

Case Study

KAM (Kris Arts & Media) Limited has decided to develop a website to bring its name and its products to the attention of businesses and the general public.

However, unlike **Lee Office Supplies** or **Frankoni T-Shirts Limited, KAM** has no stock for sale, so

the usual online ordering functionality would be inappropriate.

What would be more likely is that **KAM** would effectively create an online brochure, with an interactive gallery of images acting as a portfolio of previous work. As graphics projects tend to be bespoke (made to the specifications of the client), it would not even be appropriate to have a price list (such information would be client-confidential).

In reality, as the population becomes more **IT literate** (able to use the technology), the expectation is for companies to increasingly offer online services. Even so, some organisations are rightly reluctant to give up their high-street visibility.

Unit Link

For more on **online business** see **Unit 34** – e-Commerce.

In some cases, having an online presence would not really be feasible. For example, if your business is car maintenance, the most that you could actually do would be to put an advertisement and maybe a price list online. You would not be able to sell using this medium. In this case, you may well pay a small fee to a directory listing service that would include your organisation, along with other similar organisations in your area.

Automating manufacturing processes

Automated manufacturing, as suggested earlier in this unit, has both advantages and disadvantages.

Automated manufacturing scorecard

+ Can be active for longer hours.
+ Less potential downtime if regular maintenance is undertaken.
+ Better quality and consistent product.
− Some systems will need a programmer on staff who is capable of handling any programming anomalies or problems.
− Fewer staff required, so more unemployment

3.2 Performance

From a performance perspective, the implementation and wider use of improved IT systems has had a positive impact on the fortunes of organisations. Generally, this impact can be seen as a series of undeniable benefits.

Productivity gains

The use of IT systems:

◆ facilitates longer production periods
◆ more or less guarantees better-quality products more consistently
◆ makes processes more efficient
◆ enables processes to occur faster.

Cost reduction and increased profitability

It stands to reason that if you can reduce operating (day-to-day running) costs, production costs, distribution costs etc. that you will automatically see an increase in profitability. How has IT enabled these costs to be reduced? Examples would include:

◆ Fewer staff required as processes become automated, saving wages and salaries.
◆ Use of EDI negates the sundry expenses such as postage.
◆ Less wastage of raw material if more is successfully turned into finished product.

Efficiency

IT solutions provide opportunities for greater efficiency, particularly as the profit margin (the difference between the cost of making or doing something and how much you can sell it for) increases:

◆ Better stock efficiency with less stock tying up capital as it can be ordered closer to when it will be sold or used.
◆ Queries handled more quickly.
◆ Enhance ability to respond to opportunities and threats.

Improved management information and control

This is such an important aspect of the use of IT in business that Unit 3 – Information Systems has been dedicated to this subject area. In brief:

◆ More information is available, as greater quantities of data are being stored.
◆ Data and information are more accessible.
◆ Data is more easily manipulated and viewed from various perspectives.
◆ Information can be made available more quickly.
◆ Information will be more accurate.
◆ Historic data can be effectively used to make comparisons about performance.
◆ Decision making will be enhanced because information to support the process will be readily available.

- Control over activities is enhanced because information from all areas can be shared to improve the quality of activities across the whole organisation.

Unit Link

For more on management information and its uses see **Unit 3** – Information Systems.

Customer service

Customer service benefits from:

- a service seemingly being available for longer periods of time if the service is provided via email
- using email to quickly distribute queries and concerns to the right individuals within the organisation
- the types of calls recorded can be analysed to look for particular issues or trends, which could facilitate the organisation being proactive (anticipating the sorts of problems that customers might face and reacting accordingly).

Synergy and integration of systems

Well-developed systems where the issues of data and process integration have been considered and accommodated will produce systems that have greater synergy. This means that the **various systems** within the organisation **will work together**, almost in harmony, to produce **better-quality** data and information and therefore better services to all stakeholders within the organisation.

3.3 Managing risk

To effectively manage risk, organisations firstly need to fully understand and appreciate the risks they face! Unit 3 – Information Systems, in section 3.3 considers a range of operational issues and suggests how risks can be overcome. In addition it considers the responsibilities of data users, employees and organisations in ensuring that organisational data is safe and secure.

Cybercrime

Cybercrime (crime using computers and the Internet) is probably the fastest-growing platform for criminal activity across the world.

Typical examples include:

- **diverting financial assets**
- **sabotaging communications**
- **stealing intellectual property**
- **denial-of-service (DOS) attacks**
- **halting or diverting e-commerce transactions**.

Diverting financial assets

Quite apart from the obvious criminal activities of theft (including identity theft with a view to acquiring someone else's personal financial assets such as the contents of their savings or bank accounts), there are some more subtle crimes, such as attempting to use the general public in illegal money movement activities. An example of this occurred where a used car was put on a website for sale: the seller was contacted by a prospective buyer who insisted that they wanted to buy the car to ship abroad. The process seemed straightforward see Figure 35.19.

Suspicious about this, the seller contacts the police and discovers that this is not an uncommon activity, and it would be likely that the car would either never be collected, or would be collected and then dumped! Clearly the objective of the whole transaction was to move the money from A to B, making the tracking of the various transactions more difficult to untangle.

Sabotaging communications, DOS attacks and halting or diverting e-commerce transactions

Sometimes the unlawful activities that result in communications being sabotaged by being either diverted or deleted, are merely the actions of pranksters who simply want to cause a little mischief. They can also instigate **DOS** attacks where they bombard networks with activity to effectively slow down processing, thereby denying users the usual quality of service.

1. Buyer sends money order or cheque

2. Seller banks cheque or cashes money order which is bigger than the value required to the purchase the vehicle

3. Seller raises a money order for overpayment, and arranges for car to be collected

4. Car collected and extra money wired to an overseas account using money transfer service

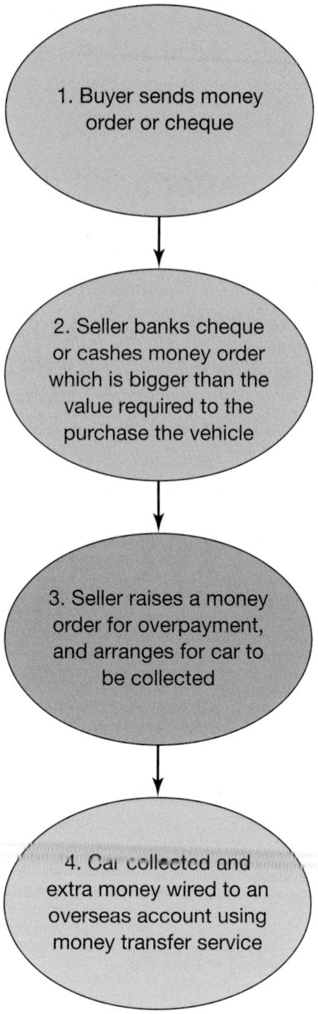

Figure 35.18 Diverting funds

However, there are more serious criminal acts such as preventing organisations from trading by disrupting their ability to do so, or diverting business transactions to other sources.

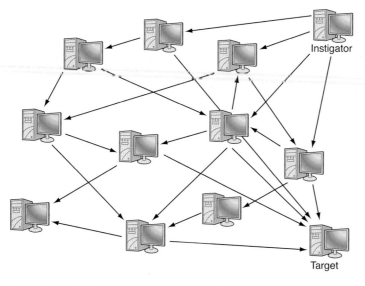

Instigator

Target

Figure 35.19 DOS attack

From a legal standpoint, it does not make any difference in law whether the crime had serious intentions or was a prank. The law will punish both activities with equal severity.

Stealing intellectual property

Most people would agree that **stealing from others** is an unacceptable act. We all understand that copying CDs or DVDs is a criminal offence. We are appalled by street crime, vehicle theft and violence.

Have you considered, however, that **directly copying information from the Internet using copy and paste** functionality, or taking information from books, word for word, to use in your coursework is also a form of stealing known as **plagiarism**? If you use information from particular sources you must reveal the original source of the material by including a **reference** to the originator and the source in what is known as a **bibliography**.

A bibliography is a list of authors, documents or web pages that have been used in the preparation of published text (which, as suggested, includes your coursework).

In fact, plagiarism is considered such a serious offence that from time to time, students who have been found guilty of plagiarism have been **excluded** from courses. Many institutions see this as unacceptable behaviour – and within education, the higher the qualification, the **more seriously** it is viewed.

Figure 35.20 Plagiarism is not allowed!

For this reason you should begin fully acknowledging your sources now!

Preventive technologies (e.g. firewalls, access control methods)

A wide range of physical and logical technologies exist which help organisations prevent criminal activity.

Physical technologies include:

◆ **surveillance systems** which discourage inappropriate behaviours because they could be seen and recorded (CCTV systems)
◆ **locked rooms** accessed through the use of swipe cards, key pads and keys
◆ **dongles**, which are physical devices that are plugged into systems and without which a user will have no access to certain software or data.

Logical technologies are largely software based and can include antivirus software such as:

◆ Bulldog Bullguard AntiVirus Firewall and Backup
◆ Sophos AntiVirus®
◆ Avast! AntiVirus 2007
◆ AVG Anti-Virus
◆ Norton AntiVirus™ 2007
◆ McAfee® Internet Security Suite 2007

As long as these utilities are regularly updated with the latest **antivirus signatures**, viruses will effectively be harmless and will not be capable of damaging your system.

Firewalls are programs that monitor a computer's incoming and outgoing data communication. Once configured, the system will automatically allow or reject data exchanges, dependent on rules that have previously been set up by the user.

Firewall software includes products such as:

◆ McAfee® Firewall Plus
◆ Zone Labs® Zonealarm 6.1.737

- Norton Personal Firewall as part of the Norton AntiVirus™ 2007 bundle
- Sygate Personal Firewall Pro User Version 5.6.

In addition, there are other software-controlled solutions that provide logical security, such as passwords and encryption.

Disaster recovery

Because organisations today rely so heavily on computer technology to undertake and record their activities, businesses must ensure that their activities are not affected by a disaster such as fire, flood or other forms of data loss resulting from activities such as hacking.

To this end the organisation should have carefully considered a **backup plan**. This is known as providing facilities for **business continuance**.

In many respects, since the development of IT systems, it has become much easier to prevent data loss, particularly as larger and larger memory devices such as Seagate® external hard drives have come on to the market and the price of this technology has come down significantly.

There is really no excuse for data loss in this age of technology (this includes the loss of coursework because you have failed to make a relevant backup)!

Unit Link

For more on preventive technologies see **Unit 15** – Organisational Systems Security, section 2.

Disaster recovery

- Potential **risks** are **identified**.
- The **organisation** fully **understands** how it will be **affected** in the event of a disaster.
- **Resolutions** will have been **sought in advance**, including strategies such as backing up data in other locations to ensure that the minimum possible amount of data is lost.
- Implement **safety strategies** (such as **backing up** data regularly).
- **Disaster** will have been **simulated** to test the plan, ensuring the plan can be modified if required.
- Ensure **staff understand** the **role** they will play in the recovery process (ensuring that they receive any appropriate training).
- The plan will be **reviewed** at regular intervals, to ensure that it remains up to date.

Activity

Your company has decided to invest in new technology which will replace the current sales and stock systems. It is quite clear that the staff in these areas, who are generally not IT-literate, are concerned about how these systems will affect their activities.

Create a short Microsoft PowerPoint® presentation that will look specifically at how the enhanced technologies will support their areas.

Once completed, show (or present) the presentation to your tutor.

Activity

To ensure that you will not be guilty of plagiarism, find out about the **Harvard method of referencing**, which is largely used in higher education (HE) institutions.

Discuss your findings with your tutor and find out whether your organisation has its own method of sourcing information in coursework.

Links

Unit 35 is a **core unit** on the BTEC National Diploma for IT Practitioners (**IT and Business route**) and a **specialist unit** for all other routes:

Software Development

Networking

Systems Support

As such it has links to a number of other units, principally:

Unit 1 – Communication and Employability Skills for IT

Unit 3 – Information Systems

Unit 7 – IT Systems Analysis and Design

Unit 15 – Organisational Systems Security

Unit 34 – e-Commerce.

So that you can monitor your own progress and achievement in each unit, a recording grid has been provided (see below). The full version of this grid is also included on the companion CD.

Achieving success

In order to achieve each unit you will complete a series of coursework activities. Each time you hand in work, your tutor will return this to you with a record of your achievement.

This particular unit has 10 criteria to meet: 5 pass, 3 merit and 2 distinction.

For a **pass**:

You must achieve **all** 5 pass criteria

For a **merit**:

You must achieve **all** 5 pass and **all** 3 merit criteria

For a **distinction**:

You must achieve **all** 5 pass, **all** 3 merit **and both** distinction criteria.

Assignment	Assignments in this unit			
	U35.01	**U35.02**	**U35.03**	**U35.04**
Referral				
Pass				
1				
2				
3				
4				
5				
Merit				
1				
2				
3				
Distinction				
1				
2				

Help with assessment

In order to **pass** this unit you will need to show that you understand the types of hardware and software that exist and which have had an impact on the way in which organisations operate. You will need to include evidence of how external factors also affect the way that organisations function internally, particularly in terms of performance. Finally, you will need to show that you understand the concept of risk to an organisation in terms of its IT systems.

For a **merit** you will need to show how you think advances in IT have had a direct effect on employers and employees, looking at issues such as home working.

And lastly, for a **distinction** you will need to show evidence that you appreciate the consequences of implementing IT solutions, and that you can identify and recommend appropriate systems and solutions for particular business situations.

Online resources on the CD

Electronic glossary for this unit
Electronic slide show of key points
Multiple choice self-test quizzes

Further reading

Textbooks

BPP Professional Education, 2005, *ACCA Paper 2.1 Information Systems@ Study Text*, BPP Professional Education, ISBN 0751723169.

Hickie, S., Bocij, P., Chaffey, D., and Greasley, A., 2005. *Business Information Systems: Technology, Development and Management for the E-Business*, 3rd edn, FT Prentice Hall, ISBN 0273688146.

McCalman, J., and Paton, R.A., 1992, *Change Management: A Guide to Effective Implementation*, Paul Chapman Publishing Limited, ISBN 1853961558.

Journal

PC World magazine

Websites

www.bbc.co.uk
www.business.timesonline.co.uk
www.computing.co.uk

Braincheck Answers

Unit 1 Braincheck answers

Braincheck answers

1 An attribute is a personal characteristic that employers expect you to have. You could have listed any of the following: creativity, problem solving, leadership qualities, team working, work with a minimum of supervision.
2 A skill is an attribute that is relatively easy to measure. You could have listed any of the following: IT skills, number skills, literacy skills.
3 A **person specification**.
4 When you can choose the hours you work within boundaries set by your employer.
5 Be observant.
   Report any hazards.
   Anticipate any possible hazards.
6 Collaboration is when you are part of a group of people who are working together to achieve a particular goal or objective. You will share ideas, share your skills and help each other to reach the required outcome.
7 Tolerance is when you respect other people's views, practices and opinions.
8 Your integrity is a measure of your honesty, sense of duty and respect.
9 A mission statement is designed to describe the basic purpose and principles of an organisation.
10 An attitude is a personal behaviour.

Braincheck answers

Term	Explanation
Spellchecking	Using software to check the accuracy of a piece of text
Yours faithfully	Closes a letter that began with Dear Sir
Indented paragraph	Where the first line is set in from the subsequent lines in a paragraph
A closed question	Where the answer can only be one of a limited number of options
Proofreading	Checking the correctness of spelling and grammar in written text
Shouting in emails	Where text is written in capital letters or emboldened
Full justification	Where both sides of text are aligned (straight)
Thesaurus	Offers a selection of alternative words that can be used to replace the word highlighted that have an identical or similar meaning
Readability test	Assessing the suitability of a piece of text for a specific age range
Yours sincerely	Closes a letter that began with Dear Mr Smith

Unit 2 Braincheck answers

Braincheck

1 Backing storage is needed to store data permanently as RAM loses its contents when power is removed.
2 Floppy disk, Hard disk, CD, DVD, USB Pen drive, Flash Memory cards etc.
3 Available data storage capacity of 1.44Mb is small by today's standards.
4 IDE (PATA), SCSI and SATA.
5 Pits and Lands.
6 Approximately 650 ~ 700MB.
7 A male USB connector, a PCB (printed circuit board) containing flash memory and a clock crystal.
8 Common types include: CompactFlash (CF), MultiMediaCard (MMC), Memory Stick (MS), Secure Digital (SD) and xD-Picture Card (xD).
9 Data access time (DAT) – how quickly specific data can be found.
10 Data transfer rate (DTR) – how quickly data moves from the device into the computer.

Braincheck

1 Base unit, monitor, keyboard and mouse.
2 BIOS is the computer system's Basic Input Output System.
3 Form factor represents a motherboard's dimensions and features.
4 PSU is the power supply unit, supplying electrical power to the motherboard and attached internal devices, in different currencies.

5 To cool the processor and by drawing excess heat away.
6 Serial sends data one bit at a time over a single wire whilst parallel sends multiple bits over parallel wires simultaneously.
7 Primary, Secondary.
8 Universal Serial Bus – a fast and popular, worldwide standard for serial device connectivity.
9 IDE means integrated drive electronics; the controlling electronics for the drive are built into the drive mechanism itself making it self-contained.
10 ROM is permanent read only memory and cannot be altered. RAM is random access memory and is alterable whilst power is present, unlike ROM it will lose its data when power is removed (it's said to be 'volatile').
11 DDR memory is a type of DIMM but is faster as it uses double the clock speed to access its data (hence the name double date rate).
12 200 Mhz
13 5,336 MBps per channel.
14 Fast memory (usually inside or near the processor) which stores recently processed or anticipated data and instructions to speed up execution.
15 Keyboard, mouse, graphics tablet, gamepad, microphone, scanner etc
16 Monitor, Printer, plotter, speakers, robot arm etc

Braincheck

1 BIOS and Applications Software.
2 Any 4 from Resource Management, User Interface, Input/Output control, Filing System, Security and Task Management.
3 On disk initially then loaded into RAM.
4 CLI (Command Line Interface) and GUI (Graphical User Interface).
5 Patching.
6 The ability to process a number of tasks (seemingly) simultaneously.
7 Disk-based memory used to complement physical RAM.
8

Objective	Windows	Linux
List files in a directory	DIR	LS
Create a new directory	MKDIR or MD	MKDIR
Delete a file	DEL or ERASE	RM
Change to the "root" directory	CD\	CD /
Examine the computer's network adaptor information	IPCONFIG	IFCONFIG

9 Price (most Linux distributions) are usually free, Virus susceptibility (Windows more prone), User learning curve (can be steep for some Linux distributions) etc.
10 It's name, size, date created, date last modified, what is file permissions are (read only, modify, delete etc).

Unit 3 Braincheck answers

Braincheck answers

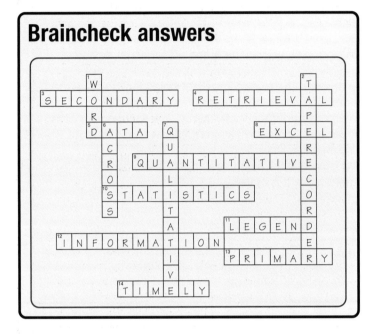

Braincheck answers

Letter	Number
A	7
B	10
C	9
D	11
E	8
F	2
G	3
H	5
I	1
J	6
K	4

Braincheck answers

Number	Issue or problem	Operational? Strategic? Tactical?
1	One of your managers has heard that a competitor is dropping prices on their main stock items next month.	**Operational** – even though this is not going to happen this week, your organisation will still need to respond quite quickly.
2	You seem to have a large amount of stock of a product that does not appear to be selling very well – should you continue to stock the product or maybe delete it?	**Tactical** – this is not urgent – if you already have the stock you have probably paid for it already. What you might want to think about is do you have another push at selling it prior to discontinuing the item?
3	Most staff in the distribution area (primarily drivers) have all called in sick with stomach upsets (suspected food poisoning) which means that out of a team of six staff, only two people are in.	**Operational** – clearly if you do not have drivers, your customers will not get their deliveries!

4	Our vehicle fleet is old and in need of significant investment. Do we want to replace the vehicles or maybe outsource this part of the organisation to a courier?	**Tactical** – this needs to be considered before the vehicles are replaced as it might be cheaper to bring in an outside company to do the deliveries for you.
5	A supplier was not paid at the end of last month and is refusing to provide any more stock.	**Operational** – if your suppliers do not supply your organisation because bills have not been paid, then you will clearly not be able to meet the needs of your customers. This should be resolved quickly.
6	A supplier has told you that they will be bringing in a whole new range of business products in about 18 months' time and has asked you whether you think your customers might be interested.	**Tactical** – you will need to do some market research and find out whether or not your customers would be interested in such products, prior to committing yourself to your supplier.
7	The distribution manager has said that we are increasingly running out of storage space in the warehouse. As there is no opportunity for physical expansion at our current premises, should we consider moving operations elsewhere?	**Strategic** – the only strategic issue Paul has at present – does the company move to larger premises? This is always a risk and the possibilities should be carefully investigated prior to making any decisions that could be detrimental to the company.

Unit 7 Braincheck answers

Braincheck answer

I, B, G, H, D, C, E, F, J, A

Braincheck answers

```
        S T R U C T U R E
                C       D
      M         R   W A T E R F A L L
      I   I     R       C       P
    P L   N     E       A       P
    S E   T   A C T I V I T Y   L
    E S   E     T               I
    U T   G   D I R E C T       C
    D O   R     V               A
  B O U N D A R I E S           T
    C E   T                     I
    O S   I                     O
    D L O G           E C O N O M I C
    E       N                   S
```

Unit 8 Braincheck answers

Braincheck answers

Decide whether the following are **PAN**, **LAN**, **MAN** or **WAN**:

A public network paid for by a city council for all its residents. **(MAN)**

A network connecting the various national branches of Lee Office Supplies. **(WAN)**

Two friends exchanging .MP3 songs via their Mobile telephones. **(PAN)**

A cluster of computer labs in a local School. **(LAN)**

A PDA transferring files to a notebook. **(PAN)**

Braincheck answers

1 There are 7 layers in the ISO OSI model.
2 Layer 4 – the Transport layer.
3 Translation, encryption and data compression.
4 Layer 1 – the Physical layer.
5 Layer 4 – the Transport layer.
6 Layer 3 – the Network layer.
7 Layer 2 – the Data Link layer.
8 Layer 3 – the Network layer.
9 Layer 2 – the Data Link layer.
10 1984.

Unit 15 Braincheck answers

Braincheck answers

Investigate the following software applications and Operating Systems and decide whether they are available as open source, freeware, shareware or commercially.

♦ OpenOffice suite **(open source)**
♦ WinZip **(shareware and commercial)**
♦ CutePDF Writer **(freeware)**
♦ AVG Antivirus **(freeware and commercial)**
♦ Apple QuickTime **(freeware and commercial)**
♦ FreeBSD **(open source)**

Braincheck answers

1 Any two from: hacking, phishing, identify theft and piggybacking.
2 A type of financial fraud committed over the Internet that tries to steal valuable personal information.
3 The act of impersonating another individual for financial gain (typically) by using their credentials.
4 Fire, flood, earthquake, hurricane, tornado etc.
5 Create an open environment where errors can be publicised (without form of recrimination) and fairly dealt with.
6 Keep it confidentially with integrity.
7 Unauthorised changing of a website's content or appearance by 3rd parties.
8 Peer to peer network – a decentralised networking methodology used to transfer data files (often illegally with copyrighted material).
9 Any 3 from loss of service, loss of business (income), increased costs and poor image.
10 Any 3 from Locked doors, security guards, CC-TV, cable shielding etc.
11 Electronic systems which authenticate users by the use of their physical characteristics.
12 Any 3 from facial structure, hand geometry, fingerprints, voice pattern, retina patterns, DNA etc.
13 A Virtual Private Network that works by transmitting private network data over a public telecommunication infrastructure.
14 Illegal duplication of sensitive data, introduction of infection threats such as a virus.
15 Email, Internet usage, software installation, purchasing etc.
16 An internal security tool used by organisations to ensure that no one employee has 100% control of a process from start to finish.
17 The act covers: Unauthorised access to computer material, unauthorised access to a computer system and Unauthorised modification of computer material.
18 The ability to **make changes** to the program's **source code**.
19 Security concerns and the personal privacy rights of the individual in society.
20 The Federation Against Software Theft; an organisation that protects a creator's intellectual property by pursuing software copyright infringement.

Unit 18 Braincheck answers

Braincheck answers

Work out whether these expressions **evaluate** to **TRUE** or **FALSE**...

10 > 5	**TRUE**
6 < 6.1	**TRUE**
'A' != 'B'	**TRUE**
FALSE == FALSE	**TRUE**
7 > 2 AND 5>=5	**TRUE**
3 < 10 OR 99 < 67	**TRUE**
"REBEKAH" == "rebekah"	**FALSE**
(10+2) >= (60/5)	**TRUE**

Braincheck answers

1 Textual, Numeric, Boolean or Date.
2 Integer or Floating point.
3 One (1) character only
4 Real numbers; ones with decimal places.
5 The mantissa represents the accuracy (the fractional part of the number).
6 255 characters.
7 Unsigned numbers represent a magnitude and are therefore neither positive or negative.
8 Boolean.
9 196.3
10 The appropriate data types are:

a	−5.8	**(Floating point)**
b	A	**(Character)**
c	+7800	**(Integer)**
d	(0120) 101000	**(String)**
e	04/09/2012	**(Date)**
f	Miss Helena Wayne	**(String)**

Braincheck answers

1 Programs should be robust, accurate, reliable and efficient.
2 Check all logical pathways, check normal, extreme and erroneous data inputs.
3 An error is a fatal (will stop compilation from completing) whilst a warning is a minor caution that may indicate a possible run-time problem.
4 Watches, Breakpoints and Traces.
5 Any 4 from: How to install, uninstall, start & end the program, use it, resolve problems and obtain further help.
6 Any 3 from: Printed documentation, .txt (text files), .pdf files and screencast videos.
7 Any 3 from: Strengths, weaknesses, review of how it meets users original needs and future improvements.
8 These may include: corrections, improvements and expansions.
9 It should be written in plain language; it is meant to be read by a typical end-user – not a developer.

Unit 20 Braincheck answers

Braincheck answers

1 Any 3 from: Visual C#, Visual C++, Visual Basic, Visual Basic .NET etc.
2 Operating System or the User.
3 Any 3 including: Low RAM, change of display settings, power mode and RTC settings.
4 Any 3 from: Flexibility, suitability for graphical user interfaces, simplicity of programming, ease of development, particularly for Rapid Application Development (RAD).
5 Any 3 from: Speed (can be slow), can be inefficient, large RAM footprint, doesn't teach developer algorithmic skills, difficult to translate into other languages, solution can be platform dependent (non-portable).

Unit 22 Braincheck answers

Braincheck answers

1 The information is gathered from the end users.
2 Critical features are "must haves". Desirable features are "would be nice" and thus less important.
3 Any 3 such as Commissioning costs, project management fees, hardware costs.
4 Software costs, consultancy costs, ongoing support and maintenance costs and training costs.
5 Any limiting factor such as time, money etc.
6 Any two such as User needs and populations, application behaviour, baseline network requirements, network loading and performance constraints.
7 Educating employees by telling them what to expect.

> 8 QoS is Quality of Service.
> 9 Any 3 such as Network data throughput, collisions and congestion, user response times, line utilisation and user satisfaction.
> 10 Network monitoring tools.

Braincheck answers

A=2, B=3, C=4, D=5, E=1

Braincheck answers

1 Any 3 server types such as Mail, Web, File, Print, Application etc.
2 HP Openview, CiscoWorks.
3 10mbps, 100mbps and 1000mbps respectively.
4 Backbone.
5 Thin client runs its services loaded from an application server (it has little in the way of locally installed software).
6 Any from 3 from mobile networking, web interfacing, RMON, VoIP, Web 2.0 etc.
7 RMON is Remote Monitoring, a standardised monitoring specification that enables different network monitors and console systems to share network-monitoring data.
8 Any 3 from: Mapping network disk drives or folders to local logical device names, redirecting printer output to a shared network printer, fixing a specified (organisational) screen saver or desktop wallpaper, deleting temporary files or automatically launching programs.
9 Any 3 from: Physical layout, network configuration, external linkage, application settings and administration/management information.
10 Any 5 from: The name and location of the device affected, who reported it, when it was reported, problems (symptoms) reported, faults diagnosed and then identified, solutions applied, who fixed the problem, when was the problem fixed, what resources were used to fix the problem and whether user acceptance has given etc.

Unit 27 Braincheck answers

Braincheck answers

A=2, B=5, C=4, D=1, E=3

Braincheck answers

1 Any 2 from: NIC, Servers (e.g. Print, Mail, File, Web, Proxy).
2 Any 2 from: Bridge, gateway, hub, modem, repeater, router, switch, wireless access point (WAP).

3 A leased line is a permanent, high speed telecommunication line between two points that is always "on".
4 Any 3 from: Coaxial, fibre optic, microwave, satellite, shielded twisted pair (STP), unshielded twisted pair (UTP) and wireless.
5 LDAP is the Lightweight Directory Access Protocol (LDAP), a TCP/IP compliant protocol that enables users to locate resources on public or private networks, given suitable access permissions.
6 Account management, asset management and authentication management.
7 IRC (or Inter Relay Chat) is a text-based service on the Internet where real-time conversations amongst multiple users take place in virtual rooms ("channels") via special IRC-clients.
8 Usenet is a distributed discussion system that operates world-wide, consisting of a number of different newsgroups.
9 IRC (Inter Relay Chat)
10 Access Control Lists (ACLs) specify which users (or groups) have access to a particular file, and what type of access they have.

# Braincheck answers
A=2, B=3, C=4, D=1

Unit 28 Braincheck answers

Braincheck answer

Braincheck answer

Braincheck answers

1 ESD stands for electrostatic discharge. This is electrical current that builds up in devices and on the human body, and which does not come from the usual electrical sources – batteries, the mains supply.
2 The Health and Safety Executive (HSE).
3 Antistatic packaging.
4 They would use an antistatic wrist strap.
5 Any or all of the following answers:
   a) hot plugs
   b) hot sockets
   c) fuses that blow for no obvious reason
   d) flickering lights
   e) scorch marks on sockets or plugs.
6 Any three of the following:
   a) badly wired plugs
   b) fraying power leads
   c) overloaded sockets
   d) trailing cables or cables in vulnerable positions
   e) water near electrics.

7 Any of the following:
   a) using a waste broker
   b) reusing (by refilling)
   c) recycling
   d) donation to charity.
8 WEEE Directive – Waste Electronic and Electrical Equipment Directive
9 Employers' Liability (Compulsory Insurance) Act 1969
10 Any six from:
   a) check that your workspace is safe and tidy;
   b) back up any data to ensure that there will be no data loss, even if you might not be working directly with hard disk devices (remember the problems associated with ESD mentioned earlier in this unit);
   c) obtain the necessary hardware, software etc. (you should be aware that some aspects of this might need to be ordered in advance, so there may be a delay before you can begin);
   d) identify and lay out the relevant tools (you should never attempt to work on a system with the wrong tools!);
   e) ensure that you have sufficient rights to access the system, particularly if you will need to be able to access the system to test it at the end of the activity;
   f) ensure that you know any configuration settings;
   g) check that any new equipment or any components are undamaged: if working on an existing system always ensure that anything you do will not invalidate any existing warranties;
   h) read the installation instructions that come with any component or equipment: these instructions may be paper-based, electronic, on a CD, or you may need to access the manufacturer's website (as suggested earlier in this unit);
   i) arrange for supervision (if appropriate).

Unit 34 Braincheck answers

Braincheck answers

1 It has given those who might ordinarily not be able to access goods or services the opportunity to do so.
2 A facility to monitor the process of a delivery.
3 Because they might not have the relevant IT skills to manipulate and use the website properly.
4 Bricks and clicks companies are ones that have outlets or branches on the high street, and enable users to trade online.
5 Any three of the following:
   ◆ global market
   ◆ 24/7 trading
   ◆ relatively low start-up and running costs
   ◆ search facilities
   ◆ gathering customer information.

6 Any four of the following:
   ◆ customer distrust
   ◆ lack of human contact
   ◆ delivery issues
   ◆ compliance with international legislation
   ◆ problems with product descriptions
   ◆ security issues.
7 A hit counter counts the number of individual times that a website, or individual web page, has been accessed.
8 The International Organisation for Standards ensures that issues such as legally defined safety standards and product standards are set, adhered to and policed.
9 The London Underground (UK) and a television (USA).
10 An organisation that sells products entirely online.

Braincheck answers

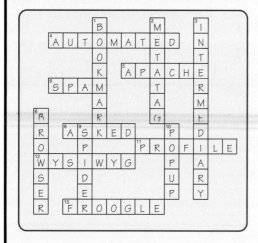

Unit 35 Braincheck answers

Braincheck answer

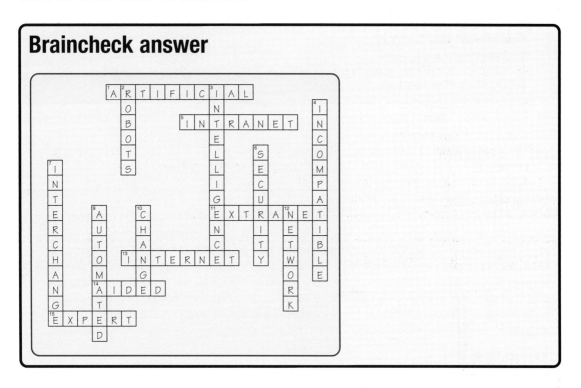

Braincheck answer

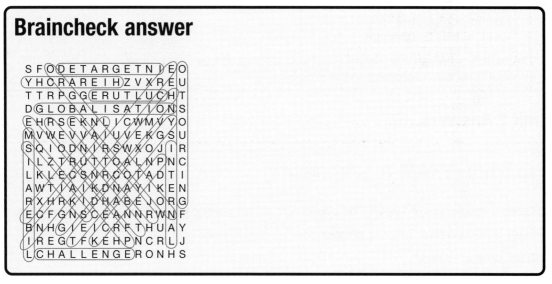

Activity Answers

Unit 1 Answers

Activity answer

Mrs Jones rang about the missing items from the last order. She says that she really isn't very happy about the way that our organisation has dealt with this issue. She says that when she dealt with Smethurst Office Supplies she never had these kinds of problems. If something was missing from an order they would courier it to her immediately. She also said that she was always given goods on account and 30 days' credit, and they didn't even chase her for an additional 15 days after the account was due. Her number is 01234 567891. She will be on this number from 3 to 4.30 pm today.

The **key facts** are:

◆ **who rang**
◆ **what about**
◆ **how to contact her**
◆ **when will be convenient.**

The remaining information **might well** be of interest to Lee Office Supplies but having this information is **not necessary** to the process.

Unit 2 Answers

Activity (VRAM requirements)

Given a **resolution** of **1024 ¥ 768 pixels** with **16 bit colour** would require 1,536 Kilobytes.

1024 × 768 pixels = 786,432 **pixels**

Each pixel = 16 **bits**

786,432 × 16 = **bits**

12,582,912 bits / 8 (bits per byte) = 1,572,864 **bytes**

1,572,864 bytes / 1024 (bytes per Kilobyte) = 1,536 **Kb**

(And optionally – 1,536 Kb /1024 (Kb per Megabyte) = 1.5 **Mb**)

Unit 3 Answers

Activity answer

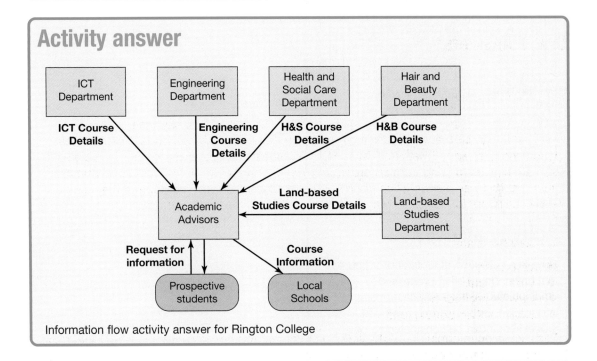

Information flow activity answer for Rington College

Activity answer

Act	Description
Data Protection Act 1998	The principles in this Act define how data about us is captured, used and stored.
Freedom of Information Act 2000	This Act gives us the right to know what data is being kept about us.
Computer Misuse Act 1990	An Act designed to discourage individuals from using computers to support criminal activities.
Terrorism Act 2000	This Act is designed to prevent groups and individuals from intimidating others for political ends.
Privacy and Electronic Communications Regulations 2003	An Act intended to reduce the instances of unsolicited communication using electronic means.

Activity answer

Activity answer

Data is a collection of facts and/or figures that have not yet been processed, manipulated or interpreted into useful information. Once the data has been processed, it can be considered to be information.

Information is therefore data that has been manipulated into ways in which it provides knowledge about something.

Unit 7 Answers

While the Level 1 DFD is relatively straightforward, the ERD reflects the t-shirt file and design file as one and the same, because these items will not be reflected individually on the subsequent order.

The invoice is then made up of a series of orders (there is no separate completed order file because you were told in the scenario that the order is stamped – it is not a new document!)

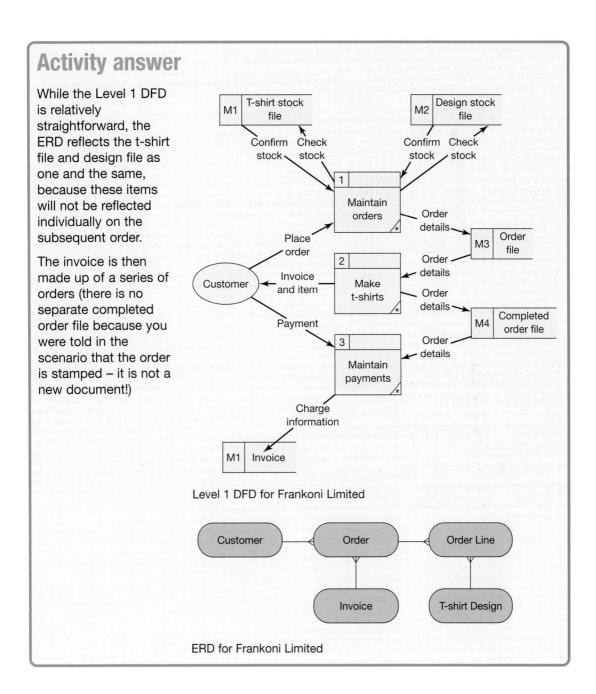

Level 1 DFD for Frankoni Limited

ERD for Frankoni Limited

Unit 29 Answers

Activity answer

Test	Normal data	Extreme data	Erroneous data
Age is between 18 and 21	19, 20	18, 21	R, 292, 0.77, #
Height is between 1.5 and 2.2 metres	1.9, 2.1	1.5, 2.2	3.4, H, £
Quantity (must not be 0)	1, 4, 6	26, 35, 50	T, -4, 62.3
Price (must be more than 0, but less than £20.00)	5.67, 3.94, 7.99, 15.42	0.50, 19.99	-59, XX
Choice must be A, B, C, D or E	C, B, D	A, E	2, -4, $
Hours worked (must be greater than 0, but less than 50)	6, 10.25, 29.75, 37.5	0.5, 49.75	L, No, -3

Activity answer

Error code	Meaning
Bad Request 400	An internet error that means the document that was requested can not be sent because of an inaccuracy in the URL (website address).
488	The user's signing-in details are invalid or have expired.
0xC000021A	Meaning Fatal System Error, this error code appears when the Microsoft Windows® log-on to system process is suddenly terminated.
5 beeps	Processor failure!
0x000000BE	The user has attempted to write to read-only memory!
Forbidden 403	An internet error meaning that you do not have access to view a particular document or page.
1 long 3 short beeps	Video failure.
Gateway timeout 503	An internet error that means an attempted connection has failed for any one of a number of reasons – the connection has not been made, so path has been closed.

Index